MFC Development
Using Microsoft Visual C++ 6.0

Microsoft
Mastering

PUBLISHED BY
Microsoft Press
A Division of Microsoft Corporation
One Microsoft Way
Redmond, Washington 98052-6399

Copyright © 2000 by Microsoft Corporation

All rights reserved. No part of the contents of this book may be reproduced or transmitted in any form or by any means without the written permission of the publisher.

Library of Congress Cataloging-in-Publication Data pending.

1 2 3 4 5 6 7 8 9   MLML   5 4 3 2 1 0

Distributed in Canada by Penguin Books Canada Limited.

A CIP catalogue record for this book is available from the British Library.

Microsoft Press books are available through booksellers and distributors worldwide. For further information about international editions, contact your local Microsoft Corporation office or contact Microsoft Press International directly at fax (425) 936-7329. Visit our Web site at mspress.microsoft.com.

Intel is a registered trademark of Intel Corporation. ActiveX, FrontPage, JScript, Microsoft, Microsoft Press, MSDN, Outlook, PowerPoint, Visual Basic, Visual C++, Visual FoxPro, Visual InterDev, Visual J++, Visual SourceSafe, Visual Studio, Windows, and Windows NT are either registered trademarks or trademarks of Microsoft Corporation in the United States and/or other countries. Other product and company names mentioned herein may be the trademarks of their respective owners.

The example companies, organizations, products, people, and events depicted herein are fictitious. No association with any real company, organization, product, person, or event is intended or should be inferred.

Acquisitions Editor: Eric Stroo
Project Editor: Wendy Zucker

Acknowledgements

Authors:
Steve Wilkins (NIIT)
Sangeeta Garg (NIIT)
Subramanian Meyyammai (NIIT)

Program Manager: Mary Anne Kobylka

Lead Subject Matter Expert: Kamran Iqbal

Lead Instructional Designer: Kathy Narvaez, Mary Anne Kobylka

Production Manager: Miracle Davis

Production Coordinator: Gale Nelson (Online Training Solutions, Inc.)

Media Production:
Geoff Harrison (Modern Digital)
Ed Stone (Modern Digital)

Editors:
Susan Filkins (S&T Onsite)
Reid Bannecker (S&T Onsite)

Build and Testing Manager: Julie Challenger

Book Production Coordinator: Kat Ford (ArtSource)

Book Design: Mary Rasmussen (Online Training Solutions, Inc.)

Book Layout:
Mary Rasmussen (Online Training Solutions, Inc.)
R.J. Cadranell (Online Training Solutions, Inc.)

Companion CD-ROM Design and Development: Jeff Brown

Companion CD-ROM Production: Kat Ford (ArtSource)

Table of Contents

Chapter 1: Introduction to Visual C++ 6.0 1
   Overview of Visual C++ and MFC 2
   Enhancements to Visual C++ 7
   Enhancements to MFC 12
   Lab 1.1: Creating an MFC-based Application 14

Chapter 2: Debugging and Error Handling 19
   Debugging 20
   Handling Errors and Exceptions 22
   Lab 2.1: Using Edit and Continue 31
   Lab 2.2: Implementing Exception Handling 33
   Self-Check Questions 38

Chapter 3: Enhancing the User Interface 39
   Enhancing Menus 40
   Enhancing Toolbars 50
   Enhancing Status Bars 54
   Enhancing Dialog Boxes 59
   Lab 3.1: Creating a Dynamic Menu 66
   Lab 3.2: Customizing the Common Dialog Class 71
   Using Modeless Dialog Boxes 83
   Using Dialog Bars 90
   Using Rebars 94
   Lab 3.3: Adding a Modeless Dialog Box 97
   Lab 3.4: Adding a Dialog Bar 114
   Lab 3.5: Adding a Rebar 122
   Sample Applications 125
   Self-Check Questions 126

Chapter 4: Implementing View Classes 129
Introduction to Views 130
Adding Multiple Views 135
Adding Scrolling Views 147
Implementing Splitter Windows 151
Lab 4.1: Adding a Splitter Bar 156
Implementing Form Views 162
Implementing Control Views 166
Creating an Explorer-Style Application 181
Coordinating Multiple Interrelated Views 183
Lab 4.2: Adding Open File Dialogs and a Rich Edit View 184
Lab 4.3 (Optional): Building a Text Viewer 196
Sample Applications 214
Self-Check Questions 216

Chapter 5: Using Controls 219
Windows Common Controls 220
Internet Explorer 4.0 Common Controls 225
ActiveX Controls 231
Controls Supplied by MFC 242
Lab 5.1: Creating Controls Dynamically 246
Lab 5.2: Adding a Progress Control 253
Lab 5.3: Using the Calendar Control 268
Sample Applications 273
Self-Check Questions 273

Chapter 6: Creating ActiveX Controls 275
Overview of ActiveX Controls 276
ActiveX Control Properties 282
ActiveX Control Methods 291
ActiveX Control Events 293
Implementing ActiveX Control Property Pages 296
Creating an Enumerated Property 304
Lab 6.1: Building an ActiveX Control Using an Existing Class 308
Data Binding in an ActiveX Control 330

Optimizing ActiveX Controls 333
Debugging and Handling Errors in ActiveX Applications 335
Sample Applications 337
Self-Check Questions 337

Chapter 7: Using OLE DB Templates for Data Access 339
Overview of OLE DB 340
Introduction to OLE DB Templates 345
Using CAccessor to Create a Consumer Application 349
Lab 7.1: Using CAccessor 360
Using CDynamicAccessor to Create a Consumer Application 368
Lab 7.2: Using CDynamicAccessor 372
Using CManualAccessor to Create a Consumer Application 377
Sample Applications 386
Self-Check Questions 387

Chapter 8: Creating ADO Database Applications 389
Introduction to ADO 390
Using Data Controls 394
Using the Data-bound Dialog Box 401
Performing Queries 429
Lab 8.1: Using the Data-Bound Dialog Box 431
Sample Applications 447
Self-Check Questions 448

Chapter 9: Building Internet Applications 451
Basic Internet Concepts 452
Using the Internet Explorer Object 455
Using the Web Browser Control 459
Using the WinInet Classes 470
Using the WinSock Classes 480
Lab 9.1: Using the Web Browser Control 486
Lab 9.2: Using the HTTP WinInet Classes 494
Lab 9.3: Adding an HTML View 501
Sample Applications 503
Self-Check Questions 504

Chapter 10: Printing and Print Preview 505
Adding Default Printer Support 506
Enhancing Printer Support 510
Lab 10.1: Adding Print and Print Preview to TextView 520
Sample Applications 531
Self-Check Questions 531

Appendix A: Self-Check Answers 533

Glossary 557

Index 597

About This Course

This book is designed to teach you how to develop applications by using Microsoft Foundation Class (MFC) Library and the Microsoft Visual C++ 6.0 development environment.

This course assumes that you are familiar with object-oriented programming (OOP) terminology and concepts, and Microsoft Windows architecture concepts. It also assumes that you have basic C++ programming skills; some programming experience with MFC Library; can use the resource editors, tools, and debugger in Microsoft Visual Studio; and are familiar with the document/view architecture and non-document/view architecture.

Course Content

The course content is organized into the following ten chapters.

Chapter 1: Introduction to Visual C++ 6.0

This chapter introduces you to the types of MFC-based applications you can build with Visual C++ 6.0. The chapter also describes the new MFC features provided in the Visual C++ 6.0-development environment and shows you the advantages that MFC and Visual C++ 6.0 offer you as a developer.

Chapter 2: Debugging and Error Handling

In this chapter, you will learn to use Visual Studio Debugger features such as Edit and Continue to identify and eliminate errors. You will also learn to write functions with built-in error-handling code, using the C++ exception-handling technique and various types of MFC exception classes to handle run-time exceptions.

Chapter 3: Enhancing the User Interface

In this chapter, you will learn to create dynamic, cascading, and ownerdraw menus. You will also learn to place dockable toolbars in an application, include graphics and additional panes in status bars, use and customize common dialog boxes, extend DDV, create tabbed dialog boxes and property sheets, invoke and display modeless dialog boxes, and create dialog bars and rebars.

Chapter 4: Implementing View Classes

In this chapter, you will learn to implement views in applications by using the CView, CScrollView, CListView, CSplitter, CTreeView, CEditView, and CRichEditView classes. You will also learn to create single-document interface (SDI) and multiple-document interface (MDI) applications with multiple views and use two interrelated views in an application.

Chapter 5: Using Controls

In this chapter, you will learn to add Windows common controls, Microsoft Internet Explorer 4.0 common controls, ActiveX controls, and controls supplied by the MFC Library to MFC-based applications.

Chapter 6: Creating ActiveX Controls

In this chapter, you will learn about the elements of an ActiveX control, the primary tasks of an ActiveX control container, and the interaction between an ActiveX control container and an ActiveX control. You will also learn to use ControlWizard to create skeletal code for your ActiveX control and use ClassWizard to define properties, methods, and events for your ActiveX control.

Chapter 7: Using OLE DB Templates for Data Access

In this chapter, you will learn to use the OLE/DB templates to create applications that access databases. You will learn to add, edit, delete, and find records in a database and handle transactions.

Chapter 8: Creating ADO Database Applications

In this chapter, you will learn to use the ADO Data Bound Dialog Wizard to create applications that implement an ADO connection to a local database.

Chapter 9: Building Internet Applications

In this chapter, you will learn about the Internet framework and the different types of Internet applications. You will also learn to create MFC-based applications that invoke Internet Explorer, use the WinInet classes to communicate across the Internet, use the synchronous and asynchronous WinSock classes, and use the Web Browser control in MFC-based applications.

About This Course

Chapter 10: Printing and Print Preview

In this chapter, you will learn about the printing process and the default printing capabilities provided by MFC for an MFC AppWizard-generated application. You will also learn to add default printer support to your application, retrieve information relating to printers and print jobs at run time, and enhance default printer support to implement custom requirements.

Labs

This course includes lab exercises that give the student hands-on experience with the skills learned in the chapter. A lab consists of one or more exercises that focus on how to use the information contained in the chapter. Lab hints, which provide code or other information that will help you complete an exercise, are indicated with the following icon in the margin.

Lab Hint Icon

Lab Setup

To complete the exercises and view the accompanying solution code, you will need to install the lab files that are found on the accompanying CD-ROM.

To complete the labs you need:

- A PC with a Pentium-class processor; Pentium 90 or higher processor
- Microsoft Visual C++ 6.0 Professional Edition or Enterprise Edition
- Microsoft Personal Web Server (PWS)

PWS is only required to complete the labs of chapter 9. To download PWS, go to the Personal Web Server page at http://www.microsoft.com/windows/ie/pws/default.htm.

xi

Self-Check Questions

This course includes a number of self-check questions at the end of each chapter. You can use these multiple-choice questions to test your understanding of the information that has been covered in the course. Answers to self-check questions are provided in Appendix A. Each answer includes a reference to the associated chapter topic, so that you can easily review the content.

CD-ROM Contents

The *Mastering MFC Development* CD-ROM that is included with this book contains multimedia, lab files, sample applications, and sample code that you may wish to view or install on your computer's hard drive. The content on the CD-ROM must be viewed by using an HTML browser that supports frames. A copy of Microsoft Internet Explorer has been included with this CD-ROM in case you do not have a browser or do not have one that supports frames, installed on your computer. Please refer to the ReadMe file on the CD-ROM for further instructions on installing Internet Explorer.

To begin browsing the content that is included on the CD-ROM, open the file, default.htm.

Lab Files

The files required to complete the lab exercises, as well as the lab solution files, are included on the accompanying CD-ROM.

Note 30 megabytes (MB) of hard disk space is required to install the labs.

Multimedia

This course provides numerous audio/video demonstrations and animations that illustrate the concepts and techniques that are discussed in this course. The following icon will appear in the margin, indicating that a multimedia title can be found on the accompanying CD-ROM.

Multimedia Icon

About This Course

In addition, at the beginning of each chapter is a list of the multimedia titles that are found in the chapter.

> **Note** You can toggle the display of the text of a demonstration or animation on and off by choosing **Closed Caption** from the **View** menu.

Sample Code

This course contains numerous code samples.

Sample code has been provided on the accompanying CD-ROM for you to copy and paste into your own projects. The following icon appears in the margin, indicating that this piece of sample code is included on the CD-ROM.

Sample Code Icon

Internet Links

The following icon appears in the margin next to an Internet link, indicating that this link is included on the accompanying CD-ROM.

Internet Link Icon

Sample Applications

A number of sample applications are included in the SampApps folder on the *Mastering MFC Development* CD-ROM.

Conventions Used In This Course

The table on the following page explains some of the typographic conventions used in this course.

xiii

Example of convention	Description
Sub, If, Case Else, Print, True, BackColor, Click, Debug, Long	In text, language-specific keywords appear in bold, with the initial letter capitalized.
File menu, **Add Project** dialog box	Most interface elements appear in bold, with the initial letter capitalized.
Setup	Words that you're instructed to type appear in bold.
Variable	In syntax and text, italic letters can indicate placeholders for information that you supply.
[expressionlist]	In syntax, items inside square brackets are optional.
{While	Until}	In syntax, braces and a vertical bar indicate a choice between two or more items. You must choose one of the items, unless all of the items are enclosed in square brackets.
``Sub HelloButton_Click()
Readout.Text = _
"Hello, world!"
End Sub```	This font is used for code.
ENTER	Capital letters are used for the names of keys and key sequences, such as ENTER and CTRL+R.
ALT+F1	A plus sign (+) between key names indicates a combination of keys. For example, ALT+F1 means to hold down the ALT key while pressing the F1 key.
DOWN ARROW	Individual direction keys are referred to by the direction of the arrow on the key top (LEFT, RIGHT, UP, or DOWN). The phrase "arrow keys" is used when describing these keys collectively.
BACKSPACE, HOME	Other navigational keys are referred to by their specific names.
C:\Vb\Samples\Calldlls.vbp	Paths and file names are given in mixed case.

Chapter 1
Introduction to Visual C++ 6.0

Multimedia

Creating an MFC-based Application Using MFC AppWizard 6

Lab 1.1 Demonstration 14

In this course you will learn to develop Microsoft Foundation Class (MFC)-based applications using Microsoft Visual C++ version 6.0.

This course assumes that you have a fundamental knowledge of Visual C++ and MFC. It builds on this knowledge to enable you to build advanced applications, such as OLE DB consumers, ADO-based database applications, and Internet-based applications.

Tip If you are not familiar with Visual C++ and MFC, you should first complete the course *Mastering MFC Fundamentals Using Visual C++*. For more information, visit the MSDN Training website at http://msdn.microsoft.com/training/.

This chapter discusses the architecture of Visual C++ version 6.0 and describes the enhancements that have been made to Visual C++ and MFC in this version.

Objectives

After completing this chapter, you will be able to:

◆ List some major features of Visual C++ and MFC Library.

◆ List the major enhancements to Visual C++ and MFC in Microsoft Visual Studio 6.0.

◆ Create, build, and run an MFC-based application.

Overview of Visual C++ and MFC

The MFC Library and Visual C++ provide an environment that you can use to create a wide variety of applications. This section provides an overview of the features of Visual C++ and MFC. It also describes the steps that you follow to create a simple MFC-based application with MFC AppWizard.

Features of Visual C++

Visual C++ helps you develop applications that address diverse business needs. It offers a wide variety of features and tools to help you develop applications using the latest technologies, such as MFC and the Component Object Model (COM).

Features of Visual C++

Features of Visual C++ include:

- Native COM support

    Visual COM editing, location- and language-independent COM browsing, MFC templates, and compiler support simplify component-based development.

- Visual Schema Designer

    Enhance your database application development productivity by remotely analyzing the schema of a Microsoft SQL Server database from your desktop.

- Microsoft Transaction Server

    Microsoft Transaction Server (MTS) helps you build high-performance transaction-based applications.

- Active document server support

    Visual C++ provides wizard and programmatic support for creating active document servers that can be invoked in any active document container, such as Microsoft Office 97 and Microsoft Internet Explorer 4.0.

Visual C++ Development Environment

Visual C++ provides an integrated environment for developing applications. Using Visual C++, you can create, test, refine, and maintain your applications.

The development environment of Visual C++ includes:

- A project workspace to help manage your projects.
- Tools for building projects.

- Editors for designing user interface and creating resources.
- Shared development components, including an optimizing compiler, an incremental linker, and an integrated debugger.

For a complete list of new features and enhancements in Visual C++ 6.0, search for "What's New for Visual C++ Version 6.0" in MSDN Library Visual Studio 6.0.

Editions of Visual C++

Visual C++ is available in three editions: Standard, Professional, and Enterprise.

Standard Edition

The Standard Edition contains all the features of the Professional Edition, except code optimizations, the Profiler, and static linking to the MFC Library.

Professional Edition

The Professional Edition enables you to develop and distribute commercial-quality software products. Features include MFC, the Active Template Library (ATL), COM, and OLE DB.

Enterprise Edition

The Enterprise Edition provides tools and components for building and validating enterprise-level COM applications. This edition contains all the features of the Professional Edition, and also includes Microsoft Transaction Server, SQL Editor and Debugger, Microsoft Visual SourceSafe, and support for ActiveX Data Objects (ADO) and Remote Data Objects (RDO).

Features of the MFC Library

The MFC Library is a collection of C++ classes and an application framework designed primarily for creating Microsoft Windows-based applications. This collection of classes extends the C++ language to include most of the basic structural elements that are used to create Windows-based applications. The application framework defines the structure of an application and handles many routine tasks for the application.

The MFC Library is built on top of the Win32 application programming interface (API). This API is a set of functions that the operating system exposes for use by applications. MFC exposes base classes that represent common objects in the Windows operating system, such as windows and menus.

MFC does not encapsulate, or wrap, the entire API. It wraps just the main structural components and commonly used components. Because MFC is written in C++, you can easily use the Win32 API to make native calls to the operating system.

Benefits of Using MFC

The MFC Library enables you to build on the work of expert Windows developers. MFC shortens development time, makes code more portable, provides support without reducing programming freedom and flexibility, and provides easy access to hard-to-program user-interface elements and technologies such as ActiveX and Internet programming. MFC simplifies database programming through OLE DB Templates and ADO, and simplifies network programming through Windows Sockets. MFC makes it easy to program such features as property sheets, print preview, and floating toolbars.

MFC offers you many advantages when developing full-featured Windows applications, database applications, ActiveX controls and components, and Internet applications, such as:

- An application framework on which you can build a Windows application.
- Compatibility with previous MFC versions and the new C++ classes.
- The largest base of reusable C++ source code in the industry.
- Integration with Visual C++.

Document/View Architecture

The MFC document/view architecture provides a single, consistent way of coordinating application data, referred to as a document, and views of that data. A document is a data object with which the user interacts in an editing session. A view is a window object through which the user interacts with the document.

MFC Class Hierarchy

MFC provides several classes that serve a wide range of programming needs. The first step in programming with MFC is to become familiar with these classes and learn how they are related to one another in the MFC hierarchy. Some classes are used directly; others serve as base classes for the classes that you create.

When learning about the MFC classes, it is helpful to organize them into categories. Some important categories of MFC classes are:

- Application architecture classes
- User-interface classes
- Database classes
- Internet classes

Message Maps

Before you start writing MFC applications, it is important to understand how MFC maps messages to the functions that will handle the messages. The application framework implements the message map data structure, which provides the link between the message ID and the function that will handle the message. Each entry consists of a message-specific macro. Standard Windows messages have predefined macros containing an implicit ID and handler name. Command message macros contain an explicit ID and handler name.

Below is an example of a message map for the **CMyView** class with two entries. Note that the base class is included to allow the framework to continue searching for a given handler if one does not exist within **CMyView**. Every standard Windows message has a macro of the form ON_WM_*xxx*, where *xxx* is the name of the message. A simple convention is used to generate the handler function name. The name of the function starts with "On", followed by the name of the message with "WM_" removed and only the first letter of each word capitalized. In the following example, the handler name for the first message would be **OnCreate**:

```
BEGIN_MESSAGE_MAP(CMyView, CView)
    ON_WM_CREATE()
    ON_COMMAND(ID_APPLY_SEQUENCE, OnApplySequence)
END_MESSAGE_MAP()
```

You can add a message map entry by using ClassWizard or WizardBar in Developer Studio. You can also add the entry manually.

Creating an MFC-based Application

Visual C++ helps you build applications that use the MFC Library. Visual C++ integrates development tools, such as wizards and editors, to provide flexibility to meet various programming needs.

 To see the demonstration "Creating an MFC-based Application Using MFC AppWizard," see the accompanying CD-ROM.

MFC AppWizard

MFC AppWizard automates the steps in creating the basic framework of a project. You choose the options you want for your project, and MFC AppWizard creates the project files and adds skeleton code. You can refine or enhance the code added by MFC AppWizard to implement custom requirements.

Workspace Window Panes

The Workspace window provides three views of a project, each in a separate pane:

- ClassView

    Lists the classes that you created to implement the application.

- FileView

    Lists the header and implementation files that constitute the project.

- ResourceView

    Lists the resources that are used in the project.

ClassWizard

ClassWizard simplifies using classes in the MFC Library by performing various routine programming tasks. Using ClassWizard, you can create and implement classes, add member functions and variables to a class, and map messages to functions.

Components and Controls Gallery

The Component and Controls Gallery contains reusable code, such as Visual C++ components, ActiveX controls, and components created by third-party vendors. When you insert a component into a project, the class definitions and code associated with the component are added to the project. You can then add code to implement the functionality of these components.

Enhancements to Visual C++

This section describes some major enhancements to the development environment in Visual C++ 6.0.

Debugger

Visual C++ 6.0 includes several new features that simplify the debugging process.

For a complete list of new debugger features, search for "What's New for Visual C++ Version 6.0, Debugger" in MSDN Library Visual Studio 6.0.

Edit and Continue

The Edit and Continue feature enables you to edit code during a debugging session without having to quit the session and rebuild the application. Changes made during a session are simply recompiled and applied to the executing application in memory.

For more information about Edit and Continue, see "Using the Edit and Continue Feature" on page 21 in Chapter 2, "Debugging and Error Handling."

GetLastError() Value Displayed as Register

A new pseudo-register, ERR, displays the last error code for the current thread. ERR is displayed as a hardware register, though actually it is not. You can view the contents of this pseudo-register in the Watch window or **Quickwatch** dialog box by using the standard procedures for displaying registers.

To display the error code in meaningful form, use the hr format specifier with ERR as shown:

```
ERR, hr
```

AfxDumpStack for Diagnosing Applications

The **AfxDumpStack** function generates an image of the current stack and dumps that image to the debug output device, such as **afxdump**. You can use this function in debug and non-debug versions of the MFC libraries to get diagnostic information, even if the debugger is not installed on the end user's computer.

New Formatting Symbols

The following table lists some new formatting symbols.

Symbol	Description
hr	Displays 32-bit values in a more meaningful way, such as S_OK or E_NOTIMPL.
st	Displays string values as ANSI or Unicode.
wm	Displays numeric values decoded into the names of windows message numbers (WM_ constants).

Variants Decoded for Display

The debugger automatically displays variants in their correct form. For example, integers are displayed numerically, and BSTRs are displayed as strings. The debugger also displays the type of the variant.

Editors

The enhancements to the Visual C++ Editor make it easier to write code for your applications.

For a complete list of new editor features, search for "What's New for Visual C++ Version 6.0, Editors" in MSDN Library Visual Studio 6.0.

Automatic Statement Completion

The text editor in Visual C++ 6.0 provides the Automatic Statement Completion feature, which uses Microsoft IntelliSense technology to help you write code for your application. When you type characters, such as "." or "->", IntelliSense presents information that helps you complete the code statement or function call.

The following illustration shows the IntelliSense information that appears when you type " (" after a function name.

```
CXDoc* CXView::GetDocument() // non-debug version is inline
{
    ASSERT(m_pDocument->IsKindOf(|
                                 BOOL IsKindOf (const CRuntimeClass *pClass)
```

Parameter Pop-Ups

In the source editor, you can get type information about a parameter by placing the mouse cursor on the parameter. Similarly, you can see the function definition by placing the cursor on a function.

Resource Editor Support for Internet Explorer 4.0 Controls

The resource editor provides support for Internet Explorer 4.0. To access the Internet Explorer 4.0 wrapper classes, you use the **Controls** toolbar in the dialog editor to add these controls to your forms and dialog boxes.

Projects

Some key enhancements relating to building projects in Visual C++ are described below.

For a complete list of new project features, search for "What's New for Visual C++ Version 6.0, Projects" in MSDN Library Visual Studio 6.0.

Dynamic Parsing

When you create a class, variable, or member function, Visual C++ updates ClassView and WizardBar to display the new items, without requiring you to save changes first.

Invoking Dialog Editor from ClassView and WizardBar

You can now go directly to the dialog editor from a class that implements a dialog box by choosing **GoTo Dialog Editor** from ClassView or WizardBar.

New Form Command

The **New Form** command generates a form and is available from the **Insert** menu, ClassView, and WizardBar. This command provides ClassWizard functionality for **CFormView, CDialog,** and the database view classes. In addition to this functionality, the **New Form** command also creates a dialog box with all the appropriate options.

Wizards

Some key enhancements to wizards, such as MFC AppWizard, are described below.

For a complete list of new wizard features, search for "What's New for Visual C++ Version 6.0, Wizards" in MSDN Library Visual Studio 6.0.

Enhancements to MFC AppWizard

MFC AppWizard offers several new options for projects that you create in Visual C++ 6.0, including:

- Single-document interface or multiple-document interface applications that are not based on the document/view architecture. This enables streamlined use of MFC for applications that are not document-based.
- Toolbars that work like Internet Explorer rebar controls.
- Active document containment.
- Windows Explorer-style applications.

Enhancements to ClassWizard

ClassWizard now enables you to add messages and variables to Internet Explorer 4.0 controls. You can also derive new classes based on MFC Internet Explorer 4.0 control classes.

For more information about these control classes, see "Internet Explorer 4.0 Common Controls" on page 225 in Chapter 5, "Using Controls."

Enhancements to the ATL Object Wizard

The ATL Object Wizard contains a new object category named Data Access, which you can use to create OLE DB consumers and providers.

For more information about building consumer applications, see Chapter 7, "Using OLE DB Templates for Data Access."

Tools

This topic provides a brief overview of some tools that are new in Visual C++ 6.0, such as Component Manager and Visual Analyzer. You will also look at enhancements to the Test Container tool.

For a complete list of new tools features, search for "What's New for Visual C++ Version 6.0, Tools" in MSDN Library Visual Studio 6.0.

Component Manager

Note Component Manager is supported only in the Enterprise Edition of Visual C++.

The Component Manager is a tool that enables you to store objects and share them between software tools and custom reusable components. The Component Manager improves support in the following areas:

- Reuse

    Support for cataloging and locating relevant designs, code and services.

- Dependency tracking

    Support for establishing and querying relationships between objects.

- Tool interoperability

    Support for publishing standardized descriptions of systems, which allows independent tools to exchange data.

- Data resource management

    Global metadata for an enterprise data warehouse, and a resource library of available services and components.

- Team development

    Support for managing concurrent activity on different versions and configurations of application design and development.

Visual Studio Analyzer

Note Microsoft Visual Studio Analyzer is supported only in the Enterprise Edition of Visual C++.

Visual Studio Analyzer server-side components provide information about the Microsoft components, such as COM, ADO, and MTS, running on a particular computer. You can use this information with the Visual Studio Analyzer client to retrieve information about a distributed application, such as what it is doing, how it is performing, and where problems are occurring.

Enhancements to Test Container

Improvements to Test Container include:

- Support for OCX 96 features, such as windowless controls, inactive controls, flicker-free activation, and quick activation.
- Microsoft Visual Basic Scripting Edition (VBScript) support for writing test scripts.
- Selective enabling/disabling of container features to simulate different container environments.
- Selective logging of events, property changes, and property edit requests.

Enhancements to MFC

This section describes some enhancements to MFC that help you build custom applications that access data sources and the Web.

Database

The two major enhancements in MFC for data access are OLE DB Templates and ActiveX Data Objects (ADO). These enhancements enable you to build powerful database applications.

OLE DB Templates

OLE DB is the latest data access methodology from Microsoft. This methodology enables you to access any kind of data source by using a set of standard data access interfaces.

Using OLE DB directly from Visual C++ involves writing a large amount of code. OLE DB template classes make OLE DB much easier to use while providing excellent performance.

For more information about OLE DB Templates, see Chapter 7, "Using OLE DB Templates for Data Access."

The new MFC class, **COleDBRecordView**, provides the functionality of OLE DB templates within the context of the MFC document/view architecture.

ActiveX Data Objects

ADO simplifies database-related operations, such as connecting to a database and retrieving rowsets. MFC supports ADO in the following ways:

- ADO Data Bound Dialog Wizard

    This wizard guides you through the process of creating a data-bound dialog box with ADO.

- ADO data control

    This control enables you to access data exposed through an OLE DB data provider application.

- Data-bound controls

    The data-bound controls, such as **DataGrid** and **DataList,** help you process the data retrieved by the data control. These controls have a **DataSource** property and can be bound to a data control. You can include these controls in your dialog boxes to display the retrieved data.

For more information about ADO, see Chapter 8, "Creating ADO Database Applications."

Internet

This topic provides a brief overview of some Internet-related enhancements in MFC. These enhancements help you build applications that access the Internet.

Dynamic HTML Control with CHtmlView

CHtmlView is a wrapper class for the Web Browser ActiveX control. The Web Browser control enables your application to display HTML pages just as a Web browser would display them. **CHtmlView** provides many browser features, including a history list, favorites (bookmarks), and security features.

For more information about using **CHtmlView,** see "Implementing HTML Views" on page 469 in Chapter 9, "Building Internet Applications."

Updates to Existing MFC Classes

The following table describes improvements to existing MFC classes that provide Internet functionality.

Class	Description
CHttpServer	Includes a function for writing data to the server.
CHttpServerContext	Includes functions that provide control over the size of chunks written to the HTTP server.
CInternetSession	Supports setting cookies for a specified URL, returning cookies for a specified URL and all its parent URLs, and retrieving the variable specifying the length of the cookie stored in the buffer.

Lab 1.1: Creating an MFC-based Application

In this lab, you will create, build, and run a simple MFC-based application in the Visual Studio development environment using AppWizard.

To see the demonstration "Lab 1.1 Demonstration," see the accompanying CD-ROM.

Estimated time to complete this lab: **20 minutes**

To complete the exercises in this lab, you must have the required software. For detailed information about the labs and setup for the labs, see "Labs" in "About This Course."

The solution code for this lab is located in the folder *<install folder>*\Labs\Ch01\Lab1.1\Ex01\Solution.

Objectives

After completing this lab, you will be able to:

- Use AppWizard to create a simple Scribble application in MFC.
- Use Visual Studio and Visual C++ to build and run the application.

Prerequisites

There are no prerequisites for this lab.

Exercises

The following exercise provides practice working with the concepts and techniques covered in this chapter:

- Exercise 1: Creating a Simple Scribble Application

    In this exercise, you will use Visual Studio, MFC AppWizard, and Visual C++ to create, build, and run a simple MFC SDI Scribble application.

Exercise 1: Creating a Simple Scribble Application

In this exercise, you will use Visual Studio, MFC AppWizard, and Visual C++ to create, build, and run a simple MFC-based single document interface (SDI) Scribble application.

▶ **Use MFC AppWizard to create a new project**

1. In Visual Studio, on the **File** menu, click **New**.
2. In the **New** dialog box, click the **Projects** tab, and then do the following:

    a. For the project type, select **MFC AppWizard (exe)**.

    b. For the project name, type **Scribble**.

    c. Set the location for your project.

    d. Accept the default platform **Win32**.

    e. Click **OK** to create the new project workspace.

    MFC AppWizard starts.

3. In MFC AppWizard Step 1, click **Single document** and **English**, leave the **Document/View architecture support** checkbox selected, and then click **Next** to go to Step 2.
4. Because this project does not need database support, accept the default **None** for database support and click **Next** to go to Step 3.
5. In Step 3, accept **None** for the document support, clear the **ActiveX Controls** check box, and then click **Next** to go to Step 4.

6. In Step 4, clear the **Printing and print preview** check box, accept the defaults (**Docking toolbar, Initial status bar, 3D controls**, and 4 files for the recent file list) and then click **Next** to go to Step 5.

7. In Step 5, leave the project style as **MFC Standard**, click **Yes, please** for generating source file comments and select **As a shared DLL** for MFC support. Click **Next** to go to Step 6.

8. In Step 6, click **Finish** to display the **New Project Information** dialog box summarizing your choices.

9. To create the application files with MFC AppWizard, click **OK**.

When MFC AppWizard is finished, you will be returned to Visual Studio. To see the classes that MFC AppWizard created, click the **ClassView** tab in the Project Workspace window.

▶ **Add message handlers for mouse messages**

1. On the **View** menu, click **ClassWizard**.

   The **MFC ClassWizard** property page appears.

2. In the **Message Maps** tab, in the combo boxes provided on the property page, select the **Scribble** project, the **CScribbleView** class, and the **CScribbleView** Object ID.

3. In the **Messages** list box, select the WM_LBUTTONDOWN message and click **Add Function**.

4. Repeat Step 3 for the WM_MOUSEMOVE and WM_LBUTTONUP messages.

5. Click **OK** to close ClassWizard.

▶ **Implement OnLButtonDown, OnMouseMove, and OnLButtonUp handlers**

1. Open ScribbleView.h.

2. In the public attributes section of the CScribbleView class declaration, define startpt and endpt as follows:

   ```
   CPoint startpt, endpt;
   ```

3. Save ScribbleView.h.

4. Open ScribbleView.cpp.

5. In the constructor, initialize startpt and endpt coordinates to −1 as follows:

   ```
   startpt=-1;
   endpt=-1;
   ```

6. Scroll to the **OnLButtonDown** handler.
7. In the **OnLButtonDown** handler, save the point where the mouse button is pressed as the start point:

   ```
   startpt.x=point.x;
   startpt.y=point.y;
   ```

8. Scroll to the **OnMouseMove** handler.
9. In the **OnMouseMove** handler, add the following code to draw a line from the previous detected point in the mouse drag to the current point:

   ```
   CClientDC dc(this);
   endpt.x = point.x;
   endpt.y = point.y;
   if (startpt.x != -1 )
   {
       dc.MoveTo(startpt.x, startpt.y);
       dc.LineTo(endpt.x, endpt.y);
       startpt.x = endpt.x;
       startpt.y = endpt.y;
   }
   ```

10. In the **OnLButtonUp** handler, add code to reinitialize the variable startpt as follows:

    ```
    startpt = -1;
    ```

▶ **Build and run the project**

1. On the **Build** menu, click **Build Scribble.exe**.

   Visual Studio displays the status of the build process as it builds your project.

2. After the build is complete, on the **Build** menu, click **Execute Scribble.exe**.

   The Scribble application starts.

The solution code for this exercise is located in the folder *<install folder>*\Labs\Ch01\Lab1.1\Ex01\Solution.

Student Notes:

Chapter 2:
Debugging and Error Handling

Multimedia

Using the Visual
    Studio Debugger 20

Using the Edit and
    Continue Technique 21

Lab 2.1 Demonstration 31

Lab 2.2 Demonstration 33

Almost all code of any significant size and complexity initially contains errors. You can use the Microsoft Visual Studio debugger to eliminate logical errors from your applications. The debugger is a powerful tool that provides several easy-to-use techniques for identifying and removing errors from your code.

In addition to errors, exceptional conditions caused by an external software or hardware environment might also affect the performance of an application. You need to anticipate and handle possible failures by adding necessary exception-handling code to ensure smooth program execution.

In this chapter, you will look at some important features of the Visual Studio debugger. You will also learn to write code to handle errors and exceptions in your applications.

Objectives

After completing this chapter, you will be able to:

- Use the Visual Studio debugger to identify and eliminate errors.
- Use the Edit and Continue feature to simplify debugging.
- Write functions with built-in error-handling code.
- Use the C++ exception-handling technique to handle run-time exceptions.
- Describe and use the various types of Microsoft Foundation Class (MFC) exception classes.

Debugging

An error is the failure of a function or process to carry out its assigned task because of some directly controllable parameter or condition. For example, **CView::GetDocument** returns a NULL pointer if the associated view is not attached to a document. You can use the Visual Studio debugger to correct the errors in your code.

This section begins with an overview of the Visual Studio debugger features. You will read about setting and managing breakpoints, viewing and modifying variables, stepping through your application, and interpreting the call stack. You will then learn how to use the Edit and Continue feature, which enables you to modify your code and continue execution of the revised code without terminating your debugging session.

Overview of the Visual Studio Debugger

The Visual Studio debugger provides a variety of features and tools to help you track down errors in your code.

Visual Studio Debugger Features

The debugging tools in Developer Studio enable you to test your C++, MFC, and mixed-language applications.

You can use the debugger to:

- Set breakpoints.
- Step through code.
- Monitor variables, registers, and memory.
- View assembly code and the call stack.
- Modify code and variable values.

To see the demonstration "Using the Visual Studio Debugger," see the accompanying CD-ROM.

Visual Studio Debugger Interface

The Visual Studio debugger interface is easy to use and consists of the following elements:

- Debugger menus

    You can find the commands related to debugging on the **Build** menu, the **Debug** menu, the **View** menu, and the **Edit** menu.

- Debugger toolbar

    Developer Studio provides the **Debug** toolbar to make common debugging tasks easier.

- Debugger windows

    During a debugging session, the debugger displays debugging information in different windows according to the type of information. You can view these windows by clicking **Debugging Windows** on the **View** menu.

- Debugger dialog boxes

    You can use the debugger dialog boxes to manipulate breakpoints, variables, threads, and exceptions.

Using the Edit and Continue Feature

Microsoft Visual C++ includes an Edit and Continue feature in the debugger. This feature enables you to change the source code during a debugging session and continue debugging without terminating the debugging session. After you make a change using this feature, you do not need to terminate the debugging process and rebuild the application. Your changes are recompiled and applied to the executing debugger in memory.

To see the demonstration "Using the Edit and Continue Technique," see the accompanying CD-ROM.

Enabling Edit and Continue

You enable or disable the Edit and Continue feature by changing the settings in the **Options** dialog box. Edit and Continue is enabled by default.

▶ **To enable Edit and Continue**
1. On the **Tools** menu, click **Options**.
2. On the **Debug** tab in the **Options** dialog box, select **Debug commands invoke Edit and Continue**.
3. On the **Project** menu, click **Settings**.
4. On the **C/C++** tab in the **Project Settings** dialog box, select **Program Database for Edit and Continue** in the **Debug Info** list.

You need to fully rebuild the project before you start the first debugging session in which you want to use Edit and Continue.

Using Edit and Continue

After modifying source code, invoke the **Step** or **Go** debugger commands to initiate Edit and Continue. If the code edit is not supported, you will be prompted to rebuild the application. If the edit is supported, the changes will be recompiled and reflected in the executing application.

Edit and Continue does not support edits to the following:

- Header files
- C++ class definitions
- Function prototypes
- Global/static code

For more information, search for "Edit and Continue" in MSDN Library Visual Studio 6.0.

Handling Errors and Exceptions

This section covers some effective techniques for handling errors and exceptions. It begins by describing the error-handling code that you can build into your functions to ensure smooth program execution. When a critical error occurs, the error-handling code stops execution of the application.

This section also describes the exception-handling technique that you can use in your MFC-based applications. The section ends with a discussion on the MFC exception classes.

Writing Robust Functions

Almost any function, including Microsoft Win32 and MFC routines, can fail. This is especially true in multitasking environments, such as Microsoft Windows or Windows NT, where applications share limited system resources. You should anticipate this possibility, and write your programs accordingly.

To properly code an application, you must anticipate possible errors by checking return values and taking appropriate action when a function fails.

Reporting Errors

Many MFC functions return special values to indicate that an error has occurred. In your functions, you should implement this mechanism to report a failure back to the calling function.

Two common techniques exist for reporting errors:

- Returning values

    Set the return value to FALSE, NULL, 0xFFFFFFFF, or − 1 to indicate a function failure.

    The following example code shows the definition of a function that returns a value indicating success or failure:

    ```
    int CMyView::GetLastWord()
    {
        ...
        if ((m_nWordCount < m_nCurrentWordNumber) || (m_nWordCount <= 0))
            return -1;
        ...
    }
    ```

- Setting global error codes

    Set a global error code indicating the type of error that occurred. Call the **SetLastError** function to set a global error code when a function fails.

When implementing error-handling code in your application, you must consider the balance between extensive error-checking and program execution speed when implementing error-handling code in your application.

Handling Errors

Handling errors involves writing code that will alter program execution when a called function reports an error. How you check for errors depends on how the function indicates an error:

- If the function returns a value, check the return value of the function.

    The following example code shows how you can decide the course of action at run time by checking for the return value:

    ```
    ...
    int b = pView.GetLastWord();
    if (b == -1)
        m_ID = ProcessEmptyDocument();
    else
        m_ID = ProcessDocument();
    ...
    return;
    ```

- If the function sets a global error code, call the **GetLastError** function to determine whether an error occurred.

Handling Exceptions

Unlike an error, an exception is an abnormal—and often unexpected—event that changes the normal flow of processing and may require special handling by the operating system. Exceptions are raised as the result of hardware or software events, which are usually undetectable during development and are beyond the direct control of the program.

Accessing a bad memory address and dividing by zero are examples of hardware exceptions. Passing an invalid parameter or insufficient memory are examples of software exceptions. You can respond to these exceptions by using special C++ syntax called exception handling.

In exception handling, the operating system and the process in which the exception occurred cooperate to resolve the exception. Exceptions are generated and handled on a thread-by-thread basis. When an exception is raised, the operating system finds an appropriate handler, and passes control to the handler to resolve the exception or terminate the process or program.

When no matching handler is found, a predefined run-time **terminate** function is called. The default action of **terminate** is to call **abort**. You can use **set_terminate** to provide your own termination routine instead.

C++ Exception-Handling Technique

C++ exception handling is the preferred method when programming C++ and MFC-based applications. It is part of the ANSI/ISO language standard, so it is available in all modern C++ implementations on all supported platforms.

C++ exception-handling code consists of three major parts: the **try** (guard) block, the **throw** statement, and the **catch** block.

In the following example, the **try** block attempts to write the headers. The catch block then handles a specific file exception, and passes all other exceptions on to the outer block with the throw macro:

```
try
{
        // Write the file header
        file.Write((LPSTR)&bmfHdr, sizeof(BITMAPFILEHEADER));
        //
        // Write the DIB header and the bits
        file.WriteHuge(lpBI, dwDIBSize);
}
catch (CFileException* e)
    {
        ::GlobalUnlock((HGLOBAL) hDib);
        throw;
    }

::GlobalUnlock((HGLOBAL) hDib);
    return TRUE;
```

Using the try Block

The **try** block is any block of code prefaced with the **try** statement and surrounded by curly brackets ({ }). To create the most robust application, any code or function calls that may generate exceptions should be contained within a **try** block.

Using the throw Statement

The **throw** statement transfers control to the exception-handler that matches the type of exception specified in the **throw** argument.

Using a catch Handler

The **catch** block is composed of a **catch** expression, immediately followed by a handler. The **catch** expression defines which exception (or exceptions) the immediately following exception handler should handle; it filters the passing exceptions. Once an exception is caught, control passes to the exception handler.

The **catch** handler has two major purposes:

- Handle the specific exception or exceptions specified by the **catch** statement appropriately.
- Delete the exception object it if was dynamically created.

A handler for a base class also handles classes derived from that class. The **catch** clause catches exceptions of any type.

To associate different code blocks with different exceptions, a single **try** block can be followed by one or more **catch** blocks. It is also possible to nest **try** blocks.

Function Exception Specifications

For documentation and software-quality purposes, if a function is capable of throwing an exception, you should specify so in its declaration. For example, a nondefault **CPen** constructor has been declared as follows:

```
CPen(int nPenStyle, int nWidth, COLORREF crColor)
    throw (CResourceException);
```

This declaration indicates that this function may throw an exception of type **CResourceException**.

For more information about handling exceptions, search for "Exception Handling" in MSDN Library Visual Studio 6.0.

Exception-Handling Process

Exception handling follows a specific path. The following illustration shows the exception-handling process.

Exception Handling Process

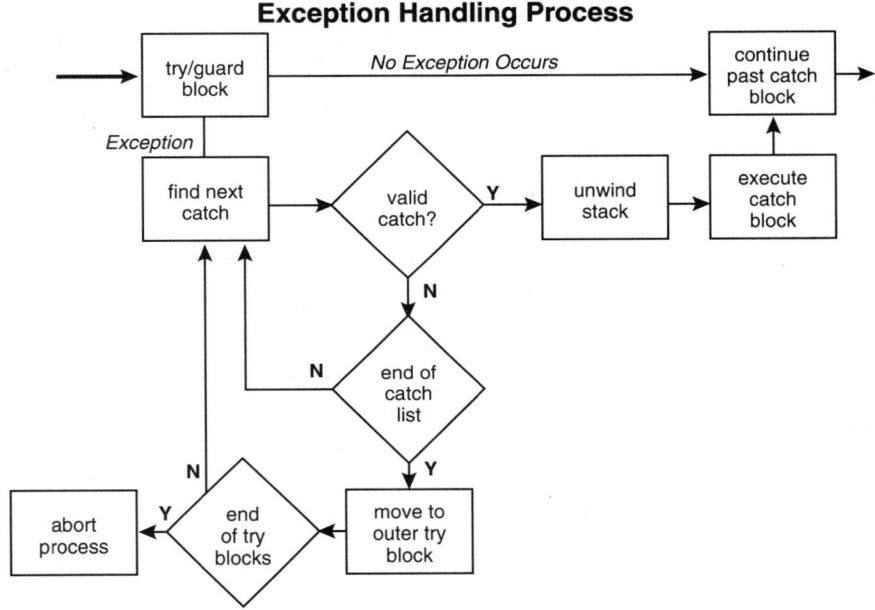

The following events occur in the exception-handling process:

- **Entering the try block**

    Control reaches the guarded section (within the **try** block) by normal flow control. The guarded section begins executing. A **try** (guard) block can throw more than one exception, though only one exception can be thrown at a time. A **catch** block can throw its own exceptions, or rethrow the caught exception.

- **If no exception is thrown**

    If no exception is thrown during execution of the guarded section, the **catch** blocks that follow the **try** block are not executed. Execution continues at the statement after the last **catch** block following the **try** block in which the exception was thrown.

- **If an exception is thrown**

    If an exception is thrown during execution of the guarded section (or in any routine the guarded section calls directly or indirectly), an exception object is created from the object created by the **throw** operand. (This implies that a copy constructor may be involved.)

- **Searching for a catch handler**

    If an exception is thrown, the compiler looks for a **catch** clause that can handle an exception of the type thrown. The **catch** handlers are examined in order of their appearance following the **try** block. If no appropriate handler is found, the next enclosing **try** block is examined. This process continues until the outermost enclosing **try** block is examined.

- **If a matching catch handler is not found**

    If a matching handler is still not found, or if another exception occurs before or during stack unwinding (but before the handler gets control), the **terminate** function is called.

- **If a matching catch handler is found**

    If a matching **catch** handler is found, the parameter is initialized to refer to the exception object.

- **Unwinding the stack**

    After the parameter is initialized, the process of unwinding the stack begins. This involves the destruction of all local objects that were constructed (but not yet destroyed) between the beginning of the **try** block associated with the **catch** handler and the exception's throw site. Destruction occurs in reverse order of construction. The **catch** handler is executed and the program resumes execution following the last handler (that is, the first statement or construct that is not a **catch** handler).

Note Control can enter a **catch** handler through a thrown exception only—never by means of a **goto** statement or a **case** label in a **switch** statement.

MFC Exception Classes

When you use C++ exceptions in an MFC-based application, you write exception handlers that use pointers to **CException** or **CException**-derived objects that can be thrown by the MFC framework or by your application.

Handler functions are polymorphic; a handler written for a base-class type will catch handlers of a derived type. To extend the exception architecture, you also can derive new exception classes from the ones provided.

Extensions to the CException Class

MFC provides the following predefined extensions to the **CException** class.

Exception class	Description	Thrown by
CMemoryException	Out of memory	**new** operator
CFileException	File exceptions	**CFile** functions
CArchiveException	Archive/serialization exception	**CArchive** functions
CNotSupportedException	Response to request for unsupported service	Any function that requests an unsupported service
CResourceException	Windows resource-allocation exception	Any function that requests a Windows resource
CDBException	ODBC database exceptions	Member functions of **ODBC** database classes
CDaoException	DAO database exceptions	Member functions of **DAO** database classes
COleException	OLE exceptions	Functions performing OLE operations
COleDispatchException	OLE dispatch (automation) exceptions	Functions performing OLE automation-related operations
CUserException	Exception that alerts the user with a message box, then throws a generic **CException**	Functions that perform operations that are likely to fail
CInternetException	Internet exception	Any function that fails in an Internet-related operation

The base class, **CException**, provides two member functions, **ReportError** and **GetErrorMessage**, to assist in handling exceptions. Many of the derived classes provide additional functionality.

For more information about **CException**, search for "CException" in MSDN Library Visual Studio 6.0.

Throwing MFC Exceptions

You can use existing MFC exception classes to throw exceptions. MFC provides a number of helper functions, such as **AfxThrowMemoryException**, to throw a preallocated exception object of the appropriate type.

The following code shows the use of these helper functions:

```
void CSomeClass::SomeFunction()
{
  char* p1 = (char*) malloc(SOME_SIZE);
  if (NULL == p1)
      AfxThrowMemoryException();
  ...
  free ( p1 );
}
```

Last Chance Exception Handling

If you do not handle an exception, program execution will abort in an undesirable manner. To prevent this behavior, you can modify the C++ **terminate** function to call a function other than **abort**. For more information about how to implement this technique, search for "set_terminate" in MSDN Library Visual Studio 6.0. The MFC Library provides the corresponding functions **AfxTerminate** and **AfxSetTerminate**, which you can use instead in an MFC-based application.

Lab 2.1: Using Edit and Continue

In this lab, you will use the Edit and Continue feature during a debugging session.

To see the demonstration "Lab 2.1 Demonstration," see the accompanying CD-ROM.

Estimated time to complete this lab: **15 minutes**

To complete the exercises in this lab, you must have the required software. For detailed information about the labs and setup for the labs, see "Labs" in "About This Course."

The code that forms the starting point for this lab is located in the folder *<install folder>*\Labs\Ch02\Lab2.1\Ex01.

Objectives

After completing this lab, you will be able to:

- Use Edit and Continue to make changes to your source code during a debugging session.

Prerequisites

There are no prerequisites for this lab.

Exercises

The following exercise provides practice working with the concepts and techniques covered in this chapter.

- Exercise 1: Using Edit and Continue

    In this exercise, you will use Edit and Continue to change source code while debugging the Scribble sample application.

Exercise 1: Using Edit and Continue

The code that forms the starting point for this exercise is in *<install folder>*\Labs\Ch02\Lab2.1\Ex01.

In this exercise, you will use Edit and Continue to change source code while debugging the Scribble sample application.

▶ Enable Edit and Continue

1. On the **Tools** menu, click **Options**, and then click the **Debug** tab.
2. On the **Debug** tab, be sure **Debug commands invoke Edit and Continue** is selected and click **OK**.
3. On the **Project** menu, click **Settings**.
4. On the **C/C++** tab, select **Program Database for Edit and Continue** in the **Debug Info** list-box and click **OK**.
5. Select **Rebuild All** from the **Build** menu.

   The application should compile without errors.

> **Tip** If you receive the error "Command line error D2016: '/ZI' and '/O2' command-line options are incompatible," do the following:
>
> 1. On the **Project** menu, click **Settings**, and then click the **C/C++** tab.
> 2. In the **Project Options** box, delete the /ZI and /O2 options and recompile.

6. Run the Scribble application.

   When you drag the mouse to draw a line, you will see that the output is different from what you expected.

7. Close the application.

> **Note** After you enable the Edit and Continue feature, you must rebuild your program before you can use the feature.

▶ Use Edit and Continue

1. In the **OnLButtonUp** function of ScribbleView.cpp, insert a breakpoint on the statement that invokes the default **OnLButtonUp** function.
2. Invoke the **Go** debugger command to run the application.

   The application enters break mode when you release the mouse button.

3. In the **OnMouseMove** function, replace the second parameter in the **MoveTo** function with StartPt.y.

4. Remove the breakpoint.
5. Invoke the **Go** command to initiate Edit and Continue.

    The new code is reflected in the running application.
6. Close the application.

For more information about Edit and Continue, see "Using the Edit and Continue Feature" on page 21 in this chapter.

Lab 2.2: Implementing Exception Handling

In this lab, you will handle exceptions thrown by **CFileException** in an application.

To see the demonstration "Lab 2.2 Demonstration," see the accompanying CD-ROM.

Estimated time to complete this lab: **15 minutes**

To complete the exercises in this lab, you must have the required software. For detailed information about the labs and setup for the labs, see "Labs" in "About This Course."

The code that forms the starting point for this lab is located in the folder *<install folder>*\Labs\Ch02\Lab2.2\Ex01.

The solution code for this lab is located in the folder *<install folder>*\Labs\Ch02\Lab2.2\Ex01\Solution.

Objectives

After completing this lab, you will be able to:

- Use **try** and **catch** blocks to handle exceptions in MFC code.

Prerequisites

There are no prerequisites for this lab.

Exercises

The following exercise provides practice working with the concepts and techniques covered in this chapter.

◆ Exercise 1: Handling Exceptions

In this exercise, you will handle exceptions thrown by **CFileException**. You will add exception-handling code to an application that enables you to choose files to compare in the two panes of a splitter window.

Exercise 1: Handling Exceptions

The code that forms the starting point for this exercise is in *<install folder>*\Labs\Ch02\Lab2.2\Ex01.

In this exercise, you will handle exceptions thrown by **CFileException**. You will add exception-handling code to an application that enables you to choose files to compare in the two panes of a splitter window.

▶ **Add exception-handling code**

1. In the **RunComparison** function of DiffDoc.cpp, set up a **try** block for the program statements that open the file lpszFile1 for reading and serialize a **CDiffView** object as shown:

   ```
   try
   {
   CFile file(lpszFile1, CFile::modeRead);
   CArchive ar(&file, CArchive::load);
   pView->Serialize(ar);
   }
   ```

Note Only the overloaded constructor of the **CFile** class, which accepts two parameters, throws an exception if an error occurs. If the file cannot be opened, an exception is thrown, which is caught by the **CFileException** handler.

Lab 2.2: Implementing Exception Handling

2. Place exception-handling code in a **catch** block as follows to determine why the open operation failed in the event that a failure occurs:

```
catch(CFileException* e)
{
    if(e->m_cause == CFileException::fileNotFound)
    {
        char errmsg[80];
        strcpy(errmsg,"File  ");
        strcat(errmsg, lpszFile1);
        strcat(errmsg," not found");
        ::MessageBox(0,errmsg,"Error",MB_OK);
    }
    else if(e->m_cause == CFileException::tooManyOpenFiles)
        ::MessageBox(0,"No more file handles available","Error",MB_OK);
    else
        ::MessageBox(0,"Open failed","Error",MB_OK);
    e->Delete();
}
```

The code in the **catch** block runs only if the code within the **try** block throws an exception of the type specified in the catch statement.

3. Repeat steps 3 and 4 for the file lpszFile2.
4. Save DiffDoc.cpp.

The following sample code shows an example of how your code should look. To copy this code for use in your own projects, see "Lab 2.1.1 RunComparison" on the accompanying CD-ROM.

```
void CDiffDoc::RunComparison (LPCSTR lpszFile1, LPCSTR lpszFile2)
{
  CMainFrame * pFrame= CDiffApp::GetApp()->GetMainFrame();
  if(pFrame)
  {
      CSplitter * pSplitter= pFrame->GetSplitter();
      if(pSplitter)
      {
          CDiffView * pView;
          pView = (CDiffView *)pSplitter->GetPane(0,0);
```

code continued on next page

code continued from previous page

```
        if (pView)
        {
            try
            {
            CFile    file(lpszFile1, CFile::modeRead);
            CArchive ar(&file, CArchive::load);
            pView->Serialize(ar);
            }
            catch(CFileException* e)
            {
            if(e->m_cause == CFileException::fileNotFound)
            {
                char errmsg[80];
                strcpy(errmsg,"File   ");
                strcat(errmsg, lpszFile1);
                strcat(errmsg,"  not found");
                ::MessageBox(0,errmsg,"Error",MB_OK);
            }
            else if(e->m_cause == CFileException::tooManyOpenFiles)
                ::MessageBox(0,"No more file handles available",
                "Error",MB_OK);
            else
                ::MessageBox(0,"Open failed","Error",MB_OK);
            e->Delete();
            }
        }
        pView = (CDiffView *)pSplitter->GetPane(0,1);
        if (pView)
        {
            try
            {
            CFile    file(lpszFile2, CFile::modeRead);
            CArchive ar(&file, CArchive::load);
            pView->Serialize(ar);
            }
            catch(CFileException* e)
            {
```

code continued on next page

Lab 2.2: Implementing Exception Handling

```
code continued from previous page
                if(e->m_cause == CFileException::fileNotFound)
                {
                    char errmsg[80];
                    strcpy(errmsg,"File   ");
                    strcat(errmsg, lpszFile2);
                    strcat(errmsg," not found");
                    ::MessageBox(0,errmsg,"Error",MB_OK);
                }
                else if(e->m_cause == CFileException::tooManyOpenFiles)
                    ::MessageBox(0,"No more file handles available",
                    "Error",MB_OK);
                else
                    ::MessageBox(0,"Open failed","Error",MB_OK);
                e->Delete();
                }
        }
        //      Flag as clean so that we won't get
        //      prompted to save
        SetModifiedFlag(FALSE);
        }
    }
}
```

For more information about exception handling, see "Exception-Handling Process" on page 27 in this chapter.

▶ **Build and test the application**

- Run your application and try to open a file that does not exist.

The solution code for this exercise is located in the folder *<install folder>*\Labs\Ch02\Lab2.2\Ex01\Solution.

Self-Check Questions

To see the answers to the Self-Check Questions, see Appendix A.

1. Which type of edit is supported by Edit and Continue?

   A. Editing header files
   B. Editing function prototypes
   C. Editing functions on the call stack
   D. Editing C++ class definitions

2. Which keyword transfers control to the matching exception handler?

   A. abort
   B. try
   C. throw
   D. catch

3. What is the base class for exception types in MFC?

   A. CMemoryException
   B. CResourceException
   C. CUserException
   D. CException

4. What is the purpose of the stack unwinding process?

   A. Delivery of the exception object to the matching **catch** handler.
   B. Destruction of automatic objects in the order in which they were created.
   C. A call to the predefined **terminate** function.
   D. Destruction of local objects in the affected part of the stack in the reverse order.

Chapter 3:
Enhancing the User Interface

Multimedia

Creating a
  Dynamic Menu 41
Creating a
  Floating Toolbar 51
Lab 3.1 Demonstration 66
Lab 3.2 Demonstration 71
Creating a Modeless
  Dialog Box 85
Implementing Dialog
  Box Communication 86
Creating and
  Implementing a
  Dialog Bar 90
Lab 3.3 Demonstration 97
Lab 3.4 Demonstration 114
Lab 3.5 Demonstration 122

In this chapter, you will learn how to enhance basic user interface (UI) elements, such as menus and toolbars, and create new UI elements, such as modeless dialog boxes and dialog bars.

This chapter begins with techniques for enhancing and extending the UI capabilities of an Microsoft Foundation Class (MFC)-based application. You will learn how to create dynamic menus, add cascading menus, and include graphics in menus and status bars.

You will also learn to extend the functionality of dialog boxes by managing Dialog Data Exchange (DDX) and Dialog Data Validation (DDV), extending DDV, and coordinating data between controls.

In the later sections of this chapter, you will learn how to create and manage modeless dialog boxes, dialog bars, and rebars.

Objectives

After completing this chapter, you will be able to:

- Create dynamic menus, cascading menus, and ownerdraw menus.
- Place dockable toolbars in an application.
- Include graphics and additional panes in status bars.
- Use and customize common dialog boxes.
- Extend DDV.
- Create tabbed dialog boxes and property sheets.
- Invoke and display modeless dialog boxes.
- Create dialog bars and rebars.

Enhancing Menus

Using the resource editor is the easiest way to create menus. However, you cannot use the resource editor to create menus at run time. Instead, you need to add the required code to your application.

The first topic in this section shows how to implement dynamic menus. Dynamic menus provide the user with an appropriate set of choices, depending on the context. They also offer you the choice of presenting the user with different options at run time.

The next topic covers how to implement cascading menus. Cascading menus enable you to provide the user with a level of depth that is easy to follow and understand.

The final topic discusses ownerdraw menus. Ownerdraw menus enable you to put bitmaps and graphical objects in a menu instead of just text. For example, you can create an ownerdraw menu to display color palettes and drawing objects in menus.

Implementing Dynamic Menus

Static menus are defined at design time using the resource editor. However, in some cases, you may want to provide context-sensitive menu options instead of making all menu items available to the user at all times. To provide menu options based on the context, you need to add and delete menus at run time.

Menus added at run time are named dynamic menus and are based on system, user, and data settings. The following illustration shows dynamic menus.

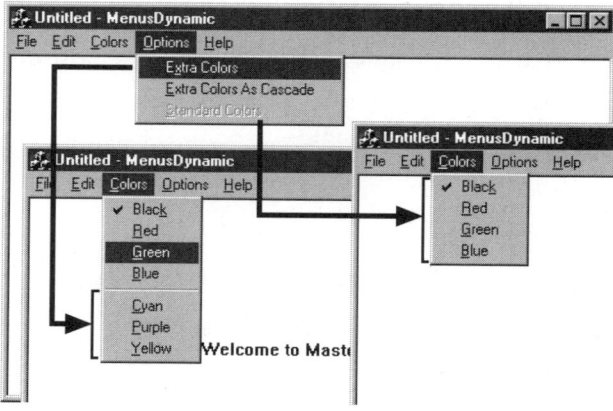

 To see the demonstration "Creating a Dynamic Menu," see the accompanying CD-ROM.

Consolidating Command Handlers into a Command Range

Before creating a dynamic menu, you need to know how to consolidate a number of command handlers into a command range. This makes creating dynamic menus easier.

Because there are many menu items, there are also many command handlers. Often, command handlers are identical or nearly identical in their functionality. When this is the case, map all the messages with similar functionality to a single handler function. Message map ranges enable you to do this for a contiguous range of messages.

You can map ranges of command IDs to:

- A command handler function.
- A command update handler function.

You can map control notification messages for a range of control IDs to a message handler function.

▶ **To consolidate command handlers**

1. Determine the maximum number of new message entries, and add symbolic constants in the resource table for each message entry.

    a. On the **View** menu, click **Resource Symbols**.

    b. In the **Resource Symbols** dialog box, click **New**.

    c. In the **New Symbol** dialog box, specify a name and a value.

2. Repeat Step 1 to add resource symbols as needed. Choose consecutive numbers for resource symbol values, and set the initial number greater than 33000 to avoid conflicts with any predefined or existing messages. At a minimum, define a beginning and ending number.

3. Add an ON_COMMAND_RANGE entry to the message map of the class that will receive the commands from the dynamic menu. Specify the beginning and ending numbers of the range that you specified in the resource symbols table as the first two arguments of the macro. For example:

```
ON_COMMAND_RANGE(ID_COLOR_CYAN, ID_COLOR_YELLOW, OnColors)
```

MFC Development Using Microsoft Visual C++ 6.0

Note ClassWizard does not support ON_COMMAND_RANGE entries. You need to add them manually.

4. Add the entry to the class's header file in the DECLARE_MESSAGE_MAP section as follows:

```
afx_msg void OnColors( UINT nID );
```

Adding a Dynamic Menu

To add a dynamic menu, you must first decide which top-level menu will display the dynamic menu. Menus are counted from left to right, starting at zero. Next, get a pointer to this top-level menu. You need to write a function to accept the commands that the dynamic menu generates. You will also need to write an update handler and an update UI function for the menu.

▶ **To add a dynamic menu**

1. Add entries to the string table to store the caption of each item on the dynamic menu.
2. Write the code that will add the menu items.

   The following sample code shows how to add menu items. To copy this code for use in your own projects, see "Adding Items to a Dynamic Menu" on the accompanying CD-ROM.

```
// Creating a menu at runtime
// Samples\CH03\Dynamenu
void CMenusDynamicView::OnOptionsExtracolors()
{
  CMenu *pAddinMenu, *pTopMenu;

  // To append to the Colors menu, we'll need a pointer
  // to it. We begin by obtaining a pointer to the top-
  // level menu.
  pTopMenu = AfxGetMainWnd()->GetMenu();

  // Colors is the 3rd menu, but that's #2 in a 0-based
  // system.
  pAddinMenu = pTopMenu->GetSubMenu(2);
  ASSERT(pAddinMenu != NULL);
```

code continued on next page

code continued from previous page

```
    // First, add a separator to separate the default
    // menus from the dynamic menus.
    pAddinMenu->AppendMenu(MF_SEPARATOR);

    // Append the 3 menu items. The captions for the menu commands
    // are stored in the string table. .
    CString prompt;
    for (int i = 0; i < 3; i++)
    {
        prompt.LoadString(ID_COLORS_CYAN + i);
        pAddinMenu->AppendMenu(MF_STRING,
                    ID_COLORS_CYAN + i, prompt);
    }
}
```

3. Write the function that will accept the commands that are generated by the additional menus.

   The following sample code shows how to write the command handler for a dynamic menu. To copy this code for use in your own projects, see "Command Handler for a Dynamic Menu" on the accompanying CD-ROM.

```
//Generic command handler for dynamic menu items
//Samples\CH03\Dynamenu
void CMenusDynamicView::OnColors(UINT nID)
{
  CMenusDynamicDoc* pDoc = GetDocument();
  ASSERT_VALID(pDoc);

  pDoc->SetColor(IDtoColorRef(nID));
  Invalidate();
}
```

code continued on next page

```
code continued from previous page

  // This function converts one of the 7 Command IDs to a
  // COLORREF value.
  COLORREF CMenusDynamicView::IDtoColorRef(int nID)
  {
    switch (nID)
    {
        case ID_COLORS_RED:
            return RED;
        case ID_COLORS_GREEN:
            return GREEN;
        case ID_COLORS_BLUE:
            return BLUE;
        case ID_COLORS_CYAN:
            return CYAN;
        case ID_COLORS_PURPLE:
            return PURPLE;
        case ID_COLORS_YELLOW:
            return YELLOW;
        default:
            return BLACK;
    }
  }
```

4. If you want an update handler for the menus you have just added, add another entry to the class's message map. For example:

   ```
   ON_UPDATE_COMMAND_UI_RANGE(ID_COLORS_CYAN, ID_COLORS_YELLOW,
   OnUpdateColors)
   ```

5. Add an entry to the header file for the class, as shown in this example:

   ```
   afx_msg void OnUpdateColors(CCmdUI* pCmdUI);
   ```

6. Finally, write the update function, as shown in this example:

   ```
   void CMenusDynamicView::OnUpdateColors(CCmdUI* pCmdUI)
   {
       CMenusDynamicDoc* pDoc = GetDocument();
       ASSERT_VALID(pDoc);

       pCmdUI->SetCheck(pDoc->GetColor() == IDtoColorRef(pCmdUI->m_nID));
   }
   ```

The code samples discussed in this topic appear in the sample application Dynamenu, which is located in the folder *<install folder>*\Samples\Ch03.

Implementing Cascading Menus

A cascading menu is a pop-up menu that appears when the user points to an item on a menu that has already been invoked. Cascading menus are useful because they display menu items hierarchically.

There is no actual limit to the number of menus that you can nest by cascading, but user interface guidelines suggest that you use no more than four levels of nesting.

The following illustration shows a cascading menu.

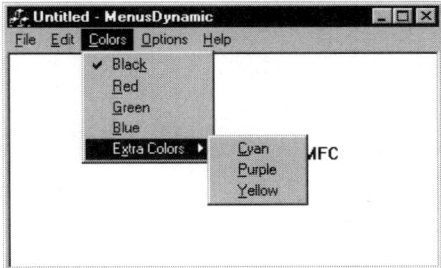

You create cascading menus at design time by using the resource editor. To implement cascading menus at run time, you need to add code to your application and use the **AppendMenu** function.

The sample code on the following page shows how to add a cascading menu at run time. To copy this code for use in your own projects, see "Creating a Cascading Menu" on the accompanying CD-ROM.

```
// Creating a cascading menu and adding menu items to it
// Samples\CH03\Dynamenu
void CMenusDynamicView::OnOptionsExtracolorsCascade()
{
    // A cascading menu is a new menu object that must
    // persist after this function terminates. Thus the
    // use of the pointer m_pExtraColors, which is a member
    // of the view class. It's needed elsewhere in this
    // class to properly delete the object allocated in
    // this function.
    m_pExtraColors = new CMenu;
    m_pExtraColors->CreatePopupMenu();

    // Next, add existing menu items to this newly
    // created menu object.
    CString prompt;
    for (int i = 0; i < 3; i++)
    {
        prompt.LoadString(ID_COLORS_CYAN + i);
        m_pExtraColors->AppendMenu(MF_STRING,
                ID_COLORS_CYAN + i, prompt);
    }

    CMenu *pTopMenu, *pSubMenu;

    pTopMenu = AfxGetMainWnd()->GetMenu();
    pSubMenu = pTopMenu->GetSubMenu(2);

    // Now that we have a pointer to the appropriate sub
    // menu, the new menu object can be appended. The
    // flag MF_POPUP tells AppendMenu how to interpret
    // the 3rd argument.
    prompt.LoadString(ID_EXTRA_COLORS);
    pSubMenu->AppendMenu(MF_STRING | MF_POPUP,
                (UINT)m_pExtraColors->m_hMenu, prompt);

    // Be sure to examine the code in
    // OnOptionsStandardcolors() to see how this menu
    // object is deleted, NOT removed! Also, examine
    // OnDestroy.
}
```

Your application must include code to delete cascading menus created at run time. Call the **DeleteMenu** function to delete menus at run time.

The following sample code shows how to delete a cascading menu. To copy this code for use in your own projects, see "Deleting a Cascading Menu" on the accompanying CD-ROM.

```
// Destroying a cascading menu and updating the view
// Samples\CH03\Dynamenu
void CMenusDynamicView::OnOptionsStandardcolors()
{
  CMenu *pAddinMenu, *pTopMenu;
  // To remove items from the Colors menu, we'll need a
  // pointer to it. We begin by obtaining a pointer to
  // the top-level menu.
  pTopMenu = AfxGetMainWnd()->GetMenu();

  // Colors is the 3rd menu, but that's #2 in a 0-based
  // system.
  pAddinMenu = pTopMenu->GetSubMenu(2);

  int i = pAddinMenu->GetMenuItemCount();

  // The cascading menu must be properly destroyed,
  // since it was allocated using CreatePopupMenu in
  // another function.

  // First delete the cascading menu. It's also
  // necessary to free the object that was allocated in
  // OnOptionsExtracolorsCascade.

  pAddinMenu->DeleteMenu(4, MF_BYPOSITION);
  delete m_pExtraColors;
  m_pExtraColors = 0;

  // Finally, set the color to black and force a
  // redraw;
  CMenusDynamicDoc* pDoc = GetDocument();
  pDoc->SetColor(BLACK);
  Invalidate();
}
```

The code samples discussed in this topic appear in the sample application Dynamenu, which is located in the folder *<install folder>*\Samples\Ch03.

Implementing Ownerdraw Menus

You can enhance a menu by displaying a bitmap or some other graphical object in place of text. For example, instead of displaying the word "Red" in a menu, you can display a rectangle that is the color red. To do this, you need to use an ownerdraw menu.

The following illustration shows an ownerdraw menu.

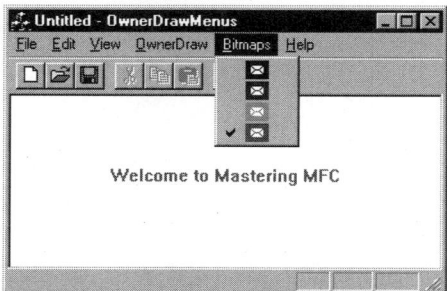

▶ **To create an ownerdraw menu**

1. Add a new class derived from **CMenu**. For example:

    ```
    class CODmenus : public CMenu
    ```

2. Add a **CODmenus** object to the **CMainFrm** class in an SDI application (or to the **CChildFrame** class in an MDI application). For example:

    ```
    CODmenus m_ownerDrawMenu;
    ```

3. Define a function that will create and attach the ownerdraw menu to the menu bar. Call this function from the **OnCreate** function of the frame class.

    The sample code on the following page shows how to create and attach an ownerdraw menu. To copy this code for use in your own projects, see "Creating and Attaching an Ownerdraw Menu" on the accompanying CD-ROM.

```
// Function to create and add an ownerdraw menu
//Samples\CH03\Owndraw
void CMainFrame::AttachOwnerDrawMenu()
{
    // Append 4 menus to the empty menu object m_ownerDrawMenu
    // (which is an object of a custom class and is a member
    // of the frame class). Each appended menu is owner drawn.
    for (int iColor = 0; iColor <= (IDR_COLOR_LAST-IDR_COLOR_FIRST);
        iColor++)
    {
        // Skip Cyan, which is the 3rd color.
        if (3 == iColor) continue;

        // 3 bit encoded RGB values
        BYTE red   = (BYTE)(((iColor & 4) != 0) * 255);
        BYTE green = (BYTE)(((iColor & 2) != 0) * 255);
        BYTE blue  = (BYTE)((iColor & 1) * 255);

        // Each appended menu has an RGB value associated with it
        // that will be passed to DrawItem in the itemData variable.
        // See DrawItem.
        m_ownerDrawMenu.AppendMenu(MF_ENABLED | MF_OWNERDRAW,
            IDR_COLOR_FIRST + iColor, (LPCTSTR)RGB(red, green, blue));
    }

    // Replace the specified menu item with a color popup
    //   (note: will only work once)
    CMenu* pMenuBar = GetMenu();
    ASSERT(pMenuBar != NULL);

    TCHAR szString[256];
    // Colors is the 4th (3rd from 0) menu. We want its string.
    pMenuBar->GetMenuString(3, szString, sizeof(szString),
                MF_BYPOSITION);

    // Make the newly created menu become the 4th menu's popup.
    pMenuBar = GetMenu();
    ASSERT(pMenuBar != NULL);
    pMenuBar->ModifyMenu(3, MF_BYPOSITION | MF_POPUP,
                (UINT)m_ownerDrawMenu.m_hMenu, szString);
}
```

4. Write a command handler to implement the ownerdraw menu items.
5. Write update UI handlers for the menu items.

The sample application Owndraw shows how to implement the functionality described above, and also shows how to place a bitmap in a menu. In the sample application, the menu items are sized and drawn. The application is located in the folder *<install folder>*\Samples\Ch03.

Enhancing Toolbars

When you use MFC AppWizard to create an application, you specify whether you want the default toolbar (IDR_MAINFRAME) added to your MFC-based application. If you choose the default toolbar, the MFC framework will add the toolbar and the default functionality.

Enabling Docking in a Frame Window

The MFC Library supports dockable toolbars. A dockable toolbar can be attached, or "docked," to any side of its parent window, or it can float in its own miniframe window (by using **CMiniFrameWnd**). The following illustration shows a floating toolbar.

If you use MFC AppWizard to generate the skeleton of your application, you can choose to use dockable toolbars. By default, MFC AppWizard generates the code to perform the following actions necessary to place a dockable toolbar in your application:

- Enable docking for the frame window.
- Enable docking for the toolbar.
- Dock the toolbar to the frame window.

If the code for any of these actions is missing, your application displays a standard toolbar. The last two actions must be performed for each dockable toolbar in your application.

To enable docking, use the **CFrameWnd::EnableDocking** function. This function takes a DWORD parameter, which is a set of style bits indicating which side of the frame window accepts docking. If a toolbar is about to be docked and there are multiple sides that can accept it, the sides are indicated in the following order: top, bottom, left, right. If you want to be able to dock control bars anywhere in the frame window, pass the CBRS_ALIGN_ANY parameter to the **EnableDocking** function.

Creating a Floating Toolbar

Floating toolbars are displayed in their own window, and they float on the parent window.

To see the demonstration "Creating a Floating Toolbar," see the accompanying CD-ROM.

▶ **To add a floating toolbar to your application**

1. Make certain that there is a command ID and a handler for every button that you place on your toolbar. The easiest way to do this is to create a menu selection for each toolbar button.

2. Use the resource editor to create a new toolbar resource. Associate each toolbar button with the ID of the command that it generates.

3. Add a menu item that will contain the code that makes the toolbar visible or invisible. Usually, you place the code in the **View** menu provided by MFC.

4. In your application's **CMainFrame** class header file, add a protected variable of type **CToolBar** as shown in the following example. This variable may be an object or a pointer. The type of variable you choose will determine the code you need to write in the frame's implementation file.

   ```
   protected:
       CToolBar * m_pColorToolbar;
   ```

5. If you made the variable in the previous step a pointer, set it to zero in the constructor for **CMainFrame**. For example:

   ```
   CMainFrame::CMainFrame()
       :m_pColorToolbar(0)
   {
   }
   ```

6. Use ClassWizard to add a command handler for the menu item that you created in Step 3. Place this handler in the **CMainFrame** class.

7. Write the code for the menu handler. The same command handler can be used to hide the control bar, which will make it function exactly like the default **CMainFrame** toolbar. You need to allow for three possible situations:

- The code is called before the toolbar is created.
- The code is called to hide the toolbar.
- The code is called to restore the toolbar.

The string table stores the error message strings.

The following sample code shows how to handle these situations. To copy this code for use in your own projects, see "Command Handler for a Floating Toolbar" on the accompanying CD-ROM.

```
// A generic command handler to create, show, and hide a floating
// toolbar
//  Samples\CH03\Toolbar
void CMainFrame::OnViewColortoolbar()
{
  // The very first time, the toolbar needs to be
  // created. m_pColorToolbar is a pointer that is a
  // member of CMainFrame. See OnDestroy for the code
  // that deletes the object allocated here.
  if (0 == m_pColorToolbar)
  {
      m_pColorToolbar = new CToolBar;
      CString ErrMsg;
      if (0 == m_pColorToolbar->Create(this))
      {
          ErrMsg.LoadString(IDS_COLORTB_CREATE);
          ::AfxMessageBox(ErrMsg);
          return;
      }
      if (0 ==
      m_pColorToolbar->LoadToolBar(IDR_COLOR_TOOLBAR))
      {
          ErrMsg.LoadString(IDS_COLORTB_LOAD);
          ::AfxMessageBox(ErrMsg);
          return;
      }
      m_pColorToolbar->EnableDocking(CBRS_ALIGN_ANY);

      DockControlBar(m_pColorToolbar);
  }
```

code continued on next page

Chapter 3: Enhancing the User Interface

```
code continued from previous page
    else
        // If the window is visible, hide it.
        if(m_pColorToolbar->IsWindowVisible() == TRUE)
            ShowControlBar(m_pColorToolbar, FALSE, FALSE);
        else
            // Otherwise, show it.
            ShowControlBar(m_pColorToolbar, TRUE, FALSE);
}
```

8. Add a UI handler to **CMainFrame** for the menu.

    The following sample code shows how to write this UI handler. To copy this code for use in your own projects, see "UI Handler for a Floating Toolbar" on the accompanying CD-ROM.

```
// Samples\CH03\Toolbar
void CMainFrame::OnUpdateViewColortoolbar(CCmdUI* pCmdUI)
{
  // Initially, the color toolbar pointer is 0, so the
  // UI handler must not call IsWindowVisible unless
  // the toolbar has been created.
  if (0 == m_pColorToolbar)
      pCmdUI->SetCheck(FALSE);
  else
      if(m_pColorToolbar->IsWindowVisible() == TRUE)
          pCmdUI->SetCheck(TRUE);
      else
          pCmdUI->SetCheck(FALSE);
}
```

9. If you created a pointer for the toolbar as shown in the sample code, use ClassWizard to add a handler for the WM_DESTROY message, and then delete the object that you created earlier.

    The following sample code shows how to delete the object. To copy this code for use in your own projects, see "Destroying a Floating Toolbar" on the accompanying CD-ROM.

53

```
//Samples\CH03\Toolbar
void CMainFrame::OnDestroy()
 CFrameWnd::OnDestroy();

 // Since the color toolbar was dynamically created,
 // it must be destroyed when the frame is destroyed.
 if (0 != m_pColorToolbar)
 {
     delete m_pColorToolbar;
     m_pColorToolbar = 0;

 }
}
```

10. Repeat the above process for additional toolbars.

The code samples discussed in this topic appear in the sample application Toolbar, which is located in the folder *<install folder>*\Samples\Ch03.

Enhancing Status Bars

Although you typically display text in status bar panes, you can also display graphics in the panes.

▶ **To enable graphics in a status bar pane**

1. Derive a new class based on **CStatusBarCtrl** as follows:

    ```
    class CCustomStatusBar : public CStatusBarCtrl
    ```

2. Add a public member variable in MainFrm.h as follows:

    ```
    CCustomStatusBar    m_wndStatusBar;
    ```

3. From **CMainFrame::OnCreate**, invoke **CStatusBarCtrl::Create** to create the status bar and establish its properties. In the call to **CStatusBarCtrl::Create**, pass AFX_IDW_STATUS_BAR as the fourth argument. This will make your status bar's pane 0 function exactly like the default status bar's pane 0. In other words, it will show menu prompts:

```
if (!m_wndStatusBar.Create(
    WS_VISIBLE | WS_CHILD | CCS_BOTTOM | SBARS_SIZEGRIP,
    rcSB, this, AFX_IDW_STATUS_BAR))
{
    TRACE0("Failed to create status bar\n");
    return FALSE;
}
```

4. Override **CStatusBarCtrl::DrawItem**. This function renders the panes that have the **Ownerdraw** property.

   The following sample code shows how to override **CStatusBarCtrl::DrawItem**. To copy this code for use in your own projects, see "Updating a Custom Status Bar" on the accompanying CD-ROM.

```
// Called when the status bar needs repainting
// Samples\CH03\CustSBar
void CCustomStatusBar::DrawItem(LPDRAWITEMSTRUCT lpdis)
{
    // Handle drawing of the ownerdraw pane(s) of the
    // CGraphicStatusBar object.

    CDC dc;
    dc.m_hDC = lpdis->hDC;

    // The parameter gives us a rectangle that needs to be drawn
    CRect rect(lpdis->rcItem);

    // itemData gives us a pointer to a structure that contains
    // the ID of the bitmap that is to be drawn in the current.
    // This structure was originally filled by CMainFrame, and
    // then changed by the View's event handler that modifies
    // the displayed color.
    CBitmap Bitmap;
    PaneTool *pt = (PaneTool *)lpdis->itemData;
    Bitmap.LoadBitmap(pt->bitmapID);
    CDC srcDC;
    srcDC.CreateCompatibleDC(NULL);
    srcDC.SelectObject(&Bitmap);
    dc.BitBlt(rect.left, rect.top, rect.Width(), rect.Height(),
              &srcDC, 0, 0, SRCCOPY);
}
```

5. Override **CStatusBarCtrl::OnSize**. This function establishes the number, type, and sizes of panes in the status bar. Use **SetText** and the **SBT_OWNERDRAW** property for any panes for which you want to assign graphics.

The following sample code shows how to override **CStatusBarCtrl::OnSize**. To copy this code for use in your own projects, see "Sizing a Custom Status Bar" on the accompanying CD-ROM.

```
//Creating the panes of the statusbar
// Samples\CH03\CustSBar
void CCustomStatusBar::OnSize(UINT nType, int cx, int cy)
{
  CStatusBarCtrl::OnSize(nType, cx, cy);

  int aWidths[5] = {cx / 2, cx / 2 + 30, cx / 2 + 100,
                    cx / 2 + 130, -1};
  SetParts(5, aWidths);

  // Pane 0's text is written by the framework for menu and
  // toolbar status, so nothing needs to be done. The framework
  // will only do this if the custom status bar is given the ID
  // AFX_IDW_STATUS_BAR in the call to Create.

  // Pane 1 shows the status of the Caps Lock key.
  // Also See CMainFrame::OnCmdMsg
  DetermineKeyboardState();

  // Pane 2 has static text.
  DetermineTextColor();

  // Pane 3 has a bitmap placed in it. Thus it has to have
  // owner draw. We pass it the address of a structure that
  // contains the bitmap's ID.
  CMainFrame * cmf = (CMainFrame *)GetParent();
  SetText((LPCTSTR) &cmf->pt, 3, SBT_OWNERDRAW);

  // Pane 4 will, width -1, takes over the rest of the
  // status bar and contains the sizing grip.
}
```

code continued on next page

code continued from previous page

```
void CCustomStatusBar::DetermineTextColor()
{
  CMainFrame * cmf = (CMainFrame *)GetParent();
  CCustomStatusBarDoc * ccsbd =
      (CCustomStatusBarDoc *)cmf->GetActiveDocument();

  CString color = "Black";

  // If the document doesn't exist yet, just set the color
  // to black.
  if (0 != ccsbd)
      // Convert an RGB value to a CString.
      switch (ccsbd->GetColor())
      {
          case RED:
              color = "Red";
              break;
          case GREEN:
              color = "Green";
              break;
          case BLUE:
              color = "Blue";
              break;
      }

  SetText(color, 2, 0);
}

void CCustomStatusBar::DetermineKeyboardState()
{
  // We completely take over writing the word CAP.
  BYTE ks[256];

  GetKeyboardState(ks);

  CRect rect;
  GetRect(1, &rect);
  rect.OffsetRect(3, 2);
```

code continued on next page

code continued from previous page

```
    CClientDC dc(this);
    CFont * cf = GetFont();
    if (cf)
        dc.SelectObject(cf);
    dc.SetBkMode(OPAQUE);
    dc.SetBkColor(GetSysColor(COLOR_MENU));

    if (ks[VK_CAPITAL] & 1)
        dc.SetTextColor(RGB(0, 0, 0));
    else
        dc.SetTextColor(RGB(127,127,127));

    dc.DrawText("CAP", rect, DT_LEFT);
}
```

6. From **CMainFrame::OnSize**, invoke **CStatusBarCtrl::MoveWindow** to reposition the status bar whenever the frame resizes.

```
    if (m_wndStatusBar.m_hWnd)
        m_wndStatusBar.MoveWindow(0, cy, cx, cy, TRUE);
```

7. Override the **OnDraw** member function of the view class to update the status bar each time the user changes the color of the text.

    The following sample code shows how to override the **OnDraw** function. To copy this code for use in your own projects, see "OnDraw Member Function" on the accompanying CD-ROM.

```
// Updating the view and invalidating the statusbar
//   Samples\CH03\CustSBar
void CCustomStatusBarView::OnDraw(CDC* pDC)
{
  CCustomStatusBarDoc* pDoc = GetDocument();
  ASSERT_VALID(pDoc);

  CRect r;
  GetClientRect(&r);
  int x = r.right / 2, y = r.bottom / 2;
```

code continued on next page

code continued from previous page

```
pDC->SetTextColor(pDoc->GetColor());
pDC->SetTextAlign (TA_CENTER | TA_BASELINE);
pDC->TextOut (x, y, pDoc->GetPhrase());

//Invalidate status bar to enable repainting
CMainFrame * cmf = (CMainFrame *)GetParent();
UINT mID;
switch(pDoc->GetColor())
{
    case RED:
        mID = IDM_REDBITMAP;
        break;
    case GREEN:
        mID = IDM_GREENBITMAP;
        break;
    case BLUE:
        mID = IDM_BLUEBITMAP;
        break;
    default:
        mID = IDM_BLACKBITMAP;
}
cmf->pt.bitmapID = mID;

// Force the status bar to be redrawn.
cmf->m_wndStatusBar.Invalidate();

}
```

The code samples discussed in this topic appear in the sample application CustSBar, which is located in the folder *<install folder>*\Samples\Ch03.

Enhancing Dialog Boxes

Microsoft Visual Studio provides a dialog box template that serves as the basic interface for a dialog box. By default, the template provides a window with a caption, a **Close** button, and **OK** and **Cancel** buttons. You add controls to the dialog box and code to your application to complete the functionality of the dialog box. In this section, you will learn how to use advanced techniques to extend the functionality of a dialog box.

Customizing Common Dialog Boxes

A common dialog box is a system-defined dialog box that users can use to perform complex operations that are common to most applications. You use common dialog boxes to make the user interface of your applications consistent with other Windows-based applications. Common dialog boxes supported by MFC include **Color, Print, Open,** and **Save As.**

For information about common dialog boxes, search for "Common Dialog Boxes" in MSDN Library Visual Studio 6.0.

You can customize a common dialog box by altering its layout or behavior to meet the requirements of your application.

Customizing a Common Dialog Box

The following general steps describe how to customize a common dialog box.

1. Create a custom dialog box template.

> **Note** For information about how to customize a common dialog box template, refer to Knowledge Base article Q132909.

> **Tip** The Microsoft Knowledge Base contains detailed technical articles and samples that are created and maintained by Microsoft Product Support Services (PSS). This database is updated daily and contains technical information about Microsoft products, fix lists, documentation errors, and answers to commonly asked technical support questions.

2. Derive a class for the dialog box template from a common dialog box class. For example, the following statement derives a class from **CColorDialog**:

   ```
   class MyColor : public CColorDialog
   ```

> **Note** Hide or disable controls in the common dialog boxes rather than deleting them.

3. Add a message map to process notification messages:
    - Add handlers for any new added controls.
    - Pass unprocessed messages to the base class.

4. Create a common dialog box object of the new class and implement it using the **DoModal** function.

Customization Complexity

A common dialog box may require significant changes before you can use it in your application, or it may require only a few minor adjustments. How you customize a common dialog box depends on the complexity of the changes you want to make.

Creating a New Template

If major changes are needed, consider starting with the dialog box template and making whatever changes you need—adding controls, deleting controls, and deriving a unique class from **CDialog**. You can make these changes to the template, but the resulting dialog box will not be a common dialog box.

Making Minor Behavioral Changes to a Common Dialog Box

To change only the behavior of a common dialog box, first consult the Microsoft Windows Software Development Kit (SDK). You can customize each common dialog box class to perform in different ways, depending on flags or settings in the construction of the object. For example, you can customize the **File Open** dialog box to hide files that are read-only.

Changing Layout and Behavior of a Common Dialog Box

Between the two levels of changes above are less significant changes to the dialog box layout and behavior. For example, if the user of a file-based application is unable to create new folders, you can safely edit the File.dlg resource and hide that particular button.

Extending Dialog Data Validation

ClassWizard implements standard DDV by adding code inside the block marked // AFX_DATA_MAP. For example, ClassWizard inserts validation statements to verify the length of an edit control string.

If you want your application to include validation capabilities that are not part of standard DDV, such as checking whether an edit control contains data, you will need to write the appropriate code.

▶ **To extend DDV**

1. Check the value of the **pDX->m_bSaveAndValidate** member variable. If it is **TRUE**, DDV is occurring.
2. If DDV is occurring, check the data variables in the dialog object.
3. If the value of the data variable is not within the proper range:

    a. Use **::AfxMessageBox** to display an error message.

    b. Call **pDX->Fail** to exit **DoDataExchange**.

The following sample code shows how to extend DDV. To copy this code for use in your own projects, see "Extending DDV" on the accompanying CD-ROM.

```
// Enhancing DDV
//   Samples\Ch03\Modeless
if(pDX->m_bSaveAndValidate)
{
  if (0 == m_strDefault.GetLength())
  {
      AfxMessageBox("Default phrase cannot be empty");
      DDX_Text(pDX, IDC_EDIT1, m_strDefault);
      pDX->Fail();
  }
  // Check other dialog class variables in a similar
  // manner.
}
```

For more information about extending DDV, search for "CDataExchange" in MSDN Library Visual Studio 6.0.

Coordinating Controls

In response to user interaction with a control, you can change the text in a static control or on a button. This requires that you create a command UI handler. For example, you can create a command UI handler to enable or disable controls, or to change the value displayed in a control.

Enabling and Disabling Controls

The **Apply** button is an example of a control that you can enable or disable in a dialog box. You disable the **Apply** button initially in the **OnInitDialog** function and enable the **Apply** button when the user changes the text in a text box.

▶ **To enable or disable a control**

1. Use the **CWnd::GetDlgItem** function to get a pointer to the control.
2. Use the **CWnd::EnableWindow** function to enable or disable the control.

The following example code enables the **Apply** button:

```
void CModelessDlg::OnChangeM1Phrase()
{
  GetDlgItem(IDC_APPLY)->EnableWindow(TRUE);
}
```

Changing the Value Displayed in a Control

The **Find** dialog box is an example of a situation where you may want to change the text displayed in a control. After the first instance of a string has been found, you can adjust the text on the search button to read **Find Again**, rather than **Find**.

▶ **To change the value displayed in a control**

- Use the **CWnd::SetDlgItemText** function to change the text that is displayed in a control.

  –or–

- Use the **CWnd::SetDlgItemInt** function to change the numeric value that is displayed in a control.

The following example code shows how you can use the **SetDlgItemInt** function to modify the numeric value of a field:

```
void CListWithItemDataDlg::OnIncrement()
{
    int m_nIncreasedValue;
    ...
    SetDlgItemInt(IDC_EDIT1, m_nIncreasedValue);
    ...
}
```

Creating Property Sheets and Tabbed Dialog Boxes

A property sheet is generally used to modify the attributes of an external object, such as the current selection in a view. Often, a property sheet is a dialog box that is made up of tabbed pages, called property pages. These pages are displayed one at a time as the user clicks the tabs at the top of the dialog box. You can use a tabbed property sheet to display a large amount of information in an organized manner.

The following illustration shows a tabbed property sheet.

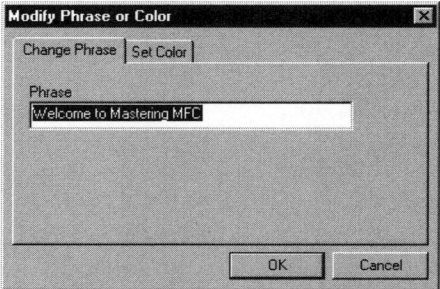

A property sheet has three main parts:

- The dialog box
- One or more property pages
- The tabs at the top of each property page that the user clicks to select the page.

For style guidelines about using property sheets in your application, search for "Guidelines, User-Interface" in MSDN Library Visual Studio 6.0.

If you do not want to use the default **CPropertyPage** object, create a dialog box by using the dialog editor. Then create a class for it, and derive the class from **CPropertyPage**. Use the derived class instead of **CPropertyPage** in the procedures that follow.

▶ **To create property pages**

1. In ResourceView, right-click the Dialog folder and click **Insert**.
2. Expand the Dialog folder and double-click **IDD_PROPPAGE_LARGE** (or **IDD_PROPPAGE_MEDIUM** or **IDD_PROPPAGE_SMALL**) to invoke the dialog bar editor.
3. Add controls to the property page.

4. Create a class for each dialog box that is derived from **CPropertyPage**. ClassWizard automates this process, but be sure to set the base class to **CPropertyPage**.

▶ **To create a property sheet**

1. Create the property page objects.
2. Create a **CPropertySheet** object that will contain the property page objects.
3. Add the property page objects. Add the largest page first because this will set the overall size of the dialog box. The tabs that appear at the top of each property sheet are inserted by the **CPropertySheet::AddPage** method. For details, see the sample code at the end of this topic.
4. If you want the property sheet to be deployed as a modal dialog box, use the **DoModal** function.

Note If the user clicks **OK**, the property sheet will extract the values from the individual property page objects.

The following sample code creates a property sheet. To copy this code for use in your own projects, see "Creating a Property Sheet" on the accompanying CD-ROM.

```
//Creating and displaying a tabbed dialog box
//Samples\CH03\Tabbed
void CTabbedColorPhraseView::OnModifyShowtabbeddialogbox()
{
  CTabbedColorPhraseDoc* pDoc = GetDocument();
  ASSERT_VALID(pDoc);

  // Create each property page object and initialize
  // as appropriate.
  CPhraseTab phraseTab;
  phraseTab.m_phrase = pDoc->GetPhrase();

  CColorTab colorTab;
  colorTab.m_color = pDoc->GetColor();
```

code continued on following page

```
code continued from previous page

    // Create the property sheet object and give it a
    // title.
    CPropertySheet cps("Modify Phrase or Color");

    // Add the largest property page first.
    cps.AddPage(&phraseTab);
    cps.AddPage(&colorTab);

    // Since this is being displayed modally instead of
    // modelessly, remove the Apply button, which
    // appears by default on Property Sheets.
    cps.m_psh.dwFlags |= PSH_NOAPPLYNOW;

    // If the user clicks on OK and either color or
    // phrase has changed, update the document and
    // invalidate the view.
    if (IDOK == cps.DoModal())
        if (pDoc->GetPhrase() != phraseTab.m_phrase ||
            pDoc->GetColor() != colorTab.m_color)
        {
            pDoc->SetColor(colorTab.m_color);
            pDoc->SetPhrase(phraseTab.m_phrase);
            Invalidate();
        }
}
```

The code samples discussed in this topic appear in the sample application Tabbed, which is located in the folder *<install folder>*\Samples\Ch03.

Lab 3.1: Creating a Dynamic Menu

In this lab, you will add items to a menu dynamically.

To see the demonstration "Lab 3.1 Demonstration," see the accompanying CD-ROM.

Estimated time to complete this lab: **20 minutes**

To complete the exercises in this lab, you must have the required software. For detailed information about the labs and setup for the labs, see "Labs" in "About This Course."

The code that forms the starting point for this lab is located in the folder *<install folder>*\Labs\Ch03\Lab3.1\Ex01.

The solution code for this lab is located in the folder *<install folder>*\Labs\Ch03\Lab3.1\Ex01\Solution.

Objectives

After completing this lab, you will be able to:

- Consolidate command handlers.
- Add menu items dynamically.

Prerequisites

There are no prerequisites for this lab.

Exercises

The following exercise provides practice working with the concepts and techniques covered in this chapter:

- Exercise 1: Creating a Dynamic Menu

    In this exercise, you will add items to a menu dynamically.

Exercise 1: Creating a Dynamic Menu

The code that forms the starting point for this exercise is in *<install folder>*\Labs\Ch03\Lab3.1\Ex01.

In this exercise, you will add items to a menu dynamically.

When a user selects the menu item **Extra Colors**, your application will add the items **Cyan**, **Purple**, and **Yellow** to the **Colors** menu.

▶ **Consolidate the command range**

1. Open the file DynaView.cpp and edit the message map of the **View** class to map the commands with their respective member functions as follows:

    ```
    ON_COMMAND(ID_OPTIONS_EXTRACOLORS, OnOptionsExtracolors)
    ON_COMMAND(ID_OPTIONS_STANDARDCOLORS, OnOptionsStandardcolors)
    ON_COMMAND_RANGE(ID_COLORS_CYAN, ID_COLORS_YELLOW, OnColors)
    ON_COMMAND_RANGE(ID_COLORS_BLACK, ID_COLORS_BLUE, OnColors)
    ```

2. Open the file DynaView.h and add the following code to the section under generated message map functions:

```
afx_msg void OnOptionsExtracolors();
afx_msg void OnColors(UINT nID);
afx_msg void OnUpdateColors(CCmdUI* pCmdUI);
afx_msg void OnUpdateOptions(CCmdUI* pCmdUI);
afx_msg void OnOptionsStandardcolors();
```

▶ **Add menu items dynamically**

1. Open DynaView.cpp and write the following code to add menu items to the **Colors** menu when the item **Extra Colors** is selected:

```
void CMenusDynamicView::OnOptionsExtracolors()
{
    CMenu *pAddinMenu, *pTopMenu;

    // To append to the Colors menu, a pointer is required.
    // Obtain a pointer to the top-level menu.
    pTopMenu = AfxGetMainWnd()->GetMenu();

    // Colors is the 3rd menu, but that's #2 in a 0-based system.
    pAddinMenu = pTopMenu->GetSubMenu(2);
    ASSERT(pAddinMenu != NULL);

    // First, add a separator to separate the default menus
    // from the dynamic menus.
    pAddinMenu->AppendMenu(MF_SEPARATOR);

    // Append the 3 menu items. They will generate consecutive
    // command IDs.
    CString prompt;
    for (int i = 0; i < 3; i++)
    {
        prompt.LoadString(ID_COLORS_CYAN + i);
        pAddinMenu->AppendMenu(MF_STRING,
                    ID_COLORS_CYAN + i, prompt);
    }
}
```

2. Add strings to the string table to store the following menu item labels.

ID	Caption
ID_COLORS_CYAN	&Cyan
ID_COLORS_PURPLE	&Purple
ID_COLORS_YELLOW	&Yellow

▶ Implement the OnColors function

- You now need to write a command handler for the dynamic menu you just created. Write the following code to handle the commands that are generated by the additional menus:

```
void CMenusDynamicView::OnColors(UINT nID)
{
   CMenusDynamicDoc* pDoc = GetDocument();
   ASSERT_VALID(pDoc);

   pDoc->SetColor(IDtoColorRef(nID));
   Invalidate();
}
```

▶ Implement the OnOptionsStandardcolors function

- When the user selects the menu item **Standard Colors**, you need to set the menu back to the standard options that were available before the menu items were added. Write code for the **OnOptionsStandardcolors** function as follows:

```
void CMenusDynamicView::OnOptionsStandardcolors()
{
   CMenu *pAddinMenu, *pTopMenu;

   // To remove items from the Colors menu, a pointer is required
   // Obtain a pointer to the top-level menu.
   pTopMenu = AfxGetMainWnd()->GetMenu();

   // Colors is the 3rd menu, but that's #2 in a 0-based system.
   pAddinMenu = pTopMenu->GetSubMenu(2);
```

code continued on next page

code continued from previous page

```
    int i = pAddinMenu->GetMenuItemCount();

    // Remove the additions to the colors menu.
    // We want to leave only 4 menu items.
    i--;                    // adjust to 0-based.
    while(i > 3)
    {
        pAddinMenu->RemoveMenu(i, MF_BYPOSITION);
        i--;
    }

    // Finally, set the color to black and force a redraw;
    CMenusDynamicDoc* pDoc = GetDocument();
    pDoc->SetColor(BLACK);
    Invalidate();
}
```

▶ Add update handlers

1. Edit the view's message map to include update handlers for the menus you have added:

   ```
   ON_UPDATE_COMMAND_UI_RANGE(ID_COLORS_CYAN, ID_COLORS_YELLOW,
   OnUpdateColors)
   ON_UPDATE_COMMAND_UI_RANGE(ID_COLORS_BLACK, ID_COLORS_BLUE,
   OnUpdateColors)
   ON_UPDATE_COMMAND_UI(ID_OPTIONS_EXTRACOLORS, OnUpdateOptions)
   ON_UPDATE_COMMAND_UI(ID_OPTIONS_STANDARDCOLORS, OnUpdateOptions)
   ```

2. Write the code for the **OnUpdateColors** handler to check the selected color in the **Colors** menu:

   ```
   void CMenusDynamicView::OnUpdateColors(CCmdUI* pCmdUI)
   {
       CMenusDynamicDoc* pDoc = GetDocument();
       ASSERT_VALID(pDoc);

       pCmdUI->SetCheck(pDoc->GetColor() == IDtoColorRef(pCmdUI->m_nID));
   }
   ```

3. Write the code for the **OnUpdateOptions** handler to check the selected menu item in the **Options** menu:

```
void CMenusDynamicView::OnUpdateOptions(CCmdUI* pCmdUI)
{
    CMenu *pAddinMenu, *pTopMenu;
    pTopMenu = AfxGetMainWnd()->GetMenu();
    pAddinMenu = pTopMenu->GetSubMenu(2);

    switch (pCmdUI->m_nID)
    {
        case ID_OPTIONS_EXTRACOLORS:
            pCmdUI->Enable(pAddinMenu->GetMenuItemCount() == 4);
            break;
        case ID_OPTIONS_STANDARDCOLORS:
            pCmdUI->Enable(pAddinMenu->GetMenuItemCount() != 4);
    }
}
```

4. Save DynaView.cpp. Build Dynamenu and run it.

The solution code for this exercise is located in the folder *<install folder>*\Labs\Ch03\Lab3.1\Ex01\Solution.

Lab 3.2: Customizing the Common Dialog Class

In this lab, you will create a customized File Open template, create a dialog class, and add custom controls and handlers for the newly created dialog class.

To see the demonstration "Lab 3.2 Demonstration," see the accompanying CD-ROM.

Estimated time to complete this lab: **75 minutes**

To complete the exercises in this lab, you must have the required software. For detailed information about the labs and setup for the labs, see "Labs" in "About This Course."

The code that forms the starting point for this lab is located in the folder *<install folder>*\Labs\Ch03\Lab3.2.

The solution code for this lab is located in the folder *<install folder>*\Labs\Ch03\Lab3.2.

Objectives

After completing this lab, you will be able to:

- Create a template to expand the functionality of a common dialog box.
- Create a class that expands the functionality of a common dialog box.
- Respond to messages sent by a common dialog box.
- Stream data into a rich edit control.
- Incorporate an expanded common dialog box into an existing application.

Prerequisites

There are no prerequisites for this lab.

Exercises

The following exercises provide practice working with the concepts and techniques covered in this chapter:

- Exercise 1: Creating a Customized File Open Template

    In this exercise, you will create a child dialog box of a common (parent) dialog box. The child dialog box will inherit all the controls of the parent dialog box.

- Exercise 2: Customizing the Dialog Class

    In this exercise, you will use the ClassWizard to create the dialog class and add custom controls and handlers for the newly created dialog class.

- Exercise 3: Implementing Dialog Class Handlers

    In this exercise, you will implement the handlers created in Exercise 2 and their supporting functions in the dialog class.

Exercise 1: Creating a Customized File Open Template

The code that forms the starting point for this exercise is in *<install folder>*\Labs\Ch03\Lab3.2\Ex01.

In this exercise, you will create a child dialog box of a common (parent) dialog box. The child dialog box will inherit all the controls of the parent dialog box.

The following illustration shows the completed template.

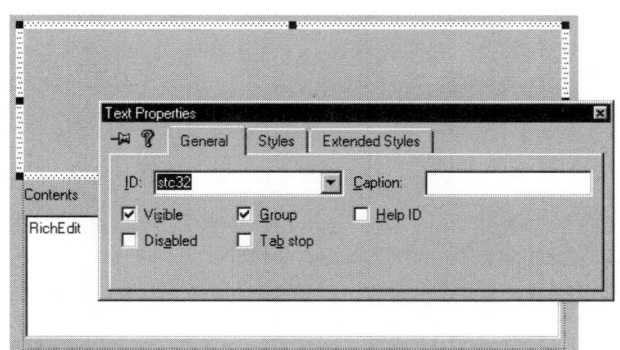

▶ **Create a new child dialog box of the common dialog box File Open**

1. On the **Insert** menu, click **Resource**, or press CTRL+R.
2. In the **Insert Resource** dialog box, click **Dialog** and click **New**.
3. Open the **Dialog Properties** dialog box and set the ID to IDD_FILEOPEN_EX.
4. On the **Styles** tab, set **Style** to **Child** and **Border** to **None**. Clear the default **Title bar** check box if it is selected. Select **Clip siblings** and **Clip children**.
5. On the **More Styles** tab, select **Visible, 3D-look,** and **Control**.

    When you select **Control**, the parent dialog box (**File Open**) can tab into the child (IDD_FILEOPEN_EX).

6. Resize the dialog box to 296 by 172. The size appears in the right pane of the status bar, as shown in the following illustration.

    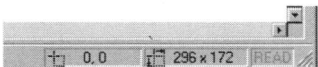

7. Delete both the **OK** and **Cancel** buttons.
8. Draw a static text control from the position 7,7 sized to 276 by 71. Set the ID to **stc32** so that Windows will draw the **File** dialog box within it. Clear its caption.
9. Draw a static text control from the position 7,84 sized to 31 by 8. Set the Caption property of the static control to **Contents**.
10. Draw a rich edit control from the position 7,98 sized to 276 by 63.
11. Set the ID property of the rich edit control to IDC_EDIT_CONTENTS.
12. Clear the **Tabstop** option.

13. Save Diff.rc.
14. Directly edit Diff.rc and set the style of the rich edit control to ES_MULTILINE | WS_BORDER | WS_VSCROLL | WS_HSCROLL.

    This style enables the user to scroll through the file.
15. Open Resource.h and remove the definition of **stc32** added by the dialog editor.

> **Lab Hint**
>
> ▶ **To open Resource.h or Diff.rc for direct editing**
>
> 1. From the **File** menu, select **open**.
> 2. Select the desired file, and from the **Open As drop down** listbox, choose **Text**.

16. Save Resource.h.
17. The constant **stc32** is defined in dlgs.h, so include dlgs.h in Diff.rc.

The solution code for this exercise is located in the folder *<install folder>*\Labs\Ch03\Lab3.2\Ex01\Solution.

Exercise 2: Customizing the Dialog Class

Continue with the files you created in Exercise 1 or, if you do not have a starting point for this exercise, the code that forms the basis for this exercise is in *<install folder>*\Labs\Ch03\Lab3.2\Ex02.

In this exercise, you will use ClassWizard to create the dialog class and add custom controls and handlers for the newly created dialog class.

▶ **Use ClassWizard to create the dialog class**

In this procedure, you will invoke the ClassWizard to create the dialog class.

> **Tip** To have ClassWizard automatically display the **Adding a Class** dialog box, open ClassWizard from the dialog editor session where you just created the new dialog resource.d.

1. Run the dialog editor on the IDD_FILEOPEN_EX dialog resource. Be sure that your dialog box template window is the active child window.

Lab 3.2: Customizing the Common Dialog Class

2. Invoke **ClassWizard**. It should automatically display the **Adding A Class** dialog box. (If for some reason this dialog box does not appear, click the **Add Class** button).

3. Click **Create a new class** option, and click **OK**. The **Create New Class** dialog box appears.

4. In the **Name** box, type **CFileOpenEx** for the name of the associated C++ dialog class.

5. In the **Base Class** box, select **CDialog**.

   The Dialog ID should already be set to IDD_FILEOPEN_EX.

   ClassWizard provides different styles of automation for dialog boxes derived from **CCommonDialog** and **CDialog**. To use ClassWizard to best effect, begin deriving from **CDialog**, and later derive from **CFileDialog**. Do this in ClassWizard and modify the class in the editor.

6. Click **OK**.

▶ Add a member variable to the dialog class

In this procedure, you will create a member variable for the new **CFileOpenEx** class.

- Right-click **CFileOpenEx** in the ClassView window. Add the following protected member variable:

  ```
  CRichEditCtrl  m_RichEdit
  ```

▶ Create handlers for the dialog class

Using ClassWizard, add a handler for **DoModal**. You will need to add the handler for **OnFileNameChange** manually.

1. Invoke ClassWizard for the Diff project.

2. Click the **Message Maps** tab in ClassWizard.

3. Create a handler for a dialog message.

   a. In the **Class Name** drop-down list box, click the dialog class **CFileOpenEx**.

   b. In the **Object ID** list box, click **CFileOpenEx** as the class name.

   c. In the **Messages** list box, click **DoModal**.

   d. Click **Add Function** and accept the default function name.

   The function name will be displayed in the **Member Functions** list box.

4. Click **OK**.

▶ **Create a handler for a function not listed in ClassWizard**

When you change the selected file in the Explorer-style list in the **File** dialog box, a CDN_SELCHANGE message is sent to the dialog box itself. (For more information about this message, see "Open and Save As Dialog Box Messages and Notifications" in the MSDN Library Visual Studio 6.0.) You will need to examine the source code for the **CFileDialog** class to determine how this message is handled.

1. In DlgFile.cpp, in the MFC source code, examine the **CFileDialog::OnNotify** handler:

   ```
   BOOL CFileDialog::OnNotify(WPARAM wParam, LPARAM lParam,
       LRESULT* pResult)
   {
       ...
       switch(pNotify->hdr.code)
       {
       ...
       case CDN_SELCHANGE:
           OnFileNameChange();
           return TRUE;
       ...
   }
   ```

   Note that when a CDN_SELCHANGE message is received, the dialog invokes **OnFileNameChange** procedure.

2. Add the **OnFileNameChange** to the **CFileOpenEx** class as a protected function as follows:

   ```
   virtual void OnFileNameChange()
   ```

3. Build your project.

The solution code for this exercise is located in the folder *<install folder>*\Labs\Ch03\Lab3.2\Ex02\Solution.

Exercise 3: Implementing Dialog Class Handlers

Continue with the files you created in Exercise 2 or, if you do not have a starting point for this exercise, the code that forms the basis for this exercise is in *<install folder>*\Labs\Ch03\Lab3.2\Ex03.

CDialogFileEx has two primary entry points:

- DoModal
- OnFileNameChange

In this exercise, you will implement each of these handlers and their supporting functions.

▶ **Change the derivation of CFileOpenEx to CFileDialog**

The **CFileDialog** class encapsulates the Windows common file dialog box. Common file dialog boxes provide an easy way to implement **File Open** and **File Save As** dialog boxes (as well as other file-selection dialog boxes) in a manner consistent with Windows standards. You can derive your own dialog class from **CFileDialog** and write a constructor for it.

1. Open FileOpenEx.h.
2. Change the parent class to **CFileDialog** as follows:

   ```
   class CFileOpenEx : public CFileDialog
   ```

3. Save FileOpenEx.h.
4. Open FileOpenEx.cpp and scroll to the **CFileOpenEx** constructor. Convert the default constructor code for **CFileDialog** from:

   ```
   CFileOpenEx::CFileOpenEx(CWnd* pParent /*=NULL*/)
       : CDialog(CFileOpenEx::IDD, pParent)
   {
       //{{AFX_DATA_INIT(CFileOpenEx)
           // NOTE: the ClassWizard will add member initialization here
       //}}AFX_DATA_INIT
   }
   ```

   To a constructor as follows:

   ```
   CFileOpenEx::CFileOpenEx( LPCTSTR lpszDefExt /*= NULL*/,
                             LPCTSTR lpszFileName /*= NULL*/,
                             DWORD dwFlags /*= OFN_HIDEREADONLY*/,
                             LPCTSTR lpszFilter /*= NULL*/,
                             CWnd* pParentWnd /*= NULL*/)
               : CFileDialog(TRUE, lpszDefExt, lpszFileName, dwFlags,
       lpszFilter, pParentWnd)
   {
   ```

code continued on following page

code continued from previous page

```
    //{{AFX_DATA_INIT(CFileOpenEx)
        // NOTE: ClassWizard will add member initialization here
    //}}AFX_DATA_INIT
}
```

5. Convert all occurrences of **CDialog** in FileOpenEx.cpp to **CFileDialog**.
6. Save FileOpenEx.cpp.
7. Open FileOpenEx.h.
8. Change the default constructor declaration from:

    ```
    CFileOpenEx(CWnd* pParent = NULL);    // standard constructor
    ```

    To reflect the new constructor declaration:

    ```
    CFileOpenEx(LPCTSTR lpszDefExt = NULL,
                LPCTSTR lpszFileName = NULL,
                DWORD dwFlags = OFN_HIDEREADONLY,
                LPCTSTR lpszFilter = NULL,
                CWnd* pParentWnd = NULL);
    ```

9. Save FileOpenEx.h.

▶ **Set up DDX**

Because a rich edit control is a custom control from the resource editor, you need to set up dialog data exchange (DDX) yourself.

1. Add a call to **DDX_Control** in **DoDataExchange** as follows:

    ```
    DDX_Control(pDX, IDC_EDIT_CONTENTS, m_RichEdit);
    ```

2. Save FileOpenEx.cpp.

The following sample code shows an example of how your code should look. To copy this code for use in your own projects, see "Lab 3.2.3 DoDataExchange" on the accompanying CD-ROM.

Lab 3.2: Customizing the Common Dialog Class

```
void CFileOpenEx::DoDataExchange(CDataExchange* pDX)
{
  CDialog::DoDataExchange(pDX);
  //{{AFX_DATA_MAP(CFileOpenEx)
  //}}AFX_DATA_MAP
      DDX_Control(pDX, IDC_EDIT_CONTENTS, m_RichEdit);
}
```

▶ Link the dialog box to the template in DoModal

DoModal associates the template you have created with the **CFileDialog** common dialog box and then calls **CFileDialog::DoModal**. ClassWizard provides an **enum** IDD that isolates your code from changes you may make in your dialog box resource.

1. Call the function **SetTemplate** as follows:

   ```
   SetTemplate(NULL, MAKEINTRESOURCE(IDD_FILEOPEN_EX));
   ```

2. Save FileOpenEx.cpp.

The following sample code shows an example of how your code should look. To copy this code for use in your own projects, see "Lab 3.2.3 DoModal" on the accompanying CD-ROM.

```
int CFileOpenEx::DoModal()
{
  SetTemplate(NULL, MAKEINTRESOURCE(IDD_FILEOPEN_EX));

  return CFileDialog::DoModal();

}
```

▶ Implement OnFileNameChange

In this procedure, you will display a file when the user selects it in the pane.

1. Get the path name from the **File** dialog box, and check to see that it is not blank:

   ```
   CString FileName = GetPathName();
   if(FileName.GetLength())
   {
   ```

2. Check to see whether the file exists:

   ```
   OFSTRUCT    of;
   if(OpenFile(FileName, &of, OF_EXIST) != HFILE_ERROR)
   ```

3. You will implement **PreviewContents** to show the file in the rich edit control later in this exercise. At this point, simply call **PreviewContents** as follows:

   ```
   PreviewContents(FileName);
   ```

4. Save FileOpenEx.cpp.

The following sample code shows an example of how your code should look. To copy this code for use in your own projects, see "Lab 3.2.3 OnFileNameChange" on the accompanying CD-ROM.

```
void CFileOpenEx::OnFileNameChange()
{
  CString FileName = GetPathName();
  if(FileName.GetLength())
  {
      OFSTRUCT of;
      if(OpenFile(FileName, &of, OF_EXIST) != HFILE_ERROR)
      {
          PreviewContents(FileName);
      }
  }
}
```

▶ **Implement a function to load the file into the preview**

CRichEditCtrl has stream-oriented input and output provided by **StreamIn** and **StreamOut**. You will use **StreamIn** to load the preview from the selected file. **StreamIn** uses a callback function to do the actual file processing, and you will specify that function as part of an EDITSTREAM structure.

1. Add **PreviewContents** to the **CFileOpenEx** class as a protected member function:

   ```
   void PreviewContents(LPCSTR lpszFilespec);
   ```

2. In the function **PreviewContents**, open the file specified in lpszFilespec as follows:

   ```
   CFile File(lpszFilespec, CFile::modeRead);
   ```

3. Declare an EDITSTREAM structure. Set the cookie to **CFile**, clear the error return, and set the callback to OpenCallback:

   ```
   EDITSTREAM es;
   es.dwCookie = (DWORD)&File;
   es.dwError=0;
   es.pfnCallback=OpenCallback;
   ```

4. Send the **StreamIn** message, specifying that the data is to be read as plain text:

   ```
   m_RichEdit.StreamIn(SF_TEXT, es);
   ```

5. Save FileOpenEx.cpp.

The following sample code shows an example of how your code should look. To copy this code for use in your own projects, see "Lab 3.2.3 PreviewContents" on the accompanying CD-ROM.

```
void CFileOpenEx::PreviewContents(LPCSTR lpszFilespec)
{
  CFile File(lpszFilespec, CFile::modeRead);

  EDITSTREAM        es;
  es.dwCookie    = (DWORD)&File;
  es.dwError     = 0;
  es.pfnCallback = OpenCallback;

  m_RichEdit.StreamIn(SF_TEXT, es);
}
```

▶ **Implement the callback function to read the file (OpenCallback)**

The callback specified in the EDITSTREAM structure does the work of reading the data stream into a buffer that **CRichEditCtrl** can process.

1. Before your implementation of **PreviewContents**, declare **OpenCallback** in FileOpenEx.cpp.

An EDITSTREAM callback takes four parameters: the DWORD parameter sent by **StreamIn**, a buffer to receive the stream, the size of the buffer, and a buffer to receive the actual count of bytes read.

```
DWORD CALLBACK OpenCallback(DWORDdwCookie,
                            LPBYTE   pbBuff,
                            LONGcb,
                            LONG*pcb )
{
```

2. Cast dwCookie to a **CFile** pointer.
3. Read cb bytes into pbBuff.
4. Return to indicate that you have processed the call.
5. Save FileOpenEx.cpp.

The following sample code shows an example of how your code should look. To copy this code for use in your own projects, see "Lab 3.2.3 OpenCallback" on the accompanying CD-ROM.

```
DWORD CALLBACK OpenCallback(DWORD   dwCookie,
                            LPBYTE  pbBuff,
                            LONGcb,
                            LONG*pcb )
{
  CFile    *pFile = (CFile *)dwCookie;

  *pcb = pFile->Read(pbBuff, cb);
  return 0;
}
```

▶ Enable CDialogFileEx

One of the advantages of maintaining a good object-oriented development style is the ease of adding, removing, or changing components. This is demonstrated in the ease of incorporating the **CFileOpenEx** class into the ShowDiff application. You only need to include the class header and change two constructor calls to enable **CFileOpenEx**.

1. Open Dlgopenf.cpp.
2. Include the **CDialogFileEx** header:

   ```
   #include "fileopenex.h"
   ```

3. In **OnButtonFile1Browse** handler, replace the **CFileDialog** declarations with **CFileOpenEx** as follows:

   ```
   CFileDialog dlg(TRUE);
   //becomes =>
   CFileOpenEx dlg;
   ```

4. Repeat Step 3 for **OnButtonFile2Browse**.
5. Save Dlgopenf.cpp.

▶ **Build and test the application**

- Build your application. Click **Open** and then click **Browse** to select a file. View the contents of a file in the **Contents** box.

The solution code for this exercise is located in the folder *<install folder>*\Labs\Ch03\Lab3.2\Ex03\Solution.

Using Modeless Dialog Boxes

You create and test modeless dialog boxes in basically the same way that you do modal dialog boxes. However, modeless dialog boxes require some additional work.

This section shows you how to create a persistent object, create and display the modeless dialog box, implement the **OK** and **Cancel** buttons, and destroy the dialog box when the user finishes with it. You will also learn how to establish communication between the dialog box and the parent application by using the **RegisterWindowMessage** function.

Initializing and Displaying a Modeless Dialog Box

This topic describes how to create and initialize a modeless dialog box. Notice that the first two steps in the process—creating and testing the dialog box template and creating the class—are the same as with modal dialog boxes.

▶ To initialize and display a modeless dialog box

1. Use the dialog editor to create and test the dialog box template.
2. Use ClassWizard to create the dialog box class and add DDX and DDV support as appropriate.
3. Declare a persistent dialog box object.

   To ensure that it will be available when needed, make the dialog box object (or pointer) an embedded member of the application class or the main window. If you use a pointer, you invoke the **New** operator and the resulting constructor to allocate and initialize storage for the object.

4. Create the dialog box object by using the **CDialog::Create** message handler.

   The first argument to **Create** is the name or the ID of the dialog box template. The second argument is a pointer to the dialog object's parent window. If the pointer is NULL, the main application window becomes the parent.

   The call to **Create** can either be in the constructor, or immediately after the invocation of the constructor.

   The following sample code shows how to create a modeless dialog box. To copy this code for use in your own projects, see "Creating a Modeless Dialog Box" on the accompanying CD-ROM.

```
//Creating and displaying a modeless dialog box
//Samples\CH03\Modeless
class CModelessView : public CView
{
...
protected:
  // CListWithItemDataDlg is the class derived from CDialog
  // for the modeless dialog box
  CListWithItemDataDlg * m_pDlg;
...
};

void CModelessView::OnModifyDisplaymodelessdialog()
{
  CModelessDoc* pDoc = GetDocument();
  ASSERT_VALID(pDoc);
```

code continued on following page

> *code continued from previous page*
>
> ```
>     // Create and initialize the dialog box object.
>     // It must be persistent (not stack-based).
>     m_pDlg = new CListWithItemDataDlg(this);
>     m_pDlg->m_color = pDoc->GetColor();
>     m_pDlg->m_phrase = pDoc->GetPhrase();
>     m_pDlg->Create(IDD_PHRASE_MODELESS);
>
>     // The call to Create has caused DDX to occur.
>     // Everything's done, show the window. Note that the
>     // DB itself has its visible property set to false
>     // in the resource editor.
>     m_pDlg->ShowWindow(SW_RESTORE);
> }
> ```

In the sample code, the dialog box is persistent rather than stack-based.

5. Display the dialog box.

    If the dialog box has the style property WS_VISIBLE, it will appear immediately. You can control the dialog box's visibility by calling the **CWnd::ShowWindow** function with the parameters SW_SHOW, SW_HIDE, and SW_RESTORE, respectively.

To see the demonstration "Creating a Modeless Dialog Box," see the accompanying CD-ROM.

Implementing Command Buttons

In a modeless dialog box, you can replace the **OK** button and override the **Cancel** button. Unlike the default version of the **OnCancel** message handler, your override of **OnCancel** should not call the **EndDialog** function to terminate the dialog box. Instead, call the **CWnd::DestroyWindow** function to terminate the modeless dialog box.

The following example code terminates a modeless dialog box:

```
void CListWithItemDataDlg::OnCancel()
{
  m_pWnd->SendMessage(m_UserMsg, ML_CANCEL);
  DestroyWindow();
}
```

Deleting the Dialog Box Object

To delete a dialog box object, override the **PostNcDestroy** (where **Nc** stands for nonclient) function. Note that the owner of the dialog box (the application that created it) probably has a pointer that will not be valid after the modeless dialog box is destroyed.

The following example code deletes a persistent dialog box object:

```
void CListWithItemDataDlg::PostNcDestroy()
{
  delete this;
  CDialog::PostNcDestroy();
}
```

Communicating with the Application

You must create a communication link between the dialog box and its parent application for modeless dialog boxes. You can use the **RegisterWindowMessage** and **SendMessage** functions to create this communication link.

To see the demonstration "Implementing Dialog Box Communication," see the accompanying CD-ROM.

The following sample code shows how to enable communication by using **RegisterWindowMessage**. To copy this code for use in your own projects, see "Implementing Modeless Dialog Box Communication" on the accompanying CD-ROM.

```
// Handlers to implement communciation between a modeless dialog box
// and its parent window
// Samples\CH03\Modeless
// Place manifest constants in the modeless
// dialog class's header file for the registered
// message and for each message that the dialog
// box will communicate back to the CWnd-derived
// object that created it.
#define MY_DIALOGBOX_MSG "LWIDMsg"
#define ML_APPLY 1
#define ML_CANCEL 2
```

code continued on next page

code continued from previous page

```
// Overload the dialog box's constructor to
// take a pointer to a CWnd object, and register
// the message in the constructor.
class CListWithItemDataDlg : public CDialog
{
  ...
public:
  CListWithItemDataDlg(CWnd *pWnd,
      CWnd* pParent = NULL);
  ...

protected:
  CWnd * m_pWnd;
  UINT m_UserMsg;
  ...
};

CListWithItemDataDlg::CListWithItemDataDlg(CWnd * pWnd,
      CWnd* pParent)
  : CDialog(CListWithItemDataDlg::IDD, pParent),
  m_pWnd (pWnd)
{
  //{{AFX_DATA_INIT(CListWithItemDataDlg)
  m_phrase = _T("");
  //}}AFX_DATA_INIT
  m_UserMsg = RegisterWindowMessage(MY_DIALOGBOX_MSG);
}
// From the dialog box's buttons, send a
// message to the object that launched the dialog
// box. Extra information may be passed in the
// third argument of the call to SendMessage.
void CListWithItemDataDlg::OnApply()
{
  UpdateData(TRUE);
  m_pWnd->SendMessage(m_UserMsg, ML_APPLY);

  // Now that the Apply button's work is done,
  // disable it.
  CButton * cb = (CButton *)GetDlgItem(IDC_APPLY);
  cb->EnableWindow(FALSE);
}
```

code continued on next page

code continued from previous page

```
void CListWithItemDataDlg::OnCancel()
{
  m_pWnd->SendMessage(m_UserMsg, ML_CANCEL);
  DestroyWindow();
}
// Include the dialog class's header file
// in the class that will receive messages from
// the modeless dialog box, and then register a
// message. In this example, the application's
// view class receives the messages.
// The class of this object must be derived from
// CWnd, since it will be receiving messages. This
// rules out anything derived from CDocument.
// Static member variables must be initialized.
// Register the message the dialog box will send to
// this object.
UINT CModelessView::m_UserMsg =
  RegisterWindowMessage(MY_DIALOGBOX_MSG);

// Add an entry to the class's message map.
// (You must do this manually; ClassWizard can't do
// this for you.)
BEGIN_MESSAGE_MAP(CModelessView, CView)
  //{{AFX_MSG_MAP(CModelessView)
  ON_COMMAND(...
  ON_UPDATE_COMMAND_UI(...
  //}}AFX_MSG_MAP
  ON_REGISTERED_MESSAGE(CModelessView::m_UserMsg, MyMessageHandler)
END_MESSAGE_MAP()

// Create the dialog box and pass in a
// pointer to the object.
class CModelessView : public CView
{
  ...
protected:
  CListWithItemDataDlg * m_pDlg;
  ...
};
```

code continued on next page

code continued from previous page

```
void CModelessView::OnModifyDisplaymodelessdialog()
{
  ...
  // Create and initialize the dialog box object.
  // It must be persistent (not stack-based).
  m_pDlg = new CListWithItemDataDlg(this);
  ...
}
// In the view's message handler, respond
// to the messages.
LRESULT CModelessView::MyMessageHandler(WPARAM wParam, LPARAM lParam)
{
  CModelessDoc* pDoc = GetDocument();
  ASSERT_VALID(pDoc);

  switch (wParam)
  {
      case ML_APPLY:
          pDoc->SetPhrase(m_pDlg->m_phrase);
          pDoc->SetColor(m_pDlg->m_color);
          Invalidate();
          break;

      case ML_CANCEL:
          // The dialog box's own code will properly
          // destroy the object, but it's important
          // that this class set its pointer to the
          // dialog box to 0.
          m_pDlg = 0;
  }
  return TRUE;
}
```

Using Dialog Bars

In this section you will learn about dialog bars and look at the steps in adding a dialog bar to your application.

Introduction to Dialog Bars

A dialog bar is a control bar with toolbar and dialog box characteristics. Because it is based on a dialog template and has the attributes of a modeless dialog box, a dialog bar can contain any kind of control that a dialog box can contain, but it behaves like a powerful toolbar.

The following illustration shows a dialog bar with a variety of controls.

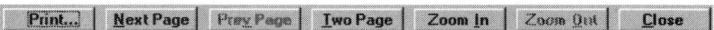

MFC supports dialog bars with the class **CDialogBar**. For more information about **CDialogBar**, search for "CDialogBar" in MSDN Library Visual Studio 6.0.

Adding a Dialog Bar

Creating and implementing a dialog bar involves several steps:

1. Add a menu item to control the display of the dialog bar.
2. Create dialog bar resources.
3. Attach the dialog bar to the **CMainFrame** class.
4. Create a **CDialogBar** class.

These steps are described in more detail below.

To see the demonstration "Creating and Implementing a Dialog Bar," see the accompanying CD-ROM.

▶ **To add a menu item to control the dialog bar**

1. Open the application in which you want to insert the dialog bar.
2. In ResourceView, expand the Menu folder.
3. Double-click **IDR_MAINFRAME** to invoke the menu editor.
4. In the menu editor, click **View**, and then double-click the empty box at the bottom of the drop-down menu (beneath the **Status Bar** option) to display the **Menu Item Properties** dialog box.

5. In the **Menu Item Properties** dialog box, set the following properties as shown.

Property	Value
ID	ID_VIEW_DIALOGBAR=0xE821
Caption	&Dialog Bar
Prompt	Show or hide the dialog bar\nToggle Dialog Bar

Note Setting ID to ID_VIEW_DIALOGBAR=0xE821 causes the associated resources to be used in calculating the layout of control bars. For a more detailed explanation of toolbar layout, search for "Control Bars" in MSDN Library Visual Studio 6.0.

▶ **To create the dialog box resources**

1. In ResourceView, right-click the Dialog folder and click **Insert**.
2. Expand the Dialog icon and double-click **IDD_DIALOGBAR** to invoke the dialog bar editor.
3. Delete the static **TODO** control from the dialog bar.
4. Drag the controls you want to add from the control palette to the dialog bar.
5. Optionally add a **Picture** control, setting properties as follows:
   - Set **Type** to **Icon**.
   - Set **Image** to the ID of an icon.
   - Set **Notify** to **True**.
   - Set **ID** to the ID of its corresponding menu item.

▶ **To attach the dialog bar to the CMainFrame class**

1. Start ClassWizard when you have finished designing the dialog bar, but before you save it.

   You will not build a new class for the control bar. Instead, you will associate the control bar with the class **CMainFrame**. This way, ClassWizard has access to the identifiers in the dialog bar so it can generate message map entries in an existing class. Without this step, you would have to edit the message map yourself.

2. In **ClassWizard**, in the **Adding a Class** dialog box, click **Select an existing class**, and then click **OK**.
3. In the **Select Class** dialog box, select the **CMainFrame** class.

   If the dialog bar's identifiers are available to the **CMainFrame** class, ClassWizard will also make them available to the view class.
4. Click **Select**, click **Yes** in the displayed message box, and then click **OK**.

▶ **To create a CDialogBar object in the CMainFrame class**

1. Right-click **CMainFrame** in ClassView and add a protected member variable as follows:

   ```
   CDialogBar  m_wndDialogBar
   ```

2. In **CMainFrame::OnCreate**, attach the dialog bar to the **CDialogBar** class. Specify the control ID of the dialog bar as the last argument. For example:

   ```
   m_wndDialogBar.Create(this, IDD_DIALOG_BAR, CBRS_TOP,
       ID_VIEW_MYDIALOGBAR);
   ```

   The first argument, this, is a handle to the window that owns the dialog bar. In this case, it is the **CMainFrame** object. The second argument, IDD_DIALOG_BAR, is the ID of the dialog box. The third argument, CBRS_TOP, defines how the dialog bar will be aligned in the associated window. The fourth argument, ID_VIEW_MYDIALOGBAR, is the control ID for the dialog bar.

3. Initialize the dialog bar and its controls as follows:

   ```
   CComboBox * p_lb =
       (CComboBox *)m_wndDialogBar.GetDlgItem(IDC_LIST_COLORS);
   p_lb->SetCurSel(0);
   ```

Implementing Command Handlers

A command handler processes an event from a menu item and calls the appropriate function based on the event.

Chapter 3: Enhancing the User Interface

▶ **To add a command handler for any list box or combo box in the dialog bar**

1. Open the dialog bar resource.

2. Invoke ClassWizard and add a command handler for any list boxes or combo boxes. Typically you need to implement the event LBN_SEL_CHANGE or CBN_SEL_CHANGE. You can choose to place the command handler in the most convenient place. The view class is a good choice, because the list box or combo box probably affects the document, and most command handlers that affect the document are placed in this class.

3. Implement the command handler. The following example code shows a sample implementation:

    ```
    void CDlgBarsView::OnSelchangeListColors()
    {
        CMainFrame * cmf = (CMainFrame *)AfxGetMainWnd();
        CComboBox * p_cb =(CComboBox *)
            cmf->m_wndDialogBar.GetDlgItem(IDC_LIST_COLORS);

        // respond to user changing selection in combo box
    }
    ```

▶ **To add command and command UI handlers to the CMainFrame class**

1. Use ClassWizard to add command and command UI handlers to the **CMainFrame** class for the **View Dialog** menu item.

2. Add code for the **OnViewDialogbar** and **OnUpdateViewDialogbar** functions that were created when you added command handlers. For example:

    ```
    void CMainFrame::OnViewDialogbar()
    {
        OnBarCheck(ID_VIEW_MYDIALOGBAR);
    }

    void CMainFrame::OnUpdateViewDialogbar(CCmdUI* pCmdUI)
    {
        OnUpdateControlBarMenu(pCmdUI);
    }
    ```

Note The functions **OnBarCheck** and **OnUpdateControlBarMenu** are members of the **CFrameWnd** class, even though they are not documented in MSDN Library Visual Studio 6.0.

93

In general, implementing command buttons or icons on a dialog bar is easy. You create a menu item that performs the same operation, and then assign the button or icon on the dialog bar the same identifier as the menu. The menu item can be a dummy menu item, but it must have a handler.

You can also add a single dialog bar from Component Gallery. When you use this method, the Component and Controls Gallery provides most of the code, but you still must do some work.

You can implement multiple dialog bars in an application. You also can create dialog bars dynamically. When doing so, the parent of a dialog bar, which is passed in as the first argument, must be **CMainFrame**. In most cases, it is sufficient to create dialog bars as described in this section.

Using Rebars

A rebar object is very similar in behavior to a toolbar object. It acts as a container for child windows such as edit boxes, toolbars, dialog bars, and list boxes.

In this section, you will learn to create and customize rebars.

Introduction to Rebars

A rebar control can contain one or more bands, with each band having any combination of a gripper bar, a bitmap, a text label, and a child window. However, bands cannot contain more than one child window.

The following illustration shows a rebar control that has two bands. One band contains a gripper bar, a text label ("Address"), and a combo box child window. The other band contains a gripper bar, a text label, and a flat toolbar (implemented with a child window).

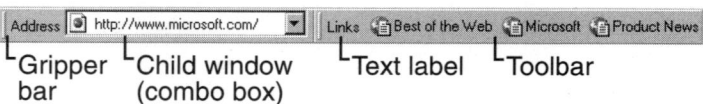

⌊Gripper   ⌊Child window   ⌊Text label   ⌊Toolbar
 bar   (combo box)

Your application can automatically resize the rebar, or the user can manually resize the rebar by clicking or dragging its gripper bar.

Rebars do not support MFC control-bar docking. If the **CRebar::EnableDocking** function is called, your application will display an error message.

Rebar Classes

MFC provides two classes for creating rebars: **CReBar** and **CReBarCtrl**. The **CReBar** class provides the functionality of the rebar common control, and it handles many of the required common control settings and structures for you. The **CReBar** class implements its functionality by using the **CReBarCtrl** class.

Creating a Rebar

You can create a rebar control in two ways. You can either use MFC AppWizard to add the code that will create the rebar at run time or manually add the code to your application to create it.

Creating a Rebar Using MFC AppWizard

You can create a rebar by choosing the **Internet Explorer ReBars** option in Step 4 of MFC AppWizard.

The following illustration shows the **MFC AppWizard - Step 4 of 6** dialog box.

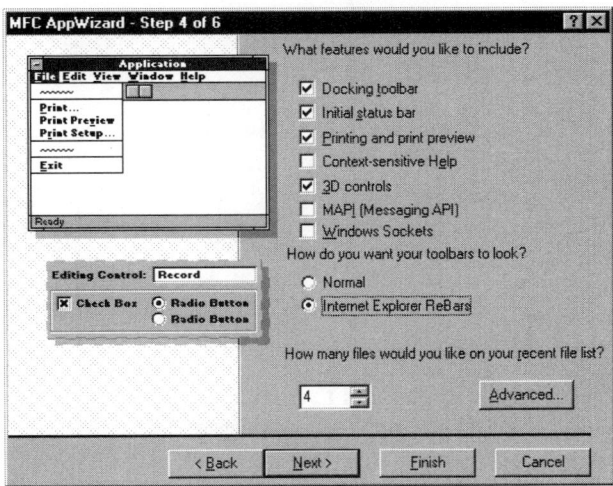

MFC AppWizard performs the following steps to create a rebar control:

♦ Defines a protected **CReBar** object as follows:

    CReBar   m_wndReBar;

- Includes the following lines of code in the **OnCreate** function of the **MainFrame** class:

```
if (m_wndReBar.Create(this))
    {
        if(m_wndReBar.AddBar(&m_wndToolBar) &&
            m_wndReBar.AddBar(&m_wndDlgBar))
            {...} //Success
        else
            {...} // Failed to add controls
    }
else
    {...} //Failed to create the rebar
```

The **Create** function creates a rebar control and attaches it to the **CReBar** object. Apart from a pointer to the parent window—normally your frame window—the **Create** function takes parameters such as the rebar control style, the rebar window styles, and the rebar's child-window ID.

For more information about **CReBar::Create**, search for "CReBar class members" in MSDN Library Visual Studio 6.0.

Creating a Rebar Without Using MFC AppWizard

You can add rebar functionality to an application by defining a protected **CReBar** object and invoking the **CReBar::Create** function from within the **OnCreate** function of the **MainFrame** class. You can add existing controls, such as toolbars and dialog bars, by using the **CReBar::AddBar** function. The next topic discusses this function in more detail.

Adding Child Windows to a Rebar

After creating a rebar control, you call the **CReBar::AddBar** function to add controls such as toolbars and dialog bars to a rebar. The function first creates a rebar band and then adds the control to the band.

The following example code shows how to use the **AddBar** member function:

```
if (!m_wndReBar.AddBar(&m_wndToolBar) ||
!m_wndReBar.AddBar(&m_wndDlgBar))
    {
        TRACE0("Failed to add controls to the rebar\n");
        return -1;      // failed to create
    }
```

For more information about **CReBar::AddBar**, search for "AddBar" in MSDN Library Visual Studio 6.0.

Customizing Rebars

You can modify the default values of a rebar by using the **CReBar::GetReBarCtrl** member function, which provides direct access to the underlying rebar control. The function returns a reference to a **CReBarCtrl** object. This enables you to use the member functions of the **CReBarCtrl** class.

For example, call the **SetBkColor** member function of **CReBarCtrl** to change the background color of the rebar, as shown in the following example code:

```
m_wndReBar.GetReBarCtrl().SetBkColor(RGB(0,0,255));
```

Lab 3.3: Adding a Modeless Dialog Box

In this lab, you will implement a modeless dialog box.

To see the demonstration "Lab 3.3 Demonstration," see the accompanying CD-ROM.

Estimated time to complete this lab: **30 minutes**

To complete the exercises in this lab, you must have the required software. For detailed information about the labs and setup for the labs, see "Labs" in "About This Course."

The code that forms the starting point for this lab is located in the folder *<install folder>*\Labs\Ch03\Lab3.3.

The solution code for this lab is located in the folder *<install folder>*\Labs\Ch03\Lab3.3.

Objectives

After completing this lab, you will be able to:

- Add a dialog box to an existing application.
- Implement the dialog box as a modeless dialog box.
- Respond to user actions from the dialog box in the application.

Prerequisites

There are no prerequisites for this lab.

Exercises

The following exercises provide practice working with the concepts and techniques covered in this chapter:

- Exercise 1: Creating the Dialog Box Template

    In this exercise, you will create a dialog box with which the user can step through the differences between two files.

- Exercise 2: Implementing the Dialog Class

    In this exercise, you will implement the dialog class, **CFindDifferenceDialog**, which you created in Exercise 1. Because this dialog box is modeless, all its actions will take place while its window still exists. Therefore, you will not need to use DDX synchronization; you can query controls directly.

- Exercise 3: Integrating the Dialog Box into an Application

    In this exercise, you will provide the code that responds to user actions in the dialog box.

Exercise 1: Creating the Dialog Box Template

The code that forms the starting point for this exercise is in *<install folder>*\Labs\Ch03\Lab3.3\Ex01.

In this exercise, you will create a dialog box with which the user can step through the differences between two files. The following illustration shows the dialog box you will create.

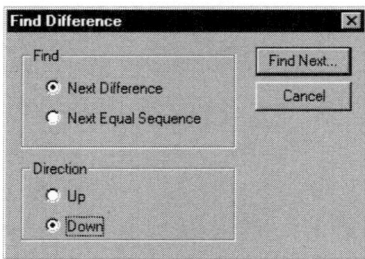

Lab 3.3: Adding a Modeless Dialog Box

There are three parts to this exercise:

1. Creating the dialog box template.
2. Adding the controls to the dialog box template.
3. Testing the dialog box and setting the tab order.

▶ **Create a new (unadorned) dialog box resource**

1. On the **Resource** toolbar, click the **New Dialog** button to create a dialog box template.
2. Set the Caption and ID properties of the dialog box as follows.

Property	Value
Caption	Find Difference
ID	IDD_NEXTDIFF

> **Tip** For the static text controls, the ampersand (&) in the static text establishes ALT key access to the control that follows in the tab order. A static control cannot have focus, so focus automatically flows to the next control in the tab-order sequence. In this case, the shortcut keys in the static-text labels provide access to the associated edit-box controls.

▶ **Add controls to the dialog box template**

1. Open the IDD_NEXTDIFF dialog box resource.
2. Add the following controls to the dialog box to create a dialog box as shown in the preceding illustration.

Control type	ID	Caption
Default command button (push button)	IDOK	Find Next...
Command button	IDCANCEL	Cancel
Group box	IDC_STATIC	Find
Option button	IDC_RADIO_NEXTDIFF	&Next Difference

table continued on next page

table continued from previous page

Control type	ID	Caption
Option button	IDC_RADIO_NEXTEQUAL	Next &Equal Sequence
Group box	IDC_STATIC	Direction
Option button	IDC_RADIO_UP	&Up
Option button	IDC_RADIO_DOWN	&Down

▶ **Group controls on the dialog box template**

1. Right-click the **Next Differences** option button and click **Properties**.
2. Click **Group**.
3. Double-click the **Up** option button and click its **Group** box.
4. Double-click the **Find Next** button and click its **Group** box.
5. Save the dialog box template.

▶ **Set the tab order for the controls on the dialog box template**

1. On the **Layout** menu, click **Tab Order**.

    The property page is hidden. The dialog editor now displays a number for each of the controls in your dialog box template. By default, the numbers indicate the order in which each control was added to the template. While setting the tab order, note that the **OK** button automatically has the **Default Button** option selected.

2. To set the tab order, click the controls in the appropriate order. For example, first click the **Next Difference** option button to set it as the first control, then click **Next Equal Sequence**, and so forth.

    Set the tab order as shown in the following illustration.

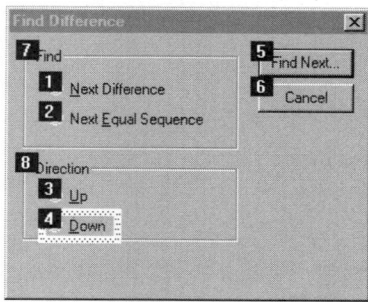

3. To end the tab-ordering operation, click inside the dialog editor window, but outside the dialog box resource. (Pressing ESC also will end the session.)

▶ **Test the dialog box resource**

In this procedure, you will test your controls.

1. Click the **Test** button on the **Dialog** toolbar.

    A simulation of the dialog box created from this resource appears.

    Note the control that has initial keyboard focus. Also note that the **Find Next** button is the default button. It is activated when the user presses the ENTER key.

2. Test the shortcut-key sequences.
3. Press the TAB key several times to cycle through the controls and verify that the tab order is correct.
4. Within the option button group, use the arrow keys to navigate among the buttons.
5. Click the **Find Next** or **Cancel** button to exit test mode.

▶ **Check and save your file**

1. Test the dialog box template again.
2. Save the current file when you are satisfied with your work.

▶ **Create a dialog class using ClassWizard**

In this procedure, you will use ClassWizard to create a dialog class in the Diff application.

> **Tip** To have ClassWizard automatically display the **Adding A Class** dialog box, open ClassWizard during the dialog editor session in which you create the new dialog resource.

1. Run the dialog editor on the IDD_NEXTDIFF dialog box resource.
2. In the dialog editor, be sure that your dialog box template window is the active child window.
3. Invoke ClassWizard.

    It should automatically display the **Adding A Class** dialog box. (If this dialog box does not appear, click the **Add Class** button).

4. Click **Create a new class**, and click **OK**.

   The **Create New Class** dialog box appears.

5. In the **Name** box, type **CFindDifferenceDialog** for the name of the associated C++ dialog class.

6. In the **Base Class** box, click **CDialog**.

   The Dialog ID should already be set to IDD_NEXTDIFF.

7. Shorten the file names FindDifferenceDialog.cpp and FindDifferenceDialog.h to FindDiff.cpp and FindDiff.h by using the **Change** button and its dialog box, and then click **OK**.

The solution code for this exercise is located in the folder *<install folder>*\Labs\Ch03\Lab3.3\Ex01\Solution.

Exercise 2: Implementing the Dialog Class

Continue with the files you created in Exercise 1 or, if you do not have a starting point for this exercise, the code that forms the basis for this exercise is in *<install folder>*\Labs\Ch03\Lab3.3\Ex02.

In this exercise, you will implement the dialog class, **CFindDifferenceDialog**, which you created in the previous exercise. Because this dialog box is modeless, all its actions will take place while its window still exists. Therefore, you will not need to use DDX synchronization; you can query controls directly.

A modeless dialog box has its own stand-alone window with its own window procedure. A modeless dialog box can communicate with its parent window in many ways; the simplest (and safest) is to use registered window messages known by the dialog class and the main application.

▶ **Set up members for control states in the dialog box**

1. Open the file FindDiff.h.

2. Create member variables to determine whether terminating or finding next difference:

   ```
   //attributes
   protected:
       BOOL m_bTerminating;
       BOOL m_bFindNext;
   ```

Lab 3.3: Adding a Modeless Dialog Box

3. Declare member functions to return the internal state to the application as follows:

   ```
   public:
       BOOL    IsTerminating() const;      //TRUE if terminating
       BOOL    SearchDown() const;         //TRUE if searching down,
                                           //FALSE if searching up
       BOOL    FindDifference() const;     //TRUE if finding next
                                           //difference
                                           //FALSE if finding next equal
       BOOL    FindNext() const;           //TRUE if find next button
                                           //pressed
   ```

4. Save FindDiff.h.
5. Open the file FindDiff.cpp.
6. Implement the **CFindDifferenceDialog::IsTerminating** function to return m_bTerminating as follows:

   ```
   BOOL CFindDifferenceDialog::IsTerminating() const
   {
       return m_bTerminating;
   }
   ```

7. Implement **CFindDifferenceDialog::SearchDown** to return the state of the **Search Down** option button as follows:

   ```
   BOOL CFindDifferenceDialog::SearchDown() const
   {
       return(IsDlgButtonChecked(IDC_RADIO_DOWN));
   }
   ```

8. Implement **CFindDifferenceDialog::FindDifference** to return the state of the **Next Difference** option button as follows:

   ```
   BOOL CFindDifferenceDialog::FindDifference() const
   {
       return(IsDlgButtonChecked(IDC_RADIO_NEXTDIFF));
   }
   ```

9. Implement **CFindDifferenceDialog::FindNext** to return m_bFindNext as follows:

    ```
    BOOL CFindDifferenceDialog::FindNext() const
    {
        return m_bFindNext;
    }
    ```

10. Save FindDiff.cpp.

▶ **Implement the Find Next button handler**

When the main application window is notified that the user has clicked a button, it will query the dialog box about the action. You could use the WPARAM parameter of the message to pass this information, but this would entail a more complicated maintenance scheme.

1. Open FindDiff.h.

2. Define a constant string for the name of the message as follows:

    ```
    const char* const FINDDIFF_MSGSTRING = "diffapp_FindDifference";
    ```

3. Save FindDiff.h.

4. Invoke ClassWizard.

5. Create a handler for BN_CLICKED on the IDOK button. Give it the name **OnFindNext**.

6. In the **OnFindNext** function, set m_bFindNext to **TRUE** as follows:

    ```
    m_bFindNext = TRUE;
    ```

7. Send the private message to the parent of the dialog box with a pointer to the dialog object in LPARAM:

    ```
    GetParent()->SendMessage(
        ::RegisterWindowMessage(FINDDIFF_MSGSTRING),
        0, (LPARAM)this);
    ```

8. Reset m_bFindNext as follows:

    ```
    m_bFindNext = FALSE;
    ```

For more information about creating a communication link between the dialog box and its parent application, see "Communicating with the Application" on page 86 in this chapter.

▶ Implement dialog initialization

1. In the constructor, initialize m_bTerminating and m_bFindNext to **FALSE** as follows:

    ```
    CFindDifferenceDialog::CFindDifferenceDialog(CWnd* pParent /*=NULL*/)
        : CDialog(CFindDifferenceDialog::IDD, pParent)
    {
        //{{AFX_DATA_INIT(CFindDifferenceDialog)
            // NOTE: ClassWizard will add member initialization here
        //}}AFX_DATA_INIT

        m_bTerminating = FALSE;
        m_bFindNext = FALSE;
    }
    ```

2. Invoke ClassWizard. Create handlers for WM_INITDIALOG message and **Create**.

3. In the **OnInitDialog** handler, click the **Next Difference** and **Down** option buttons as follows:

    ```
    BOOL CFindDifferenceDialog::OnInitDialog()
    {
        CDialog::OnInitDialog();

        //  Our initialization
        CheckDlgButton(IDC_RADIO_NEXTDIFF, TRUE);
        CheckDlgButton(IDC_RADIO_DOWN, TRUE);

        return TRUE;  // return TRUE unless you set the focus to a control
                      // EXCEPTION: OCX Property Pages should return FALSE
    }
    ```

4. Delete the parameters from the **Create** handler. Because all the members are set up in **CDialog::CDialog**, the call to the **Create** function uses these variables:

    ```
    BOOL CFindDifferenceDialog::Create()
    {
        //  m_lpszTemplateName and m_pParent are set
        //  up by CDialog during construction
        return CDialog::Create (m_lpszTemplateName, m_pParentWnd);
    }
    ```

5. Save FindDiff.cpp.
6. In the file FindDiff.h, remove the parameters from **Create**.
7. Save FindDiff.h.

For more information about creating a modeless dialog box, see "Initializing and Displaying a Modeless Dialog Box" on page 83 in this chapter.

▶ **Implement dialog shutdown**

1. Use ClassWizard to create handlers for BN_CLICKED on the IDCANCEL button (**OnCancel**) and the **PostNcDestroy** messages.
2. Edit the code of **CFindDifferenceDialog::OnCancel**. Use **CWnd::DestroyWindow** to close the window when the **Cancel** button is pressed:

```
void CFindDifferenceDialog::OnCancel()
{
    DestroyWindow();
}
```

3. Edit the code of **CFindDifferenceDialog::PostNcDestroy**. **PostNcDestroy** is sent by **CWnd** after the window has been destroyed. Because your window no longer exists, you cannot follow your window tree with **CWnd::GetParent**. You will use the stored m_mParentWnd handle to communicate with the parent window. Set the m_bTerminating member to **TRUE**, and then send the message to your parent window:

```
m_bTerminating = TRUE;
m_pParentWnd->SendMessage(
    ::RegisterWindowMessage(FINDDIFF_MSGSTRING),
    0, (LPARAM)this);
```

4. As the last step, delete your object:

```
delete this;
```

5. Save FindDiff.cpp.

    The following sample code shows an example of how your code should look. To copy this code for use in your own projects, see "Lab 3.3.2 PostNcDestroy" on the accompanying CD-ROM.

```
void CFindDifferenceDialog::PostNcDestroy()
{
 m_bTerminating = TRUE;
 m_pParentWnd->SendMessage(
     ::RegisterWindowMessage(FINDDIFF_MSGSTRING),
     0, (LPARAM)this);

 delete this;
}
```

6. Build your project.

The solution code for this exercise is located in the folder *<install folder>*\Labs\Ch03\Lab3.3\Ex02\Solution.

Exercise 3: Integrating the Dialog Box into an Application

Continue with the files you created in Exercise 2 or, if you do not have a starting point for this exercise, the code that forms the basis for this exercise is in *<install folder>*\Labs\Ch03\Lab3.3\Ex03.

A modeless dialog box shares code with its parent window. In this exercise, you will provide the code that responds to actions in the dialog box. This code is placed in the **CMainFrame** class for simplicity; however, any **CWnd**-derived window (such as **CDiffView**) could be used as the target.

▶ **Resolve dependencies on CDifferenceDialog in Mainfrm.h**

- You will add reference to **CFindDifferenceDialog** class in MainFrm.h. You will need to include FindDiff.h in any file that includes MainFrm.h prior to that include. Add the include statements to these files.
  - MainFrm.cpp
  - DiffView.cpp
  - DiffDoc.cpp
  - Diff.cpp

▶ Add menu items to the IDR_MAINFRAME menu

1. Open the IDR_MAINFRAME menu.
2. Add a separator to the end of the **Edit** menu.
3. Add these two menu items after the separator:

ID	Caption
ID_EDIT_FIND	&Find...
ID_EDIT_FINDDIFF	Find &Difference...

4. Save Diff.rc.

▶ Integrate CFindDifferenceDialog into CMainFrame

1. Open MainFrm.h.
2. Declare a pointer to a **CFindDifferenceDialog** object in the protected implementation section:

   ```
   CFindDifferenceDialog*   m_pFindDiffDlg;
   ```

3. Declare a handler for the FINDDIFF_MSGSTRING registered message before DECLARE_MESSAGE_MAP as follows:

   ```
   afx_msg LRESULT OnFindDifferenceCmd (WPARAM, LPARAM lParam);
   ```

4. Declare a member function to find the next difference as follows:

   ```
   void OnFindNextDifference(BOOL bSearchDown,
                             BOOL bNextDifference);
   ```

5. Save MainFrm.h.
6. Open MainFrm.cpp.
7. Initialize a variable to hold the ID of the registered message:

   ```
   static const UINT nMsgFindDifference =
                   ::RegisterWindowMessage(FINDDIFF_MSGSTRING);
   ```

8. Map the message to **CMainFrame** as follows:

   ```
   ON_REGISTERED_MESSAGE (nMsgFindDifference, OnFindDifferenceCmd)
   ```

9. Using ClassWizard, add a command handler for ID_EDIT_FINDDIFF (**OnEditFindDiff**).

10. In the constructor, set m_pFindDiffDlg to NULL as follows:

    ```
    m_pFindDiffDlg = NULL;
    ```

▶ **Implement the menu handler for ID_EDIT_FINDDIFF**

1. Edit the code for **CMainFrame::OnEditFindDiff**. Check to see whether the dialog box is already displayed:

   ```
   if(m_pFindDiffDlg == NULL)
   ```

2. Dynamically construct a **CFindDifferenceDialog** instance and assign the pointer to m_pFindDiffDlg if the dialog box is not already displayed:

   ```
   m_pFindDiffDlg = new CFindDifferenceDialog(this);
   ```

3. Once you have constructed the dialog box, call **CFindDifferenceDialog::Create** to initialize it as follows:

   ```
   if(m_pFindDiffDlg)
   {
       m_pFindDiffDlg->Create();
   }
   ```

4. Display the dialog window as follows:

   ```
   if(m_pFindDiffDlg)
   {
       m_pFindDiffDlg->SetActiveWindow();
       m_pFindDiffDlg->ShowWindow(SW_SHOW);
   }
   ```

The sample code on the following page shows an example of how your code should look. To copy this code for use in your own projects, see "Lab 3.3.3 OnEditFindDiff" on the accompanying CD-ROM.

```
void CMainFrame::OnEditFindDiff()
{
  // Create the dialog if needed

  if(m_pFindDiffDlg == NULL)
  {

    m_pFindDiffDlg = new CFindDifferenceDialog(this);
    if(m_pFindDiffDlg)
    {
        m_pFindDiffDlg->Create();
    }
  }

  // Show it

  if(m_pFindDiffDlg)
  {
      m_pFindDiffDlg->SetActiveWindow();
      m_pFindDiffDlg->ShowWindow(SW_SHOW);
  }
}
```

▶ **Implement a handler for the registered message**

1. In the MainFrm.cpp file, define **CMainFrame::OnFindDifferenceCmd**:

   ```
   LRESULT CMainFrame::OnFindDifferenceCmd(WPARAM, LPARAM lParam)
   ```

2. Cast LPARAM to a pointer to **CFindDifferenceDialog**:

   ```
   CFindDifferenceDialog* pDialog = (CFindDifferenceDialog *)lParam;
   ```

3. The dialog box sends its message when the **Find Next** button is clicked, or when the dialog box is closing. In the latter case, clear m_pFindDiffDlg:

   ```
   if (pDialog->IsTerminating())
   {
      m_pFindDiffDlg = NULL;
   }
   ```

4. When the **Find Next** button is clicked, check the state of the option buttons and dispatch to **CMainFrame::OnFindNextDifference** as follows:

   ```
   else if (pDialog->FindNext())
   {
       OnFindNextDifference(pDialog->SearchDown(),
                            pDialog->FindDifference());
   }
   ```

5. Return 0 for the message.
6. Save MainFrm.cpp.

   The following sample code shows an example of how your code should look. To copy this code for use in your own projects, see "Lab 3.3.3 OnFindDifferenceCmd" on the accompanying CD-ROM.

```
LRESULT CMainFrame::OnFindDifferenceCmd(WPARAM, LPARAM lParam)
{
    CFindDifferenceDialog* pDialog = (CFindDifferenceDialog *)lParam;

    if (pDialog->IsTerminating())
    {
        m_pFindDiffDlg = NULL;
    }
    else if (pDialog->FindNext())
    {
        OnFindNextDifference(pDialog->SearchDown(),
                             pDialog->FindDifference());
    }

    return 0;
}
```

▶ **Implement visual feedback**

Since the difference is simulated, finding the next difference also will need to be simulated. You will simply move randomly forward or backward through the current view in response to the message from the dialog box.

1. In the MainFrm.cpp file, define **CMainFrame::OnFindNextDifference**:

   ```
   void CMainFrame::OnFindNextDifference(BOOL bSearchDown,
                                         BOOL bNextDifference)
   ```

2. Get the active view:

   ```
   CDiffView * pView = (CDiffView *)GetActiveView();
   if(pView)
   {
   ```

3. Find out which line (if any) is currently highlighted:

   ```
   int nLineCnt = pView->GetRichEditCtrl().GetLineCount();
   LONG lStart = 0;
   LONG lEnd   = 0;
   pView->GetRichEditCtrl().GetSel(lStart, lEnd);
   LONG lCurLine = pView->GetRichEditCtrl().LineFromChar(lStart);
   ```

4. Find a line randomly between the current line and the end of the text if you are searching forward; find a line randomly between the current line and the beginning of the text if you are searching backward:

   ```
   int nNewLine;
   if(bSearchDown)
   {
       nNewLine = lCurLine + (rand() % (nLineCnt-lCurLine)+1);
   }
   else
   {
       nNewLine = rand() % (lCurLine+1) + 1;
   }
   ```

5. Find the starting and ending characters of that line and select them as follows:

   ```
   lStart = pView->GetRichEditCtrl().LineIndex(nNewLine);
   lEnd = lStart + pView->GetRichEditCtrl().LineLength(nNewLine);

   pView->GetRichEditCtrl().SetSel(lStart, lEnd);
   ```

6. There is no difference between the next difference and the next equal text in this simulation. Use the status bar text to show the current option as follows:

   ```
   if (bNextDifference)
   {
       m_wndStatusBar.SetWindowText(_T("Found next difference"));
   }
   else
   {
       m_wndStatusBar.SetWindowText(_T("Found next equal run"));
   }
   ```

7. Save MainFrm.cpp.

   The following sample code shows an example of how your code should look. To copy this code for use in your own projects, see "Lab 3.3.3 OnFindNextDifference" on the accompanying CD-ROM.

```cpp
void CMainFrame::OnFindNextDifference(BOOL bSearchDown,
                                     BOOL bNextDifference)
{
  CDiffView * pView = (CDiffView *)GetActiveView();
  if(pView)
  {
      int nLineCnt = pView->GetRichEditCtrl().GetLineCount();
      LONG lStart = 0;
      LONG lEnd   = 0;
      pView->GetRichEditCtrl().GetSel(lStart, lEnd);
      LONG lCurLine = pView->GetRichEditCtrl().LineFromChar(lStart);

      int nNewLine;
      if(bSearchDown)
      {
          nNewLine = lCurLine + (rand() % (nLineCnt-lCurLine)+1);
      }
      else
      {
          nNewLine = rand() % (lCurLine+1) + 1;
      }

      lStart = pView->GetRichEditCtrl().LineIndex(nNewLine);
      lEnd = lStart + pView-
>GetRichEditCtrl().LineLength(nNewLine);

      pView->GetRichEditCtrl().SetSel(lStart, lEnd);

      if (bNextDifference)
      {
          m_wndStatusBar.SetWindowText(_T("Found next difference"));
      }
      else
      {
          m_wndStatusBar.SetWindowText(_T("Found next equal run"));
      }
  }
}
```

▶ Build and test the application

- Build your application. Choose menu items under **Edit**, set the focus in either pane, and find the next difference between the files either forward or backward.

The solution code for this exercise is located in the folder *<install folder>*\Labs\Ch03\Lab3.3\Ex03\Solution.

Lab 3.4: Adding a Dialog Bar

In this lab, you will create the dialog bar resources for an application and implement a dialog bar.

To see the demonstration "Lab 3.4 Demonstration," see the accompanying CD-ROM.

Estimated time to complete this lab: **60 minutes**

To complete the exercises in this lab, you must have the required software. For detailed information about the labs and setup for the labs, see "Labs" in "About This Course."

The code that forms the starting point for this lab is located in the folder *<install folder>*\Labs\Ch03\Lab3.4.

The solution code for this lab is located in the folder *<install folder>*\Labs\Ch03\Lab3.4.

Objectives

After completing this lab, you will be able to:

- Create the resources to support a dialog bar.
- Use a menu command to toggle the dialog bar on and off.
- Use a combo box drop-down list in the dialog bar to display information.
- Use an event handler to handle dialog bar events.
- Use **CWnd::OnCommand** to handle dialog bar events.

Prerequisites

Before working on this lab, you should be familiar with the following:

- Menus and command handlers
- Combo boxes

Exercises

The following exercises provide practice working with the concepts and techniques covered in this chapter:

- Exercise 1: Creating Dialog Bar Resources

  In this exercise, you will create the dialog bar resources for an application.

- Exercise 2: Implementing a Dialog Bar

  In this exercise, you will implement a nonfunctional dialog bar, which includes a menu to turn the dialog bar on and off.

- Exercise 3: Implementing a Combo Box for the Dialog Bar

  In this exercise, you will implement a combo box on the left side of the dialog bar by manually adding a message-map entry and its associated command handler.

- Exercise 4: Implementing a Combo Box with Command Handlers

  In this exercise, you will implement a combo box on the right side of the dialog bar by using an **OnCommand** handler.

Exercise 1: Creating Dialog Bar Resources

The code that forms the starting point for this exercise is in *<install folder>*\Labs\Ch03\Lab3.4\Ex01.

In this exercise, you will create the dialog bar resources for an application.

▶ **Add a menu and dialog bar to the ShowDiff application**

1. Use ResourceView to open the menu resource IDR_MAINFRAME for editing.
2. In the menu editor, choose the top-level item, **View**, and then double-click the empty box at the bottom (beneath the status bar).

3. Set the menu item ID to ID_VIEW_DIALOGBAR=0xE821. This ID will cause the associated resources to be used in calculating the layout of toolbars. If you do not want a menu item to toggle the dialog bar, you can use **View Resource Symbols** to insert the name and ID of the menu item.

   For a more detailed explanation of toolbar layout, see Technical Note TN031: Control Bars in the MSDN Library Visual Studio 6.0.

4. Set the **Caption** to &Dialog Bar.

5. Set the **Prompt** to Show or hide the dialog bar\nToggle Dialog Bar.

▶ **Create the dialog bar resources**

1. Use ResourceView to insert a new dialog bar resource. Right-click the Dialog folder and click **Insert**.

2. Expand the Dialog folder by clicking the plus (+) symbol, and choose IDD_DIALOGBAR.

3. Delete the static **TODO** control from the dialog bar.

4. Drag a combo box from the control palette to the dialog. Place the combo box in the upper-left corner. The position of the combo box should be 10, 1 and its size should be 142 by 12. Set its ID to **IDC_LEFT**. Set its styles to Type **Drop List**, and select the **Auto HScroll** check box.

5. Select the combo box. Use the menu to copy and paste a second combo box. Name the second box IDC_RIGHT. Place it slightly to the right of the first combo box. Align the top edges of the combo boxes, then reduce the size of the dialog box to just contain the combo boxes.

6. Save your work.

▶ **Provide prompts and ToolTips for the combo boxes**

1. Open the string table.

2. Add a new string with an ID of IDC_LEFT and a caption of **Select a file to display in the left window\nDisplay on Left**.

3. Add a new string with an ID of IDC_RIGHT and a caption of **Select a file to display in the right window\nDisplay on Right**.

4. Save your work.

The solution code for this exercise is located in the folder *<install folder>*\Labs\Ch03\Lab3.4\Ex01\Solution.

Exercise 2: Implementing a Dialog Bar

Continue with the files you created in Exercise 1 or, if you do not have a starting point for this exercise, the code that forms the basis for this exercise is in *<install folder>*\Labs\Ch03\Lab3.4\Ex02.

In this exercise, you will implement a nonfunctional dialog bar, which includes a menu to turn the dialog bar on and off.

▶ **Associate the dialog bar resource with the CMainFrame class**

1. Use ResourceView to open the dialog bar resources. Highlight IDD_DIALOGBAR with a single click.

2. Start Class Wizard. Click **Select an existing class,** click **CMainFrame,** and then click **Select.**

3. Click **Yes** to create an association between **CMainFrame** and **CDialog.** Close ClassWizard, and then restart it.

4. In ClassWizard, make sure that the selected class name is **CMainFrame.** In the **Object IDs** list, select ID_VIEW_DIALOGBAR and double-click **COMMAND** in the Messages window. Accept the default name of **OnViewDialogbar.** (Do not select Edit Code yet.)

5. Double-click UPDATE_COMMAND_UI. Accept the default name of **OnUpdateViewDialogbar.**

6. Exit ClassWizard.

▶ **Add a protected variable to the CMainFrame class**

- Right-click **CMainFrame** in ClassView and add a protected variable:

    ```
    CDialogBar m_wndDialogBar
    ```

▶ **Implement the dialog bar in the CMainFrame::OnCreate function**

1. In the function **CMainFrame::OnCreate,** call **CDialogBar::Create** using the data member m_wndDialogBar. Place the code at the bottom of the function, just before the return 0 statement, as follows:

    ```
    m_wndDialogBar.Create( this, IDD_DIALOGBAR, CBRS_TOP,
        ID_VIEW_DIALOGBAR );
    ```

2. Because a dialog bar is similar to a toolbar, copy the code that MFC AppWizard created for the toolbar to set docking and styles, and to set ToolTips. Change the variable name of the toolbar to that of the dialog bar variable. Place this code after the call to **CDialogBar::Create**. Edit the docking style of the dialog bar to allow docking at only the top or bottom of the frame:

   ```
   m_wndDialogBar.EnableDocking(CBRS_ALIGN_TOP|CBRS_ALIGN_BOTTOM);
   EnableDocking(CBRS_ALIGN_ANY);
   DockControlBar(&m_wndDialogBar);
   m_wndDialogBar.SetBarStyle(m_wndDialogBar.GetBarStyle() |
       CBRS_TOOLTIPS | CBRS_FLYBY);
   ```

3. Open the header file for **CMainFrame**. Remove the following statement from the beginning of the file (if it is there):

   ```
   #define _BASELINE_CODE_
   ```

4. While you have the **CMainFrame** header file open, locate the definition of the enumerated values LEFT and RIGHT. Now that you have added controls with the identifiers IDC_LEFT and IDC_RIGHT, you can complete the declaration of this enumerated type as follows:

   ```
   enum { LEFT = IDC_LEFT, RIGHT = IDC_RIGHT };
   ```

5. Build and run the application. If it is working correctly, the dialog bar should start docked beneath the standard toolbar. It should tear away, float, and dock. If you float the dialog bar, and then close it, you will not be able to open it again.

▶ **Implement the menu to turn the dialog bar on and off**

   1. Find the stub implementation of **CMainFrame::OnViewDialogbar**. Use the functions **CDialogBar::ShowControlBar** and **CWnd::IsWindowVisible** to turn the dialog bar on and off:

      ```
      ShowControlBar( & m_wndDialogBar,! m_wndDialogBar.IsWindowVisible( ),
          FALSE );
      ```

   2. Find the stub implementation of **CMainFrame::OnUpdateViewDialogbar**. Use the functions **CCmdUI::SetCheck** and **CWnd::IsWindowVisible** to update the menu item:

      ```
      pCmdUI->SetCheck( m_wndDialogBar.IsWindowVisible( ) );
      ```

3. Build and run the application. Verify that the menu turns the dialog bar on and off.

The solution code for this exercise is located in the folder <install folder>\Labs\Ch03\Lab3.4\Ex02\Solution.

Exercise 3: Implementing a Combo Box for the Dialog Bar

Continue with the files you created in Exercise 2 or, if you do not have a starting point for this exercise, the code that forms the basis for this exercise is in <install folder>\Labs\Ch03\Lab3.4\Ex03.

In this exercise, you will implement a combo box on the left side of the dialog bar by manually adding a message-map entry and its associated command handler.

▶ **Create message map entries for the left combo box**

The combo box contains a list of files opened by the user. When the user selects a file name from the list, the application will open and display that file.

1. Right-click the CMainFrame icon in the ClassView pane. Click **Add Member function** to add the following function header:

    ```
    afx_msg void OnSelendokLeft();
    ```

2. Insert a message map entry in the **CMainFrame** implementation file. Place the entry between the end of the code section created by ClassWizard and the end of the Message Map as follows:

    ```
    //}}AFX_MSG_MAP
        ON_CBN_SELENDOK ( IDC_LEFT, OnSelendokLeft )
    END_MESSAGE_MAP()
    ```

▶ **Code the function CMainFrame::OnSelendokLeft**

You added this message handler in the previous step. In this handler, you will extract the selected string from the combo box, and then use that string as an argument to the function **CMainFrame::ResetFile**. **ResetFile** is not part of MFC; it is part of the baseline code written for this application.

1. Assign a pointer to the combo box using **CWnd::GetDlgItem** and the enum **CMainFrame::LEFT**.

2. Create a **CString** variable.
3. Call the function **CWnd::GetWindowText** to modify the **CString** variable.
4. Invoke **CMainFrame:: ResetFile** using the enum and the string variable.

   The following sample code shows an example of how your code should look. To copy this code for use in your own projects, see "Lab 3.4.3 OnSelendokLeft" on the accompanying CD-ROM.

```
void CMainFrame::OnSelendokLeft()
{
  // TODO: Add your control notification handler code here
  CComboBox * pCmb =
      ( CComboBox * ) m_wndDialogBar.GetDlgItem( LEFT );
  CString str;
  pCmb->GetWindowText( str );   //Get the selected text
  ResetFile( LEFT, str );
}
```

5. Build and run the application. Use **File Open** at least twice. Drop the left list box to choose a file name. If the application is working correctly, when you click the name, the indicated file will load into the view.

The solution code for this exercise is located in the folder *<install folder>*\Labs\Ch03\Lab3.4\Ex03\Solution.

Exercise 4: Implementing a Combo Box with Command Handlers

Continue with the files you created in Exercise 3 or, if you do not have a starting point for this exercise, the code that forms the basis for this exercise is in *<install folder>*\Labs\Ch03\Lab3.4\Ex04.

In this exercise, you will implement a combo box on the right side of the dialog bar by using an OnCommand handler.

▶ **Add a command handler to the CMainFrame class**

Use ClassWizard to add a handler to the **CMainFrame** class for the message event **OnCommand**. The parameter, wParam, contains the identifier of the message source in its low-order word. The high-order word of wParam contains the notification code. When the message is the selection notification from the right-hand combo box, get the selected file name from the combo box. Display the selected file in the right-side view.

1. Initialize an int variable with the message value. Use the HIWORD macro to extract the message.
2. Create a second int variable. Use LOWORD to extract and store the control ID in the variable.
3. If the message is CBN_SELENDOK and the control is IDC_RIGHT, then get the selected text from the combo box.
4. Load the right-side view using the function **CMainFrame::ResetFile**. The completed code for adding the command handler and writing the code for this function follows:

```
BOOL CMainFrame::OnCommand(WPARAM wParam, LPARAM lParam)
{
    // TODO: Add your specialized code here and/or call the base class

    int msg  = HIWORD( wParam );   //Get the message
    int ctrl = LOWORD( wParam );   //Get the message source

    //Check for notification message from the right-side combo
    if ( CBN_SELENDOK == msg && IDC_RIGHT == ctrl )
    {
        CString str;
        CComboBox * pCmb =
            ( CComboBox * ) m_wndDialogBar.GetDlgItem( ctrl );
        pCmb->GetWindowText( str );   //Get selected text
        ResetFile( ctrl, str );       //Change to the selected file
    }
    return CFrameWnd::OnCommand(wParam, lParam);
}
```

5. Build and run the application. Use **File Open** at least twice. Drop the right list box to choose a file name. If the application is working correctly, the indicated file will be displayed when you click on the name. The left list box should work the same way.

The solution code for this exercise is located in the folder *<install folder>*\Labs\ Ch03\Lab3.4\Ex04\Solution.

Lab 3.5: Adding a Rebar

In this lab, you will implement a rebar.

To see the demonstration "Lab 3.5 Demonstration," see the accompanying CD-ROM.

Estimated time to complete this lab: **15 minutes**

To complete the exercises in this lab, you must have the required software. For detailed information about the labs and setup for the labs, see "Labs" in "About This Course."

The code that forms the starting point for this lab is located in the folder *<install folder>*\Labs\Ch03\Lab3.5\Ex01.

The solution code for this lab is located in the folder *<install folder>*\Labs\Ch03\Lab3.5\Ex01\Solution.

Objectives

After completing this lab, you will be able to:

- Create a **CReBar** object.
- Add a dialog bar and a toolbar to rebar.

Prerequisites

Before working on this lab, you should be familiar with the following:

- Toolbars
- Dialog bars

Exercises

The following exercise provides practice working with the concepts and techniques covered in this chapter:

- Exercise 1: Implementing a Rebar

  In this exercise, you will create a rebar and add a toolbar and a dialog bar to it.

Exercise 1: Implementing a Rebar

The code that forms the starting point for this lab is in *<install folder>*\Labs\Ch03\Lab3.5\Ex01.

In this exercise, you will create a rebar and add a toolbar and a dialog bar to it.

▶ **Implement a rebar**

1. Open the file MainFrm.h.
2. Add a protected **CReBar** member to the class definition:

   ```
   CReBar m_wndReBar;
   ```

3. Open MainFrm.cpp and scroll to the **OnCreate** function.
4. Create a **CReBar** object and add controls to it by using the **AddBar** function as follows:

   ```
   if (!m_wndReBar.Create(this) ||
           !m_wndReBar.AddBar(&m_wndToolBar) ||
           !m_wndReBar.AddBar(&m_wndDialogBar))
       {
           TRACE0("Failed to create rebar\n");
           return -1;      // fail to create
       }
   ```

The following sample code shows an example of how your code should look. To copy this code for use in your own projects, see "Lab 3.5.1 OnCreate" on the accompanying CD-ROM.

```
int CMainFrame::OnCreate(LPCREATESTRUCT lpCreateStruct)
{
  if (CFrameWnd::OnCreate(lpCreateStruct) == -1)
     return -1;

  if (!m_wndToolBar.Create(this) ||
      !m_wndToolBar.LoadToolBar(IDR_MAINFRAME))
  {
      TRACE0("Failed to create toolbar\n");
      return -1;      // fail to create
  }
```

code continued on next page

code continued from previous page

```
    if (!m_wndStatusBar.Create(this) ||
        !m_wndStatusBar.SetIndicators(indicators,
            sizeof(indicators)/sizeof(UINT)))
    {
        TRACE0("Failed to create status bar\n");
        return -1;      // fail to create
    }

    m_wndToolBar.SetBarStyle(m_wndToolBar.GetBarStyle() |
        CBRS_TOOLTIPS | CBRS_FLYBY);


    m_wndDialogBar.Create( this,  //Parent window is the main frame
                IDD_DIALOGBAR,   //The graphic resource
                CBRS_TOP,        //Align to the top of the frame
                ID_VIEW_DIALOGBAR);  //Control's ID

    m_wndDialogBar.SetBarStyle(m_wndDialogBar.GetBarStyle() |
        CBRS_TOOLTIPS | CBRS_FLYBY);
    if (!m_wndReBar.Create(this) ||
        !m_wndReBar.AddBar(&m_wndToolBar) ||
        !m_wndReBar.AddBar(&m_wndDialogBar))
    {
        TRACE0("Failed to create rebar\n");
        return -1;      // fail to create
    }
    return 0;
}
```

5. Build and run the application.

For more information about creating rebars, see "Creating a Rebar" on page 95 in this chapter.

The solution code for this exercise is located in the folder *<install folder>*\Labs\Ch03\Lab3.5\Ex01\Solution.

Sample Applications

The following table describes the sample applications related to this chapter. These sample applications are located in the folder *<install folder>*\Samples\Ch03.

Sample application	This sample application shows you how to:
Dynamenu	Manage menus dynamically.
Owndraw	Implement ownerdraw menus by drawing menus that include bitmaps.
Custsbar	Replace the default status bar with a custom status bar. This custom status bar duplicates the functionality of the default status bar (CAPS state, status line) and has graphics drawn in one of its panes.
Toolbar	Add a floating, dockable toolbar.
Tabbed	Implement a modal tabbed dialog box with three property sheets.
Modeless	Implement a modeless dialog box.
Dlgbars	Add a dialog bar featuring buttons, icons, and combo boxes.

Self-Check Questions

To see the answers to the Self-Check Questions, see Appendix A.

1. **Which function adds menu items to a cascading menu?**

    A. AppendMenuItems

    B. AddPopupItems

    C. AppendMenu

    D. AddMenu

2. **To create a dockable toolbar, which steps must you complete?**

    A. You only need to enable docking for the frame window.

    B. You only need to enable docking for each toolbar you want to be dockable.

    C. You only need to add code to dock the toolbar to a frame window.

    D. You must complete all three steps: enable docking for the frame, enable docking for each toolbar you want to be dockable, and dock the toolbar to the frame.

3. **Which drawing type must you specify to include graphics in a status bar?**

    A. SBT_IMAGES

    B. SBT_OWNERDRAW

    C. SBT_NOBORDERS

    D. SBT_POPOUT

4. **How do you invoke modal and modeless dialog boxes?**

    A. Invoke modal dialog boxes with **CDialog::DoModal**. Invoke modeless dialog boxes with **CDialog::Create**.

    B. Invoke modal dialog boxes with **CDialog::DoModal**. Invoke modeless dialog boxes with **CDialog::DoModeless**.

    C. Invoke modal dialog boxes with **CModal::Create**. Invoke modeless dialog boxes with **CModeless::Create**.

    D. Invoke modal dialog boxes with **CDialog::Create**. Invoke modeless dialog boxes with **CDialog::DoModal**.

5. What is the advantage of using common dialog boxes?

 A. Makes your code portable across operating systems.

 B. Improves run-time performance of your applications.

 C. Reduces time needed to build property sheets and tabbed dialog boxes.

 D. Makes the user interface of your applications consistent with other Windows-based applications.

6. Which is the base class of a dialog bar control?

 A. CDlgCtrl

 B. CReBar

 C. CDialog

 D. CDialogBar

7. Which function adds controls to a rebar?

 A. SetReBarCtrl()

 B. AddReBar()

 C. AddBar()

 D. GetReBarCtrl()

Student Notes:

Chapter 4:
Implementing View Classes

Multimedia

Creating an Application
with a Scrolling View 148

Dynamic Vs. Static
Splitter Windows 152

Creating a Dynamic Splitter
Window 153

Lab 4.1 Demonstration 156

Creating a Tree View
Application 173

Lab 4.2 Demonstration 184

Lab 4.3 Demonstration 196

This chapter examines the different types of view classes available in the Microsoft Foundation Class (MFC) Library. The chapter begins with a general discussion of how views fit into the document/view architecture, and continues with sections on some of the views.

The **CHTMLView** class, which provides Internet browsing functionality, is not covered in this chapter. For information about **CHTMLView**, see "Implementing HTML Views" on page 469 in Chapter 9, "Building Internet Applications."

Objectives

After completing this chapter, you will be able to:

- Describe the purpose of documents, views, templates, and frames within the document/view architecture, and explain how they interact.
- Describe the various types of view classes in MFC.
- Implement applications that use the following view classes:
  - CView
  - CScrollView
  - CListView
  - CSplitter
  - CTreeView
  - CEditView
  - CRichEditView
- Create single-document interface (SDI) and multiple-document interface (MDI) applications with multiple views.
- Use two interrelated views in an application.

Introduction to Views

The view class, **CView**, physically represents the client area of the application. Logically, **CView** represents a viewport of the information contained in the document class. It also allows user input through the mouse or keyboard.

MFC supports a wide variety of views. The following illustration shows the hierarchy of MFC view classes.

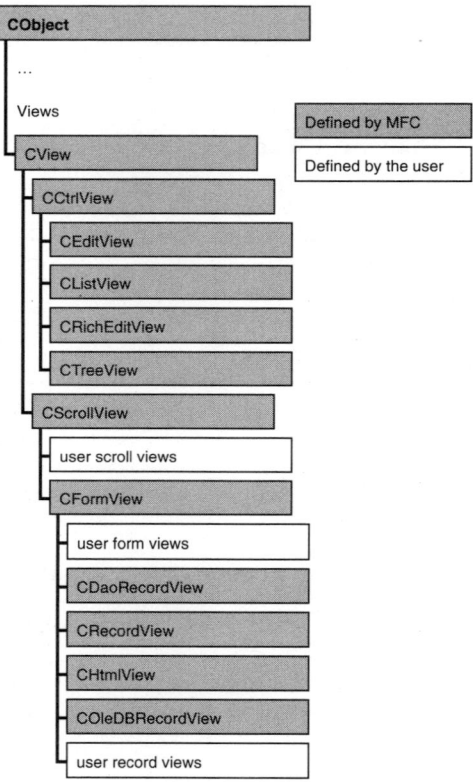

By deriving your application's view from one of these classes, the view inherits support for interaction with the application framework. This section provides information on the **CView** class and how it fits into document/view architecture. It also introduces the relationship between the view and the document.

The **CView** class simplifies the implementation of printing and print preview for your documents. For more information about implementing printing features, see Chapter 10, "Printing and Print Preview."

The CView Class

The **CView** class provides the basic functionality for user-defined view classes.

A view is attached to a document and acts as an intermediary between the document and the user. The view renders an image of the document on the screen or printer and interprets user input as operations on the document.

A view is a child of a frame window. More than one view can share a frame window, as in the case of a splitter window. When the user opens a new window or splits an existing one, the framework constructs a new view and attaches it to the document.

Relationship Between a View and a Document

A view can be attached to only one document, but a document can have multiple views attached to it at once, as when the contents of the document are displayed in a splitter window or in multiple child windows in an MDI application.

A view displays a document's data. The document provides the view with the necessary details about its data. You can have the view access the document's data members directly, or you can provide member functions in the document class for the view class to call.

Coordinating the Views of a Document

To manage the complex process of creating documents with their associated views and frame windows, the framework uses two document template classes:

- CSingleDocTemplate

    You use **CSingleDocTemplate** with single-document interface (SDI) applications to create and store one document of one type.

- CMultiDocTemplate

    You use **CMultipleDocTemplate** with multiple-document interface (MDI) applications to create and store multiple documents of one type.

When a document's data changes, the view responsible for the changes typically calls the **CDocument::UpdateAllViews** function for the document, which notifies all the other views by calling the **OnUpdate** member function for each view. The default implementation of **OnUpdate** invalidates the view's entire client area. You can override this function to invalidate only those parts of the client area that you want to redraw.

Managing Document/View Interaction

To manage the interaction between a document and its view, you must complete the following steps.

1. Establish communication between the document and view.
2. Display data in the view.
3. Update the view when data in the document changes.

Establishing Communication

To establish communication between the current document and a view, create a pointer to the appropriate type of document and call the view's **GetDocument** member function, as shown in the following example code:

```
// Samples\CH04\Mdiapp
// Mdiview.cpp
void CMDIAppView::OnDraw(CDC* pDC)
{
  // Get pointer to current document
  CMDIAppDoc* pDoc = GetDocument();
  ASSERT_VALID(pDoc);

  // Use document pointer as required
  // to access document data and functions

  // ... remainder of drawing code goes here
}
```

Displaying Data

To display data in a view, override the **OnDraw** function. The sample code on the following page overrides the **OnDraw** function. To copy this code for use in your own projects, see "Overriding OnDraw" on the accompanying CD-ROM.

```
// Overriding the OnDraw function to display data in a view
// Samples\CH04\Mdiapp
// Mdiview.cpp

void CMDIAppView::OnDraw(CDC* pDC)
{
  // Get pointer to current document
  CMDIAppDoc* pDoc = GetDocument();
  ASSERT_VALID(pDoc);

  // Calculate position to display text
  CRect r;
  GetClientRect(&r);
  int x = r.right / 2, y = r.bottom / 2;

  // Set text characteristics
  pDC->SetTextColor(pDoc->GetColor());
  pDC->SetTextAlign (TA_CENTER | TA_BASELINE);

  // Display text to the view
  pDC->TextOut (x, y, pDoc->GetPhrase());
}
```

Updating the View

To update the view(s) when data in the document changes, use either one of these procedures:

- **CWnd::Invalidate** (or **CDocument::UpdateAllViews**)

  Use in applications that use a single view.

- **CDocument::UpdateAllViews**

  Use in applications that use multiple views.

In applications that use views of different types, calling the **UpdateAllViews** function may not be the easiest solution for updating data. For information about a method that bypasses the **UpdateAllViews** function, see "Coordinating Multiple Interrelated Views" on page 183 in this chapter.

Tip You can use the pHint and lHint parameters of **UpdateAllViews** to pass information to the views about the modifications made to the document. You can encode information by using lHint, and you can define a **CObject**-derived class to store information about the modifications and pass an object of that class by using pHint. Override the **CView::OnUpdate** member function in your **CView**-derived class to optimize the updating of the view's display, based on the information passed.

For more information about the **UpdateAllViews** function, search for "UpdateAllViews" in MSDN Library Visual Studio 6.0.

The following sample code shows how an MDI application uses the **UpdateAllViews** function to ensure that all views associated with the current document are correctly repainted when the user changes the color of the text displayed in the view. To copy this code for use in your own projects, see "Updating the Views in an MDI Application" on the accompanying CD-ROM.

```
// Repainting all views of a document when the user changes the text
// color in one of the views
// Samples\CH04\Mdiapp
// Mdiview.cpp

void CMDIAppView::OnColors(UINT nID)
{
  CMDIAppDoc* pDoc = GetDocument();
  pDoc->SetColor(IDtoColorRef(nID));

  // If this were an SDI app then you could call
      // Invalidate();
  // Since it's an MDI app, you have to call
  pDoc->UpdateAllViews(NULL);
}
```

For more information about functions used to update views, search for "Updating Views" in MSDN Library Visual Studio 6.0.

Adding Multiple Views

It is possible to support more than one view of a single document. To help you implement multiple views, a document object keeps a list of its views, provides member functions for adding and removing views, and supplies the **UpdateAllViews** member function, which sends a message to the views when the user changes the data in a document.

This section explains how to create multiple views of the same document for SDI and MDI applications. In the sample applications for this section, multiple views share a single frame window. The views are constructed from different classes, each view providing a different way to display the same document. For example, one view might show the text in a document in a normal mode, while the other view shows the text in italic.

Adding Multiple Views to an SDI Application

In an SDI application, you can have multiple views of the same document. The views are constructed from different classes, each view providing a different way to display the same document. Several steps are required to add a second view to an SDI application.

▶ **To create an SDI application with two views of the same document**

1. Build an SDI application the way you normally would. For an application with more than one view class, like the one discussed in these steps, place the command handlers in the **CMainFrame** class. Placing the command handlers in **CMainFrame** ensures that they will be available regardless of which view is active. If you place the command handlers in the view class, the handlers will not be available unless that view object is active.

> **Tip** In an application with only one view class, place command handlers in the view class. In an application with more than one view class, place command handlers in the **CMainFrame** (SDI) or **CChildFrame** (MDI) class. The functions **CFrameWnd::GetActiveView** and **CFrameWnd::GetActiveDocument** facilitate accessing the view of the document from your main frame or child frame.

2. Add a new view class derived from **CView**.

3. Add debug and nondebug versions of the **GetDocument** function.

   Use the **GetDocument** functions from your existing view class as a model.

4. Add a public constructor.

   ClassWizard provides the new view class with a protected constructor. Make sure the constructor differs from the existing constructor in a way other than scope.

5. Make the destructor provided by Class Wizard public.

   The protected destructor is not necessary, and the new constructor you have added is already public.

6. Include the document class header file in the source file of the new view class.

7. Add a handler for the **OnDraw** event of the new view class.

8. Include the header file of the new view class in Mainfrm.cpp.

9. Add two protected variables in the **CMainFrame** class.

   These variables will be pointers to the two view objects your application uses. Initialize these pointers to NULL (0) in the constructor of **CMainFrame**, as shown in the following example code:

   ```
   class CMainFrame : public CFrameWnd
   {
       ...
   protected:
       CItalicsView * m_pItalicsView;
       CDefaultView * m_pDefaultView;
       ...
   }
   CMainFrame::CMainFrame()
   {
       // To give this SDI app 2 views, the main frame stores
       // pointers to them both.
       m_pItalicsView = 0;
       m_pDefaultView = 0;
   }
   ```

10. Add two menu selections to permit the application to switch between the two views.

    The **View** menu is a good place to insert the menu selections, but you can choose any of the drop-down menus.

11. Add command handlers to **CMainFrame** for the two new menu items.

    The following sample code shows how to add the command handler to switch to the new view. To copy this code for use in your own projects, see "Command Handler to Switch to New View" on the accompanying CD-ROM.

```
// To switch to the new view and hide the default view
// Samples\CH04\SDI2VIEWS
void CMainFrame::OnViewItalics()
{
  CDocument* pDoc = GetActiveDocument();

  // Only need to do this one time.
  if (0 == m_pItalicsView)
  {
      m_pDefaultView = (CDefaultView *)GetActiveView();
      // This object is destroyed in main frame's d'tor.
      m_pItalicsView = new CItalicsView(NULL);

      m_pItalicsView->Create(NULL, NULL, AFX_WS_DEFAULT_VIEW,
            rectDefault, this, AFX_IDW_PANE_FIRST + 1);
  }

  pDoc->AddView(m_pItalicsView);

  // Set the child i.d. of the italics view to AFX_IDW_PANE_FIRST,
  // so that CFrameWnd::RecalcLayout will allocate to this
  // "first pane" that portion of the frame window's client area
  // not allocated to control bars.  Set the child i.d. of the
  // default view to AFX_IDW_PANE_FIRST + 1
  m_pItalicsView->SetDlgCtrlID(AFX_IDW_PANE_FIRST);
  m_pDefaultView->SetDlgCtrlID(AFX_IDW_PANE_FIRST+1);

  // Show the italics view and hide the default view.
  m_pItalicsView->ShowWindow(SW_SHOW);
  m_pDefaultView->ShowWindow(SW_HIDE);

  SetActiveView(m_pItalicsView);

  // See comment in OnViewDefault.
  pDoc->RemoveView(m_pDefaultView);
  RecalcLayout();
}
```

The following sample code shows how to add the command handler that restores the default view. To copy this code for use in your own projects, see "Command Handler to Restore Default View" on the accompanying CD-ROM.

```
// To switch to the default view and hide the second view (the italics
// view)
//   Samples\CH04\SDI2VIEWS
void CMainFrame::OnViewDefault()
{
  CDocument* pDoc = GetActiveDocument();

  // The UI handler will prevent this function executing before
  // OnViewItalics, but just in case...
  ASSERT (m_pItalicsView != 0);
  ASSERT (m_pDefaultView != 0);

  pDoc->AddView(m_pDefaultView);

  m_pDefaultView->ShowWindow(SW_SHOW);
  m_pItalicsView->ShowWindow(SW_HIDE);

  m_pDefaultView->SetDlgCtrlID(AFX_IDW_PANE_FIRST);
  m_pItalicsView->SetDlgCtrlID(AFX_IDW_PANE_FIRST + 1);

  SetActiveView(m_pDefaultView);
  pDoc->RemoveView(m_pItalicsView);
  RecalcLayout();
}
```

You can choose to leave the inactive view in the application, or you can remove the inactive view from your application. The previous sample code uses **CDocument::RemoveView** to remove the inactive view. Removing it means that when the document object is changed and **CDocument::UpdateAllViews** is called, the inactive view object's **OnDraw** function will not be called.

Removing the inactive view is not required, but it makes the application more efficient. If the inactive view is not removed from the document object's list of attached views, nothing detrimental will happen when the inactive view's **OnDraw** function executes. In an application with only two views, each with simple **OnDraw** functions, you will not be able to tell much difference.

12. Enable and disable the two menu items, as shown in the following example code:

```
void CMainFrame::OnUpdateViewDefault(CCmdUI* pCmdUI)
{
    // Only enable the default view menu if the current view
    // is the italics view. The isKindOf function checks if the
    // active view is derived from CItalicsView
    RUNTIME_CLASS macro
    pCmdUI->Enable(
        GetActiveView()->IsKindOf(RUNTIME_CLASS(CItalicsView)));
}

void CMainFrame::OnUpdateViewItalics(CCmdUI* pCmdUI)
{
    // Only enable the italics view menu if the current view
    // is the default view.
    pCmdUI->Enable(
        GetActiveView()->IsKindOf(RUNTIME_CLASS(CDefaultView)));
}
```

The code samples discussed in this topic appear in the sample application SDI2VIEWS, which is located in the folder *<install folder>*\Samples\Ch04.

Adding Multiple Views to an MDI Application

In this section, you will learn how to create an MDI application with two or more views of the same document. The views are constructed from different classes, each view providing a different way to view the data stored in the document.

Building an MDI Application

An MDI application provides the interface to open and work on more than one document simultaneously. You can create multiple views of different types and attach them to these documents.

▶ **To build an MDI application with two views**

1. Build an MDI application by using MFC AppWizard. AppWizard will create a skeleton MDI application with a single view.
2. Add a new class derived from the **CView** class.
3. Add debug and nondebug versions of the **GetDocument** function.

   Use the **GetDocument** functions from your existing view class as a model.

4. Include the header file for the document class in the source file of the new view class.

5. Place the command handlers in the **CChildFrame** class.

   It is easier to access the view or the document from **CChildFrame** rather than from the view class. Use the **CFrameWnd::GetActiveView** and **CFrameWnd::GetActiveDocument** functions to access the views and the document.

6. Add a handler for the **OnDraw** event of the new view class.

   At this point, you must decide whether you want users to select the type of view at application startup, or whether you want to have your application start with a default view. In either case, the user can select another view at run time.

Starting an Application with the Default View

If the users of your application are likely to use one view more often than another, you can define the frequently used view as the default view. When you provide a default view for your application, you must manage the document template without the help of ClassWizard.

▶ **To start an application with a default view**

1. Add a variable to the **CMainFrame** class in your application. For example:

    ```
    class CMainFrame : public CMDIFrameWnd
    {
        ...
    protected:
        CDocTemplate* m_pItalicsTemplate;
        ...
    }
    ```

2. Initialize the variable in the constructor of **CMainFrame** as shown in the following example:

    ```
    CMainFrame::CMainFrame()
    {
        m_pItalicsTemplate = 0;
    }
    ```

3. Add a menu item for a visible child window.

   Add a menu item to be used when the application is displaying a visible child window. You can choose the menu to which you add the item; however, do not place the item in the IDR_MAINFRAME menu. The **Window** menu is a good choice, because that is where MFC AppWizard places the menu item that creates another window of the same type as the default.

4. Add a command handler for the new menu item to the **CMainFrame** class.

   The following sample code shows the menu command handler. To copy this code for use in your own projects, see "Displaying Italics View" on the accompanying CD-ROM.

```
// Menu Command Handler for displaying Italics View
// Samples\CH04\MDI2Views
void CMainFrame::OnWindowItalics()
{
  if (0 == m_pItalicsTemplate)
  {
      m_pItalicsTemplate = new CMultiDocTemplate(
          IDR_XXXXTYPE,
          RUNTIME_CLASS(CXXXXViewsDoc),
          RUNTIME_CLASS(CChildFrame),
          RUNTIME_CLASS(CItalicsView));
  }

  CMDIChildWnd* pActiveChild = MDIGetActive();
  CDocument* pDocument;
  if (NULL == pActiveChild ||
     (pDocument = pActiveChild->GetActiveDocument()) == NULL)
  {
      TRACE0("Warning: No active document.\n");
      AfxMessageBox(AFX_IDP_COMMAND_FAILURE);
      return;     // command failed
  }

  CFrameWnd* pFrame = m_pItalicsTemplate->
                  CreateNewFrame(pDocument, pActiveChild);
  if (NULL == pFrame)
  {
      TRACE0("Warning: failed to create new frame.\n");
      return;     // command failed
  }

  m_pItalicsTemplate->InitialUpdateFrame(pFrame, pDocument);
}
```

The code in the previous example determines when the template object needs to be created. It then obtains pointers to the current document, and the current active child window. These two pointers are needed to call the **CDocTemplate::CreateNewFrame** function. The **CDocTemplate::InitialUpdateFrame** function is called to finish creating the document template.

5. Destroy any dynamically allocated objects.

   In this process, some objects have been dynamically allocated and must be destroyed. The following example code shows the destructor in **CMainFrame**:

   ```
   CMainFrame::~CMainFrame()
   {
       if (0 != m_pItalicsTemplate)
       {
           delete m_pItalicsTemplate;
           m_pItalicsTemplate = 0;
       }
   }
   ```

The code samples discussed in this topic appear in the sample application MDI2VIEWS, which is located in the folder *<install folder>*\Samples\CH04.

Selecting a View for Application Startup

Rather than define a default view for documents, you can provide users with an option to select the view at application startup. This will also provide the user with an option for a new view when selecting **New** on the **File** menu.

▶ **To select a view for application startup**

1. Add another document template to the **CWinApp** class. Store pointers to the new and existing templates in the application class as shown in the following example code:

   ```
   class CMDI2ViewsBApp: public CWinApp
   {
   public:
       CMultiDocTemplate * m_pItalicsTemplate;
       CMultiDocTemplate * m_pDefaultTemplate;
       ...
   }
   ```

2. Modify the **InitInstance** function in the application class. For example:

   ```
   BOOL CMDI2ViewsBApp::InitInstance()
   {
       ....
       m_pDefaultTemplate = new CMultiDocTemplate(
           IDR_MDI2VITYPE,
           RUNTIME_CLASS(CMDI2ViewsBDoc),
           RUNTIME_CLASS(CChildFrame),
           RUNTIME_CLASS(CDefaultView));
       AddDocTemplate(m_pDefaultTemplate);
       m_pItalicsTemplate = new CMultiDocTemplate(
           IDR_MDI2VITYPE2,
           RUNTIME_CLASS(CMDI2ViewsBDoc),
           RUNTIME_CLASS(CChildFrame),
           RUNTIME_CLASS(CItalicsView));
       AddDocTemplate(m_pItalicsTemplate);
       ....
   }
   ```

   The application framework takes care of any cleanup for these dynamically allocated objects.

3. Create a menu, icon, and document template string for the new document template.

   The second template needs its own menu, icon, and document template string. Copy the existing IDR_XXXXTYPE menu and icon and give each an appropriate name, such as IDRXXXTYPE2. Make any changes to the menu before copying it. The table entry for the document template string must be changed slightly. If the string IDR_XXXXTYPE looks like this:

   ```
   \nXXXX\nDefault\n\n\nXXXXViews.Document\nXXXX Document
   ```

   Then the string IDRXXXTYPE2 must look like this:

   ```
   \nXXXX\nItalics\n\n\nXXXXViews.Document\nXXXX Document
   ```

4. Add a menu entry to the Microsoft Windows menu that will display the new view.

   Use ClassWizard to install a command handler for the new menu entry in the **CMainFrame** class. Then use ClassWizard to install a command handler for the **OnWindowNew** ID, and give the handler the same name and location as the handler that displays the other view. In effect, you will have two entries in the message map pointing to the same function.

The following sample code shows how to determine which menu invoked the command handler. To copy this code for use in your own projects, see "Determine Which Menu Invoked Command Handler" on the accompanying CD-ROM.

```
// Generic command handler to handle view display in an application
// that lets the user choose the view on application startup and
// using a menu item
//  Samples\CH03\MDI2VIEWSB
void CMainFrame::OnWindowItalics()
{
  // We'll need a pointer to the active child...
  CMDIChildWnd* pChild = MDIGetActive();
  if (NULL == pChild)
  {
      TRACE0("Warning: No active child.\n");
      AfxMessageBox(AFX_IDP_COMMAND_FAILURE);
      return;      // command failed
  }

  // and to the active document...
  CDocument* pDoc = pChild->GetActiveDocument();
  if (NULL == pDoc)
  {
      TRACE0("Warning: No active document.\n");
      AfxMessageBox(AFX_IDP_COMMAND_FAILURE);
      return;      // command failed
  }

  // and to the application object.
  CMDI2ViewsBApp * pApp = (CMDI2ViewsBApp *)AfxGetApp();

  // Since both menu selections end up here (see message map)
  MSG const * pMsg = GetCurrentMessage();
  CMultiDocTemplate * pTemplate;

  // we need to know how we got here to figure out which template
  // to use...
  if (LOWORD(pMsg->wParam) == ID_WINDOW_ITALICS)
      pTemplate = pApp->m_pItalicsTemplate;
  else
      pTemplate = pApp->m_pDefaultTemplate;
```

code continued on next page

```
code continued from previous page
    // so that finally we can create a new frame...
    CFrameWnd* pFrame = pTemplate->CreateNewFrame(pDoc, pChild);
    if (NULL == pFrame)
    {
        TRACE0("Warning: failed to create new frame.\n");
        return;     // command failed
    }

    // which is then updated.
    pTemplate->InitialUpdateFrame(pFrame, pDoc);
}
```

The code samples discussed in this topic appear in the sample application MDI2VIEWSB, which is located in the folder *<install folder>*\Samples\Ch04.

Suppressing Automatic Creation of a Child Window

When MFC AppWizard generates an MDI application, it automatically creates a new child window. You can suppress this feature with an addition to the **InitInstance** member of the application class, as shown in the following example code:

```
CCommandLineInfo cmdInfo;
ParseCommandLine(cmdInfo);

//Insert this statement in your application:
if (CCommandLineInfo::FileNew == cmdInfo.m_nShellCommand)
  cmdInfo.m_nShellCommand = CCommandLineInfo::FileNothing;

if (!ProcessShellCommand(cmdInfo))
  return FALSE;
```

If the user specifies a parameter on the command line, then you would not want to change m_nShellCommand. The example code shows how to determine whether a command-line parameter was specified and skip the change to m_nShellCommand if a parameter was specified.

Setting Titles for Child Frame Windows

You can define the title that should be displayed on child windows when the user opens a document or chooses to open a new window for a document that is already open.

145

Setting Titles for New Documents

The default title of a child window in an MDI application is a concatenation of the document title and a sequence number. The source of the document title is the second substring of the document template string.

Note The document template string is the string table entry with the name IDR_XXXXXXTYPE. Set the contents of each of the IDR_XXXXXXTYPE substrings by clicking the **Advanced** button in Step 4 of MFC AppWizard. You can modify these substrings later by editing the string table. For more information, search for "CDocTemplate::GetDocString" and "CDocTemplate::SetDefaultTitle" in MSDN Library Visual Studio 6.0, or read the Knowledge Base article Q129095.

Tip The Microsoft Knowledge Base contains detailed technical articles and samples that are created and maintained by Microsoft Product Support Services (PSS). This database is updated daily and contains technical information about Microsoft products, fix lists, documentation errors, and answers to commonly asked technical support questions.

The document class provides functions to access the document title: **CDocument::GetTitle** and **CDocument::SetTitle**. Typically, an application calls **CDocument::SetTitle** from the **OnNewDocument** function.

Setting Titles for New Windows

When you click **New Window** on an MDI application's **Window** menu, no new document is created, so **OnNewDocument** is not invoked. The title of the new window is the document title for that document object, with ":2" appended after the title. The existing document window has ":1" appended to its title. The titles of new windows on that document will be appended sequentially starting with ".3." When you close any window on that document, the framework renumbers all the remaining windows.

If the default numbering is not appropriate for your application, you can create your own titles for new windows. The steps necessary to change the title of an MDI child window frame are as follows:

1. Override the **PreCreateWindow** function of the child frame class, as shown in this example:

   ```
   BOOL CChildFrame::PreCreateWindow(CREATESTRUCT &cs)
   {
       cs.style&=~(LONG)FWS_ADDTOTITLE;
       if (!CMDIChildWnd::PreCreateWindow(cs))
           return FALSE;
       return TRUE;
   }
   ```

2. Override the **OnInitialUpdate** function of the view class, as shown in this example:

   ```
   void CXXXXView::OnInitialUpdate()
   {
       CView::OnInitialUpdate();
       GetParent()->SetWindowText(GetDocument()->GetTitle()+
           " - This is a test!");
   }
   ```

Run the application. The first view displays "*XXXX*1 - This is a test!" Titles of other views will be identical except for the document name.

Adding Scrolling Views

A document has a logical size. A view, which is inherently limited to a physical area on a given device, can often display only part of the document. The following illustration shows a scrolling view and the underlying document.

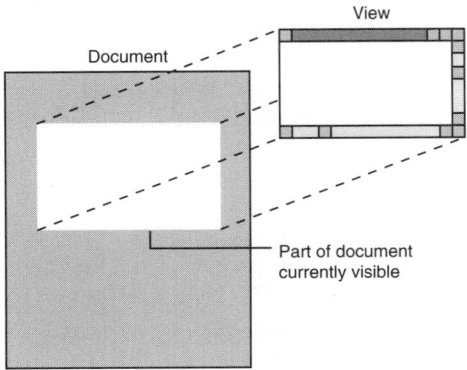

The user controls how much of the document to view by shrinking or enlarging the viewport, and selects which part of the document to view by manipulating the horizontal and vertical scroll bars.

Introduction to Scrolling Views

MFC encapsulates the functionality of a scrolling view in the **CScrollView** class.

To see the demonstration "Creating an Application with a Scrolling View," see the accompanying CD-ROM.

▶ **To add a scrolling view to your application**

1. Set the application's base view class to **CScrollView**.
2. Adjust the scrolling characteristics to set the mapping mode and document size appropriately.
3. Handle the conversion between logical and physical (device) coordinates as required by your application.

Converting the Application View to a Scrolling View

You specify **CScrollView** as the base class for the view in your application to make it a scrolling view.

The following illustration shows the **MFC AppWizard - Step 6** dialog box with the base view class set to **CScrollView**.

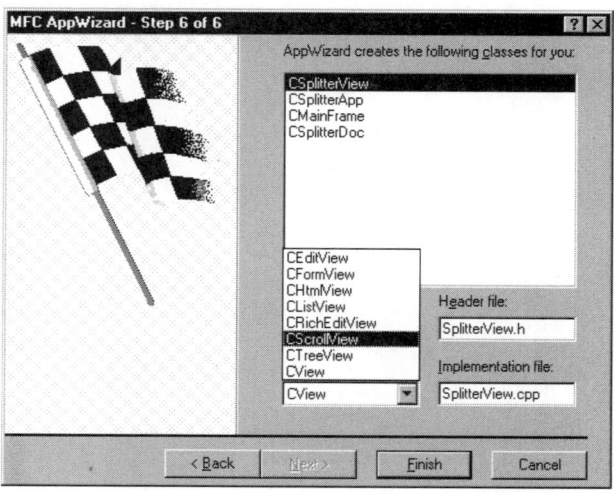

If you have an existing application that uses **CView** and you want to convert it to a scrolling view, do the following:

- Replace all occurrences of **CView** with **CScrollView** in your existing view's header file.
- Replace all occurrences of **CView** with **CScrollView** in your existing view's implementation file.

Adjusting Scrolling Characteristics

You can adjust the scrolling characteristics of an application with the **OnInitialUpdate** or **OnUpdate** function of the application's view class. Call **CScrollView::SetScrollSizes** to set the mapping mode and the size of the document appropriately.

The following sample code sets the mapping mode and document size in the **OnInitialUpdate** function. To copy this code for use in your own projects, see "Adjusting Scrolling Characteristics" on the accompanying CD-ROM.

```
// Setting mapping mode and document size of an application with
// scrolling view
// Samples\CH04\Scroll

void CMyScrollView::OnInitialUpdate()
{
  CScrollView::OnInitialUpdate();
  CSize sizeTotal;

  sizeTotal.cx = sizeTotal.cy = 200;
  SetScrollSizes(MM_TEXT, sizeTotal);

  // Optional: To resize the frame to exactly fit the view at
  // application startup

  GetParentFrame()->RecalcLayout();
  ResizeParentToFit();
}
```

For information about scrolling functions, search for "Scrolling functions" in MSDN Library Visual Studio 6.0.

Converting Coordinates

When specifying view coordinates, you can generally use logical coordinates. However, there are times when your application receives information in physical coordinates. This often happens in an application with a scrolling view. When the user scrolls through the document, the viewport origin no longer coincides with the origin of the document—that is, the window origin in logical space.

For example, in mouse button event handlers, your application receives the position of the mouse in terms of physical coordinates stored in a **CPoint** object. You can use the **CDC** functions **DPtoLP** and **LPtoDP** to convert between the coordinate systems of logical and physical space as required by your application.

The following sample code shows how to use the **DPtoLP** function in the **OnLButtonDown** handler to convert coordinates for an application using a scrolling view. To copy this code for use in your own projects, see "Converting Coordinates" on the accompanying CD-ROM.

```
// Converting physical coordinates to logical coordinates to implement
// a scroll view
// Samples\CH04\Scroll

void CMyScrollView::OnDraw(CDC* pDC)
{
  CScrollDoc * pDoc = GetDocument();
  CPoint pt = pDoc->GetLocation();
  pDC->TextOut(pt.x, pt.y, pDoc->GetPhrase());
}

// The CPoint argument represents the location of the mouse in
// device (physical) coordinates. OnDraw, which will be called
// as a result of the call to Invalidate at the end of this
// function, always draws to logical space. Therefore, the CPoint
// argument must be converted to logical coordinates before storing
// the new location into the document object. To show the necessity
// of doing this, comment out the first 3 lines of code in this
// function, re-compile and execute.
```

code continued on following page

code continued from previous page

```
void CMyScrollView::OnLButtonDown(UINT nFlags, CPoint point)
{
  // Create a client dc that points to the current view
  CClientDC dc(this);

  // Given that this is a scroll view, call OnPrepareDC to
  // adjust attributes of the device context appropriately.
  OnPrepareDC(&dc);

  dc.DPtoLP(&point);

  // Store the new location in the document and invalidate the view.
  CScrollDoc * pDoc = GetDocument();
  pDoc->SetLocation(point);

  Invalidate();

  CScrollView::OnLButtonDown(nFlags, point);
}
```

Implementing Splitter Windows

MFC provides the **CSplitterWnd** class for creating splitter windows.

The following illustration shows an application with splitter windows.

This section begins with a discussion on the different types of splitter windows and proceeds to describe the steps in implementing them in your application.

Introduction to Splitter Windows

There are two types of splitter windows: dynamic and static.

In dynamic splitter windows, additional panes are created and destroyed as the user splits and unsplits the views.

In static splitter windows, the panes are created when the window is created, and the order and number of panes never change. The panes are separated by a splitter bar that can change the relative sizes of the panes.

To see the demonstration "Dynamic Vs. Static Splitter Windows," see the accompanying CD-ROM.

The following table describes the two types of splitter windows.

Characteristics	Dynamic splitter window	Static splitter window
Maximum number of panes	four (two rows x two columns)	256 panes (16 rows x 16 columns)
Different types of views	Can associate only a single type of view with all the panes.	Can associate different types of views with the panes.

Microsoft Excel, Word, and the source code editor provided with Microsoft Developer Studio all use dynamic splitter windows. Windows 95 Explorer is an example of an application that has a static splitter window.

For more information, search for "Splitter windows" in MSDN Library Visual Studio 6.0.

Creating Dynamic Splitter Windows

You can create a dynamic splitter window in the following ways:

- Use MFC AppWizard.
- Use the Components and Controls Gallery.
- Add code manually.

Chapter 4: Implementing View Classes

▶ **To create a dynamic splitter window by using MFC AppWizard**

- In MFC AppWizard, click **Advanced Options** in Step 4, click the **Window Styles** tab, select the **Use split window** check box, and click **Close**.

▶ **To create a dynamic splitter window by using the Components and Controls Gallery**

- In the Components and Controls Gallery, double-click the **Visual C++ Components** folder, click **Split Bars**, and click **Insert**.

▶ **To create a dynamic splitter window by adding code manually**

1. Add a **CSplitterWnd** object to the **CMainFrm** class in an SDI application (or to the **CChildFrame** class in an MDI application).
2. In the **OnCreateClient** function of the frame class, initialize the **CSplitterWnd** object by calling the **CSplitterWnd::Create** function.

When one of the views changes data in the document, use the **CDocument::UpdateAllViews** function to propagate the changes to the other panes.

To see the demonstration "Creating a Dynamic Splitter Window," see the accompanying CD-ROM.

The following sample code shows how to implement a dynamic splitter window. To copy this code for use in your own projects, see "Implementing a Dynamic Splitter Window" on the accompanying CD-ROM.

```
// Implementing a dynamic splitter window in an MFC application
// Samples\CH04\Splitter
// MainFrm.h : interface of the CMainFrame class

class CMainFrame : public CFrameWnd
{
  ...
protected:
  CSplitterWnd m_wndSplitter;
  ...
};

// SAMPLES\CH03\splitter
// MainFrm.cpp : implementation of the CMainFrame class
```

code continued on following page

153

code continued from previous page

```
BOOL CMainFrame::OnCreateClient(LPCREATESTRUCT lpcs,
      CCreateContext* pContext)
{
  CSize minWindow(10, 10);

  // These variables must both be 1 or 2 for dynamic splitters.
  int nRows = 2, nColumns = 1;

  return m_wndSplitter.Create(this, nRows, nColumns,
                                    minWindow, pContext);
//
}
```

Creating Static Splitter Windows

A static splitter window is constructed along with the frame window at application startup. The user cannot create or destroy a static splitter window.

▶ **To create a static splitter window**

1. Add a **CSplitterWnd** object to the **CMainFrm** class in an SDI application (or to the **CChildFrame** class in an MDI application).

> **Note** You can use MFC AppWizard or the Component and Controls Gallery to add the splitter object. However, you will need to replace the code generated by MFC AppWizard or the Component and Controls Gallery to make it appropriate for a static splitter window.

2. Add the classes for the additional views that you want in your application.

> **Note** You can use ClassWizard to add new view classes.

3. Associate each view with the appropriate pane of the splitter window.

When you use MFC AppWizard to create an application, you choose the base class for the view in Step 6. MFC AppWizard adds this single view class to your application. You can then use ClassWizard to derive other view classes from appropriate view base classes and display each in a pane of a static splitter window.

Chapter 4: Implementing View Classes

▶ **To implement a static splitter window in an application**

1. Initialize the **CSplitterWnd** object by calling the **CSplitterWnd::CreateStatic** function in the **OnCreateClient** function of the frame class.

2. Associate the appropriate views with each pane. To do so, call the **CSplitterWnd::CreateView** function for each pane that you created in the call to **CSplitterWnd::CreateStatic**.

The following sample code shows how to create and implement a static splitter window by using the **OnCreateClient** function. To copy this code for use in your own projects, see "Implementing a Static Splitter Window" on the accompanying CD-ROM.

```
// Implementing an application with a static splitter window
// Samples\CH04\Splitter
// MainFrm.h : interface of the CMainFrame class

class CMainFrame : public CFrameWnd
{
  ...
protected:
  CSplitterWnd m_wndSplitter;
  ...
};

// Samples\CH03\Splitter
// MainFrm.cpp : implementation of the CMainFrame class

BOOL CMainFrame::OnCreateClient(LPCREATESTRUCT lpcs,
    CCreateContext* pContext)
{
// ...
  // This is the code for a static splitter.
  CRect cr;
  GetClientRect(&cr);

  CSize paneSize(cr.Width(), cr.Height() / 2);

  int rc;
  m_wndSplitter.CreateStatic(this, 2, 1);
```

code continued on next page

155

```
code continued from previous page
    rc = m_wndSplitter.CreateView(0, 0,
                                  RUNTIME_CLASS(CSplitterView),
                                  paneSize, pContext);
    if (FALSE == rc)
        return rc;

    rc = m_wndSplitter.CreateView(1, 0,
                                  RUNTIME_CLASS(CItalicsView),
                                  paneSize, pContext);
    return rc;
}
```

Command Handler Issues

In a dynamic splitter application, command handlers are generally placed in the view class. The view class has the easiest access to the document, and commands often modify the data in the document.

However, a static splitter application generally has multiple views. Depending on what is appropriate for your application, you must decide where to place your command handlers. If you want the same commands enabled regardless of which view has focus, place the handlers in the frame class. If you want each view to have its own set of handlers, add the appropriate handlers to each view class.

Coordinating Updates in the Views

In applications that use different types of views, calling **UpdateAllViews** is not the easiest solution for updating data. For information about coordinating multiple views, see "Coordinating Multiple Interrelated Views" on page 183 in this chapter.

Lab 4.1: Adding a Splitter Bar

In this lab, you will add a splitter bar to a single document interface (SDI) application.

To see the demonstration "Lab 4.1 Demonstration," see the accompanying CD-ROM.

Estimated time to complete this lab: **20 minutes**

To complete the exercises in this lab, you must have the required software. For detailed information about the labs and setup for the labs, see "Labs" in "About This Course."

The code that forms the starting point for this lab is located in the folder *<install folder>*\Labs\Ch04\Lab4.1\Ex01.

The solution code for this lab is located in the folder *<install folder>*\Labs\Ch04\Lab4.1\Ex01\Solution.

Objectives

After completing this lab, you will be able to:

- Add a class to an application using ClassWizard.
- Add a static splitter bar to a window to create a split pane.

Prerequisites

There are no prerequisites for this lab.

Exercises

The following exercise provides practice working with the concepts and techniques covered in this chapter:

- Exercise 1: Adding a Splitter Window

    In this exercise, you will add a splitter bar to an SDI window.

Exercise 1: Adding a Splitter Window

The code that forms the starting point for this exercise is in *<install folder>*\Labs\Ch04\Lab4.1\Ex01.

In this exercise, you will add a splitter bar to an SDI application.

▶ **Create a new CSplitter class**

1. On the **View** menu, click **ClassWizard**.
2. Click **Add Class**, and then click **New**.
3. Set the name of the class to **CSplitter**, and base the class on the generic **CWnd** class. Accept the defaults for the other fields. Click **OK**.

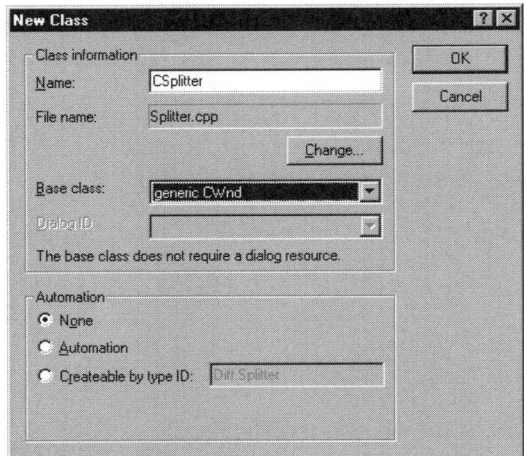

 **Note** ClassWizard does not present **CSplitterWnd** as a base class. You can change the base class directly.

4. Edit the file Splitter.h. Click **CSplitter** in FileView, then click **Go to Definition**. Change the declaration line of **CSplitter** from:

    ```
    class CSplitter : public CWnd
    ```

    to:

    ```
    class CSplitter : public CSplitterWnd
    ```

5. Add a method to get the protected width of the splitter window to the public attributes section of the **CSplitter** definition as follows:

    ```
    int GetSplitterWidth() const { return m_cxSplitter; }
    ```

6. Open the file Splitter.cpp and update the message map declaration. It reads:

    ```
    BEGIN_MESSAGE_MAP(CSplitter, CWnd)
        //{{AFX_MSG_MAP(CSplitter)
    ```

7. Change the first line to reference **CSplitterWnd** instead of **CWnd** as follows:

    ```
    BEGIN_MESSAGE_MAP(CSplitter, CSplitterWnd)
    ```

Lab 4.1: Adding a Splitter Bar

▶ **Add a reference to the splitter in the MainFrame object**

1. Open the file MainFrm.h.

2. Add a protected **CSplitter** member to the class definition as follows:

   ```
   // splitter bar embedded members
   CSplitter    m_wndSplitter;
   ```

3. Use ClassWizard to add an **OnCreateClient** handler. ClassWizard creates a reference to the **OnCreateClient** handler in MainFrm.h and a blank implementation in the file MainFrm.cpp.

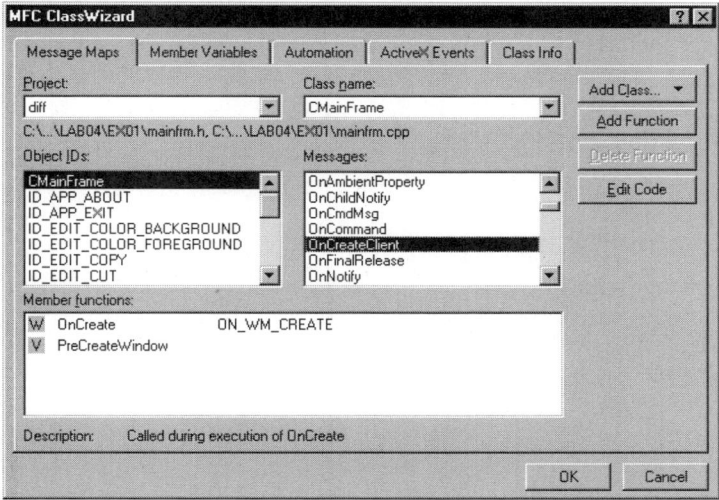

The major implementation task in adding a splitter bar to an application is to create the split window itself. Because only two files are allowed to be active, you use static splitter windows. Put the bar in the middle of the frame. For more information, see "Multiple Document Types, Views, and Frame Windows" under "Static splitter windows" in the MSDN Library Visual Studio 6.0.

▶ **Add code to the OnCreateClient handler to create the splitter window**

1. Create the static splitter window by adding a call to **CSplitterWnd::CreateStatic** as follows:

   ```
   m_wndSplitter.CreateStatic (this, 1, 2, WS_CHILD);
   ```

   CSplitterWnd::CreateStatic sets up a constant number and arrangement of splitter panes.

2. Size the splitter windows to two equal panes as follows:

```
SIZE size;
CRect rect;
GetClientRect(&rect);
size.cx = (rect.right - m_wndSplitter.GetSplitterWidth())/2;
size.cy = rect.bottom;
```

3. Attach the views to the windows as follows:

```
m_wndSplitter.CreateView(0,0,RUNTIME_CLASS(CDiffView), size,
    pContext);
m_wndSplitter.CreateView(0,1,RUNTIME_CLASS(CDiffView), size,
    pContext);
SetActiveView((CView *)m_wndSplitter.GetPane(0,1));
```

4. Show the splitter window as follows:

```
m_wndSplitter.ShowWindow(SW_SHOWNORMAL);
m_wndSplitter.UpdateWindow();
return TRUE
```

The following sample code shows an example of how your code should look. To copy this code for use in your own projects, see "Lab 4.1.1 OnCreateClient" on the accompanying CD-ROM.

```
BOOL CMainFrame::OnCreateClient(LPCREATESTRUCT /*lpcs*/,
  CCreateContext* pContext)
{
  // Create a static splitter window with two side-by-side panes

  if(!m_wndSplitter.CreateStatic (this,1,2,WS_CHILD))
  {
      return FALSE;
  }

  // Calculate the size of the splitter panes
  SIZE size;
  CRect   rect;
  GetClientRect(&rect);
```

code continued on next page

code continued from previous page

```
    size.cx = (rect.right - m_wndSplitter.GetSplitterWidth())/2;
    size.cy = rect.bottom;

    //set the views
    m_wndSplitter.CreateView(0,0,RUNTIME_CLASS(CDiffView), size,
        pContext);
    m_wndSplitter.CreateView(0,1,RUNTIME_CLASS(CDiffView), size,
        pContext);
    SetActiveView((CView *)m_wndSplitter.GetPane(0,1));

    //show the splitter
    m_wndSplitter.ShowWindow(SW_SHOWNORMAL);
    m_wndSplitter.UpdateWindow();

    return TRUE;
}
```

▶ Build, and run the Diff application

1. In MainFrm.cpp, include Splitter.h, the file DiffDoc.h., and the file DiffView.h. Splitter.h must be included before MainFrm.h, because there is a **CSplitter** member of **CMainFrame**.

   ```
   #include "splitter.h"
   #include "MainFrm.h"
   #include "diffdoc.h"
   #include "diffview.h"
   ```

2. In the file Diff.cpp, include Splitter.h before MainFrm.h

   ```
   #include "splitter.h"
   #include "MainFrm.h"
   ```

3. Build and run the application. You will notice that you can reposition the splitter bar, but you cannot delete or add splitters.

The solution code for this exercise is located in the folder *<install folder>*\Labs\Ch04\Lab4.1\Ex01\Solution.

Implementing Form Views

The **CFormView** class provides a window whose client area contains dialog box controls. These controls support entering, viewing, or altering data that is usually found in a form-based, data-access application.

In this section, you will look at creating and implementing form views derived from the **CFormView** class. This section also provides an overview of the database view classes.

User-Defined Form Views

To create a user-defined form view, you must create controls on the form, and handle updating the view and the document. Optionally, you can provide customized printing support.

Choosing **CFormView** as the base class for your application in Step 6 of MFC AppWizard provides a "blank" form, which you can customize with the appropriate controls. The following illustration shows the **MFC AppWizard - Step 6** dialog box with **CFormView** selected.

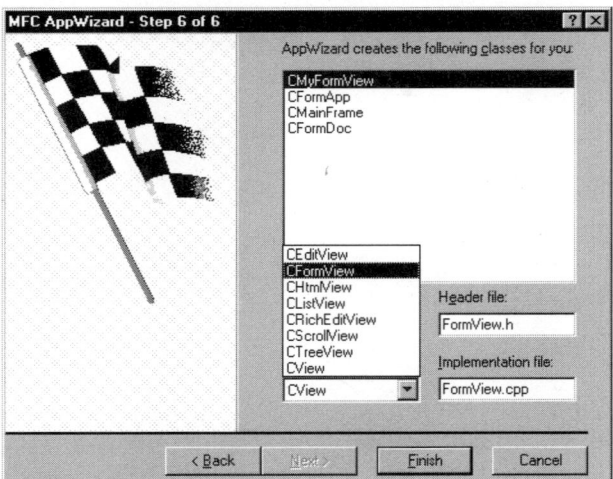

Use the resource editor to open the dialog box resource in the .rc file that is associated with your application view, and to create the controls that you want on the form.

It is important to note that certain properties for the form itself are set by MFC AppWizard and should not be changed. The following table lists the required property settings for a form.

Property name	Value
Style	Child
Border	None
Titlebar	Off
Visible	Off

Use ClassWizard to add member variables to the form view class. For example, add **CString** variables for edit controls, **BOOL** variables for option buttons, and so on.

Tip If you have an existing Visual Basic-based application with a form similar to one that you want to use in your form view application, you can import the Visual Basic form into your Visual C++ project. For more information, search for "Using Custom Controls in a Dialog Box" and specifically, "Importing Visual Basic Forms" in MSDN Library Visual Studio 6.0.

Override the **OnInitialUpdate** function of your view class to perform the initialization you want to occur at application startup, such as resizing the frame to fit the view. Override the **OnUpdate** function of your view class to initialize the controls on the form with data from the document, as required.

Add message handlers in the view class to respond to messages generated by the controls contained in the view. Typically, you add code to the message handlers to move data from your view to your document. For example, if your document class contains a string, you would place an edit box on the form. Next, in the **OnUpdate** function, you would initialize the edit control with the current value of the string. Finally, in the handler for the EN_CHANGE message for each edit control, you would add the code to store the new string value in the appropriate member variable in the document.

The sample code on the following page implements a form view with an edit control and three check boxes. To copy this code for use in your own projects, see "Implementing a Form View Application" on the accompanying CD-ROM.

```
// Samples\CH04\Form
// FormView.cpp : implementation of the CMyFormView class

void CMyFormView::OnInitialUpdate()
{
  CFormView::OnInitialUpdate();

  // These next 2 calls make the main frame exactly the size
  // of form object.
  GetParentFrame()->RecalcLayout();
  ResizeParentToFit();
}

void CMyFormView::OnUpdate(CView* pSender, LPARAM lHint, CObject* pHint)
{
  // Obtain a pointer to the document object.
  // Note that OnDraw isn't used, since controls in a dialog
  // box can paint themselves.
  CFormDoc * pDoc = (CFormDoc *)GetDocument();

  // Set the dialog class's member variables to those in the document.
  m_dlgPhrase = pDoc->GetPhrase();
  m_blue = GetBValue(pDoc->GetColor()) == 255;
  m_green = GetGValue(pDoc->GetColor()) == 255;
  m_red = GetRValue(pDoc->GetColor()) == 255;

  // Cause DDX to occur from dialog object to dialog box.
  UpdateData(FALSE);
}
void CMyFormView::OnChangeWelcome()
{
  // Cause DDX to occur from dialog box to dialog object.
  UpdateData(TRUE);

  // Set the document's member variables to those in the dialog object.
  CFormDoc * pDoc = (CFormDoc *)GetDocument();
  pDoc->SetPhrase(m_dlgPhrase);
}
```

code continued on next page

code continued from previous page

```
void CMyFormView::OnColor(UINT nID)
{
  // Cause DDX to occur from dialog box to dialog object.
  UpdateData(TRUE);

  // Determine the state of the color check boxes, build an RGB
  // value, and store it back into the document.
  int r, g, b;
  r = m_red ? 255 : 0;
  g = m_green ? 255 : 0;
  b = m_blue ? 255 : 0;

  CFormDoc * pDoc = (CFormDoc *)GetDocument();
  pDoc->SetColor(RGB(r,g,b));

  // Now, invalidate the edit control so it repaints itself.
  CWnd * pWnd = GetDlgItem(IDC_WELCOME);
  pWnd->Invalidate();
}

HBRUSH CMyFormView::OnCtlColor(CDC* pDC, CWnd* pWnd, UINT nCtlColor)
{
  HBRUSH hbr = CFormView::OnCtlColor(pDC, pWnd, nCtlColor);

  // Note that this function is called before all controls on
  // the form are painted. The intent is to only change the
  // color of the edit box, so it's necessary to clarify for
  // which control this function is being called.
  if (GetDlgItem(IDC_WELCOME)->m_hWnd == pWnd->m_hWnd)
  {
      CFormDoc * pDoc = (CFormDoc *)GetDocument();
      pDC->SetTextColor(pDoc->GetColor());
  }

  return hbr;
}
```

Optionally, override the **OnPrint** function in your view class as required.

For more information, search for "CFormView" in MSDN Library Visual Studio 6.0.

Database View Classes

The **COleDBRecordView** class is derived from **CFormView** and displays database records in controls. For information about **COleDBRecordView**, see "COleDBRecordView Class" on page 355 in Chapter 7, "Using OLE DB Templates for Data Access."

In addition, MFC provides the following view classes:

- **CRecordView**

  Provides database forms for applications that use the MFC ODBC classes.

- **CDaoRecordView**

  Provides database forms for applications that use the MFC DAO classes.

Implementing Control Views

This section describes the view classes that are derived from the **CCtrlView** class and shows how to implement them in an application.

Introduction to Control Views

The **CCtrlView** class makes it possible to treat the client area of a view as if it were filled by a single control. The following illustration shows the classes derived from **CCtrlView**.

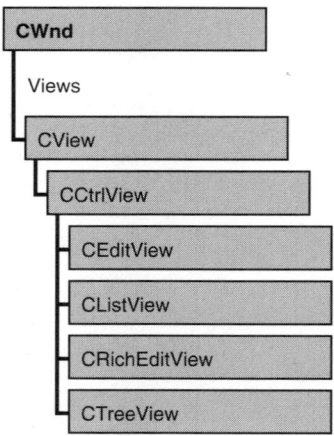

The following illustration shows the different types of views that you can select in the **MFC AppWizard - Step 6** dialog box.

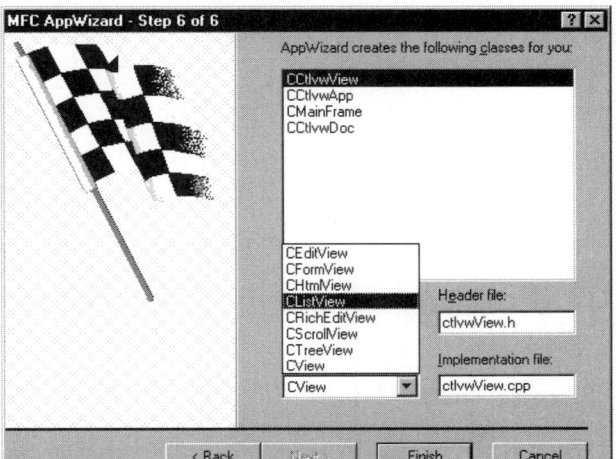

All four classes derived from **CCtrlView** have two member functions in common: a default constructor and an accessor function that returns a reference to the embedded common control object. With that reference, you can operate on the client area as if you were working with a single dialog box control.

The following example code uses the **GetListCtrl** accessor function in the **CListView** class to change the style of the list control that is embedded in the list view:

```
void CMyListView::OnInitialUpdate()
{
  // ...

  // Get a reference to the list control
  // embedded in the view
  CListCtrl & clc = GetListCtrl();

  // Use the reference to call member functions
  // of the embedded control
  clc.ModifyStyle(NULL, LVS_SORTASCENDING | LVS_REPORT);

  // ...do rest of initialization steps
}
```

When working with the **CCtrlView**-derived view classes, typically you will also use members of the control classes that they encapsulate. The available public members for these controls can be found in their respective classes, which are shown in the following table.

View class	Common control name	Common control class
CListView	List control	**CListCtrl**
CTreeView	Tree control	**CTreeCtrl**
CEditView	Edit control	**CEdit**
CRichEditView	Rich edit control	**CRichEditCtrl**

In many of the other view classes that are derived more directly from **CView**, typically you add your drawing code to the **OnDraw** member function of the view class.

The view classes with embedded controls handle most of the drawing for you in their customized versions of **OnDraw**. Typically, you do not override **OnDraw** to handle painting, but you may want to override it for printing/print preview. To handle updates by the user in a view, place code in the appropriate message handlers.

Overview of CListView

The **CListView** class simplifies the use of the list control and **CListCtrl**, the class that encapsulates list-control functionality, with the MFC document/view architecture.

A list control displays a collection of items, each consisting of an optional icon and a label. List views provide several ways of arranging items and displaying individual items. For example, additional information about each item can be displayed in columns to the right of the icon and label.

The illustration on the following page shows an example of an application with a report-style list view.

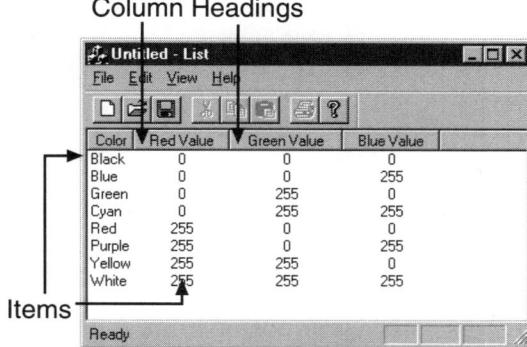

Column Headings

Items

The main steps in creating a list view application are as follows:

1. Run the MFC AppWizard. In Step 6, choose **CListView** as the base for your view class.
2. Edit the **OnInitialUpdate** function and add code to set the characteristics for the list view.
3. Edit the **OnUpdate** function and add code to populate the list.

For more information about **CListView**, search for "CListView" in MSDN Library Visual Studio 6.0.

Implementing CListView

To implement an application whose view class has been derived from **CListView**, you need to customize the characteristics of the list control and populate it.

Customizing a List Control

You customize a list control by editing the **OnInitialUpdate** function as follows:

1. Use the **GetListCtrl** function to get a reference to the list control that is embedded in the view, so that you can call the list control's **ModifyStyle** member function.
2. Use **ModifyStyle** to set the list view type. (The example in this section uses a report style.)

 Tip You can combine the LVS_SORTASCENDING or LVS_SORTDESCENDING value with other style values you pass as the second parameter to **ModifyStyles** to create a sorted list.

3. Add columns to the list control by creating a LV_COLUMN structure and setting the members with the values that your application requires. You can then set up a loop and use the **InsertColumn** member function of the list control object to insert each column with its specific characteristics, such as heading, format, width, and so on.

The following sample code creates a four-column list in report style. To copy this code for use in your own projects, see "Setting List View Characteristics" on the accompanying CD-ROM.

```
// Setting the properties of a list view that displays a columnar
// report
// Samples\CH04\List
// ListView.cpp : implementation of the CMyListView class

void CMyListView::OnInitialUpdate()
{
  int i;
  CString s;
  LV_COLUMN lv;
  CListCtrl & clc = GetListCtrl();

  clc.ModifyStyle(NULL, LVS_SORTASCENDING | LVS_REPORT);

    lv.mask = LVCF_FMT | LVCF_TEXT | LVCF_WIDTH;
    lv.fmt = LVCFMT_LEFT;

  // Create 4 columns in the list control and
  // give each column a header string.
  for (i = ID_COLUMN1; i <= ID_COLUMN4; i++)
  {
      s.LoadString(i);
      lv.cx = 15 * clc.GetStringWidth(s) / 10;
      lv.pszText = (char *) (const char *)s;
      clc.InsertColumn(i - ID_COLUMN1, &lv);
      lv.fmt = LVCFMT_CENTER;
  }

  CListView::OnInitialUpdate();
}
```

Populating a List Control

You populate a list control by editing the **OnUpdate** function as follows:

1. Erase the outdated list.

   Use the **GetListCtrl** function to get a reference to the list control that is embedded in the view. Then call the list control's **DeleteAllItems** member function to prepare to refresh the list.

2. Populate the list with the current data, as follows:

   a. Create a new row and use the **InsertItem** member function of the list control to insert data into column 0.

   b. Use a loop to fill in the other columns of this row.

   c. Use the **SetItemText** member function to set the text of each column.

For more information about **CListView**, search for "CListView" in MSDN Library Visual Studio 6.0.

The following sample code populates the rows in a list with information about RGB values for various colors. To copy this code for use in your own projects, see "Populating the List in a List View" on the accompanying CD-ROM.

```
// Populating a list that displays a columnar report
// Samples\CH04\List
// ListView.cpp
void CMyListView::OnUpdate(CView* pSender, LPARAM lHint, CObject* pHint)
{
  CListCtrl & clc = GetListCtrl();
  CString s;

  // Remove all the list's data. Since OnUpdate will be called
  // when the list's data changes, this call is necessary before
  // rebuilding the list.
  clc.DeleteAllItems();
```

code continued on next page

code continued from previous page

```
    // Each iteration of the loop builds 1 row. InsertItem fills
    // column 0, SetItemText fills the other columns.
    for (int i = ID_BLACK; i <= ID_WHITE; i++)
    {
        s.LoadString(i);
        // row will be 0-7, which corresponds to the 8 basic colors.
        int row = i-ID_BLACK;
        // insert the string
        clc.InsertItem(row, s);

        // Convert the color to its component RGB values.
        int mask = 4;
        for (int col = 1; col <= 3; col++)
        {
            // Determine if a bit is on or not.
            s.Format("%d", row & mask ? 255 : 0);
            clc.SetItemText(row, col, s);
            mask /= 2;
        }
    }
}
```

Overview of CTreeView

The **CTreeView** class simplifies the use of the tree control and **CTreeCtrl**, the class that encapsulates tree-control functionality.

A tree control is a window that displays a hierarchical list of items, such as the headings in a document, the entries in an index, or the files and folders on a disk. Each item consists of a label and an optional bitmapped image, and each item can have a list of subitems associated with it. By clicking an item, the user can expand and collapse the associated list of subitems.

Use **CTreeView** when you want the tree control to act like a view window in document/view architecture as well as a tree control. A tree view occupies the entire client area of a frame window or pane of a splitter window. It automatically resizes when its parent window is resized, and it can process command messages from menus, accelerator keys, and toolbars. Because a tree control contains the data necessary to display the tree, the corresponding document object does not have to be complex; you can even use **CDocument** as the document type in your document template.

The tree control (and therefore, the **CTreeCtrl** class) is available only to applications running under Windows 95 and Windows NT versions 3.51 and later.

The following illustration shows a tree view.

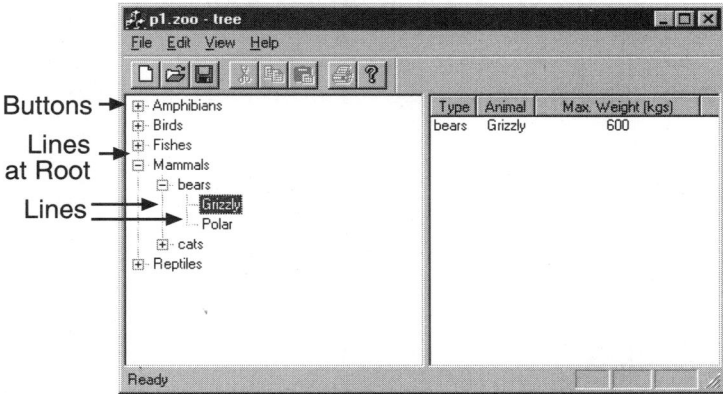

To see the demonstration "Creating a Tree View Application," see the accompanying CD-ROM.

In the demonstration, the tree control has an image list associated with it. Associating an image list with the tree control is optional.

The main steps in creating a tree view application are as follows:

1. Run MFC AppWizard. In Step 6, choose **CTreeView** as the base for your view class.
2. Edit **OnInitialUpdate** and add code to set the characteristics for the tree view.
3. If you want to have images associated with the nodes, create an image list and associate it with the tree control.
4. Edit **OnUpdate** and add code to populate the tree.

For more information about **CTreeView**, search for "CTreeView" in MSDN Library Visual Studio 6.0.

Implementing CTreeView

To implement an application that uses a view based on **CTreeView**, you need to customize the properties of the tree control and populate it. If you want to display images in the tree view, then you must build an image list and associate it with the view.

Customizing Tree View Characteristics

Use **CTreeView::GetTreeCtrl** to call the **ModifyStyle** member function of the tree control that is embedded in the view. Use **ModifyStyle** to include buttons and horizontal and vertical lines in the tree control, as shown in the following example code:

```
void CTreeWithImagesView::OnInitialUpdate()
{
  ...
  GetTreeCtrl().ModifyStyle(NULL,
      TVS_HASBUTTONS | TVS_HASLINES | TVS_LINESATROOT);
  ...
}
```

Associating an Image List with the Tree Control

To display images with the nodes, you must complete the following steps:

1. Use the Resource editor to create the bitmaps to be used in the image list, and add them to your project.
2. Build an image list.
3. Associate the image list with the tree control.
4. As you insert a node, select an image to use for each of the two states of a node: selected and unselected.

The following sample code builds an image list and associates it with the tree control. To copy this code for use in your own projects, see "Associating an Image List with a Tree Control" on the accompanying CD-ROM.

```
// Samples\CH04\Treewimg
// TimgView.cpp

void CTreeWithImagesView::InsertBitmaps()
{
  CImageList *cim;
  cim = new CImageList();   //dynamically allocate list
  cim->Create(BITMAP_WIDTH, BITMAP_HEIGHT, TRUE,
              NUM_BITMAPS, 0);
```

code continued on next page

Chapter 4: Implementing View Classes

code continued from previous page

```
    CBitmap bitmap;  // Temporary holding area for current
                     // for bitmap being loaded

    // Load the bitmaps and add them to the image list.
    for (int i = IDB_AMPHIBIAN; i <=
                    IDB_REPTILE_SELECTED; i++)
    {
        bitmap.LoadBitmap(i);
        cim->Add(&bitmap, (COLORREF)0xFFFFFF);
        bitmap.DeleteObject();
    }

    // Associate the image list with the tree control.
    GetTreeCtrl().SetImageList(cim, TVSIL_NORMAL);
}
```

Populating the Tree Control

To populate the tree control, add code to the **OnUpdate** function to refresh the control. Refreshing the tree control consists of two steps:

1. Delete all data from the tree control.
2. Populate the tree control (with the updated items).

The following sample code populates the tree control. To copy this code for use in your own projects, see "Populating a Tree Control" on the accompanying CD-ROM.

```
// Samples\CH04\Treewimg
// TimgView.cpp

void CTreeWithImagesView::InsertAnimals()
{
    static char * classes[] = { "amphibians", "birds", "fishes",
                                "mammals", "reptiles", NULL };
    static char * types[][4] = { "frogs", "toads", "salamanders", NULL,
                                 "eagles", "owls", "falcons", NULL,
                                 "trout", "perch", "bass", NULL,
                                 "bears", "whales", "rodents", NULL,
                                 "snakes", "turtles", "lizards", NULL };
```

code continued on next page

175

code continued from previous page

```
    HTREEITEM hSubTree;
    int ImageListIndex = 0;

    CTreeCtrl & ctc = GetTreeCtrl();

    for (int r = 0; r < 5; r++)
    {
        hSubTree = ctc.InsertItem(classes[r], TVI_ROOT, TVI_SORT);
        ctc.SetItemImage(hSubTree, ImageListIndex, ImageListIndex + 1);
        // The string from the classes array is placed at the root...
        // and the newly-inserted node serves as parent to the types.
        InsertNodes(hSubTree, types[r], ImageListIndex,
                                    ImageListIndex + 1);
        ImageListIndex += 2;
    }

    static char * beartypes[] = { "grizzly", "polar", "black", NULL };
    HTREEITEM hSubTree2;

    // Now that the tree is built, the bears node will have children
    // added to it. This requires 2 lookup operations.
    hSubTree = FindNode(ctc.GetRootItem(), classes[3]);
    if (NULL != hSubTree)
    {
        hSubTree2 = FindNode(hSubTree, types[3][0]);
        if (NULL != hSubTree2)
            InsertNodes(hSubTree2, beartypes, MAMMAL, MAMMAL + 1);
    }
}

// The function iterates over the children of ParentNode looking
// for a match.
// If ParentNode is NULL, the search starts in the root, otherwise
// it starts
// in the designated node. Returns NULL if not found, the HTREEITEM
// if found.

HTREEITEM CTreeWithImagesView::FindNode(const HTREEITEM ParentNode,
                                    const CString &str) const
{
  CTreeCtrl & ctc = GetTreeCtrl();
  HTREEITEM node;
  CString s;
```

code continued on next page

code continued from previous page

```
    if (NULL == ParentNode)
        node = ctc.GetRootItem();
    else
        if (ctc.GetRootItem() == ParentNode)
            node = ParentNode;
        else
            node = ctc.GetChildItem(ParentNode);

    while (node != NULL)
    {
        s = ctc.GetItemText(node);
        // Halt the search when we find what we're looking for.
        if (0 == s.CompareNoCase(str))
            return node;
        node = ctc.GetNextItem(node, TVGN_NEXT);
    }
    // If we get to here, string was never found, and node == NULL.
    return node;
}

// This function inserts the array of strings pointed to by the 2nd
// argument into the tree at the node represented by the first
// argument. All nodes have the same 2 image IDs.
void CTreeWithImagesView::InsertNodes(const HTREEITEM hSubTree,
        char ** AnimalClass, const int ImageID, const int
SelectedImageID)
{
    HTREEITEM node;
    CTreeCtrl & ctc = GetTreeCtrl();

    int i = 0;
    while (AnimalClass[i])
    {
        // Insert a node as a child of hSubTree and set its images.
        node = ctc.InsertItem(AnimalClass[i++], hSubTree, TVI_SORT);
        ctc.SetItemImage(node, ImageID, SelectedImageID);
    }
}
```

This sample code does not enable the user to change the data that is associated with the control.

Overview of CEditView

The **CEditView** class provides the functionality of a **CEdit** control with the following enhanced editing features: printing; find and replace; **Cut, Copy, Paste, Clear,** and **Undo** commands; and **File Save** and **File Open** commands. You can use **CEditView** to implement a simple text-editor view.

The following illustration shows an edit view application.

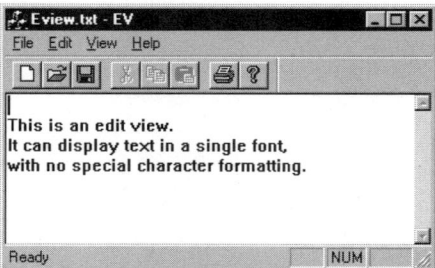

Implementing CEditView

Objects of type **CEditView** (or of types derived from **CEditView**) have the following limitations:

- **CEditView** does not implement true WYSIWYG (what you see is what you get) editing.

    Where there is a choice between readability on the screen and matching printed output, **CEditView** opts for screen readability.

- **CEditView** can use only one font to display text.

    No special character formatting is supported. Use the **CRichEditView** class for greater capabilities.

- The amount of text that a **CEditView** object can contain is limited. It can store only 64KB of text.

 Tip Note that you can make the edit control "read-only" by calling the **SetReadOnly** member function of your application's **CEdit** class in the view's **OnInitialUpdate** function.

 **Note** If you want support for serialization as well as the behavior of the **CEdit** control, use a **CEditView**-derived view instead of an edit control on a dialog box or form view.

For more information about **CEditView**, search for "CEditView" in MSDN Library Visual Studio 6.0.

Overview of CRichEditView

A rich text file is a file that contains encoded, formatted text and graphics for easy transfer between applications. The rich-text encoding format is commonly used by document-processing programs such as Microsoft Word for Windows and for generating online Help files. Rich-text format files usually have an .rtf file extension.

A rich edit control is a window in which the user can:

- Enter and edit text that can be assigned character and paragraph formatting.
- Include embedded ActiveX objects.

The rich edit control covers a large subset of the full RTF specification.

For more information about **CRichEditView**, search for "CRichEditView" in MSDN Library Visual Studio 6.0.

Implementing CRichEditView

The MFC class **CRichEditCtrl** encapsulates the rich edit control. The rich edit control (and therefore the **CRichEditCtrl** class) is available only to applications running under Windows 95 and Windows NT versions 3.51 and later.

The **CRichEditView**, **CRichEditDoc**, and **CRichEditCntrItem** classes provide the functionality of the rich edit control within the context of MFC's document/view architecture as follows:

- **CRichEditView** maintains the text and formatting characteristic of text.
- **CRichEditDoc** maintains the list of ActiveX client items that are in the view and, like any **CDocument**-derived object, provides support for serialization.
- **CRichEditCntrItem** provides container-side access to the ActiveX client item.

The following illustration shows how these classes interrelate.

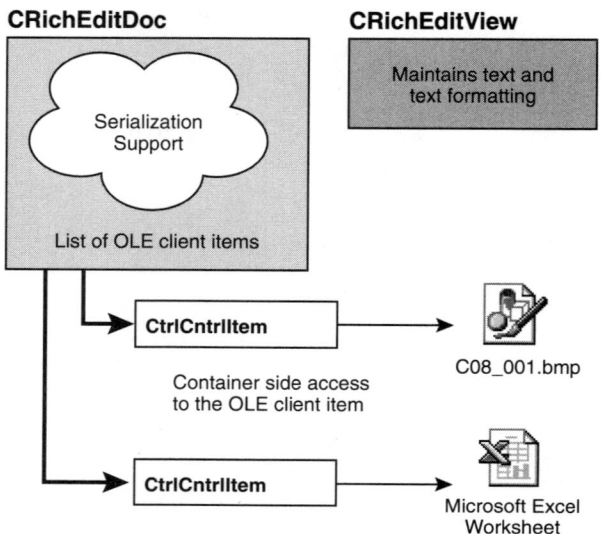

The **CRichEditView** class provides numerous member functions that are wrappers for member functions of the **CRichEditCtrl** class. You use these wrappers to simplify the code that implements a given functionality.

If you use MFC AppWizard to generate an application that uses **CRichEditView** as the base class for the view, MFC AppWizard will change the base class for the document and will also add the class required for ActiveX container support. The following illustration shows an example of a rich edit view application.

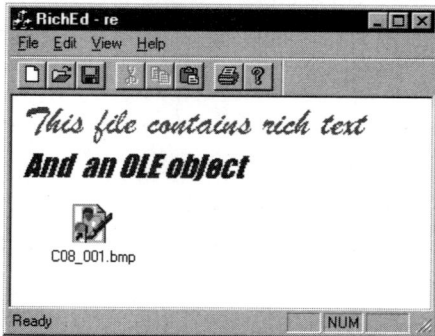

Rich edit controls provide a programming interface for formatting text. However, you must implement any user-interface components necessary to make formatting operations available to the user.

Implementing the Drag-and-Drop Feature

The drag-and-drop technique is used to transfer data between applications, between windows in an application, or within a window. An MFC AppWizard-generated application that uses **CRichEditView** as the base class for its view includes drop target functionality. This means it can accept an OLE object that is dropped into a view.

For example, the user might select several files in the Windows 95 Explorer and drop them into the view of your application. You must add one or more handlers to your application to provide the appropriate response.

If your application contains a single view, add an **OnDropFiles** handler for the WM_DROPFILES message to your view class. If your application contains multiple views, consider having each view's **OnDropFiles** function send a WM_DROPFILES message to the frame class and implement the common functionality for handling dropped files in the frame's **OnDropFiles** function.

Creating an Explorer-Style Application

Many Windows system applications use the Explorer user interface, in which the client area is split vertically. The left side of the client area shows an overview pane, which makes navigation and browsing possible, while the right side of the client area shows details about the selection in the left pane.

You can create an Explorer-Style application by using MFC AppWizard and selecting the **Windows Explorer** option in Step 5.

The following illustration shows the **MFC AppWizard - Step 5** dialog box.

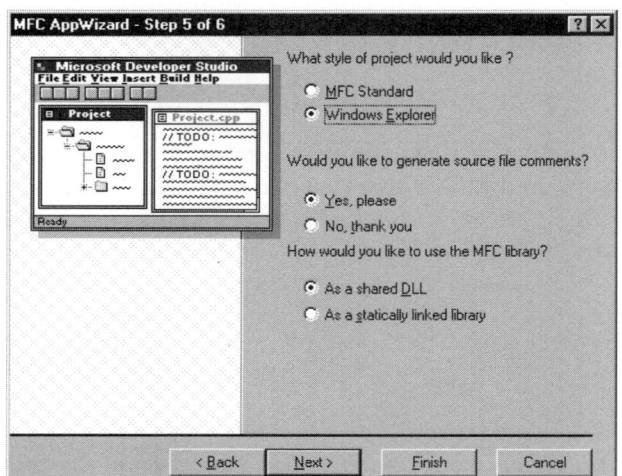

MFC AppWizard generates code so that each frame window that the application creates is split vertically using the **CSplitterWnd** object. The left pane always contains a tree view control. The right pane contains a list view control by default. You can modify the view type of the right pane to customize the display detail of the selected item in the left pane.

The following illustration shows the **MFC AppWizard - Step 6** dialog box with a list of view types.

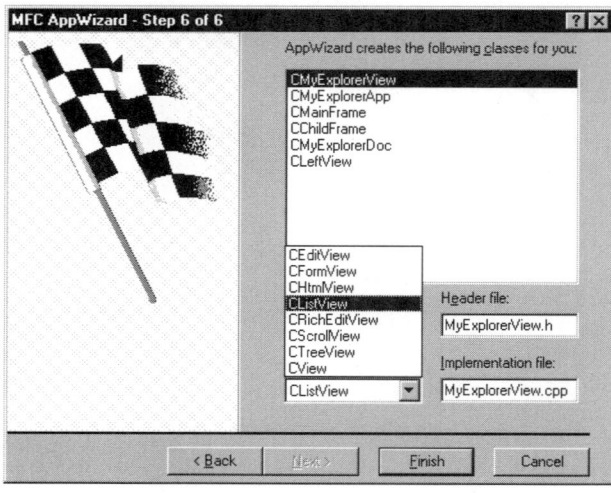

If you use the MFC AppWizard default list view in the right pane, the wizard creates additional menu choices and toolbar buttons to switch the view's style among report mode, small icon mode, and list mode.

Coordinating Multiple Interrelated Views

If your application uses two or more views of different types, you need to ensure that the display of data in the views is always synchronized.

There are two methods for coordinating the data in the views. The first method uses the **UpdateAllViews** function to update the views, whereas the second method updates the views without using this function. Which method you use depends on the requirements of your application.

Coordinating Data Using the UpdateAllViews Function

Using **UpdateAllViews** takes advantage of the document/view architecture as provided by MFC. Suppose that the user does something in a list view that causes a change in a form view. The list view packages the information it needs to pass to the form in a class derived from **CObject**. The list then calls **UpdateAllViews**, passing three parameters: a pointer to itself, NULL (0), and a pointer to the object where information is packaged.

The document object then calls the form's **OnUpdate** function, and passes the second and third arguments of **UpdateAllViews** to the form. The document does not call the list's **OnUpdate** function, because the list specified a pointer to itself in the first argument to **UpdateAllViews**.

Coordinating Data Without Using the UpdateAllViews Function

The second method requires you to manually control the process of coordinating the data. With this method, the document stores pointers to the two view objects. Each view initializes this pointer to itself in its **OnCreate** function. Each view also has as many public functions, with as many parameters as are needed, to respond to changes requested by the other view. When, for instance, the list needs to cause the form to change its display, the list obtains the pointer to the form from the document and calls a specific function in the form, passing arguments as required. Using this method may be much easier than packaging information in a class and passing that class by using the **UpdateAllViews** function as described in the first method.

Lab 4.2: Adding Open File Dialogs and a Rich Edit View

In this lab, you will use a **Common Open File** dialog box and a rich edit view in an application.

To see the demonstration "Lab 4.2 Demonstration," see the accompanying CD-ROM.

Estimated time to complete this lab: **60 minutes**

To complete the exercises in this lab, you must have the required software. For detailed information about the labs and setup for the labs, see "Labs" in "About This Course."

The code that forms the starting point for this lab is located in the folder *<install folder>*\Labs\Ch04\Lab4.2.

The solution code for this lab is located in the folder *<install folder>*\Labs\Ch04\Lab4.2.

Objectives

After completing this lab, you will be able to:

- Modify the base classes of views and documents.
- Use a **Common Dialogs Library Open** dialog box.
- Use a rich edit view in an application.
- Process a dropped file on the edit control.

Prerequisites

There are no prerequisites for this lab.

Exercises

The following exercises provide practice working with the concepts and techniques covered in this chapter:

- Exercise 1: Modifying the Base Classes of Views and Documents

    In this exercise, you will use the text editors of Visual C++ to modify the **Document** and **View** classes to inherit from their respective rich edit classes.

- Exercise 2: Handling the Common Open File Dialog Box

    In this exercise, you will add a handler for the **Open File** dialog box in the **ShowDiff** application.

- Exercise 3: Using the Rich Edit Views in the Application

    In this exercise, you will use the rich edit views to display the file that the user chooses in the File dialog box. You will create a function that serializes the text data into the rich edit views, and drive that function from the **OnFileOpen** handler.

- Exercise 4: Managing Drag-and-Drop Editing

    In this exercise, you will modify the behavior of **CRichEdit** so that it will open a file that is dragged from Windows Explorer to the window pane of the running application.

Exercise 1: Modifying the Base Classes of Views and Documents

The code that forms the starting point for this exercise is in *<install folder>*\Labs\Ch04\Lab4.2\Ex01.

In this exercise, you will use the text editors of Visual C++ to modify the **Document** and **View** classes to inherit from their respective rich edit classes.

▶ **Replace CDocument with CRichEditDoc**

1. Open the file DiffDoc.cpp.
2. Replace all instances of **CDocument** with **CRichEditDoc**.
3. Save DiffDoc.cpp.
4. Repeat this procedure with the file DiffDoc.h.

▶ **Replace CView with CRichEditView**

1. Open DiffView.cpp.
2. Replace all instances of **CView** with **CRichEditView**.
3. Save DiffView.cpp.
4. Repeat this procedure with DiffView.h.

▶ Add the #includes that support rich edit classes to the file Stdafx.h

1. Open Stdafx.h.
2. The **CRichEditDoc** class inherits from **COleDocument, COleLinkingDoc,** and **COleServerDoc**. The definitions for these classes and their support functions need to be included before the rich edit definitions. To the end of Stdafx.h, add:

   ```
   #include <afxole.h>
   #include <afxodlgs.h>
   ```

3. The definitions for rich edit control are in the file Afxrich.h. To the end of Stdafx.h, after the file Afxodlgs.h, add:

   ```
   #include <afxrich.h>
   ```

4. Save Stdafx.h.

▶ Add the support for CRichEditCntrItem

Derived classes from **CRichEditDoc** need to provide a pointer to a control item (the class that contains the rich edit control itself). This simple function is implemented in DiffDoc.h.

1. Open DiffDoc.h.
2. Add this code to the overrides section (after the //}AFX_VIRTUAL tag):

   ```
   virtual CRichEditCntrItem* CreateClientItem(REOBJECT* preo) const;
   ```

3. Save DiffDoc.h.
4. Open DiffDoc.cpp.
5. Add this code right after the destructor (**CDiffDoc::~CDiffDoc**):

   ```
   CRichEditCntrItem* CDiffDoc::CreateClientItem(REOBJECT* preo) const
   {
       return new CRichEditCntrItem();
   }
   ```

6. Save DiffDoc.cpp and build the project.

The solution code for this exercise is located in the folder *<install folder>*\Labs\Ch04\Lab4.2\Ex01\Solution.

Exercise 2: Handling the Common Open File Dialog Box

Continue with the files you created in Exercise 1 or, if you do not have a starting point for this exercise, the code that forms the basis for this exercise is in *<install folder>*\Labs\Ch04\Lab4.2\Ex02.

In this exercise, you will add a handler for the **Open File** dialog box to the ShowDiff application.

▶ **Add an OnFileOpen handler for CDiffDoc**

1. On the **View** menu, click **ClassWizard** or press CTRL+W. Click the **Message Maps** tab.
2. Select the **CDiffDoc** class, the ID_FILE_OPEN menu object ID, and the COMMAND message, and click **Add Function**, as shown in this figure.

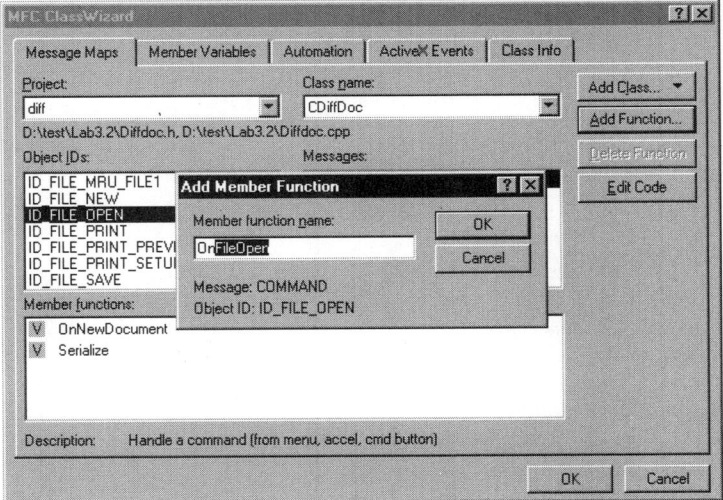

3. Accept the default **OnFileOpen** function name in the **Add Member Function** dialog box, and click **OK**.
4. In ClassWizard, click **OK** to create the function.

▶ **Declare protected file name members**

- Right-click **CDiffDoc** in ClassView and add these two protected variables:

    CString m_File1
    CString m_File2

▶ **Complete the OnFileOpen handler**

1. In the **OnFileOpen** handler of the file DiffDoc.cpp, define the filter for the **File** dialog box. In this example, you will filter for C++ source files (*.cpp and *.h) and for all files:

   ```
   static char BASED_CODE szFilter[] =
       "All Files (*.*)|*.*|C++ Files (*.cpp, *.h)"\
       "|*.cpp;*.h||";
   ```

2. Construct the **File** dialog box as an open dialog box with this filter:

   ```
   CFileDialog dlg(TRUE,NULL,NULL,NULL,szFilter);
   ```

3. Show the **File** dialog box as a modal dialog box, and check to see whether **OK** was clicked.
4. When the user clicks **OK**, assign the path to m_File1 and m_File2.
5. Save DiffDoc.cpp.

The following sample code shows an example of how your code should look. To copy this code for use in your own projects, see "Lab 4.2.2 OnFileOpen" on the accompanying CD-ROM.

```
void CDiffDoc::OnFileOpen()
{

  static char BASED_CODE szFilter[] =
      "All Files (*.*)|*.*|C++ Files (*.cpp, *.h)| "\
      "*.cpp;*.h||";

  CFileDialog dlg(TRUE,NULL,NULL,NULL,szFilter);

  if (dlg.DoModal() == IDOK)
  {
      m_File1 = m_File2 = dlg.GetPathName();
  }
}
```

The solution code for this exercise is located in the folder *<install folder>*\Labs\Ch04\Lab4.2\Ex02\Solution.

Exercise 3: Using the Rich Edit Views in the Application

Continue with the files you created in Exercise 2 or, if you do not have a starting point for this exercise, the code that forms the basis for this exercise is in *<install folder>*\Labs\Ch04\Lab4.2\Ex03.

In this exercise, you will use the rich edit views to display the file that the user chooses in the **File** dialog box. You will create a function that serializes text data into the rich edit views, and drive that function from the **OnFileOpen** handler.

▶ **Get the application and the main frame**

1. Open the file Diff.h.

2. Add a forward reference to **CMainFrame** before the definition of **CDiffApp** as follows:

   ```
   class CMainFrame;
   ```

3. Define a public method to return a pointer to the application as follows:

   ```
   public:
   static CDiffApp * GetApp()
   {
       return (CDiffApp *)AfxGetApp();
   }
   ```

4. Define a public method to a pointer to the main frame as follows:

   ```
   CMainFrame * GetMainFrame()
   {
       return (CMainFrame *)m_pMainWnd;
   }
   ```

   Note that the purpose of steps 3 and 4 is to simplify writing the code for the rest of this lab.

5. Save Diff.h.

▶ **Initialize the file members and set the views to text only**

1. Open the file DiffDoc.cpp and scroll to **CDiffDoc::CDiffDoc**.

2. Initialize m_File1 and m_File2 as empty strings as follows:

   ```
   m_File1 = _T("");
   m_File2 = _T("");
   ```

3. The m_bRTF member of **CRichEditDoc** defines whether the streams should store formatting. Because you will only be dealing with text, set this member to **FALSE** as follows:

   ```
   m_bRTF = FALSE;
   ```

4. Save DiffDoc.cpp.

▶ **Add the function to display the files in the views**

1. Right-click **CDiffDoc** in ClassView and add the following public function:

   ```
   void RunComparison(LPCSTR lpszFile1, LPCSTR lpszFile2)
   ```

2. Open DiffDoc.cpp. Include DiffView.h, the file Splitter.h, and the file MainFrm.h after the statement that includes DiffDoc.h as follows:

   ```
   #include "diffdoc.h"
   #include "diffview.h"
   #include "splitter.h"
   #include "mainfrm.h"
   ```

▶ **Write the code for the Run Comparison function**

1. Get the splitter:

   ```
   CMainFrame * pFrame = CDiffApp::GetApp()->GetMainFrame();
   CSplitter * pSplitter = pFrame->GetSplitter();
   ```

2. Get the first pane as follows:

   ```
   CDiffView * pView;
   pView = (CDiffView *)pSplitter->GetPane(0,0);
   ```

3. Stream the first file into the first pane as follows:

   ```
   CFile   file(lpszFile1, CFile::modeRead);
   CArchive ar(&file, CArchive::load);
   pView->Serialize(ar);
   ```

4. Repeat the procedure for the second pane.

Lab 4.2: Adding Open File Dialogs and a Rich Edit View

5. Mark the document as "clean" so as not to save it:

   ```
   SetModifiedFlag(FALSE);
   ```

6. Save DiffDoc.cpp.

The following sample code shows an example of how your code should look. To copy this code for use in your own projects, see "Lab 4.2.3 RunComparison" on the accompanying CD-ROM.

```
void CDiffDoc::RunComparison (LPCSTR lpszFile1,
                              LPCSTR lpszFile2)
{
  CMainFrame * pFrame = CDiffApp::GetApp()->GetMainFrame();

  if(pFrame)
  {
      CSplitter * pSplitter = pFrame->GetSplitter();

      if(pSplitter)
      {
          CDiffView * pView;

          pView = (CDiffView *)pSplitter->GetPane(0,0);

          if(pView)
          {
              CFile    file(lpszFile1, CFile::modeRead);
              CArchive ar(&file, CArchive::load);
              pView->Serialize(ar);
          }

          pView = (CDiffView *)pSplitter->GetPane(0,1);

          if(pView)
          {
              CFile    file(lpszFile2, CFile::modeRead);
              CArchive ar(&file, CArchive::load);
              pView->Serialize(ar);
          }
          //Flag as clean so that we won't get prompted to save
          SetModifiedFlag(FALSE);
      }
  }
}
```

▶ **Call RunComparison from OnFileOpen**

1. Scroll to the end of **CDiffDoc::OnFileOpen**.
2. Add a call to **RunComparison** with the two files as shown:

   ```
   RunComparison (m_File1, m_File2);
   ```

3. Save DiffDoc.cpp.

▶ **Set the rich edit control to read-only**

1. Open ClassWizard.
2. Add a handler for **OnInitialUpdate** to **CDiffView**.
3. Open the file DiffView.cpp.
4. Add a call to **SetReadOnly** to the end of **OnInitialUpdate** as follows:

   ```
   GetRichEditCtrl().SetReadOnly();
   ```

5. Save DiffView.cpp.

▶ **Make the changes to CMainFrame**

1. Open MainFrm.h.
2. Add a public attribute method to return the splitter object as follows:

   ```
   CSplitter * GetSplitter() { return &m_wndSplitter; }
   ```

3. Save MainFrm.h.
4. In the **CMainFrame::OnCreateClient** function of the file MainFrm.cpp, comment out **SetActiveView** as follows:

   ```
   //SetActiveView((CView *)m_wndSplitter.GetPane(0,1));
   ```

5. Save MainFrm.cpp.

▶ **Build and test the application**

- Run your application and open a file. You will see that the file appears in the two panes of the window.

The solution code for this exercise is located in the folder *<install folder>*\Labs\Ch04\Lab4.2\Ex03\Solution.

Exercise 4: Managing Drag-and-Drop Editing

Continue with the files you created in Exercise 3 or, if you do not have a starting point for this exercise, the code that forms the basis for this exercise is in *<install folder>*\Labs\Ch04\Lab4.2\Ex04.

In this exercise, you will modify the behavior of **CRichEdit** so that it will open a file that is dragged from Windows Explorer to the window pane of the running application. For purposes of this exercise, you will process dropped files only if two files are dropped. Ignore any additional files beyond the first two.

▶ Implement CMain Frame::OnDropFiles

1. Add a handler for WM_DROPFILES to **CMainFrame** using ClassWizard.
2. Determine the number of files being dropped:

   ```
   UINT nFileCount =
       ::DragQueryFile (hDropInfo,0xFFFFFFFF, NULL, 0);
   ```

3. Determine whether two or more files have been dropped:
   ```
   if (nFileCount >= 2)
   ```

▶ Edit CMainFrame::OnDropFiles to get the first two dropped files and pass them to CDiffDoc::RunComparison

1. Get the path of the first file:

   ```
   CString File1;

   ::DragQueryFile(hDropInfo,
                   0,
                   File1.GetBufferSetLength(_MAX_PATH),
                   _MAX_PATH);
   File1.ReleaseBuffer();
   ```

2. Repeat the process for the second file.
3. Call **CDiffDoc::RunComparison**:

   ```
   ((CDiffDoc *)GetActiveDocument())->
                   RunComparison(File1, File2);
   ```

4. Finish drag-and-drop processing:

   ```
   ::DragFinish(hDropInfo);
   ```

The following sample code shows an example of how your code should look. To copy this code for use in your own projects, see "Lab 4.2.4 CMainFrame::OnDropFiles" on the accompanying CD-ROM.

```
void CMainFrame::OnDropFiles(HDROP hDropInfo)
{
  UINT nFileCount = ::DragQueryFile (hDropInfo,
                                      0xFFFFFFFF,
                                      NULL, 0);
  ASSERT(nFileCount !=0);

  // We must have at least two files for this function;
  // we will grab only the first two

  if (nFileCount >= 2)
  {
      CString File1;
      CString File2;

      ::DragQueryFile(hDropInfo,
                      0,
                      File1.GetBufferSetLength(_MAX_PATH),
                      _MAX_PATH);
      File1.ReleaseBuffer();

      ::DragQueryFile(hDropInfo,
                      1,
                      File2.GetBufferSetLength(_MAX_PATH),
                      _MAX_PATH);
      File2.ReleaseBuffer();

      ((CDiffDoc *)GetActiveDocument())->
                      RunComparison(File1, File2);

      ::DragFinish(hDropInfo);
  }
}
```

▶ **Add a handler for WM_DROPFILES to CDiffView**

- Use ClassWizard to add a handler for WM_DROPFILES to **CDiffView**.

Lab 4.2: Adding Open File Dialogs and a Rich Edit View

▶ **Pass the WM_DROPFILES message to CMainFrame from CDiffView**

1. In **CDiffView::OnDropFiles**, get the main frame window:

   ```
   CDiffApp::GetApp()->GetMainFrame()
   ```

2. Send WM_DROPFILES to it:

   ```
   CDiffApp::GetApp()->GetMainFrame()->SendMessage( WM_DROPFILES,
                   (WPARAM)hDropInfo );
   ```

3. Comment out the default **OnDropFiles** behavior so OLE embedding will not be invoked:

   ```
   //CRichEditView::OnDropFiles(hDropInfo);
   ```

   The following sample code shows an example of how your code should look. To copy this code for use in your own projects, see "Lab 4.2.4 CDiffView::OnDropFiles" on the accompanying CD-ROM.

```
void CDiffView::OnDropFiles(HDROP hDropInfo)
{
  CDiffApp::GetApp()->GetMainFrame()->
          SendMessage (WM_DROPFILES,
                       (WPARAM)hDropInfo);
  // Don't call the default—we don't want OLE embedding behavior
  //CRichEditView::OnDropFiles(hDropInfo);
}
```

4. In the file DiffView.cpp, include the file splitter.h and the file mainfrm.h after the file diffView.h:

   ```
   #include "splitter.h"
   #include "mainfrm.h"
   ```

▶ **Build and test the application**

1. Run the application.
2. Invoke Windows Explorer and drag any two files from Windows Explorer to the window pane of the running application.

   You will see that the files appear in the two panes of the window.

MFC Development Using Microsoft Visual C++ 6.0

The solution code for this exercise is located in the folder *<install folder>*\Labs\Ch04\Lab4.2\Ex04\Solution.

Lab 4.3 (Optional): Building a Text Viewer

In this lab, you will implement a text viewer and control fonts for on-screen display.

To see the demonstration "Lab 4.3 Demonstration," see the accompanying CD-ROM.

Estimated time to complete this lab: **30 minutes**

To complete the exercises in this lab, you must have the required software. For detailed information about the labs and setup for the labs, see "Labs" in "About This Course."

The solution code for this lab is located in the folder *<install folder>*\Labs\Ch04\Lab4.3.

Objectives

After completing this lab, you will be able to:

- Implement supporting code for a viewer.
- Display streams of text.
- Control fonts for on-screen display.

Prerequisites

Before working on this lab, you should be familiar with the following:

- Member functions of **CDC** class

You may find it helpful to review the MSDN Library Visual Studio 98 Help topics on graphics before attempting this lab.

Exercises

The following exercises provide practice working with the concepts and techniques covered in this chapter:

- Exercise 1: Implementing a Basic Text Viewer
  In this exercise, you will add text display capability to a viewer.

196

◆ Exercise 2: Adding Font Support

In this exercise, you will implement a user interface for the text viewer you created in Exercise 1.

Exercise 1: Implementing a Basic Text Viewer

In this exercise, you will add text display capability to a viewer based on **CScrollView**. There are four parts to this exercise:

1. Creating a multiple-document interface (MDI) application with MFC AppWizard
2. Adding file-handling to the document
3. Calculating the basic metrics of the view
4. Displaying the text

At the end of this exercise, you will have created an MDI text viewer with file selection, display, and scrolling.

▶ Use MFC AppWizard to create an MDI application

1. Name the new project workspace **Text**.
2. In Step 6, derive **CTextView** from **CScrollView**, rather than **CView**.

Finish and create the new project. Build it at this point.

In the Text.exe file, **CTextDoc** is little more than a holder for **CStringList**, into which you will read the lines of a selected file. **CDocument** provides the menu and the **File Open** dialog box. You will provide the file-handling code and the parsing of the file into **CStringList**.

▶ Prepare CTextDoc for file reading

1. Open the file TextDoc.h.
2. Declare a protected **CStringList** member:

    ```
    CStringList m_LineList;
    ```

3. Declare a public member function to return a pointer to m_LineList:

    ```
    CStringList*GetLineList() { return &m_LineList; }
    ```

4. Save TextDoc.h.

5. **CTextDoc::OnNewDocument** is called when the application starts and when a user action occurs. Because Text.exe is a read-only application, disable this function in the file TextDoc.cpp:

   ```
   BOOL CTextDoc::OnNewDocument()
   {
       return FALSE;
   }
   ```

▶ **Implement OnOpenDocument**

1. **CTextDoc::OnOpenDocument** will read the selected text file, line by line, into the **CStringList** member. **OnOpenDocument** is called from the application after **CTextApp** has queried the user with a **File Open** dialog box. Create **CTextDoc::OnOpenDocument** from ClassWizard or WizardBar. Edit the code to remove the default handler.

2. Reading a file into memory one line at a time could take a while. Show the wait cursor with **CCmdTarget::BeginWaitCursor**:

   ```
   BeginWaitCursor();
   ```

3. Clear all the items from m_LineList:

   ```
   m_LineList.RemoveAll();
   ```

4. **CStdioFile** provides stream-oriented file access with line-oriented file access. Open the file passed in lpszPathName by constructing a **CStdioFile** object as follows:

   ```
   CStdioFile  file(lpszPathName,
                    CFile::modeRead | CFile::typeText);
   ```

5. Declare a **CString** variable into which to read each line as follows:

   ```
   CString strLine;
   ```

6. **CStdioFile::ReadString** returns **TRUE** if anything was read and **FALSE** if the end of the file was encountered before reading any data. Read data as long as there is anything to read:

   ```
   while (file.ReadString(strLine) != NULL)
   {
   ```

Lab 4.3: (Optional) Building a Text Viewer

7. Clean up the ends of the lines for white space and control characters as follows:

   ```
   int nLastCharIndex = strLine.GetLength()-1;
   while (nLastCharIndex >= 0 && strLine[nLastCharIndex] < ' ')
   {
       strLine.SetAt(nLastCharIndex-, '\0');
   }
   ```

8. Once the string is clean, add it to the end of m_LineList as follows:

   ```
   m_LineList.AddTail(strLine);
   ```

9. At the end of the read loop, restore the cursor as follows:

   ```
   EndWaitCursor();
   ```

10. Return **TRUE** to indicate that you have handled the message:

    ```
    return TRUE;
    ```

11. Save TextDoc.cpp and TextDoc.h.

The following sample code shows an example of how your code should look. To copy this code for use in your own projects, see "Lab 4.3.1 OnOpenDocument" on the accompanying CD-ROM.

```
BOOL CTextDoc::OnOpenDocument(LPCTSTR lpszPathName)
{
  //  Could be a big file
  BeginWaitCursor();

  //  Clear List, this will cleanup the CString objects
  m_LineList.RemoveAll();

  //  Read the file and store as a list
  //  of CStrings
  CStdioFile   file(lpszPathName,
                 CFile::modeRead | CFile::typeText);
```

code continued on next page

```
code continued from previous page

    CString strLine;
    while (file.ReadString(strLine) != NULL)
    {
        //remove the noise characters at the end of the line
        int nLastCharIndex = strLine.GetLength()-1;
        while (nLastCharIndex >= 0 && strLine[nLastCharIndex] < ' ')
        {
        strLine.SetAt(nLastCharIndex-, '\0');
        }

        //  Add to CStringList
        m_LineList.AddTail(strLine);
    }

    EndWaitCursor();
    return TRUE;
}
```

▶ **Declare the basic metrics members**

You will need to have a number of basic metrics for the text view. These do not need to be calculated each time you draw text on the screen if you hold them in member variables.

1. Right-click **CTextView** in ClassView and add the following protected variables:

   ```
   CSize    m_ViewCharSize
   CSize    m_DocSize
   CFont*   m_pFont
   ```

2. Right-click **CTextView** in ClassView and declare a public function as follows:

   ```
   CFont*    GetFont()
   ```

3. Right-click **CTextView** in ClassView and declare a protected function as follows:

   ```
   void ComputeViewMetrics()
   ```

4. Add public member functions manually to the file CTextView.h as follows:

   ```
   CSize       GetDocSize() const { return m_DocSize; }
   CSize       GetCharSize() const { return m_ViewCharSize; }
   ```

5. Open the file TextView.cpp.
6. Initialize m_ViewCharSize, m_DocSize, and m_pFont in the constructor. The constructor looks like the following:

```
CTextView:: CTextView()
    :   m_ViewCharSize(0,0),
        m_DocSize(0,0)
{
    m_pFont = NULL;
}
```

7. Save TextView.cpp.

▶ **Get the current font**

1. In TextView.cpp, define the **GetFont** function as follows:

    ```
    CFont*  CTextView::GetFont()
    ```

2. If no font has been created, construct a new font as follows:

    ```
    if(m_pFont == NULL)
    {
        m_pFont = new Cfont;
    }
    ```

3. Create a nine-point Arial font in m_pFont as follows:

    ```
    if(m_pFont)
    {
        // Default to 9 pt Arial
        m_pFont->CreatePointFont(90, "Arial");
    }
    ```

4. Return m_pFont. Save TextView.cpp.

The sample code on the following page shows an example of how your code should look. To copy this code for use in your own projects, see "Lab 4.3.1 GetFont" on the accompanying CD-ROM.

```
CFont *  CTextView::GetFont()
{
  if(m_pFont == NULL)
  {
      m_pFont = new CFont;
      if(m_pFont)
      {
          // Default to 9 pt Arial
          m_pFont->CreatePointFont(90, "Arial");
      }
  }
  return m_pFont;
}
```

▶ **Compute the basic metrics for the view by defining ComputeViewMetrics**

1. Get the pointer to the screen device context (DC) and save the state of the DC as follows:

   ```
   CDC* pDC = CDC::FromHandle(::GetDC(NULL));
       int nSaveDC = pDC->SaveDC();
   ```

2. Set the mapping mode to MM_LOENGLISH as follows:

   ```
   pDC->SetMapMode(MM_LOENGLISH);
   ```

3. Select the display font into the DC and get the font's text metrics as follows:

   ```
   CFont* pPreviousFont = pDC->SelectObject(GetFont());
   TEXTMETRIC tm;
   pDC->GetTextMetrics(&tm);
   ```

4. Calculate the height of a font element (character) as the sum of its internal height (tmHeight) and the space between lines (tmExternalLeading):

   ```
   m_ViewCharSize.cy = tm.tmHeight + tm.tmExternalLeading;
   m_ViewCharSize.cx = tm.tmAveCharWidth;
   ```

5. Get a pointer to a document so you can access the **CStringList** member that holds the data:

   ```
   CTextDoc* pDoc = GetDocument();
   ```

6. Initialize the document width to 0. To calculate the document height, multiply the number of lines by the height of a line:

   ```
   m_DocSize.cx = 0;
   m_DocSize.cy = m_ViewCharSize.cy *
                  pDoc->GetLineList()->GetCount();
   ```

7. The longest line has to be calculated by looking at each line of the document using the current font. Declare variables for a loop to interrogate each line as follows:

   ```
   CString Line;
   CSize size;
   ```

8. Because **CStringList** is a collection with an iterator, you will use a POSITION pointer to iterate through the list:

   ```
   POSITION pos = pDoc->GetLineList()->GetHeadPosition();
   while( pos != NULL )
   ```

9. Get the current line, and from it get its text extent as follows:

   ```
   Line = pDoc->GetLineList()->GetNext( pos );
   size = pDC->GetTextExtent(Line, Line.GetLength());
   ```

10. Set the width of the document to the largest size found as follows:

    ```
    m_DocSize.cx = max(size.cx, m_DocSize.cx);
    ```

11. After the loop is closed, add a four-pixel margin as follows:

    ```
    m_DocSize.cx += 4 * m_ViewCharSize.cx;
    ```

12. Select the application font out of the DC as follows:

    ```
    if(pPreviousFont)
        {
        pDC->SelectObject(pPreviousFont);
        }
    ```

13. Restore the DC to its original state as follows:

    ```
    pDC->RestoreDC(nSaveDC);
    ```

14. Release the DC as follows:

    ```
    ::ReleaseDC(NULL, pDC->GetSafeHdc());
    ```

15. Save TextView.cpp and TextView.h.

    The following sample code shows an example of how your code should look. To copy this code for use in your own projects, see "Lab 4.3.1 ComputeViewMetrics" on the accompanying CD-ROM.

```
void CTextView::ComputeViewMetrics()
{
  // get a CDC* for the screen
  CDC* pDC = CDC::FromHandle(::GetDC(NULL));
  int nSaveDC = pDC->SaveDC();


  // select mapping mode
  pDC->SetMapMode(MM_LOENGLISH);

  // select the font and get its metrics
  CFont* pPreviousFont = pDC->SelectObject(GetFont());
  TEXTMETRIC tm;
  pDC->GetTextMetrics(&tm);

  //   Calculate view character size
  m_ViewCharSize.cy = tm.tmHeight + tm.tmExternalLeading;
  m_ViewCharSize.cx = tm.tmAveCharWidth;

  // convert to device units to minimize round off error
  pDC->LPtoDP(&m_ViewCharSize);

  //   Calculate document size
  CTextDoc* pDoc = GetDocument();
  m_DocSize.cy = m_ViewCharSize.cy *
                 pDoc->GetLineList()->GetCount();
```

code continued on next page

```
code continued from previous page

    // loop through the document and find the longest line
    CString Line;
    CSize size;
    POSITION pos = pDoc->GetLineList()->GetHeadPosition();
    while( pos != NULL )
    {
        Line = pDoc->GetLineList()->GetNext( pos );
        size = pDC->GetTextExtent(Line, Line.GetLength());
        m_DocSize.cx = max(size.cx, m_DocSize.cx);
    }

    // Account for our simple margin
    m_DocSize.cx += 4 * m_ViewCharSize.cx;

    // clean up
    if(pPreviousFont)
    {
        pDC->SelectObject(pPreviousFont);
    }
    pDC->RestoreDC(nSaveDC);
    ::ReleaseDC(NULL,pDC->GetSafeHdc());
}
```

▶ Implement the OnDraw function

In the **OnDraw** function, you need to calculate the number of lines that can fit into the window and paint only those lines. In addition, you will need to process the OnUpdate message that is sent when the view window is resized.

1. Move to the top of **CTextView::OnDraw**. Delete the contents of the function and declare variables to store the first and last lines of the visible text:

   ```
   int nFirstLn, nLastLn;
   ```

2. Calculate the lines to draw by calling **ComputeVisibleLines** as follows:

   ```
   ComputeVisibleLines(pDC, nFirstLn, nLastLn);
   ```

3. Calculate the position of the first line relative to the origin of the window as follows:

   ```
   int nYPos = - nFirstLn * GetCharSize().cy;
   int nXPos = 4 * GetCharSize().cx;
   ```

4. Call the core **OnDraw** handler as follows:

   ```
   OnDraw(pDC, nFirstLn, nLastLn,nXPos,nYPos);
   ```

5. Save TextView.cpp.

The following sample code shows an example of how your code should look. To copy this code for use in your own projects, see "Lab 4.3.1 OnDraw" on the accompanying CD-ROM.

```
void CTextView::OnDraw(CDC* pDC)
{
  int nFirstLn, nLastLn;

  ComputeVisibleLines(pDC, nFirstLn, nLastLn);

  int nYPos = - nFirstLn * GetCharSize().cy;
  int nXPos = 4 * GetCharSize().cx;
  OnDraw(pDC, nFirstLn, nLastLn,nXPos,nYPos);
}
```

▶ Implement the ComputeVisibleLines function

1. Right-click **CTextView** in ClassView and add **ComputeVisibleLines** as a protected function:

   ```
   void ComputeVisibleLines(CDC* pDC, int& nFirst, int& nLast)
   ```

2. Begin writing the code for the **ComputeVisibleLines** function by getting the number of lines in the **CStringList** as folllows:

   ```
   int nLineCount = GetDocument()->GetLineList()->GetCount();
   ```

3. Get the viewport origin in logical coordinates as follows:

   ```
   CPoint pt = pDC->GetViewportOrg();
   pDC->DPtoLP(&pt,1);
   ```

4. Get the clipping region in logical coordinates as follows:

   ```
   CRect rc;
   pDC->GetClipBox(&rc);
   ```

Lab 4.3: (Optional) Building a Text Viewer

5. Get the line height as follows:

    ```
    CSize CharSize = GetCharSize();
    ```

6. The algorithm for the first visible line accomplishes these points:

    a. Calculates the distance from the top of the viewport to the top of the clipping region.

    b. Divides this distance by the height of a line, giving the number of lines.

    c. Ensures that at least one line will be shown.

    The code is written as follows:

    ```
    nFirst = min(abs((rc.top - pt.y)/CharSize.cy),
            nLineCount-1);
    ```

7. The algorithm for the last visible line accomplishes these points:

    a. Calculates the number of lines that will fit into the clipping region.

    b. Adds that to the starting line.

    c. Adds one more line to make sure that partial lines are displayed.

    d. Ensures that this is less than the total number of lines.

    The code is written as follows:

    ```
    nLast = min(abs(rc.Height())/CharSize.cy + nFirst + 1,
            nLineCount-1);
    ```

8. Save TextView.cpp.

The following sample code shows an example of how your code should look. To copy this code for use in your own projects, see "Lab 4.3.1 ComputeVisibleLines" on the accompanying CD-ROM.

```
void CTextView::ComputeVisibleLines(CDC* pDC, int& nFirst, int& nLast)
{
  int nLineCount = GetDocument()->GetLineList()->GetCount();

  // Get the viewport origin, convert to logical coordinates
  CPoint pt = pDC->GetViewportOrg();
  pDC->DPtoLP(&pt,1);
```

code continued on next page

```
code continued from previous page
    // Get the clipping region, in logical coordinates
    CRect rc;
    pDC->GetClipBox(&rc);

    // Get the logical line height
    CSize CharSize = GetCharSize();

    // Compute the first visible line
    nFirst = min(abs((rc.top - pt.y)/CharSize.cy),
                 nLineCount-1);

    // Compute the last visible line
    nLast = min(abs(rc.Height())/CharSize.cy + nFirst + 1,
                nLineCount-1);
}
```

▶ **Implement the core OnDraw handler**

1. Declare a second **OnDraw** handler in TextView.h as follows:

    ```
    virtual void OnDraw(CDC* pDC, int nFirstLn, int nLastLn,
                        int nXPos = 0, int nYPos = 0);
    ```

2. Define the second **OnDraw** handler in TextView.cpp as follows:

    ```
    void CTextView::OnDraw(CDC* pDC, int nFirstLn, int nLastLn,
                           int nXPos /*= 0*/, int nYPos /*= 0*/)
    ```

3. Select your chosen font into the DC as follows:

    ```
    CFont* pPreviousFont = pDC->SelectObject(GetFont());
    ```

4. Get the size of the font as follows:

    ```
    CSize CharSize = GetCharSize();
    ```

5. Get the string list from the document as follows:

    ```
    CStringList *pLineList = GetDocument()->GetLineList();
    ```

6. You will loop through the lines in pLineList from the first line passed (which will be an index) to the last line passed, drawing the text on the screen and moving down the screen (that is, to lower y-coordinate values). Declare the necessary variables:

   ```
   CString strLine;
   POSITION    pos;
   ```

7. Control the loop as follows:

   ```
   while (nFirstLn <= nLastLn)
   ```

8. Find the item in the list as follows:

   ```
   if( ( pos = pLineList->FindIndex( nFirstLn )) != NULL )
   ```

9. If you have a valid item, copy it to the string and display it as follows:

   ```
   strLine = pLineList->GetAt(pos);
   pDC->TabbedTextOut(nXPos, nYPos, strLine, 0, NULL, 0);
   ```

10. Decrement the y-coordinate and increment the line count as follows:

    ```
    nYPos -= CharSize.cy;
    nFirstLn++;
    ```

11. Back outside the loop, select your font out of the DC:

    ```
    if(pPreviousFont)
    {
        pDC->SelectObject(pPreviousFont);
    }
    ```

12. Save TextView.cpp.

The sample code on the following page shows an example of how your code should look. To copy this code for use in your own projects, see "Lab 4.3.1 core OnDraw" on the accompanying CD-ROM.

MFC Development Using Microsoft Visual C++ 6.0

```
void CTextView::OnDraw(CDC* pDC, int nFirstLn, int nLastLn,
                        int nXPos /*= 0*/, int nYPos /*= 0*/)
{
  // Select specified font
  CFont* pPreviousFont = pDC->SelectObject(GetFont());

  // Needed for height of each line
  CSize CharSize = GetCharSize();

  // Get list of strings from the document
  // and output them to the display context
  CStringList *pLineList = GetDocument()->GetLineList();

  CString strLine;
  POSITION pos;
  while (nFirstLn <= nLastLn)
  {
      if( ( pos = pLineList->FindIndex( nFirstLn )) != NULL )
      {
          strLine = pLineList->GetAt(pos);
          pDC->TabbedTextOut(nXPos, nYPos, strLine, 0, NULL, 0);
          nYPos -= CharSize.cy;
          nFirstLn++;
      }
  }

  // Cleanup and restore original GDI Objects
  if(pPreviousFont)
  {
      pDC->SelectObject(pPreviousFont);
  }
}
```

▶ **Implement OnUpdate**

1. Using ClassWizard, delete **CTextView::OnInitialUpdate** and manually remove the associated code.

2. Using ClassWizard or WizardBar, add **CTextView::OnUpdate**. Edit the code to compute the view metrics as follows:

    ```
    ComputeViewMetrics();
    ```

3. **CScrollView::SetScrollSizes** sets the mapping mode for the scroll view. Because **CTextView::ComputeViewMetrics** uses MM_LOENGLISH for its calculations, you will need to use that mode here. It also sets the scrolling ranges. Get these ranges from the document size:

   ```
   SetScrollSizes( MM_LOENGLISH, GetDocSize());
   ```

4. **CView::OnUpdate** is sent whenever the view window is changed. Invalidate the window so that **CTextView::OnDraw** will be called to appropriately redisplay the text:

   ```
   Invalidate();
   ```

5. Save TextView.cpp.

   The following sample code shows an example of how your code should look. To copy this code for use in your own projects, see "Lab 4.3.1 OnUpdate" on the accompanying CD-ROM.

```
void CTextView::OnUpdate(CView* pSender, LPARAM lHint, CObject* pHint)
{
  ComputeViewMetrics();

  SetScrollSizes(MM_LOENGLISH, GetDocSize());
  Invalidate();
}
```

6. Save TextView.h and TextView.cpp.
7. Build your application.

The solution code for this exercise is located in the folder *<install folder>*\Labs\Ch04\Lab4.3\Ex01\Solution.

Exercise 2: Adding Font Support

Continue with the files you created in Exercise 1 or, if you do not have a starting point for this exercise, the code that forms the basis for this exercise is in *<install folder>*\Labs\Ch04\Lab4.3\Ex02.

In this exercise, you will implement a user interface to **CTextView.m_pFont**.

▶ Add a menu item for Font

1. Open the IDR_TEXTTYPE menu resource.
2. Add a menu between the **View** and **Window** menus. Give it the caption **Font**.
3. Add a menu item below the font menu, giving it the ID **ID_FORMAT_FONT** and the prompt, **Change Font**.
4. Save the file Text.rc.

▶ Add a handler for the menu message

- Use ClassWizard or WizardBar. Add a handler for ID_FORMAT_FONT to **CTextView**, and accept the default **OnFormatFont** function name.

▶ Implement CTextView::OnFormatFont

1. Go to the head of **OnFormatFont**. Get (or create, if it has not yet been created) the current font with **GetFont** as follows:

   ```
   CFont * pFont = GetFont();
   ```

2. Retrieve a LOGFONT structure with the font information as follows:

   ```
   LOGFONT lf;
   pFont->GetObject(sizeof(LOGFONT), &lf);
   ```

3. Use this structure to initialize a common font dialog box as follows:

   ```
   CFontDialog dlg(&lf, CF_SCREENFONTS | CF_INITTOLOGFONTSTRUCT);
   ```

4. Show the dialog box modally:

   ```
   if(dlg.DoModal() == IDOK)
   ```

5. If the user closed the font dialog box with **OK**, delete the current font (remember that this font is selected out of a device context (DC) each time it is selected in, so this deletion is safe):

   ```
   if(m_pFont)
   {
       delete m_pFont;
   }
   ```

6. Construct the new font and initialize it using the LOGFONT structure returned from **CFontDialog** as follows:

```
m_pFont = new CFont;
if(m_pFont)
{
    m_pFont->CreateFontIndirect(&lf);
}
```

7. Finally, you must recalculate all the metrics and invalidate the view's window to redisplay the file using the new font. You already have a function that does this, **OnUpdate**, but it will take some significant amount code to set up the call. The simplest way to accomplish this is to call **CDocument::UpdateAllViews**. Because there is only one view of this document, this will be the equivalent of calling **OnUpdate** directly:

```
GetDocument()->UpdateAllViews(NULL);
```

8. Save TextView.cpp.

The following sample code shows an example of how your code should look. To copy this code for use in your own projects, see "Lab 4.3.2 OnFormatFont" on the accompanying CD-ROM.

```
void CTextView::OnFormatFont()
{
    CFont * pFont = GetFont();

    LOGFONT lf;
    pFont->GetObject(sizeof(LOGFONT), &lf);

    CFontDialog dlg(&lf, CF_SCREENFONTS | CF_INITTOLOGFONTSTRUCT);
```

code continued on next page

```
code continued from previous page
    if(dlg.DoModal() == IDOK)
    {
        if(m_pFont)
        {
            delete m_pFont;
        }

        m_pFont = new CFont;
        if(m_pFont)
        {
            m_pFont->CreateFontIndirect(&lf);
        }

        // This will cause OnUpdate() to be called ensuring
        // that our cached metrics and scrolling get updated
        GetDocument()->UpdateAllViews(NULL);
    }
}
```

▶ **Build and test your application**

- Run your application and open a file. The view class supports scrolling and changes of fonts. Select the **font** option to change the text font.

The solution code for this exercise is located in the folder *<install folder>*\Labs\Ch04\Lab4.3\Ex02\Solution.

Sample Applications

The following table describes the sample applications related to this chapter. These sample applications are located in the folder *<install folder>*\Samples\Ch04.

Sample application subfolder	Description of application
Mdiapp	Shows how document class tracks all views attached to that class.
SDI2VIEWS	An SDI application with two views available. User can toggle between those two views at run time.

table continued on next page

table continued from previous page

Sample application subfolder	Description of application
MDI2VIEWS	Shows how to implement an MDI application with two views of its data. Defaults at startup to one view, and the user can choose another from a menu selection.
MDI2VIEWSB	Similar to MDI2VIEWS, except that the user is asked when the application starts, and when opening a new document, which view to use.
List	Implements an SDI application with its view based on **CListView**. Shows how to populate a report-style list control.
Form	Implemented using **CFormView** as the base class for the view. Also shows how to change text color in an edit box.
Scroll	An SDI application with **CScrollView** as its base class. Shows how to adjust the frame to fit the view. Also shows how converting device points to logical points.
Splitter	An SDI application with a static splitter bar and different views in each pane. **CMainFrame::OnCreateClient** also contains commented source code for a dynamic splitter.
Tmpgraph	An SDI application with a static splitter bar and different views in each pane. Shows the document/view concept of different views of data. Uses persistence. Demonstrates minimal graphing capabilities.
Treewimg	An SDI application that uses **CTreeView** as the base for its view class. Shows how to create a **CImageList** and attach it to a tree control. Also shows how to populate a tree control.
Treelist	An SDI application that shows how to build an application with an interface like Windows Explorer: a vertical splitter and a tree view in its left pane and list view in its right pane.

Self-Check Questions

To see the answers to the Self-Check Questions, see Appendix A.

1. **What is the relationship between views and other framework classes?**

    A. A view is owned by the mainframe object.

    B. A view is embedded in its corresponding document object.

    C. A view is refreshed by the mainframe object.

    D. A view displays the contents of a document object.

2. **How do you enhance an existing application to support a scrolling view?**

    A. By adding code to the **OnInitialUpdate** function

    B. By setting the base class of the view to **CScrollView**

    C. By calling CView::SetScrollSizes

    D. By adding a scrollbar object to the view

3. **What differentiates a dynamic splitter window from a static splitter window?**

    A. Static splitters cannot have different views associated with each pane, whereas dynamic splitters can.

    B. Dynamic splitters have no maximum number of panes, but static splitters are limited to 256 panes.

    C. You must declare a **CDynSplitterWnd** object for a dynamic splitter and a **CSplitterWnd** object for static splitters.

    D. Dynamic splitter windows can be destroyed at run time, whereas static splitter windows cannot.

4. **Which property name-value pairs is set by AppWizard for a form view?**

    A. Style: Popup

    B. Border: None

    C. Titlebar: On

    D. System Modal: On

5. Which class is used as the base class for control views?

    A. CControlView
    B. CCtrlView
    C. CListView
    D. CView

Student Notes:

Chapter 5:
Using Controls

Multimedia

Using ActiveX Controls 233

Communication Between
ActiveX Controls 235

Adding an ActiveX Control to an
Application 236

Lab 5.1 Demonstration 246

Lab 5.2 Demonstration 253

Lab 5.3 Demonstration 268

Controls are interactive objects that you can place on dialog boxes, toolbars, and other windows. Users interact with controls to manipulate and enter data. When you build an application with Microsoft Foundation Class (MFC), you can use the following types of controls.

- Microsoft Windows common controls

    These controls are provided by the Windows operating system. The (MFC) Library encapsulates these controls, so that they can be programmed and used in dialog boxes and other Windows controls.

- Microsoft Internet Explorer 4.0 common controls

    These controls include **CComboBoxEx, CIPAddressCtrl, CMonthCalCtrl, CProgressCtrl,** and **CReBar.**

- Microsoft ActiveX controls

    You can use ActiveX controls in applications for Windows or in HTML pages on the World Wide Web. These controls are reusable and must be loaded into a control container.

- Control classes supplied by the MFC Library

    These classes include **CBitmapButton, CCheckListBox,** and **CDragListBox.**

This chapter describes the procedure for adding controls to an MFC-based application.

Objectives

After completing this chapter, you will be able to:

◆ Add Windows common controls to MFC-based applications.

◆ Add Internet Explorer 4.0 common controls to MFC-based applications.

◆ Add ActiveX controls to MFC-based applications.

◆ Add controls supplied by the MFC Library to MFC-based applications.

Windows Common Controls

Windows common controls are provided by the Windows operating system. These controls are programmable and can be added to dialog boxes and other windows. MFC provides a number of classes to encapsulate Windows common controls.

In this section, you will learn to create Windows common controls, set control attributes, and process notification messages.

MFC Classes for Windows Common Controls

MFC provides a number of control classes that encapsulate Windows common controls. These controls include **CSliderCtrl, CSpinButtonCtrl, CListCtrl, CToolBarCtrl, CStatusBarCtrl, CAnimateCtrl, CHeaderCtrl, CHotKeyCtrl,** and **CRichEditCtrl**. The **CWnd** class is the base class for all these controls.

The following table provides a brief description of some Windows common controls.

Type of control	MFC control class	Description
Edit controls	**CRichEditCtrl**	A window in which the user can enter and edit text. The characters and paragraph in the control can be formatted, and the control can include embedded ActiveX objects.

table continued on next page

table continued from previous page

Type of control	MFC control class	Description
Controls that represent numbers	**CSliderCtrl**	A window containing arrow buttons and a slider, which the user moves to select a value.
	CSpinButtonCtrl	A pair of arrow buttons that the user can click to increment or decrement a value.
Lists	**CListCtrl**	Displays a collection of items, each consisting of an icon and a label, in a manner similar to the right pane of the Windows 95 Explorer.
Toolbars and Status Bars	**CToolBarCtrl**	Provides the functionality of the Windows toolbar common control. Most MFC-based applications use **CToolBar** instead of this class.
	CStatusBarCtrl	A horizontal window usually divided into panes, in which an application can display status information. Most MFC-based applications use **CStatusBar** instead of this class.
Miscellaneous controls	**CAnimateCtrl**	Displays a simple video clip.
	CHotKeyCtrl	Displays a text representation of the key combination the user types into the hot key control. **CHotKeyCtrl** is often used in dialog boxes that prompt the user to assign a hot key. You must program the control to retrieve the values describing the hot key and associate the hot key with a window or thread.
	CHeaderCtrl	Displays titles or labels for columns.

For information about these controls, search for "Windows common controls" in MSDN Library Visual Studio 6.0.

Creating Windows Common Controls

MFC provides classes to wrap common controls. There are two ways you can create a common control in an MFC-based application:

- Use code to create the control by creating an instance of the MFC control class and then calling the object's **Create** function.
- Use the dialog editor to add the control to a dialog box.

▶ **To create a Windows common control object by using code**

1. Create an instance of the control in a dialog box or frame-window object.
2. Call the control's **Create** member function in the **OnInitDialog** function for dialog boxes and in the **OnCreate** function for frame windows.

The following example shows the declaration of a **CEdit** object and a **CSpinButtonCtrl** object:

```
class CSpinEditDlg : public CDialog
{
  protected:
    CEdit m_wndCEdit; // Embedded edit object
    CSpinButtonCtrl m_wndCSpinButton; // Embedded Spin Button object
  public:
    Virtual BOOL OnInitDialog();
};
```

The sample code on the following page creates an edit control and a spin button control. To copy this code for use in your own projects, see "Creating a Spin Button Control" on the accompanying CD-ROM.

Chapter 5: Using Controls

```
//Samples\CH05\SpinButton
//Creates a spin button and its buddy window
BOOL CSpinEditDlg::OnInitDialog()
{
 CDialog::OnInitDialog();
 CRect rect1(10, 30, 100, 55);
 CRect rect2(101, 30, 110, 55);
 m_wndCEdit.Create(WS_CHILD | WS_VISIBLE | WS_TABSTOP |
    ES_AUTOHSCROLL | WS_BORDER, rect1, this, IDC_BUDDY);
 m_wndCSpinButton.Create(WS_CHILD | WS_VISIBLE | WS_TABSTOP |
    ES_AUTOHSCROLL | WS_BORDER|UDS_SETBUDDYINT,
 rect2, this, IDC_SPIN_BUTTON);
 m_wndCSpinButton.SetFocus();
 m_wndCSpinButton.SetBuddy(&m_wndCEdit);
 m_wndCSpinButton.SetRange(0,100);
 m_pCStaticCm = (CStatic*)GetDlgItem(IDC_LENGTH_CM);
 m_pMph=(CProgressCtrl*)GetDlgItem(IDC_MPH);
 m_pKmph=(CProgressCtrl*)GetDlgItem(IDC_KMPH);
 m_pMph->SetRange(0,200);
 m_pKmph->SetRange(0,200);
 m_pMph->SetStep(1);
 m_pKmph->SetStep(1);
 SetDlgItemInt(IDC_BUDDY,m_wndCSpinButton.GetPos());
 return TRUE;
}
```

In the previous sample code, the **OnInitDialog** function sets up two rectangles. The first rectangle is for the edit control and the second is for the spin button control. Calling the **Create** function creates the edit control and the spin button control as shown in the following example:

```
m_wndCEdit.Create(WS_CHILD|WS_VISIBLE|WS_TABSTOP|ES_AUTOHSCROLL|
    WS_BORDER, rect1, this, IDC_EDIT1);

m_wndCSpinButton.Create(WS_CHILD|WS_VISIBLE|WS_TABSTOP|ES_AUTOHSCROLL|
    WS_BORDER|UDS_SETBUDDYINT, rect2, this, IDC_BUTTON1);
```

The style UDS_SETBUDDYINT causes the spin button control to set the text of the buddy window when the user clicks the spin button. A buddy window is an edit control that displays the value of the current position of the spin button control. You associate an edit control with a spin button control by using the **SetBuddy** function.

223

After you create the object, call the **SetFocus** function to set focus to the spin button control.

▶ **To create a Windows common control by using the dialog editor**

1. Open the application in which you want to add the common control.
2. Invoke the dialog editor.
3. Insert a dialog box by using the **Insert** command on the **Resource** menu.
4. Drag the control you want to add from the **Controls** palette onto the dialog box. This adds the specifications for the control to the dialog box resource.

The framework creates the controls when you construct a dialog object and make a call to its **Create** function or to its **DoModal** function.

Setting Windows Common Control Attributes

All Windows common controls have a set of attributes. The attributes for a control depend on the type of control. For example, the spin button control has a range attribute, which you can set by using the **SetRange** member function as shown in the following example:

```
m_wndCSpinbutton.SetRange(0,10);
```

The **GetRange** member function retrieves the integer values for the range set for the spin button control, as shown in the following example:

```
m_wndCSpinbutton.GetRange(nLower,nUpper);
```

The **SetBuddy** member function sets the buddy window for a spin button control that has been created by using the UDS_SETBUDDYINT style. The following example sets the buddy window of the spin button control **m_wndCSpinbutton** to the edit control **m_wndCEdit**:

```
m_wndCSpinbutton.SetBuddy(&m_wndCEdit);
```

Processing Notification Messages from Windows Common Controls

Applications depend on messages to determine what course of action to take. Whenever an event occurs, such as clicking a button, a message is sent from the control to its parent window. The parent window can be a frame window or a dialog box. All controls are child windows. With the exception of Windows 3.*x* controls, controls send their messages as WM_NOTIFY messages. The **OnNotify** function of the parent window handles these messages. **OnNotify** dispatches the notification message to **OnCmdMsg** for handling in message maps. The message-map entry for handling notifications is ON_NOTIFY.

The following example shows the overridden **OnNotify** function that handles the WM_NOTIFY message:

```
BOOL CSpinEditDlg::OnNotify(WPARAM wParam, LPARAM lParam,
    LRESULT* pResult)
{
  if(wParam==IDC_SPIN_BUTTON)
  {
      ...
      m_Pos=m_wndCSpinButton.GetPos();
      ...
  }
  return CDialog::OnNotify(wParam, lParam, pResult);
}
```

The first parameter to **OnNotify**, wParam, identifies the control that sent the message. The second parameter is a pointer to a notification structure NMHDR. The NMHDR structure contains a handle to the control sending the message, the identifier of the control, and a notification code that is specific to a control type.

Internet Explorer 4.0 Common Controls

Internet Explorer 4.0 common controls include the IP address control, progress control, extended combo box control, month calendar control, and the rebar control.

In this section, you will learn to create Internet Explorer 4.0 common controls, set control attributes, and process notification messages.

MFC Classes for Internet Explorer 4.0 Controls

MFC implements Internet Explorer 4.0 common controls through the classes **CIPAddressCtrl**, **CProgressCtrl**, **CComboBoxEx**, **CMonthCalCtrl**, and **CReBar**.

CIPAddressCtrl Class

The **CIPAddressCtrl** class implements the IP address control. This control is available only to applications running under Microsoft Internet Explorer 4.0 and later. **CIPAddressCtrl** is implemented in version 4.71 and later of Comctl32.dll.

The IP address control is similar to the edit control. It enables you to enter and edit an Internet Protocol (IP) address. IP addresses consist of four three-digit fields. Each field contains zero-based numbers. The IP control enables the user to enter numeric text in each field. When three digits have been entered in a given field, focus automatically moves to the next field. However, if fewer than three digits are required by the application, the user can enter the value and press the RIGHT ARROW key to move to the next field. The default range for each field is 0 to 255. The following illustration shows a sample IP Address control.

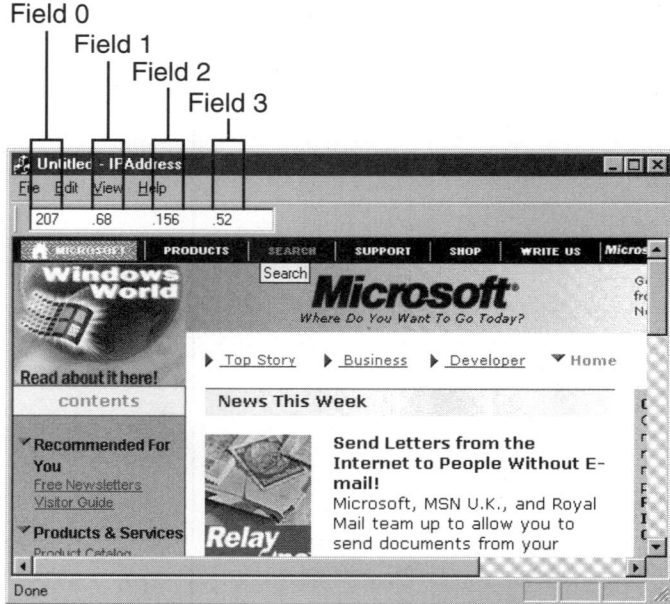

CProgressCtrl Class

The **CProgressCtrl** class implements the progress control, which is available only to applications running under Windows 95 and Windows NT version 3.51 and later.

A progress control is used to indicate the progress of a lengthy operation. It consists of a rectangle that is gradually filled, from left to right, with the system highlight color as an operation progresses. The following illustration shows a sample progress control.

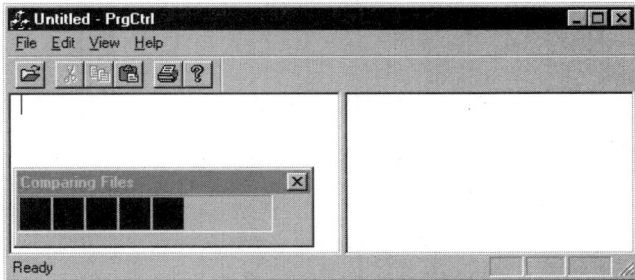

A progress control has a range, which represents the entire duration of the operation, and a current position, which represents the progress the application has made toward completing the operation. Both range and current position are represented as signed integers.

CComboBoxEx Class

The **CComboBoxEx** class extends the combo box control. It provides support for image lists. The advantage of using **CComboBoxEx** is that you do not have to implement your own image drawing code. **CComboBoxEx** can access images from an image list. The following illustration shows a sample combo box control.

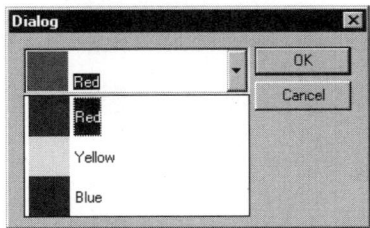

CMonthCalCtrl Class

The **CMonthCalCtrl** class implements the functionality of the month calendar control. The month calendar control provides a calendar interface from which the user can select a date. The following illustration shows a sample month calendar control.

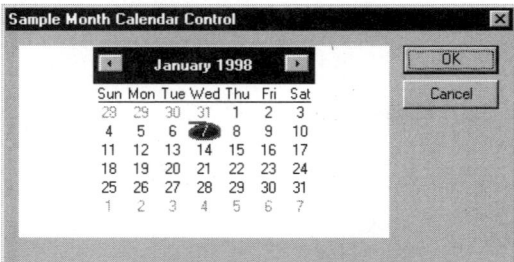

You can apply a variety of styles when you create the calendar control object. The control can display more than one month and can indicate special dates in bold.

CReBar Class

The **CReBar** class implements the rebar control. Rebars act as containers for child windows and other controls, such as toolbars and dialog bars. For information about rebars, see "Using Rebars" on page 94 in Chapter 3, "Enhancing the User Interface."

Creating Internet Explorer 4.0 Controls

To create any of the Internet Explorer 4.0 common controls, except the rebar control, you can use either the dialog editor or code. To create the rebar control, you must use code.

▶ **To insert an Internet Explorer 4.0 common control by using the dialog editor**

1. Open the application in which the control is to be added.
2. Create a dialog box.
3. Add the control to the dialog box.

▶ **To create an Internet Explorer 4.0 common control by using code**

1. Embed the Internet Explorer 4.0 common control object in a frame-window object or dialog box as shown in the following example:

   ```
   class CProgressDlg : public CDialog
   {
       .....
   protected:
       CProgressCtrl m_wndProgCtrl;
       .....
   };
   ```

2. Call the control's **Create** member function in the **OnCreate** function for frame windows or the **OnInitDialog** function for dialog boxes as shown in the following example:

   ```
   BOOL CProgressDlg::OnInitDialog()
   {
       CDialog::OnInitDialog();

   m_wndProgCtrl.Create(WS_CHILD|WS_VISIBLE,CRect(0,0,200,40),this,
       IDC_PROGRESS);
       ....
       return TRUE;
   }
   ```

Setting Internet Explorer 4.0 Control Attributes

Like Windows common controls, Internet Explorer 4.0 common controls possess attributes, which you can set by using member functions. Each control has a specific set of attributes. The class that implements the control provides functions that you invoke to set these attributes.

For example, a progress control has attributes that indicate range and a current position. The range specifies the duration of the operation, and the current position represents the progress made by the application toward completing the operation. The **CProgressCtrl** class provides functions that you invoke to set these attributes.

To initialize the progress control, call the **SetRange** and the **SetStep** functions in the **InInitDialog** function of your dialog class. The following example sets the range of the progress control **m_pProgCtrl** between 1 and 100, and sets the step increment for the progress control to one:

```
BOOL CProgressDlg::OnInitDialog()
{
  CDialog::OnInitDialog();
  m_pProgCtrl=(CProgressCtrl*)GetDlgItem(IDC_PROGRESS);
  m_pProgCtrl->SetRange(1,100);
  m_pProgCtrl->SetStep(1);
  return TRUE;
}
```

To advance the progress control by the step increment and redraw the control, call the **StepIt** function. The following example determines the range that has been set for the progress control and advances the control until the upper limit is reached:

```
int upper, lower;
m_pProgCtrl->GetRange(lower, upper);
for(; m_pProgCtrl->StepIt() < upper - 1;);
```

Processing Notification Messages from Internet Explorer 4.0 Common Controls

Internet Explorer 4.0 common controls send notification messages to their parent windows just as other controls do. The notification messages generated are specific to a control. The following table lists some of the notification messages generated by Internet Explorer 4.0 common controls.

Control class	Notification message	Description
CMonthCalCtrl	MCN_GETDAYSTATE	Requests information about which dates should be displayed in bold.
	MCN_SELCHANGE	Notifies the parent window that the selected date or range of the date has been changed.
	MCN_SELECT	Notifies the parent window that an explicit date selection has been made.

table continued on next page

table continued from previous page

Control class	Notification message	Description
CComboBoxEx	CBEN_BEGINEDIT	Notifies the parent window when the user activates the drop-down list or clicks the control's edit box.
	CBEN_ENDEDIT	Sent when the user has concluded an operation within the edit box or has selected an item from the control's drop-down list.
	CBEN_INSERTITEM	Sent when a new item has been inserted in the control.
	CBEN_DELETEITEM	Sent when an item has been deleted.
CIPAddressCtrl	IPN_FIELDCHANGED	Sent when the user tabs from one IP address field to another.
CProgressCtrl	NM_OUTOFMEMORY	Sent when the control could not complete an operation because there is not enough memory available.
CReBar		Notification messages are processed for the individual controls the rebar contains.

ActiveX Controls

An ActiveX control is a reusable software component that supports a wide variety of functionality and can be customized to fit many software needs. An ActiveX control can be developed and reused for a variety of tasks, such as database access, data monitoring, or graphing.

This section compares ActiveX controls and common controls and explains how you can use an ActiveX control in an MFC-based application.

ActiveX Controls vs. Custom Controls

Before the ActiveX technology was developed, Windows programmers designed and used custom controls when they needed to extend the set of dialog box controls.

Custom Controls

Custom controls have several limitations:

- No cross-platform support

    A custom control can be used only on and by the platform for which it was developed.

- No interaction with the container's user interface
- Not based on a standard program interface

ActiveX Controls

ActiveX controls are designed to overcome the limitations of custom controls and greatly extend a control's usability. The benefits of ActiveX controls include:

- 32-bit support
- Cross-platform capabilities

    With little or no modification, ActiveX controls can be used by environments other than the Windows operating system. This is limited by the capabilities of the target system, such as the availability and capability of the graphical interface, and the support it provides for OLE 2.0.

- Support for Automation
- Ability to send event notifications to the container
- Standardized interfaces that allow unrelated components to interconnect, much like standardized jacks on a component stereo system

Using Automation

Automation technology enables you to programmatically control objects that are defined outside the application that uses the objects. Automation enables programmability by exposing properties and methods of objects.

Before you implement an ActiveX control, you should understand some of the features of ActiveX controls. ActiveX controls have properties and methods that are exposed to the application in which they are contained, and can trigger events that notify the container application when an action occurs. When you develop an ActiveX control, you define the properties, methods, and events that the control will support.

To see the demonstration "Using ActiveX Controls," see the accompanying CD-ROM.

Properties

Properties are values that are maintained by the control and that change the appearance or behavior of an ActiveX control. You can programmatically set and retrieve properties of a control. Examples of control properties are background color and the property-enabled state.

In addition to properties exposed by a control, the ActiveX control container can expose a set of ambient properties to the control. These properties maintain the characteristics or state of the container itself, such as its background color. A control can use these properties to blend into the container's look and feel. For example, a control can set its own background color to the background color of the container.

Methods

Methods are actions that the control can perform at the request of the container. For example, a calculator control can have a method called **Calculate** that uses the current properties to compute an answer.

Events

Events are notifications that the control can send to an ActiveX control container in response to user interaction or some other occurrence. For example, when a user clicks the mouse on a control, the control sends a **Click** event notification to the container.

Type Library

For a container to use an ActiveX control, the container must know what properties and methods the control supports. The control's type library provides this information. A type library file contains prototyping information about an object's properties and methods. Using the prototyping information, ClassWizard generates a wrapper class that contains member functions for each method and property.

When you use ControlWizard to create an ActiveX control project, an .ocx file and an .odl (Object Description Language) file are created. The .ocx file is the ActiveX control and the .odl file is a text file that provides the specification for the interface that an object supports, including its properties, methods, and events. When you compile the control, the information from the .odl file is placed in a binary type-library (.tlb) file to provide the control with a common interface for many different kinds of applications.

Applications and browsers can access the type library to determine the interfaces, properties, methods, and events that a control supports.

ActiveX Control Containers

An ActiveX control is implemented as an in-process (DLL) server that you can use in any control container. A control container is a special type of application that supports embedding of ActiveX controls and can receive and process event notifications from the control.

For each embedded control, the control container creates an associated client site object through which the control and container interact. The control container interacts with the control through exposed methods and properties. The control interacts with the container by firing events to notify the container that an action has occurred.

The requirements of a control container are extensive and complex. MFC supplies complete control container support, which hides much of the complexity from you.

ActiveX Control and Container Communication

When you use an ActiveX control within a control container, two types of communication are exposed:

- Communication from the container to the ActiveX control
- Communication from the ActiveX control to the container

Communication from the Container to the ActiveX Control

The control container communicates with the ActiveX control by setting properties and invoking methods of the control. In effect, the container calls the appropriate functions in the control. An ActiveX control provides the **IDispatch** interface to handle properties and methods. **IDispatch** exposes objects, methods, and properties to a container application by providing member functions such as **Invoke**. **Invoke** provides access to properties and methods exposed by an object.

Communication from the ActiveX Control to the Container

The ActiveX control communicates with the control container by sending event notifications to the control container. A container provides a dispatch interface to handle events.

To see the animation "Communication Between ActiveX Controls," see the accompanying CD-ROM.

Implementing an ActiveX Control Container

MFC provides many features that hide the complexity of creating container applications from you. However, creating a useful application that acts as a control container is a fairly complicated process. Consider a word processor, for example. Providing control container support is only one issue. You must also consider the word processor text formatting, text wrapping, merging text with the control, and user interaction with the control. These are complex issues, beyond simply allowing controls to be embedded.

You can implement a control container in three ways:

1. Use MFC AppWizard to create your application and, in Step 3, select **ActiveX Control**.
2. Manually add support by modifying your application to include Afxdisp.h in the Stdafx.h file, and update the derived **CWinApp** class **InitInstance** function by making a call to **AfxEnableControlContainer**, as shown in the following example.

```
// CContainerApp initialization
BOOL CContainerApp::InitInstance()
{
    AfxEnableControlContainer();
...
}
```

3. Use the Add ActiveX Control Containment component in the Components and Controls Gallery.

To use an ActiveX control in your control container application, you must first add the control to your application's project. In Microsoft Visual C++, you use the Components and Controls Gallery to add an ActiveX control to a project. The ActiveX control is then placed in the Controls palette, where you can use it to create an instance of the control on a form.

Using an ActiveX Control in an MFC-based Application

To use an ActiveX control in an MFC-based application, you follow these general steps:

1. Register the control.
2. Add the control to the project.
3. Add the control to the application.
4. Access the control's methods and properties.
5. Add event handlers for the control.

These steps are described in more detail below. The steps assume that you are using an ActiveX control that was built with the MFC ActiveX ControlWizard. An ActiveX control built this way has type information embedded in the .ocx file, and the MFC class **COleControl** provides much of the control's essential functionality. To see the demonstration "Adding an ActiveX Control to an Application," see the accompanying CD-ROM.

Registering the Control

If the control was built on another computer, you will need to register the control before you start Microsoft Visual Studio. Place the control in the appropriate folder, such as C:\Windows\System, and then run Regsvr32.exe and pass the control file name as a parameter to register the control.

Adding the Control to the Project

1. Start Visual Studio and load your application.

    If you will use the control directly on the application, set your application type to be a dialog-based application or an SDI or MDI application with its view class derived from **CFormView**.

    If you will use the control in one of your application's dialog boxes, it does not matter what type of application you build.

2. Locate the control in the Components and Controls Gallery and add it to the project.

    Visual Studio reads the control's type information and builds a wrapper class to expose the control's properties, methods, and events. The wrapper class is then inserted into the project in the usual manner, with an implementation and a header file.

    For example, adding the **Clock** control to an MFC project adds two files, Clock.cpp and Clock.h, to the project. The **Clock** control can be found in *<install folder>*\Samples\Ch06\Clock. The following sample code shows the contents of Clock.h. To copy this code for use in your own projects, see "Adding the Control to the Project" on the accompanying CD-ROM.

```
//Samples\CH06\Clock
//Clock.h - header file

class CClock : public CWnd
{
protected:
  DECLARE_DYNCREATE(CClock)
public:
  CLSID const& GetClsid()
  {
      static CLSID const clsid
          = { 0x6eb850a3, 0x263c, 0x11cf,
              { 0xa1, 0x51, 0x0, 0xaa, 0x0, 0x37, 0x4d, 0xd8 } };
      return clsid;
  }
```

code continued on next page

code continued from previous page

```cpp
    virtual BOOL Create(LPCTSTR lpszClassName,
        LPCTSTR lpszWindowName, DWORD dwStyle,
        const RECT& rect,
        CWnd* pParentWnd, UINT nID,
        CCreateContext* pContext = NULL)
            { return CreateControl(GetClsid(), lpszWindowName,
                        dwStyle, rect, pParentWnd, nID); }

    BOOL Create(LPCTSTR lpszWindowName, DWORD dwStyle,
        const RECT& rect, CWnd* pParentWnd, UINT nID,
        CFile* pPersist = NULL, BOOL bStorage = FALSE,
        BSTR bstrLicKey = NULL)
            { return CreateControl(GetClsid(), lpszWindowName,
                        dwStyle, rect, pParentWnd, nID,
                    pPersist, bStorage, bstrLicKey); }
// Attributes

public:
    short GetAlarmHour();
    void SetAlarmHour(short);
    short GetAlarmMinute();
    void SetAlarmMinute(short);
    short GetAlarmType();
    void SetAlarmType(short);
    CString GetAlarmSound();
    void SetAlarmSound(LPCTSTR);
    CString GetAlarmCommand();
    void SetAlarmCommand(LPCTSTR);
    BOOL GetAlarmSet();
    void SetAlarmSet(BOOL);
    BOOL Get_AlarmSet();
    void Set_AlarmSet(BOOL);
    OLE_COLOR GetBackColor();
    void SetBackColor(OLE_COLOR);

// Operations
public:
    void SetAlarmTime(short hour, short nNewValue);
    void TestAlarm();
    void AboutBox();
};
```

Adding the Control to the Application

You can use an ActiveX control directly on the application or in the application's dialog box. If you add a control to a dialog box, you can size the control and set design-time properties as needed. Use ClassWizard to add a variable to the class that contains the dialog box. For instance, in an SDI application whose view class is derived from **CFormView**, add a member variable to the application's view class. The following illustration shows the addition of a member variable of type **CClock**.

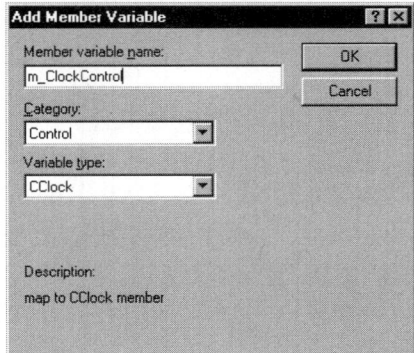

Accessing the Control's Methods and Properties

Once you have added the control to your application, you can write code to access the control's methods and properties.

The following example code sets the **AlarmHour** property of the **Clock** control:

    m_ClockControl.SetAlarmHour(10);

The following example code retrieves the **AlarmHour** property of the **Clock** control:

    short hours = m_ClockControl.GetAlarmHour();

To set a parameterized property, controls typically expose a method that accepts multiple arguments. For example, the **Clock** control provides the **SetAlarmTime** method, which takes two arguments. This method sets the parameterized property **AlarmTime**. The following example invokes the **SetAlarmTime** method:

    m_ClockControl.SetAlarmTime(10, 23);

The control's methods, like its properties, are member functions of the wrapper class that Visual Studio created from the control's type library. The following example tests the alarm and sets the command to be executed when the alarm triggers:

```
m_ClockControl.TestAlarm();
m_ClockControl.SetAlarmCommand("calc.exe");
```

Adding Event Handlers for the Control

Use ClassWizard to add event handlers for events the control fires. On the **Message Maps** tab in the **ClassWizard** dialog box, set the **Class name** list box to the class that contains the ActiveX control. Set the **Object IDs** list box to the ActiveX control. The events associated with the control will be displayed in the **Messages** dialog box. Add a function to receive that event, just as you would add a command handler. The following illustration shows the **Messages** dialog box.

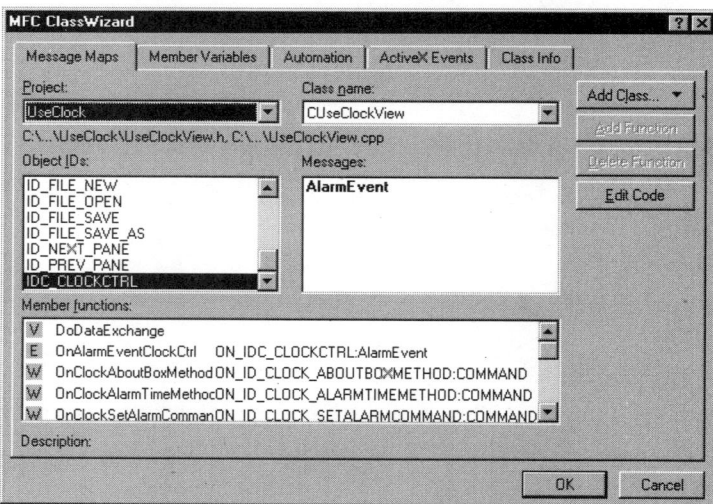

ClassWizard handles events differently than messages. ClassWizard inserts an event sink map in the class, with an entry for each event handler you install using ClassWizard, as shown in the following example:

```
BEGIN_EVENTSINK_MAP(CUseClockView, CFormView)
  ON_EVENT(CUseClockView, IDC_CLOCKCTRL, 1,
           OnAlarmEventClockCtrl, VTS_NONE)
END_EVENTSINK_MAP()
```

Write the event handler code as needed for the control:

```
void CUseClockView::OnAlarmEventClockCtrl()
{
  MessageBeep(-1);
  MessageBox("The control has fired its alarm event!");
}
```

For a complete application that uses the **Clock** control and shows how to access all its methods, properties, and events, see the sample application UseClock, which is located in the folder *<install folder>*Samples\Ch06\UseClock.

Using ActiveX Controls on the Internet

Many of the ActiveX controls that you create and use in MFC can be used on Web pages. You can use Microsoft FrontPage 98 to create Web applications with controls embedded in them.

Performance Issues

When selecting or creating ActiveX controls for use on the Internet, you must consider whether the control is suitable for the environment. The size of an ActiveX control dramatically affects its usability and performance on a Web page. Consider the size of the sample MFC-based **Clock** control found in *<install folder>*\Samples\ Ch06\Clock. A release version of the **Clock** control is about 30 KB. There are two DLLs required of all MFC-based applications or components: Mfc42.dll and Msvcrt.dll. Therefore, the size of the **Clock** control and its auxiliary files is approximately 1.2 MB—a large application to download from a Web page.

Note The sizes specified here are uncompressed. Microsoft CAB compression typically reduces file sizes by half.

Fortunately, the files that need to be downloaded for a specific control usually are not this large. The MFC DLLs will already be present on any computer using Internet Explorer 3.0 or later. If they are not present because the user has another browser installed, then your Web page must download the MFC DLLs. For information about how to do this, search for "Internet First Steps: Upgrading an Existing ActiveX Control" in MSDN Library Visual Studio 6.0.

Modifying ActiveX Controls for the Internet

When you use an ActiveX control on a Web page, it should download quickly and be as small as possible. For information about how to make your control small and fast, search for "ActiveX Controls: Optimization" in MSDN Library Visual Studio 6.0.

If your control has large amounts of persistent data, such as images or video data, you can improve its downloading times by downloading the data asynchronously. You can add this feature to your control in Step 2 of the MFC ActiveX ControlWizard by clicking the **Advanced** button and choosing **Loads Properties Asynchronously**. The manual process for adding asynchronous downloading to a control's properties is complex and is beyond the scope of this course.

Using the Active Template Library (ATL)

You can also use the ATL COM AppWizard to build ActiveX controls. This method requires more manual programming than creating controls using ControlWizard. However, you can build a much smaller, faster control that has only the components it needs. For information about building ActiveX controls using the ATL COM AppWizard, search for "Using the ATL COM AppWizard" in MSDN Library Visual Studio 6.0.

Controls Supplied by MFC

Apart from Windows common controls, Internet Explorer 4.0 common controls, and ActiveX controls, MFC provides the following three controls that you can use in your applications:

- **CBitmapButton**

  Bitmap buttons are controls that are labeled with bitmapped images instead of text.

- **CCheckListBox**

  Check list boxes are similar to list boxes, but each item in the list has a check box next to it, which can be selected or cleared.

- **CDragListBox**

  Drag list boxes are similar to list boxes, with the additional capability of allowing the user to order the items in the list by dragging them to change their positions.

This section describes how to create and handle notification messages from a bitmap button.

Adding a Bitmap Button to an Application

The **CBitmapButton** class implements the bitmap button. Objects created from the **CBitmapButton** class can contain four images, which correspond to the four states of the button: up, down, focused, and disabled. Only the bitmap for the up state is required. The following illustration shows a bitmap button on a dialog bar.

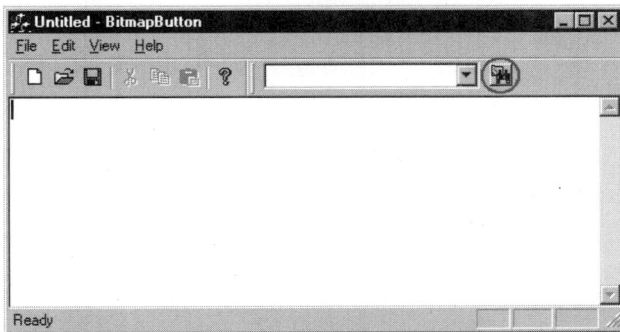

You can create **CBitmapButton** controls by calling either the **Create** function or the **AutoLoad** function.

▶ **To add a bitmap button control by using Create**

1. Create a bitmap image for the button. You can create additional images for the button, in case you want to display a different image for each state.

2. Declare a **CBitmapButton** object in the mainframe class.

3. In the **OnCreate** function of the mainframe class, call the **Create** function to create the bitmap control and attach it to the **CBitmapButton** object as shown in the following example:

   ```
   m_wndBitmapButton.Create("",BS_OWNERDRAW|WS_VISIBLE,
               CRect(200,0,232,32),&m_wndDlgBar,ID_FINDTEXT);
   ```

4. After the bitmap button is constructed, call the **LoadBitmaps** member function to load the bitmap resources as shown in the following example:

   ```
   m_wndBitmapButton.LoadBitmaps(IDB_FINDU);
   ```

▶ **To add a bitmap button control in a dialog bar by using AutoLoad**

1. In the mainframe class, declare a **CBitmapButton** object.
2. Using the dialog editor, create a dialog bar and add a command button to it. Position the command button where you want the bitmap button to appear. Set the command button's style to owner draw by using the properties dialog box.
3. Set the button's caption (for example, IDB_RED).
4. Create a bitmap image for the button. You can create additional images for the button, in case you want to display a different image for each state.
5. In the properties dialog box for each image, assign each image an ID.

   The ID for each image which represents a state of the bitmap button, is assigned by taking the caption of the command button created in step 2, and appending one of the letters "U," "D," "F," or "X" to it to indicate the state that the image represents.

   The following table lists the letters to be appended while assigning IDs to the images that represent the states of a bitmap button:

Letter	State	Example
U	Up	"IDB_REDU"
D	Down	"IDB_REDD"
F	Focused	"IDB_REDF"
X	Disabled	"IDB_REDX"

   When assigning IDs to the images, make sure that the IDs are within double quotes; otherwise, the image will fail to load.

6. Call the **CBitmapButton** object's **AutoLoad** function, using as parameters the button's control ID and the address of the dialog bar as shown in the following example:

   ```
   m_wndBitmapButton1.AutoLoad(ID_COLORS_RED,&m_wndDlgBar);
   ```

   In this example, ID_COLORS_RED is the name of the button.

Processing Notification Messages from Controls Supplied by MFC

Bitmap buttons generate the same notification messages as control buttons do. Possible message-map entries include ON_BN_CLICKED and ON_BN_DOUBLECLICKED.

▶ **To handle notification messages from a bitmap button on a dialog bar**

1. Add derived object message-map entries to the class in which the bitmap-button messages are to be handled. This could be the mainframe class or the view class as shown in the following example:

   ```
   BEGIN_MESSAGE_MAP(CBitmapButtonView, CEditView)
       //{{AFX_MSG_MAP(CBitmapButtonView)
       ....
       ON_BN_CLICKED(ID_FINDTEXT,OnBnClicked)
   END_MESSAGE_MAP()
   ```

2. Add message-handler functions to the class in which the bitmap-button messages are being handled.

Notification messages from a bitmap-button on a dialog bar can also be handled in the view, as shown in the following example:

```
void CBitmapButtonView::OnBnClicked()
{
  if(!m_Text.IsEmpty())
  {
      OnFindNext(m_Text,TRUE,TRUE);
  }
}
```

The function **OnBnClicked** is invoked in response to the message ON_BN_CLICKED. You must add the following message-map entry in the message map of the view class:

```
ON_BN_CLICKED(ID_FINDTEXT,OnBnClicked)
```

The function invokes the **OnFindNext** function to search the view for the text contained in m_Text. If m_Text is empty, no search occurs.

> **Note** If the bitmap button is part of a dialog box, add the message-map entry and the message-handler to the dialog object.

Lab 5.1: Creating Controls Dynamically

In this lab, you will create a bitmap button control dynamically.

To see the demonstration "Lab 5.1 Demonstration," see the accompanying CD-ROM.

Estimated time to complete this lab: **30 minutes**

To complete the exercises in this lab, you must have the required software. For detailed information about the labs and setup for the labs, see "Labs" in "About This Course."

The code that forms the starting point for this lab is located in the folder *<install folder>*\Labs\Ch05\Lab5.1\Ex01.

The solution code for this lab is located in the folder *<install folder>*\Labs\Ch05\Lab5.1\Ex01\Solution.

Objectives

After completing this lab, you will be able to:

- Create the resources to support a bitmap button control.
- Create a bitmap button control dynamically.
- Handle the BN_CLICKED notification message sent by the bitmap button control.

Prerequisites

Before working on this lab, you should be familiar with the following:

- Combo boxes
- Dialog bars
- Rebars

Exercises

The following exercise provides practice working with the concepts and techniques covered in this chapter:

- Exercise 1: Creating a Bitmap Button Control Dynamically

    In this exercise, you will create a bitmap button control dynamically and handle the BN_CLICKED notification message sent by the control.

Exercise 1: Creating a Bitmap Button Control Dynamically

The code that forms the starting point for this exercise is in *<install folder>*\Labs\Ch05\Lab5.1\Ex01.

In this exercise, you will create a bitmap button control dynamically and handle the BN_CLICKED notification message sent by the control. You will create a button that will allow the user to search for a string in a document.

▶ **Create an ID for the bitmap button control**

1. Use ResourceView to open the String table folder.
2. Open the properties window by double-clicking **String table**.
3. Display the properties for the blank line at the end of the String table resource. Set **ID** to ID_BITMAPBUTTON and **Caption** to Search string\nSearch.
4. Save the file BitmapButton.rc.

▶ **Create the dialog bar resources**

1. Use ResourceView to insert a new dialog resource.
2. Expand the Dialog icon and click **IDD_DIALOG1**.
3. Delete both the **OK** and **Cancel** buttons.
4. Open the **Dialog Properties** dialog box.
5. On the **General** tab, clear the caption.
6. On the **Styles** tab, set **Style** to Child and **Border** to None.
7. Resize the dialog box to 266 by 18 pixels.
8. Draw a combo box from the position 2,1 sized to 146 by 12 pixels.

9. On the **Styles** tab, set **Type** to Dropdown and **Owner draw** to No. Click **Vertical Scroll**.
10. Save BitmapButton.rc.

▶ Add a protected variable to CMainFrame class

In this procedure, you will create a **CReBar** object.

- Right-click **CMainFrame** in ClassView and add a protected variable as follows:

  ```
  CReBar m_wndReBar;
  ```

▶ Create a bitmap button

1. Open the file MainFrm.h and create a **CBitmapButton** object in the public attributes section as follows:

   ```
   CBitmapButton m_ctlBitmapButton;
   ```

2. Open the file MainFrm.cpp and declare a **CDialogBar** object after the declaration of the status line indicators as follows:

   ```
   CDialogBar m_wndDialogBar;
   ```

3. In the **OnCreate** function, call the **CDialogBar::Create** function using the data member m_wndDialogBar. Place the code after the call to **CToolBar::CreateEx** as follows:

   ```
   if (!m_wndDialogBar.Create(this, IDD_DIALOG1, CBRS_ALIGN_TOP,
       AFX_IDW_DIALOGBAR))
   {
       TRACE0("Failed to create dialogbar\n");
       return -1;      // fail to create
   }
   ```

4. Create the bitmap button control as follows:

   ```
   m_ctlBitmapButton.Create("Search",WS_CHILD | WS_VISIBLE | BS_OWNERDRAW,
       CRect(230,3,262,32),&m_wndDialogBar,ID_BITMAPBUTTON);
   ```

5. Call the **LoadBitmaps** member function to load the bitmap resources after the bitmap button is constructed as follows:

   ```
   m_ctlBitmapButton.LoadBitmaps( IDB_BITMAP1,IDB_BITMAP2,0,0);
   ```

Lab 5.1: Creating Controls Dynamically

6. Create a **CReBar** object and add controls to it using the **AddBar** function as follows:

```
if (!m_wndReBar.Create(this) ||
    !m_wndReBar.AddBar(&m_wndToolBar) ||
    !m_wndReBar.AddBar(&m_wndDialogBar))
{
    TRACE0("Failed to create rebar\n");
    return -1;      // fail to create
}
```

The following sample code shows an example of how your code should look. To copy this code for use in your own projects, see "Lab 5.1.1 CMainFrame::OnCreate" on the accompanying CD-ROM.

```
int CMainFrame::OnCreate(LPCREATESTRUCT lpCreateStruct)
{
  if (CFrameWnd::OnCreate(lpCreateStruct) == -1)
      return -1;
      if (!m_wndToolBar.CreateEx(this) ||
          m_wndToolBar.LoadToolBar(IDR_MAINFRAME))
  {
      TRACE0("Failed to create toolbar\n");
      return -1;      // fail to create
  }

  if (!m_wndDialogBar.Create(this, IDD_DIALOG1, CBRS_ALIGN_TOP,
      AFX_IDW_DIALOGBAR))
  {
      TRACE0("Failed to create dialogbar\n");
      return -1;      // fail to create
  }
  m_ctlBitmapButton.Create("Search",WS_CHILD | WS_VISIBLE |
BS_OWNERDRAW,CRect(230,3,262,32),&m_wndDialogBar,ID_BITMAPBUTTON);
  m_ctlBitmapButton.LoadBitmaps( IDB_BITMAP1,IDB_BITMAP2,0,0);

  if (!m_wndReBar.Create(this) ||
      !m_wndReBar.AddBar(&m_wndToolBar) ||
      !m_wndReBar.AddBar(&m_wndDialogBar))
  {
      TRACE0("Failed to create rebar\n");
      return -1;      // fail to create
  }
```

code continued on next page

```
code continued from previous page
    if (!m_wndStatusBar.Create(this) ||
        !m_wndStatusBar.SetIndicators(indicators,
           sizeof(indicators)/sizeof(UINT)))
    {
        TRACE0("Failed to create status bar\n");
        return -1;      // fail to create
    }
    m_wndToolBar.SetBarStyle(m_wndToolBar.GetBarStyle() |
    CBRS_TOOLTIPS | CBRS_FLYBY);

    return 0;
}
```

▶ **Create message map entries for the combo box**

1. Run the dialog editor on the IDD_DIALOG1 dialog resource and select the combo box.

2. Invoke ClassWizard.

   The **Adding a class** dialog box will automatically appear. Click **Cancel** to dismiss this dialog box.

3. In the **Message Maps** tab, set **Class name** to CBitmapButtonView, set **Object ID** to IDC_COMBO1, and set **Message** to CBN_KILLFOCUS.

4. Click **Add Function** and accept the default name of **OnKillfocusCombo1**.

▶ **Create message map entries for the Windows notification message BN_CLICKED**

1. Open the file BitmapButtonView.h and add the following line after the // {{AFX_MSG message block:

   ```
   afx_msg void OnBnClicked();
   ```

2. Insert a message map entry for the **OnBnClicked** function in the **CBitmapButtonView** implementation file. Place the entry between the end of the code section created by ClassWizard and the end of the message map as follows:

   ```
   //{{AFX_MSG_MAP(CBitmapButtonView)
   ON_CBN_KILLFOCUS(IDC_COMBO1, OnKillfocusCombo1)
   //}}AFX_MSG_MAP
   ON_BN_CLICKED(ID_BITMAPBUTTON,OnBnClicked)
   END_MESSAGE_MAP()
   ```

For more information about handling notification messages from a bitmap button, see "Processing Notification Messages from Controls Supplied by MFC" on page 245 in this chapter.

▶ Add a protected variable to the CBitmapButtonView class

- Right-click **CBitmapButtonView** in ClassView and add a protected variable as follows:

```
CString m_text;
```

▶ Add an extern declaration for CDialogBar

- Because m_wndDialogBar is declared in MainFrm.cpp, add the following declaration to the CBitmapButtonView.h before the definition of **CBitmapButtonView**:

```
extern CDialogBar m_wndDialogBar;
```

▶ Write the code for the OnKillfocusCombo1 function

In this handler, you will add the string typed by the user to the combo box if it is a new string.

- Write the code for the **OnKillfocusCombo1** function as follows:

```
CComboBox *ptr;
ptr=(CComboBox*)m_wndDialogBar.GetDlgItem(IDC_COMBO1);
m_wndDialogBar.GetDlgItemText(IDC_COMBO1,m_text);

if(ptr)
{
   if(ptr->FindStringExact(0,m_text)==CB_ERR&&
!m_text.IsEmpty())
        ptr->AddString(m_text);
}
```

▶ **Write the code for the OnBnClicked function**

In this handler, you will search for the entered string in a document.

- Write the code for the **OnBnClicked** function as follows:

```
void CBitmapButtonView::OnBnClicked()
{
if(!m_text.IsEmpty())
   OnFindNext(m_text,TRUE,TRUE);
else
::MessageBox(0,"Enter search string","Search",MB_OK);
}
```

▶ **Override OnTextNotFound function to change the default implementation**

In the default implementation, the **OnFindNext** function calls the **OnTextNotFound** function if the string is not found.

1. Add the **OnTextNotFound** function to the **CBitmapButtonView** class as a protected function. It should be added after the //{{AFX_VIRTUAL block:

   ```
   virtual void OnTextNotFound(LPCTSTR lpszFind);
   ```

2. Write the code for the **OnTextNotFound** function as follows:

   ```
   ::MessageBox(0,"End of file reached","End of file",MB_OK);
   ```

▶ **Build and test the application**

- Build your application. Open a file or enter text in EditView. Enter the string to be searched and click **Search**. If the string is found, it should be highlighted. If the string is not found, a message box indicating the end of file should appear.

The solution code for this exercise is located in the folder *<install folder>*\Labs\Ch05\Lab5.1\Ex01\Solution.

Lab 5.2: Adding a Progress Control

In this lab, you will create and implement a progress control.

To see the demonstration "Lab 5.2 Demonstration," see the accompanying CD-ROM.

Estimated time to complete this lab: **45 minutes**

To complete the exercises in this lab, you must have the required software. For detailed information about the labs and setup for the labs, see "Labs" in "About This Course."

The code that forms the starting point for this lab is located in the folder *<install folder>*\Labs\Ch05\Lab5.2.

The solution code for this lab is located in the folder *<install folder>*\Labs\Ch05\Lab5.2.

Objectives

After completing this lab, you will be able to:

- Create a progress control.
- Create and control a label for a progress control.
- Display both the control and its label in the context of the status bar.

Prerequisites

There are no prerequisites for this lab.

Exercises

The following exercises provide practice working with the concepts and techniques covered in this chapter:

- Exercise 1: Creating a Progress Control

    In this exercise, you will add a progress control to the default status bar that MFC AppWizard provides as part of the mainframe class. You will also provide the progress control with a label.

- Exercise 2: Implementing the Progress Control

  In this exercise, you will provide the supporting code and resources to use the **CProgressStatusBar** class in the ShowDiff application.

Exercise 1: Creating a Progress Control

The code that forms the starting point for this exercise is in *<install folder>*\Labs\Ch05\Lab5.2\Ex01.

In this exercise, you will add a progress control to the status bar that MFC AppWizard provides as part of the mainframe class. You will also add a label to the progress control as shown in the following illustration.

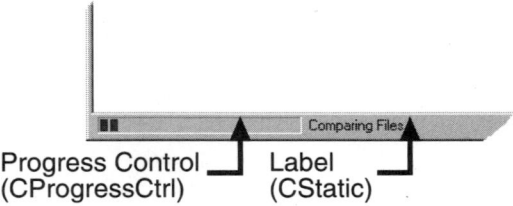

Progress Control (CProgressCtrl)   Label (CStatic)

▶ **Create a new CProgressStatusBar class derived from the generic CWnd class**

1. Invoke ClassWizard.
2. Click **Add Class**, click **New**, and add **CProgressStatusBar**. Base it on the generic **CWnd class**.
3. Click **OK** to create the new class.
4. Close ClassWizard.

▶ **Edit the generated files to derive CProgressStatusBar from CStatusBar**

1. Open the file ProgressStatusBar.h.
2. On the **Edit** menu, click **Replace**.
3. Replace all instances of **CWnd** with **CStatusBar**.
4. Save ProgressStatusBar.h.
5. Repeat this procedure with the file ProgressStatusBar.cpp.

Lab 5.2: Adding a Progress Control

▶ Add new members to CProgressStatusBar

CProgressStatusBar needs to track the member controls in the derived class, and the state and position of these member controls. Right-click **CProgressStatusBar** in ClassView and add four protected variables:

1. Add a member variable for the progress control itself:

    ```
    CProgressCtrl    m_ProgressCtrl;
    ```

2. Add a member variable for the static control that displays the label:

    ```
    CStatic m_ProgressLabel;
    ```

3. **CProgressStatusBar** suppresses the default painting of its **CStatusBar** parent when you display the progress indicator. To track default painting, add a member variable that is set when a progress control is in use:

    ```
    BOOL m_bProgressMode;
    ```

4. Add a member variable to enable **CProgessStatusBar** to store the width of the progress control to position the label:

    ```
    int m_nProgressCtrlWidth;
    ```

▶ Create a method to set the width of the progress control

1. Right-click **CProgressStatusBar** in ClassView and select **Go to Definition**. Immediately before the class definition, add the following three constants:
   First, declare a constant for the default width of the progress control as follows:

    ```
    const int PROGRESS_CTRL_CX = 160;
    ```

    Declare constants for the horizontal and vertical margins and the width of the progress control as follows:

    ```
    const int X_MARGIN = 5;  // X value used for margins
                             // and control spacing
    const int Y_MARGIN = 2;  // Y value used for margins
                             // and control spacing
    ```

2. Right-click **CProgressStatusBar** in ClassView and add a public member function to set the control width:

   ```
   void SetProgressCtrlWidth(int nWidth = PROGRESS_CTRL_CX)
   ```

3. Write the function body to set **m_nProgressCtrlCX** to the passed parameter as follows:

   ```
   void SetProgressCtrlWidth(int nWidth)
   {
           m_nProgressCtrlWidth = nWidth;
   }
   ```

4. Save ProgressStatusBar.cpp.

▶ **Create a method to lay out the progress control and its label**

1. Right-click **CProgressStatusBar** in ClassView and add a public member function:

   ```
   void RecalcProgressDisplay()
   ```

2. Write the code for the **RecalcProgressDisplay** function to get the client rectangle of the status bar as follows:

   ```
   CRect ControlRect;
   CRect ClientRect;
   GetClientRect(&ClientRect);
   ControlRect = ClientRect;
   ```

   You can assume that both the progress control and its labels have been created when this function is called.

3. Adjust the rectangle for the progress control so that it reflects the x and y margins, and the progress control width as follows:

   ```
   // First the Progress bar

   ControlRect.left += X_MARGIN;
   ControlRect.right = ControlRect.left + m_nProgressCtrlWidth;
   ControlRect.top += Y_MARGIN;
   ControlRect.bottom -= Y_MARGIN;
   ```

Lab 5.2: Adding a Progress Control

4. Position the progress control within this rectangle as follows:

   ```
   m_ProgressCtrl.MoveWindow(ControlRect, FALSE);
   ```

5. Adjust the rectangle so that it occupies the space remaining to the right of the progress control, except for the x margins as follows:

   ```
   ControlRect.left = ControlRect.right + X_MARGIN;
   ControlRect.right = ClientRect.right - X_MARGIN;
   ```

6. Position the label within this rectangle as follows:

   ```
   m_ProgressLabel.MoveWindow(ControlRect, FALSE);
   ```

7. Save ProgressStatusBar.cpp.

The following sample code shows an example of how your code should look. To copy this code for use in your own projects, see "Lab 5.2.1 RecalcProgressDisplay" on the accompanying CD-ROM.

```
void CProgressStatusBar::RecalcProgressDisplay()
{
  // Adjust the postions of the Label and Progress Controls
  // Place the Label Control to the right of the
  // Progress Control
  //
  //      [Progress Control] Label Text...

  CRect ControlRect;
  CRect ClientRect;
  GetClientRect(&ClientRect);
  ControlRect = ClientRect;

  // First the Progress bar

  ControlRect.left += X_MARGIN;
  ControlRect.right = ControlRect.left + m_nProgressCtrlWidth;
  ControlRect.top += Y_MARGIN;
  ControlRect.bottom -= Y_MARGIN;

  m_ProgressCtrl.MoveWindow(ControlRect, FALSE);
```

code continued on next page

```
code continued from previous page

//   Then the text label using the rest of the status
//   bars client area

ControlRect.left = ControlRect.right + X_MARGIN;
ControlRect.right = ClientRect.right - X_MARGIN;

m_ProgressLabel.MoveWindow(ControlRect, FALSE);
}
```

▶ **Create a method to set the label for the progress control**

1. Right-click **CProgressStatusBar** in ClassView and add a public member function:

   ```
   void SetProgressLabel(LPCSTR lpszProgressLabel)
   ```

2. In the **SetProgressLabel** function, set the text of the static label control to the passed parameter as follows:

   ```
   m_ProgressLabel.SetWindowText(lpszProgressLabel);
   ```

3. If the program displays the progress bar at the time of the call, update the display as follows:

   ```
   if(m_bProgressMode)
   {
       RecalcProgressDisplay();
       Invalidate();
       UpdateWindow();
   }
   ```

4. Save ProgressStatusBar.cpp.

The sample code on the following page shows an example of how your code should look. To copy this code for use in your own projects, see "Lab 5.2.1 SetProgressLabel" on the accompanying CD-ROM.

```
void CProgressStatusBar::SetProgressLabel(LPCSTR
                                          lpszProgressLabel)
{
  m_ProgressLabel.SetWindowText(lpszProgressLabel);

  // If were currently displaying progress, update
  // placement of label and progress control

  if(m_bProgressMode)
  {
      RecalcProgressDisplay();
      Invalidate();
      UpdateWindow();
  }
}
```

▶ **Create a method to show or hide the progress control**

1. Right-click **CProgressStatusBar** in ClassView and add **ShowProgressDisplay** as a public member function:

   ```
   void ShowProgressDisplay(BOOL bShow = TRUE)
   ```

2. In the **ShowProgressDisplay** function, set the mode to the passed parameter as follows:

   ```
   m_bProgressMode = bShow;
   ```

3. To show the progress control, recalculate the display as follows:

   ```
   if(m_bProgressMode)
   {
       RecalcProgressDisplay();
   }
   ```

4. Show or hide the static and the progress control, as appropriate:

   ```
   m_ProgressLabel.ShowWindow(m_bProgressMode ?  SW_SHOW : SW_HIDE);
   m_ProgressCtrl.ShowWindow(m_bProgressMode ?   SW_SHOW : SW_HIDE);
   ```

5. Invalidate and update the status bar as follows:

   ```
   Invalidate();
   UpdateWindow();
   ```

6. Save ProgressStatusBar.cpp.

The following sample code shows an example of how your code should look. To copy this code for use in your own projects, see "Lab 5.2.1 ShowProgressDisplay" on the accompanying CD-ROM.

```
void CProgressStatusBar::ShowProgressDisplay(BOOL bShow)
{
  m_bProgressMode = bShow;
  if(m_bProgressMode)
  {
      RecalcProgressDisplay();
  }
  m_ProgressLabel.ShowWindow(m_bProgressMode ? SW_SHOW : SW_HIDE);
  m_ProgressCtrl.ShowWindow(m_bProgressMode ? SW_SHOW : SW_HIDE);
  Invalidate();
  UpdateWindow();
}
```

▶ **Create a handler for the WM_CREATE message**

1. Invoke ClassWizard and create a handler for the WM_CREATE message in **CProgressStatusBar**.

2. Edit this handler to create the progress control with no positions or percentages:

```
if(!m_ProgressCtrl.Create(
            0,                  // Style - Don't Show
                                //   Position or Percent
            CRect(0,0,0,0),     //Initial position
            this,               // Parent ID
            0))                 // Child ID
{
    return -1;
}
```

Lab 5.2: Adding a Progress Control

3. Create the static label control as follows:

    ```
    if(!m_ProgressLabel.Create(
                    NULL,                   // Text
                    WS_CHILD|SS_LEFT,       // Style
                    CRect(0,0,0,0),         // Initial position
                    this))                  // Parent
    {
        return -1;
    }
    ```

4. Set the font of the static label to the same font as that of the status bar:

    ```
    m_ProgressLabel.SetFont(GetFont());
    ```

5. Return 0 to the calling function to indicate success:

    ```
    return 0;
    ```

6. Save ProgressStatusBar.cpp.

The following sample code shows an example of how your code should look. To copy this code for use in your own projects, see "Lab 5.2.1 OnCreate" on the accompanying CD-ROM.

```
int CProgressStatusBar::OnCreate(LPCREATESTRUCT
                                     lpCreateStruct)
{
  if (CStatusBar::OnCreate(lpCreateStruct) == -1)
      return -1;

    //  Create the Progress Control - we'll calculate its  //size and
position later - in response to a
    //  ShowProgressDisplay() call.

    if(!m_ProgressCtrl.Create(
                0,                      // Style - Don't Show
                                        //   Position or Percent
                CRect(0,0,0,0),  //Initial position
                this,                   // Parent ID
                0))                     // Child ID
```

code continued on next page

```
code continued from previous page
    {
        return -1;
    }

    // Create the Progress Label - we'll calculate its
    // size and position later - in response to a
    //ShowProgressDisplay() call.

    if(!m_ProgressLabel.Create(
                    NULL,                // Text
                    WS_CHILD|SS_LEFT,    // Style
                    CRect(0,0,0,0),      // Initial position
                    this))               // Parent
    {
        return -1;
    }

    // Use the same font as the Status Bar

    m_ProgressLabel.SetFont(GetFont());

    return 0;
}
```

▶ Create a handler for the WM_PAINT message

1. Invoke ClassWizard and create a handler for the WM_PAINT message in **CProgressStatusBar**.

2. Pass the WM_PAINT message as follows if the progress control does not get displayed:

   ```
   if(!m_bProgressMode)
   {
       CStatusBar::OnPaint();
   }
   ```

3. Save ProgressStatusBar.cpp.

The sample code on the following page shows an example of how your code should look. To copy this code for use in your own projects, see "Lab 5.2.1 OnPaint" on the accompanying CD-ROM.

```
void CProgressStatusBar::OnPaint()
{
  // If were displaying the progress control, then we
  // need to handle painting of the Status Bar,
  // otherwise defer to the base class

  if(!m_bProgressMode)
  {
      CStatusBar::OnPaint();
  }
}
```

▶ **Update the constructor to set defaults**

1. Set the mode to **FALSE** and the control width to the declared default:

   ```
   m_bProgressMode = FALSE;
   m_nProgressCtrlWidth = PROGRESS_CTRL_CX;
   ```

2. Save ProgressStatusBar.cpp.
3. Build your project.

The solution code for this exercise is located in the folder *<install folder>*\Labs\Ch05\Lab5.2\Ex01\Solution.

Exercise 2: Implementing the Progress Control

Continue with the files you created in Exercise 1 or, if you do not have a starting point for this exercise, the code that forms the basis for this exercise is in *<install folder>*\Labs\Ch05\Lab5.2\Ex02.

In this exercise, you will provide the supporting code and resources to use the **CProgressStatusBar** class in the ShowDiff application.

▶ **Make the status bar available to other classes**

1. In the file MainFrm.cpp, include the file ProgressStatusBar.h before the file Splitter.h.
2. Save MainFrm.cpp.
3. Open MainFrm.h.

4. Add a method to return a pointer to the status bar:

   ```
   CProgressStatusBar *GetStatusBar()
       { return &m_wndStatusBar; }
   ```

5. Change the status bar type from **CStatusBar** to **CProgressStatusBar**.
6. Save MainFrm.h.
7. In ProgressStatusBar.h, add a method to return a pointer to the progress control itself as follows:

   ```
   CProgressCtrl * GetProgressCtrl()
       { return &m_ProgressCtrl; }
   ```

8. Save ProgressStatusBar.h.
9. Include ProgressStatusBar.h before Splitter.h in Diff.cpp, DiffDoc.cpp, and DiffView.cpp.
10. Save Diff.cpp, DiffDoc.cpp, and DiffView.cpp.

▶ **Use String table editor to add a label string**

1. Open the String table resource.
2. Display the properties for the blank line at the end of the String table resource.
3. Set the **ID** to IDS_COMPARING, and the **Caption** to Comparing files.
4. Save the String table.

▶ **Set the label of the status bar to the resource string**

1. In the implementation of **CDiffDoc::RunComparison**, add code as described in the following steps. Place all the code you add before the code that is already there.
2. In **RunComparison**, before processing the files, get the status bar as follows:

   ```
   CProgressStatusBar *pStatus = CDiffApp::GetApp()->
               GetMainFrame()->GetStatusBar();
   ```

3. Add a statement to determine whether pStatus is valid as follows:

   ```
   if (pStatus)
   {
   ```

4. Declare a **CString** variable as follows:

   ```
   CString Label;
   ```

5. Load the resource string as follows:

   ```
   Label.LoadString(IDS_COMPARING);
   ```

6. Set the label of the progress bar as follows:

   ```
   pStatus->SetProgressLabel(Label);
   ```

▶ Show the status bar

- After setting the label, set the status bar to **Progress mode** as follows:

  ```
  pStatus->ShowProgressDisplay(TRUE);
  ```

▶ Step the status bar through its range

Normally, you update a status bar as the result of an action that your program performs. In this procedure, you will simulate that action with a timing loop.

1. Get a pointer to the progress control as follows:

   ```
   CProgressCtrl *pProgress = pStatus->GetProgressCtrl();
   ```

2. Set the range of the progress control to ten steps, starting at 0:

   ```
   pProgress->SetRange(0,10);
   ```

3. Display the first step of the range as follows:

   ```
   pProgress->SetStep(1);
   ```

4. Do ten steps of the progress control as follows:

   ```
   while (pProgress->StepIt() != 10)
   {
       ::Sleep(200);
   }
   ```

▶ Restore the status bar to its normal behavior

1. After you stop the progress control, send the status bar a message to turn off the progress bar as follows:

   ```
   pStatus->ShowProgressDisplay(FALSE);
   ```

2. Save DiffDoc.cpp.

The following sample code shows an example of how your code should look. To copy this code for use in your own projects, see "Lab 5.2.2 RunComparison" on the accompanying CD-ROM.

```
void CDiffDoc::RunComparison (LPCSTR lpszFile1, LPCSTR lpszFile2)
{
  CProgressStatusBar *pStatus = CDiffApp::GetApp()->
      GetMainFrame()->GetStatusBar();

  if(pStatus)
  {
      CString Label;
      Label.LoadString(IDS_COMPARING);
      pStatus->SetProgressLabel(Label);

      // Flip the StatusBar into Progress Mode
      pStatus->ShowProgressDisplay(TRUE);

      // Simulate some bogus progress
      CProgressCtrl *pProgress = pStatus->GetProgressCtrl();
      if(pProgress)
      {
          pProgress->SetRange(0, 10);
          pProgress->SetStep(1);
          while(pProgress->StepIt() != 10)
          {
              ::Sleep(200);
          }
      }
      pStatus->ShowProgressDisplay(FALSE);
  }
}
```

code continued on next page

code continued from previous page

```
    CMainFrame * pFrame = CDiffApp::GetApp()->GetMainFrame();
    if(pFrame)
    {
        CSplitter * pSplitter = pFrame->GetSplitter();

        if(pSplitter)
        {
            CDiffView * pView;
            pView = (CDiffView *)pSplitter->GetPane(0,0);
            if (pView)
            {
                CFile file(lpszFile1, CFile::modeRead);
                CArchive ar(&file, CArchive::load);
                pView->Serialize(ar);
            }

            pView = (CDiffView *)pSplitter->GetPane(0,1);
            if (pView)
            {
                CFile file(lpszFile2, CFile::modeRead);
                CArchive ar(&file, CArchive::load);
                pView->Serialize(ar);
            }
            //      Flag as clean so that we won't get
            //      prompted to save
            SetModifiedFlag(FALSE);
        }
    }
}
```

▶ **Build and run your application**

- Click **Open** on the **File** menu and select two files to compare. The status bar will run when comparisons are being simulated between the two files which you have chosen.

The solution code for this exercise is located in the folder *<install folder>*\Labs\Ch05\Lab5.2\Ex02\Solution.

Lab 5.3: Using the Calendar Control

In this lab, you will use the **Calendar** control in your MFC-based application.

To see the demonstration "Lab 5.3 Demonstration," see the accompanying CD-ROM.

Estimated time to complete this lab: **20 minutes**

To complete the exercises in this lab, you must have the required software. For detailed information about the labs and setup for the labs, see "Labs" in "About This Course."

The solution code for this lab is located in the folder *<install folder>*\Labs\Ch05\Lab5.3\Ex01\Solution.

Objectives

After completing this lab, you will be able to:

- Create an MFC-based application that is a control container.
- Use the Components and Controls Gallery to add the **Calendar** control to your project.
- Use the **Calendar** control in your application.

Prerequisites

There are no prerequisites for this lab.

Exercises

The following exercise provides practice working with the concepts and techniques covered in this chapter:

- Exercise 1: Using the Calendar Control

    In this exercise, you will create a simple control container application and use the Components and Controls Gallery to add the **Calendar** control to the project. You will include the **Calendar** control in your application and invoke a method and set properties of the control.

Exercise 1: Using the Calendar Control

In this exercise, you will create a simple control container application and use the Microsoft Components and Controls Gallery to add the **Calendar** control to the project. You will include the **Calendar** control in your application and invoke a method and set properties of the control.

▶ **Create a control container application**

1. Start Microsoft Visual Studio and then on the **File** menu, click **New**.
2. In the **New** dialog box, click the **Projects** tab, and select **MFC AppWizard (exe)**.
3. In the Location field, type the directory path in which to save the files, set Project Name to **UseCal**, accept the default option, create new workspace, then click **OK**.
4. In Step 1 of MFC AppWizard, set the type of application to create to **Single Document**, then click **Next**.
5. In Step 2, accept the default settings and click **Next**.
6. In Step 3, accept the default of None for compound document support and under other support, make sure that the **ActiveX Controls** check box is selected.
7. In Step 4, clear the **Printing and print preview** check box.
8. In Step 5, accept the default options.
9. In Step 6, derive **CUseCalView** from **CFormView**, rather than **CView**, and click **Finish**.

▶ **Add the Calendar control to your project**

1. On the **Project** menu, click **Add To Project**, and then click **Components and Controls**.

    In the **Components and Controls Gallery** dialog box, double-click the Registered ActiveX Controls folder to see the controls currently registered.

2. Select **Calendar Control 8.0**, and click **Insert**.
3. In the **Confirm Classes** dialog box, click **OK**.
4. In the **Components and Controls Gallery** dialog box, click **Close**.

    The **CCalendar** and **COleFont** classes are added to the list of classes in the UseCal application.

5. In the Visual Studio ClassView pane, expand the **CCalendar** class to view properties and methods of the class.

▶ Add the Calendar control to your application

1. In the ResourceView pane of your project workspace, open the IDD_USECAL_FORM dialog box resource.
2. Delete the Static **TODO** control and add a **Calendar** control to the dialog box.
3. Size and position the **Calendar** control appropriately.
4. Change the ID of the control to IDC_CALENDARCTRL.
5. You need to add a member variable for the **Calendar** control to the class that contains the dialog box. In this case, add a member variable to your application's view class as follows:
   a. Invoke ClassWizard.
   b. On the **Member Variables** tab, click **Add Variable**.
   c. In the **Add Member Variable** dialog box, type **m_CalControl** in the **Member variable name** text box and click **OK**.
   d. Click **OK** to close the ClassWizard dialog box.

▶ Add a Calendar menu to your application

1. Open the IDR_MAINFRAME menu resource.
2. In the menu editor, click the empty placeholder in the menu bar and drag it to the position between the **View** and **Help** items.
3. Double-click the dotted box to display the **Menu Item Properties** property sheet. Set the **Caption** to **Calendar**.
4. Add three menu items to the **Calendar** menu with the captions **Show Current Date**, **Set Back Color**, and **Toggle Title**, respectively.
5. Close the **Menu Item Properties** property sheet.

▶ Add handlers for the menu items

1. Invoke ClassWizard.
2. On the **Message Maps** tab, select CUseCalView as the class name, ID_CALENDAR_SHOWCURRENTDATE as the object ID, and COMMAND as the message. Create a new function and accept the default **OnCalendarShowcurrentdate** as the function name.
3. Repeat this procedure to add the default handlers for the ID_CALENDAR_SETBACKCOLOR and ID_CALENDAR_TOGGLETITLE messages.

Lab 5.3: Using the Calendar Control

▶ **Invoke a method and set properties of the Calendar control**

1. In the **OnCalendarShowcurrentdate** function of the file UseCalView.cpp, add code to invoke the **Calendar** control's **Today** method as follows:

   ```
   m_CalControl.Today();
   ```

2. In the **OnCalendarSetbackcolor** function, add the following code to change the background color of the **Calendar** control:

   ```
   OLE_COLOR current_color = m_CalControl.GetBackColor();
   COLORREF old_color;
   // OLE_COLOR must be converted to a COLORREF for use
   // by CColorDialog.
   if (S_OK != ::OleTranslateColor(current_color,
                                   NULL, &old_color))
       return;

   CColorDialog dlg(old_color);

   if (IDOK == dlg.DoModal())
   {
       // No translation is needed from COLORREF to OLE_COLOR
       COLORREF new_color = dlg.GetColor();
       if (new_color != old_color)
       {
           current_color = new_color;
           m_CalControl.SetBackColor(current_color);
       }
   }
   ```

3. In the **OnCalendarToggleTitle** function, add the following code to toggle the display of the title on the **Calendar** control:

   ```
   BOOL bTitleState = m_CalControl.GetShowTitle();
   m_CalControl.SetShowTitle(! bTitleState);
   ```

▶ **Add an event handler for the Calendar control**

In this procedure, you will add and implement a handler for the double-click event to enable the user to set the system date.

1. Invoke ClassWizard.

2. On the **Message Maps** tab, select CUseCalView as the Class name, IDC_CALENDARCTRL as the Object ID and DbClick as the Message.

3. Click **Add Function** and accept the default name of **OnDblClickCalendarctrl**. ClassWizard will insert an event sink map in the class with an entry for the double-click event.

4. Write the code for the **OnDblClickCalendarctrl** function to change the system date as follows:

```
short year = m_CalControl.GetYear();
short month = m_CalControl.GetMonth();
short day = m_CalControl.GetDay();
WORD hh,min,sec,mlsec;
SYSTEMTIME mtime;

GetSystemTime(&mtime);
hh=mtime.wHour;
min=mtime.wMinute;
sec=mtime.wSecond;
mlsec=mtime.wMilliseconds;

mtime.wYear= (WORD)year;
mtime.wMonth= (WORD)month;
mtime.wDay= (WORD)day;
mtime.wHour=hh;
mtime.wMinute=min;
mtime.wSecond=sec;
mtime.wMilliseconds=mlsec;

CString str;
str.Format("Set system date to: %d/%d/%d ?",month,day,year);

int i=::MessageBox(0,str,"Date",MB_YESNO);
if(i==IDYES)
    ::SetSystemTime(&mtime);
```

▶ **Build and test your application**

- Run your application and test the options under the **Calendar** menu. Double-click a date on the control and try changing the system date.

The solution code for this exercise is located in the folder <install folder>\Labs\Ch05\Lab5.3\Ex01\Solution.

Sample Applications

The following table describes the sample applications related to this chapter. These sample applications are located in the folder *<install folder>*\Samples\Ch05.

Sample application subfolder	Description of application
BitmapBut	Uses the bitmap-button control to change the color of text displayed.
ComboBoxEx	Uses an extended **ComboBox** control to change the color of text displayed.
ProgressCtrl1	Displays the extent of progress of comparing two files in a dialog box. The progress control is created using the dialog editor.
ProgressCtrl2	Displays the extent of progress in comparing two files in a dialog box. The progress control is created using code rather than the dialog editor.
Spinbutton	Displays the product of two numbers, one from a spin control and the other from an edit control.

Self-Check Questions

To see the answers to the Self-Check Questions, see Appendix A.

1. What are events?

   A. The actions that the ActiveX control can perform at the request of the container

   B. The settings that change the appearance or behavior of an ActiveX control

   C. The notifications that an ActiveX control container sends to an ActiveX control in response to user interaction or some other occurrence

   D. The notifications that an ActiveX control sends to an ActiveX control container in response to user interaction or some other occurrence

2. What does a .odl file contain?

A. The specification for the interface that an object supports, including its properties, methods, and events, in text format

B. Information to provide a common interface for the control with many different kinds of applications, in binary format

C. Executable code for the ActiveX control

D. Dynamic-link library routines that are loaded with the ActiveX control

3. Which notification message is sent if the progress control cannot complete an operation because there is not enough memory available?

A. MCN_GETDAYSTATE
B. IPN_FIELDCHANGED
C. NM_OUTOFMEMORY
D. CMemoryException

Chapter 6:
Creating ActiveX Controls

Multimedia

Using the MFC ActiveX
  Control Wizard 277

Adding Properties
  with ClassWizard 287

Adding Methods
  with ClassWizard 293

Adding Events with
  ClassWizard 295

Adding Custom
  Property Pages 302

Lab 6.1 Demonstration 308

Microsoft ActiveX controls offer you an ideal way to create reusable code. Additionally, ActiveX controls inherit and support ActiveX function-ality, such as in-place activation, Automation, and drag-and-drop editing.

This chapter focuses on the Microsoft Foundation Class (MFC) implementation of ActiveX controls. You will learn how to implement ActiveX controls by using MFC ActiveX ControlWizard.

Objectives

After completing this chapter, you will be able to:

◆ Describe the advantages of ActiveX control technology.

◆ Describe the elements of an ActiveX control.

◆ Explain the features of ControlWizard in creating an ActiveX control.

◆ Describe the primary tasks of an ActiveX control container.

◆ Explain the interaction between an ActiveX control container and an ActiveX control.

◆ Use ControlWizard to create skeletal code for your ActiveX control.

◆ Use ClassWizard to define properties, methods, and events for your ActiveX control.

Overview of ActiveX Controls

This section explains how to create ActiveX controls by using the MFC ActiveX ControlWizard. Using ControlWizard, you can create up to 99 separate controls per project and set individual options for each control.

Advantages of ActiveX Controls

ActiveX technology makes it easy to develop platform-independent components. ActiveX controls are components that you can plug into many different types of applications called ActiveX control containers. Microsoft Access, Microsoft Visual Basic, Microsoft Visual C++, and HTML Web pages are examples of ActiveX control containers. The more you use ActiveX controls, the easier it is to develop and implement applications.

Benefits for Developers

ActiveX controls offer several benefits to developers:

- Your productivity can increase because you develop the code for a feature only once.

- Once an ActiveX control has been developed, support for it is immediately provided through any ActiveX control container, with no customization required.

- You can add standard or custom ActiveX controls to HTML Web pages. ActiveX controls enable the Web user to interact with the page or enter data on the page, rather than just view its contents.

Benefits for Users

As the user of a an ActiveX control, you gain the following benefits:

- You can select from a wide range of advanced features and quickly add them to your applications without having to develop the idea or the code for the features from the ground up.

- You can easily use the expertise and efforts of others to improve your applications.

Using the MFC ActiveX ControlWizard

The MFC ActiveX ControlWizard is provided with Microsoft Visual C++ 6.0. ControlWizard creates the skeleton code and the necessary project files for an ActiveX control and implements the code for selected options.

▶ **To launch ControlWizard**

1. On the **File** menu, click **New**, and then click the **Projects** tab.
2. Enter a name for your project and double-click **MFC ActiveXControlWizard** to start creating your control.

To see the demonstration "Using the MFC ActiveX ControlWizard," see the accompanying CD-ROM.

▶ **To complete Step 1 of ControlWizard**

1. Choose the number of controls for your project. Each control has a control class and a property page class.
2. Choose whether you want the controls in your project to have a run-time license.
3. Choose whether you want ControlWizard to generate comments in the source file that will guide you in creating your control.
4. Choose whether you want ControlWizard to generate files for context-sensitive Help. Help support requires that you use the Help compiler, which is provided with Visual C++.
5. Click **Finish** to create the ActiveX control, or proceed to Step 2 by clicking **Next**.

The following illustration shows the **MFC ActiveX ControlWizard - Step 1 of 2** dialog box.

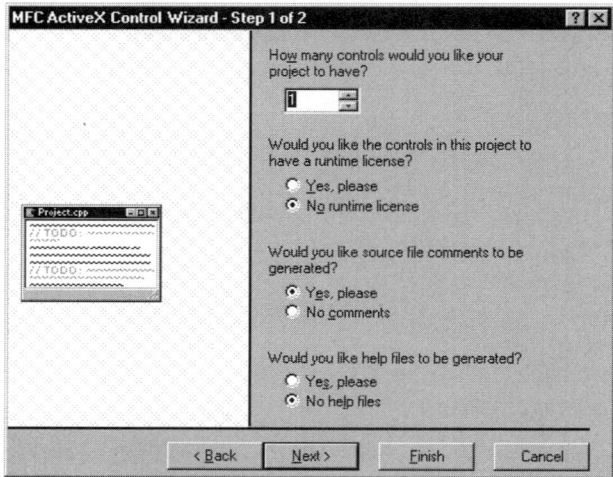

▶ **To complete Step 2 of ControlWizard**

1. If you added more than one control to your project and want to edit the names of the classes or files they use, select the control you want to edit from the list and click **Edit Names**. Repeat this procedure for each control you want to edit.

2. Select the features for each control.

3. Select the window class, if any, that each control should subclass.

4. Click **Advanced** to add enhanced ActiveX features to your control. The **ActiveX Advanced Features** dialog box will appear as shown in the following illustration.

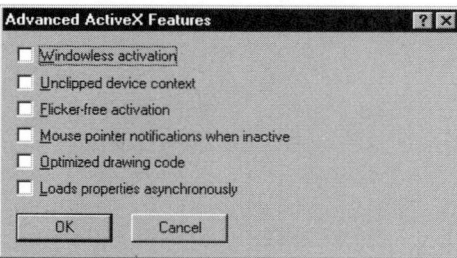

5. Select the advanced features for your control and click **OK**.

6. Click **Finish** to create the project files for your control.

7. Click **OK** to place your control in the appropriate folder and prepare it for use.

The following illustration shows the **MFC ActiveX ControlWizard - Step 2 of 2** dialog box.

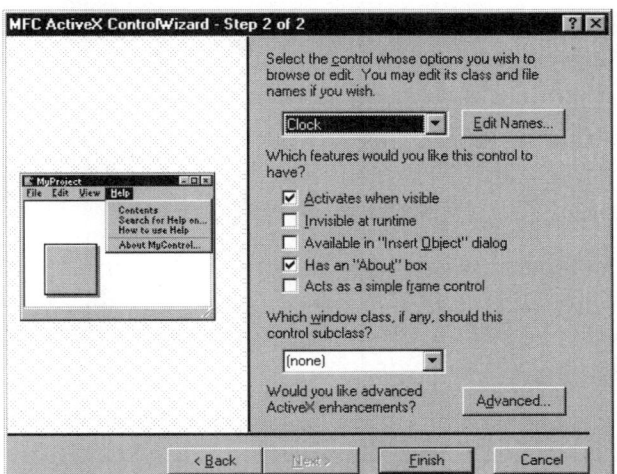

What ControlWizard Provides

ControlWizard generates a set of core project files that every control must have, plus any additional files that are required for optional features, such as context-sensitive Help or licensing.

Additionally, ControlWizard generates three main classes for each control, as shown in the following table.

Class	Description
Control module	Used to initialize the ActiveX control DLL. Typically, you do not need to modify this class. The default class name is **CXxxApp**, where **Xxx** is the name of the control.
Control	Provides control-specific behavior, including drawing and user interaction code. The default class name is **CXxxCtrl**, where **Xxx** is the name of the control.
Property page	Default property page for the control. Generally available at application design time, the property page(s) enables the developer to expediently initialize the properties of a control. The default class name is **CXxxPropPage**, where **Xxx** is the name of the control.

What MFC Provides

MFC provides the **COleControl** class, a powerful base class that encapsulates much of the required implementation for an ActiveX control. Derived from **CWnd**, this class inherits all the functionality of a Windows window object, plus additional functionality specific to ActiveX, such as event firing and the ability to support methods and properties.

Registering an ActiveX Control

One requirement for success in using component technology is having a single, searchable location that contains information about available components and their capabilities. This location is an operating system database known as the registry, which is available in Microsoft Windows 95 and Windows NT.

For a control to be available for general use, it must register itself in the HKEY_CLASSES_ROOT section of the registry. When your ActiveX control is created with ControlWizard, the code that is necessary to accomplish registration is provided in the control module class. The control automatically registers itself every time it is loaded into memory. Registering the control automatically every time it is loaded minimizes the possible damage if a user mistakenly corrupts the registry database.

> **Tip** The HKEY_CLASSES_ROOT section of the registry lists various items, including the name of the various OLE controls. A CLSID entry appears as a subkey under each item. Selecting this entry displays a large number consisting of 128-bit hexadecimal numbers. These numbers are known as globally unique identifiers (GUIDs) and are statically guaranteed to be unique when generated randomly. Specifically, they are known as class IDs, or CLSIDs, and uniquely identify each control and property page. Each class ID maps to an entry under the HKEY_CLASSES_ROOT\CLSID key, which completely defines the control information that is stored in the registry, including: its location, whether the control appears in the **Insert Object** dialog box, and so on.

You can register any DLL function by adding a shortcut to RegSvr32.exe in the \Windows\Sendto folder. After you add the shortcut, right-click the ActiveX control's .ocx file, click **Send To** on the shortcut menu, and then click **Shortcut to RegSvr32.exe**. The ActiveX control will be registered.

Painting an ActiveX Control

Some controls provide meaningful functionality but require no visible user interface. However, many of the controls require painting code to display information to the user.

The OnDraw Function

The framework provides an **OnDraw** function in your control class, complete with an appropriate device context (DC). The header file for the **COleControl::OnDraw** function contains the following arguments:

>   **OnDraw(CDC*** pDC, **const CRect&** rcBounds, **const CRect&** rcInvalid)

The pDC argument contains a DC in which the drawing occurs. The rcBounds argument defines the rectangular area of the control, including the border. The rcInvalid argument defines the rectangular area of the control that is invalid.

The **OnDraw** function is called whenever the framework or control container determines that the control is dirty and needs repainting. However, not only does the control display its information, it must also blend with the control container; that is, it should appear to be part of the container.

To blend with a container, an ActiveX control can query the control container for ambient properties such as background color, text color, and current font, and set its own properties to match those of the container.

MFC provides a function called **COleControl::InvalidateControl** that is analogous to the **CWnd::Invalidate** function. **InvalidateControl** forces immediate repainting of either the whole control window or just the rectangle specified in the function call. **InvalidateControl** is frequently called in functions that are used to set visual properties of the control.

Using OnDraw at Run Time vs. Design Time

The **OnDraw** function of an ActiveX control is called under two different circumstances: at run time and at design time.

Run Time

When the application that contains the control is running, **OnDraw** is invoked in a manner similar to an MFC-based application's view class. OnDraw: WM_PAINT messages are routed to **COleControl::OnPaint**, which creates a DC and then calls **OnDraw**. When a control is painted during run time, it is considered active.

Design Time

When a control is being used in a design environment, such as Visual Basic or the Visual C++ dialog editor, the application in which the control will eventually be used is not running; however, the control still must be drawn on the screen. Your control's **OnDraw** function is used, but the mechanism that calls **OnDraw** is different. When a control is painted at design time, it is considered inactive.

When the control is inactive, its window is invisible or nonexistent, so it cannot receive a paint message. Instead, the control container directly calls the **OnDraw** function of the control, passing the DC of the control container and the coordinates of the rectangular area occupied by the control. This differs from an active control's painting process in that the **COleControl::OnPaint** member function is never called.

Modifying the OnDraw Function

Whether the control is active or inactive, the framework calls the **OnDraw** member function. You add the majority of your painting code to this member function.

The rectangle passed by the framework to the **OnDraw** member function contains the area occupied by the control. If the control is active, the upper-left corner is (0, 0) and the DC passed is for the child window that contains the control. If the control is inactive, the upper-left corner is not necessarily (0, 0) and the DC passed is for the control container.

When you modify **OnDraw**, remember that the rectangle's upper-left corner may not necessarily be (0, 0), and that you draw only inside the rectangle passed to **OnDraw**. Unexpected results can occur if you draw outside the defined rectangle area.

Note When painting a control, do not make assumptions about the state of the DC passed as the pDC parameter to the **OnDraw** function. Occasionally, the DC is supplied by the container application and will not necessarily be initialized to the default state. In particular, explicitly select the pens, brushes, colors, fonts, and other resources on which your drawing code depends.

ActiveX Control Properties

Control properties, as opposed to ambient properties, are properties that the control exposes to its container. This section describes the two types of control properties: stock properties and custom properties.

This section explains how to use ClassWizard to implement control properties. You will also learn how to access ambient properties and how to set and return control properties at run time.

Stock Properties

Properties that are typically supported by all ActiveX controls are referred to as stock properties. ControlWizard provides standard implementations of stock properties to make developing controls easier. The following table describes some common stock properties.

Property	Description
BackColor	Determines the color used to paint the background of the control.
BorderStyle	Determines what sort of border the control should have.
FillColor	Determines the color used to fill in shapes.
Font	Determines the font the control uses for text output.
Enabled	Determines whether the control is enabled.
Text or Caption	Determines the text/caption assigned to the control. (These properties represent the same characteristic.)

Tip For a complete list of stock properties, see the Olectl.h file. This file can be found in the Include subfolder of Microsoft Visual Studio.

Adding Stock Properties

Although standard implementations of stock properties are provided, you are not required to support them. Use ClassWizard to add only those properties that your ActiveX control will support.

▶ **To add a stock property to an ActiveX control**

1. Open the project file and start ClassWizard.
2. On the **Automation** tab, select the control class and click **Add Property**.

3. Select the property name from the **External name** box, and then click **OK**. The names enumerated in the **External name** box are the stock properties.

The following illustration shows the **Automation** tab in the **MFC ClassWizard** dialog box.

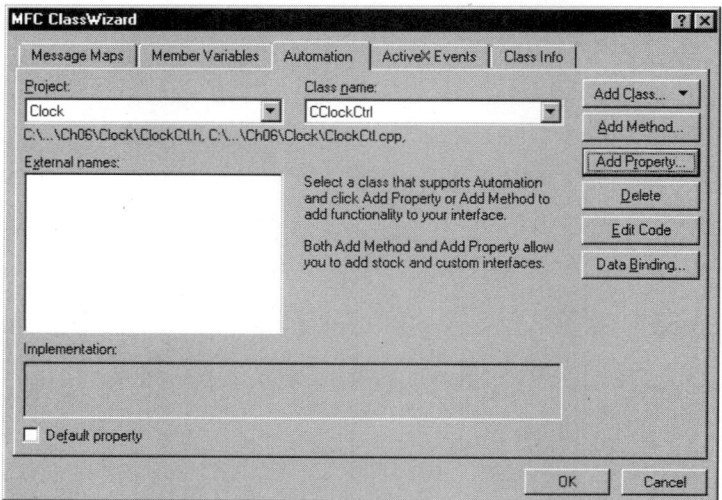

The following illustration shows the **Add Property** dialog box.

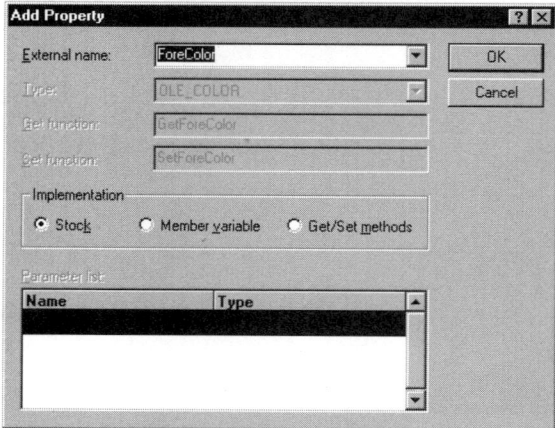

What ClassWizard Provides

For each stock property that you include, ClassWizard adds a **DISP_STOCKPROP_xxx** entry to the dispatch map of the control, where **xxx** is the property name. For example, **DISP_STOCKPROP_FORECOLOR** is added to provide support for the **ForeColor** stock property, as shown in the following example:

```
BEGIN_DISPATCH_MAP(CClockCtrl, COleControl)
  //{{AFX_DISPATCH_MAP(CClockCtrl)
  DISP_STOCKPROP_FORECOLOR()
  //}}AFX_DISPATCH_MAP
END_DISPATCH_MAP()
```

When a stock property is modified, it may be important for your application to be notified. Most stock properties have an associated notification function that, by default, calls **InvalidateControl** to force the control to repaint. For example, the **BackColor** stock property has an **OnBackColorChanged** notification function that can be overridden by your control class to get explicit notification that the backcolor has changed, as shown in the following example:

```
void CClockCtrl::OnBackColorChanged()
{
  MessageBox("Background Color Changed");
  COleControl::OnBackColorChanged();
}
```

The **BackColor** property is added in very much the same manner as the **ForeColor** property.

Custom Properties

Custom properties are properties you define as you develop an ActiveX control. Through custom properties, your ActiveX control assumes its unique characteristics.

The table on the following page describes the four custom control implementations.

Type	Dispatch map entry macro	When to use
Member variable with notification	DISP_PROPERTY_NOTIFY	Use when you need to be notified that a property value has changed. The controller changes the property directly, but a notification function is called to inform the control. ClassWizard adds the data member.
Member variable	DISP_PROPERTY	Use when it is not important to know when the property value changes. The controller changes the property directly. ClassWizard adds the data member, but you must delete the notification function in the **Add Property** dialog box to set this property.
Get/Set methods	DISP_PROPERTY_EX	Use when you need to compute the value of a property at run time, perform validation, or implement read-only or write-only properties. Use the **Get/Set** methods to add the variable to the control class.
Parameterized	DISP_PROPERTY_PARAM	Use to access a set of values through a single control property. You must add the data member. This implementation allows **Get/Set** methods to add as many arguments to the control as needed to expose a property.

The **Get** and **Set** methods are the most widely used implementation. They give the ActiveX control explicit handling of property interaction by the control container. Typically, the container will not necessarily call the **Get** or **Set** function; the appropriate function will be called depending on the use of the property in the container. For sample code that shows how to use a control's properties in Visual C++, see "Using an ActiveX Control in an MFC-based Application" on page 236 in Chapter 5, "Using Controls."

Adding Custom Properties

Adding custom properties to your ActiveX control is similar to adding stock properties. The main difference between the two is that when you add a custom property, you must enter a custom property name and parameters.

▶ **To add a custom property to an ActiveX control**

1. Load your control's project and start ClassWizard.
2. On the **Automation** tab, choose the control's class from the **Class name** box and click **Add Property**.
3. In the **External name** box, type a name for the custom property.
4. On the **Implementation** tab, select **Member Variable** or **Get/Set Methods**.
5. Select a type for the property, and set other options specific to the desired implementation.
6. Choose **OK** to close the **Add Property** dialog box.
7. Choose **OK** to confirm your choices and close ClassWizard.

To see the demonstration "Adding Properties with ClassWizard," see the accompanying CD-ROM.

Using Get/Set Methods to Implement Control Properties

When you implement a control property by using the **Get/Set** methods, the following two functions are created for you:

◆ Get

This function is called when the control user requests the value of the control's property.

◆ **Set**

This function is called when the control user requests that the control's property be changed.

The following example sets the alarm hour to a new value:

```
void CClockCtrl::SetAlarmHour(short nNewValue)
{
  if (nNewValue < 0 || nNewValue >= 24)
  {
      ThrowError(CTL_E_INVALIDPROPERTYVALUE, "AlarmHour must be
          between 0 and 23, inclusive");
  }

  m_AlarmHour = nNewValue;
  SetModifiedFlag();
}
```

The following code sample returns the value of the alarm hour that has been set.

```
short CClockCtrl::GetAlarmHour()
{
  return m_AlarmHour;
}
```

When you select the **Get/Set** methods implementation in ClassWizard, you can either accept the default name of these functions, or specify unique names.

Implementing Read-Only and Write-Only Properties

By using ClassWizard, you can easily make a control property read-only or write-only by deleting the **Get** or **Set** function in the **Get/Set** methods implementation. To create a read-only property, you delete the **Set** function. To create a write-only property, you delete the **Get** function

When the DISP_PROPERTY function is added to the dispatch map, the function that was cleared will default to the function **SetNotPermitted** or **GetNotPermitted**, as appropriate. These functions simply throw an appropriate error back to the container and notify it that the attempted **Set** or **Get** is not supported for the property.

Parameterized Properties

A parameterized property (also called a property array) enables you to specify a set of values for a single property. When this property is used by the control container application, individual values are accessed using array notation. For sample code showing how to use a parameterized property in an MFC-based application, see "Using an ActiveX Control in an MFC-based Application" on page 236 in Chapter 5, "Using Controls."

▶ **To add a parameterized property by using ClassWizard**

1. Add a new property using the **Get/Set** method.
2. In the **Parameter** list, use the grid control to add parameters and specify the type you want for each. (You can use up to 15 parameters.)

When specifying parameter values that are dynamic, the control will usually expose read-only properties for the row and column parameters. For example, if you build a temperature control using the number of hours in a day (24) as the row parameter and the maximum days in a month (31) as column parameter, the control will expose "hours in day" and "days in month" as read-only properties. If the control container passes invalid values, the control will generally use the function **ThrowError** to notify the container of the problem.

Accessing Ambient Properties

Often, you will want a visible ActiveX control to blend into the control container application's display. To accomplish this, the control must be able to determine some of the visual properties used by the control container. For example, determining the background color used by the container allows the control to set its own background property to match that of the container. The properties exposed by the control container to a control are known as ambient properties.

Some ambient properties allow the control to determine environmental variables for the control container, such as design mode or run mode in Visual Basic. Based on the mode, the control may behave in a particular manner.

MFC provides a single function call, **COleControl::GetAmbientProperty,** to access any ambient property by specifying its dispatch ID. Some of the more commonly used ambient properties have dedicated functions available, as listed in the table on the following page.

COleControl function	Description
AmbientBackColor	The container's backcolor.
AmbientDisplayName	The container's name for the control.
AmbientFont	The ambient font; note that the caller must call the **Release** function on the returned font.
AmbientForeColor	The container's forecolor.
AmbientLocaleID	The locale identifier that allows the control to localize itself.
AmbientScaleUnits	Displays positions or dimensions, labeled with the chosen unit, such as twips or centimeters.
AmbientTextAlign	The container's text alignment.
AmbientUserMode	Used by containers that support two modes of operation; for example, design mode or run mode in Visual C++.
AmbientUIDead	Allows the control to determine whether the container wants it to react to user-interface operations.
AmbientShowHatching	Determines whether the container allows the control to display itself with a hatched pattern when the user interface is active.
AmbientShowGrabHandles	Determines whether the container allows the control to display grab handles for itself when active.

Tip For a complete list of the dispatch IDs for the standard set of ambient properties, see the Olectl.h file. This file can be found in the Include subfolder of Microsoft Visual Studio.

A control container does not need to provide information about the ambient properties. In this case, you can use a reasonable default value for any ambient property values not supplied.

ActiveX Control Methods

Methods enable a control container to request that an ActiveX control perform some action.

In this section, you will learn how to use ClassWizard to add ActiveX control methods. You will also learn about the stock methods available for use by your control, and how to add custom methods. Finally, this section describes the syntax used by the control container application when ActiveX control methods are invoked.

Adding Stock Methods

ClassWizard provides implementations for the stock methods **DoClick** and **Refresh** as follows.

Method	Description
DoClick	Simulates the action of clicking the left mouse button. This method causes the **COleControl** member function **OnClick** to be called and causes the **Click** event to be called (if supported).
Refresh	Calls **COleControl::Refresh**, which causes the control to be repainted.

You are not required to support these methods, but most ActiveX controls support them.

You use ClassWizard to add stock methods to an ActiveX control much as you would to add properties.

▶ **To add a stock method to an ActiveX control**

1. In the **MFC ClassWizard** dialog box, click the **Automation** tab.
2. Choose the control's class from the **Class name** box, and click **Add Method**.
3. In the **External name** box, select a stock method name from the drop-down list, then click **OK** to close the **Add Method** dialog box.
4. Click **OK** to confirm your choices and close ClassWizard.

The following illustration shows the **Add Method** dialog box.

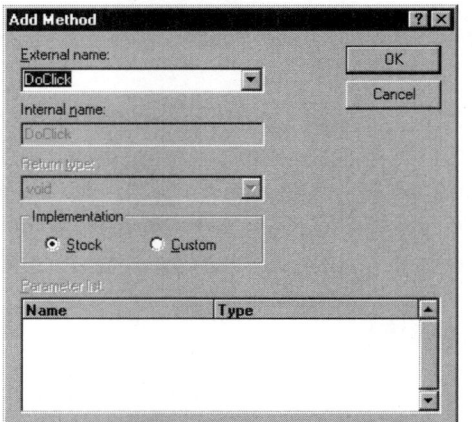

As with stock properties, no additional code is added to your application, except that an appropriate entry is inserted into the control's dispatch map. The code necessary to handle the method is part of the base class.

Adding Custom Methods

Use custom methods to define control-specific actions for your ActiveX control. Custom methods typically perform a specific task. For example, the **Clock** control uses an **AlarmTest** method for testing the alarm setting.

In ClassWizard, you can create a custom method, and define a return value type (if desired) and the parameters that will be passed to the method.

▶ **To add a custom method to an ActiveX control**

1. Load your control's project.
2. In the **MFC ClassWizard** dialog box, on the **Automation** tab, choose the control's class from the **Class name** box and click **Add Method**.
3. In the **External name** box, type a name for the custom method. (By not selecting a method from the drop-down box, you are defining a custom method.)
4. In the **Internal name** box, type the name of the method's internal function, or use the default value provided by ClassWizard.
5. In the **Return Type** box, select a data type.

6. In the **Parameter** list, add any parameters you want and select a data type for each parameter.
7. Click **OK** to close the **Add Method** dialog box.
8. Click **OK** to confirm your choices and close ClassWizard.

As when adding a stock method, an appropriate entry is added to the dispatch map of the control. Additionally, a skeletal function is provided in the control class; you must update this function to provide the behavior you want for the method.

To see the demonstration "Adding Methods with ClassWizard," see the accompanying CD-ROM.

ActiveX Control Events

Properties and methods enable the control container to request or submit information and ask the ActiveX control to perform actions. Events provide a way for the ActiveX control to communicate with the control container, without requiring an explicit request from the container. Events also are important when communicating errors to the container.

An event can take up to 15 parameters, which enable it to pass information about itself to the control container. However, you cannot return results to the ActiveX control through event invocations.

This section describes how to add stock and custom events to a control by using ClassWizard.

Adding Stock Events

Stock events are events that the **COleControl** class handles automatically. It is not required that you support all these events, in your ActiveX control. The following table describes some of the stock events that ClassWizard can implement for you.

Event	Event fires when:
Click	The user clicks the control.
DblClick	The user double-clicks the control.
Error	The control wants to notify its container that an error has occurred.

table continued on next page

table continued from previous page

Event	Event fires when:
KeyDown	The user presses a key while the control has focus.
KeyUp	The user releases a key while the control has focus.
MouseDown	The user clicks a mouse button over the control.
MouseMove	The user moves the mouse over the control.
MouseUp	The user releases a mouse button over the control.

▶ **To add a stock event to an ActiveX control**

1. Load your control's project, and start ClassWizard.
2. On the **ActiveX Events** tab, select the control's class from the **Class name** box.
3. Click **Add Event**, and select one of the stock events from the **External name** box.
4. Click **OK** to close the **Add Method** dialog box.
5. Click **OK** to confirm your choices and close ClassWizard.

ClassWizard adds an entry in the event map section of the control's implementation file. For example, if the **Click** event is added to the **Clock** control, ClassWizard adds the following code to the event map section of the file ClockCtrl.cpp:

```
BEGIN_EVENT_MAP(CClockCtrl, COleControl)
    //{{AFX_EVENT_MAP(CClockCtrl)
    EVENT_STOCK_CLICK()
    //}}AFX_EVENT_MAP
END_EVENT_MAP()
```

Adding Custom Events

Using custom events, you can define unique ways for your control to notify its container that something has occurred. A custom event can be based on events that are visual in nature and occur as a result of some user action, such as clicking a particular portion of the control. Custom events can also be based on other occurrences, such as the passing of time or a ringing telephone line.

Stock events are fired by **COleControl** at the appropriate times. Custom events must be fired explicitly by the derived control class. For example, when an alarm is signaled in the **Clock** control, the control must explicitly fire the custom alarm event for the control container to receive notification of the event.

Adding Custom Events

As with stock events, you implement custom events by using the **ActiveX Events** tab in ClassWizard.

▶ **To add a custom event to a control**

1. Load your control's project.
2. Start ClassWizard.
3. On the **ActiveX Events** tab, choose the name of the control class from the **Class name** box and click **Add Event**.
4. In the **External name** box, type the name of your event.
5. The **Internal name** box displays the default name for the event firing function, **FireXxxx**, where "Xxxx" is the name of your event. You can accept the default name, or enter a different name.
6. Add parameters you want to the **Parameter** list.
7. Click **OK** to close the **Add Event** dialog box.
8. Click **OK** again to confirm your choices and close ClassWizard.

The following occurs when you use ClassWizard to add a custom event:

- A function called **FireXxxx** is created (where "Xxxx" is the name of the custom event). This function calls **COleControl::FireEvent,** passing to it the custom event and any parameters that have been defined.
- An entry is made to the control's event map that maps the custom event to the **FireXxxx** function.
- A line of code is added to the control's .odl file that assigns the custom event a specific ID number. This entry allows the control container to anticipate the event. For example, if the control is used in a Visual Basic-based application, the event will be listed in the code window's procedure list box.

Once the custom event is in place, you can call the **FireXxxx** function at any point in your code where that event has occurred.

To see the demonstration "Adding Events with ClassWizard," see the accompanying CD-ROM.

Implementing ActiveX Control Property Pages

This section describes how to implement ActiveX control property pages. It discusses default, stock, and custom property pages, and also explains how to transfer data between controls and property pages. A sample **Clock** control is used to show how to implement the code to modify and set the properties for a control.

Introduction to ActiveX Control Property Pages

A control container supports access to a control's properties at design time. However, different containers provide different implementations to set design-time properties. For example, Visual Basic provides a Properties window that may not be available in other containers. To ensure that developers can set properties at design time regardless of the type of control container your ActiveX control is used in, you should implement a container-independent method to set properties.

With ActiveX control property pages, you can display and alter a control's properties without affecting the control container displaying the control. ActiveX control property pages will work with any type of container control.

Using property pages also enables you to provide a dialog-type interface for setting properties.

The following illustration shows an example of a property page for an ActiveX control.

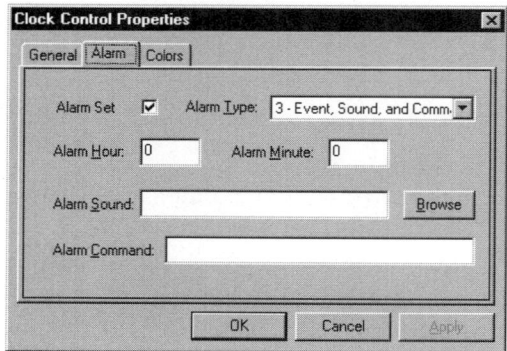

Implementing the Default Property Page

When you create an ActiveX control by using ControlWizard, the template provides for one default property page. This includes both an empty property page resource and the code to invoke the property page.

A property page appears as a tabbed page on a dialog box that acts very much like a standard dialog box. You can add controls to the default property page, and add more pages to suit the needs of your ActiveX control.

To view the default property page for any ActiveX control, right-click the control and select **Properties** on the context menu.

To add controls to a property page, you follow nearly the same set of steps as you would to add a control to a dialog box.

▶ **To add a control to a property page**

1. In the Dialog section in ResourceView, open the appropriate property page template.
2. Add a control to the template that will be associated with a control property.
3. Start ClassWizard to add a member variable to hold the property value.
4. Click the **Member Variables** tab.
5. In the **Control IDs** list, select the control for which the member variable is to be added and click **Add Variable**.
6. Enter the member variable name in the **Add Member Variable** dialog box.
7. Set the category to **value** and ensure that the variable type is accurate.
8. In the **Optional Property Name** combo box, enter the name of the ActiveX control property associated with this variable, or choose a stock property, and click **OK**.

As it does when creating dialog boxes, ClassWizard performs several tasks in this situation. First, it declares and initializes member variables. Second, it adds an appropriate entry to the **DoDataExchange** function to transfer information between the member variables and the controls, as appropriate. However, **DoDataExchange** takes on an additional task when implementing default property pages, as described in the following section.

Exchanging Data Between Controls and Property Pages

DoDataExchange is designed to transfer data between controls on the property page and the member variables in the property page class to link property page values with the actual values of properties in the ActiveX control. The DDX group of functions handles these transfers. You must map the appropriate property page fields to their respective control properties to establish links. This enables the property page object to get and set control properties, as an ActiveX container would.

You use the property page DDP functions to map property page fields to control properties. The DDP functions work much like the DDX functions used in standard MFC dialog boxes, with one exception: In addition to the reference to a member variable, DDP functions take the name of the control property. The following is a typical entry in the **DoDataExchange** function for a property page:

```
DDP_Text(pDX, IDC_CAPTION, m_caption, _T("Caption"));
```

This function associates the property page's *m_caption* member variable with the **Caption** property of the ActiveX control.

The following table describes the DDP functions available in MFC.

Function name	Purpose
DDP_CBIndex	Links the selected string's index in a combo box with a control property.
DDP_CBString	Links the selected string in a combo box with a control property. The selected string can begin with the same letters as the property's value, but need not match it fully.
DDP_CBStringExact	Links the selected string in a combo box with a control property. The selected string and the property's string value must match exactly.
DDP_Check	Links a check box with a control property.
DDP_LBIndex	Links the selected string's index in a list box with a control property.

table continued on next page

table continued from previous page

Function name	Purpose
DDP_LBString	Links the selected string in a list box with a control property. The selected string can begin with the same letters as the property's value, but need not match it exactly.
DDP_LBStringExact	Links the selected string in a list box with a control property. The selected string and the property's string value must match exactly.
DDP_Radio	Links a radio button with a control property.
DDP_Text	Links text with a control property.

The following sample code shows the **DoDataExchange** function. To copy this code for use in your own projects, see "Exchanging Data Between Controls and Property Pages" on the accompanying CD-ROM.

```
//Transfers data between controls on the property page
//and the member variables in the property page class
//Samples/CH06/Clock

void CAlarmPropPage::DoDataExchange(CDataExchange* pDX)
{
  // NOTE: ClassWizard will add DDP, DDX, and DDV calls here
  //      DO NOT EDIT what you see in these blocks of generated code !
  //{{AFX_DATA_MAP(CAlarmPropPage)
  DDP_Text(pDX, IDC_ALARM_HOUR, m_AlarmHour, _T("AlarmHour") );
  DDX_Text(pDX, IDC_ALARM_HOUR, m_AlarmHour);
  DDV_MinMaxInt(pDX, m_AlarmHour, 0, 23);
  DDP_Text(pDX, IDC_ALARM_MINUTE, m_AlarmMinute, _T("AlarmMinute") );
  DDX_Text(pDX, IDC_ALARM_MINUTE, m_AlarmMinute);
  DDV_MinMaxInt(pDX, m_AlarmMinute, 0, 59);
  DDP_Text(pDX, IDC_ALARM_SOUND, m_AlarmSound, _T("AlarmSound") );
  DDX_Text(pDX, IDC_ALARM_SOUND, m_AlarmSound);
```

code continued on next page

code continued from previous page

```
    DDP_Text(pDX,IDC_ALARM_COMMAND,m_AlarmCommand,_T("AlarmCommand"));
    DDX_Text(pDX, IDC_ALARM_COMMAND, m_AlarmCommand);
    DDP_Check(pDX, IDC_ALARM_SET, m_bAlarmSet, _T("AlarmSet") );
    DDX_Check(pDX, IDC_ALARM_SET, m_bAlarmSet);
    DDP_CBIndex(pDX, IDC_ALARM_TYPE, m_AlarmType, _T("AlarmType") );
    DDX_CBIndex(pDX, IDC_ALARM_TYPE, m_AlarmType);
    //}}AFX_DATA_MAP
    DDP_PostProcessing(pDX);
}
```

Your property page's **DoDataExchange** function includes a call to **DDP_Processing** to complete the transfer of data to the control.

Adding Stock Property Pages

Beginning with Windows 3.1, Microsoft has provided implementation for a set of commonly used dialog boxes, such as those used when you open and save files. Use of these common dialog boxes eliminates a significant amount of work that was previously required of programmers, and provides a consistent interface to the user across all applications. Similarly, MFC provides implementation for several commonly used property pages that you can use in your application. These stock property pages include the font chooser, the color chooser, and the picture chooser.

To invoke a stock property page, update the control's property page macro set in the property page map by:

◆ Adding a PROPPAGEID entry with the appropriate class ID for the stock property page, as shown in the following table.

Stock property page	Class ID
Font chooser	**CLSID_CFontPropPage**
Picture chooser	**CLSID_CPicturePropPage**
Color chooser	**CLSID_CColorPropPage**

◆ Incrementing the number of property pages in the BEGIN_PROPPAGEIDS macro.

The following illustration shows the color chooser stock property page.

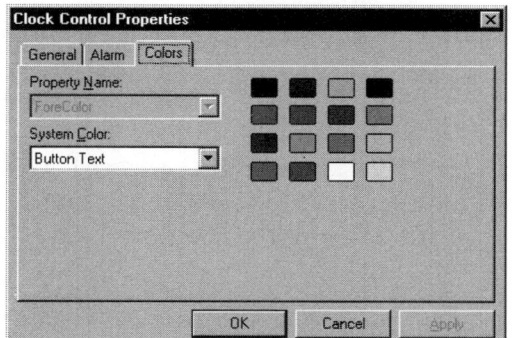

The following sample code contains a property page macro set that uses the color chooser property page for a sample **Clock** control. The complete code for the **Clock** control is located in *<install folder>*\Samples\Ch06\Clock.

```
BEGIN_PROPPAGEIDS(CClockCtrl, 3)
  PROPPAGEID(CClockPropPage::guid)
  PROPPAGEID(CAlarmPropPage::guid)
  PROPPAGEID(CLSID_CColorPropPage)
END_PROPPAGEIDS(CClockCtrl)
```

For the changes to the property pages to be enabled, your ActiveX control will need to be reregistered. Beginning with Visual C++ 4.0, this is done by default when the project is rebuilt; otherwise, use RegSvr32.exe.

Adding Custom Property Pages

In addition to stock property pages, you can also add custom property pages to your ActiveX control. As you create additional property pages for your ActiveX control, consider the following suggestions:

- Keep the number of pages to a minimum.
- Try to minimize the complexity of each property page and keep it uncluttered.
- Keep related information together on the same page.

Adding additional property pages requires four main steps:

1. Create the new property page.
2. Add controls to the property page.

MFC Development Using Microsoft Visual C++ 6.0

3. Create the new property page class.
4. Add the property page to the control's property page list.

To see the demonstration "Adding Custom Property Pages," see the accompanying CD-ROM.

The following steps show how to create the new property page without the ActiveX Control Property Page component in the Components and Controls Gallery. A sample application for a **Clock** control is used to show how the completed code should look.

▶ To create the dialog resource for the property page

1. Use the Resource editor to create a new dialog resource.
2. Name the dialog box IDD_PROPPAGE_Xxxx (where "Xxxx" is a name that describes the topic of the property page).
3. Set the dialog box style to create a child window with a thin border.
4. Make sure the **Titlebar** and **Visible** options are cleared.
5. Size the dialog box to be 250 x 62 or 250 x 110 dialog units.

   Although not mandatory, this step will eliminate compiler warnings that the property page is a nonstandard size.

Note If you create your property page using the IDD_OLE_PROPPAGE_SMALL or IDD_OLE_PROPPAGE_LARGE templates, the resource editor will set the size and properties appropriately.

▶ To create the new property page class

1. Start ClassWizard and select **Create a New Class**.
2. Provide the name for the new class and ensure that **COlePropertyPage** is the base class.
3. Click **OK**.

▶ To associate a property page name and caption

1. Use the string table editor to add an entry for the property page name. For example, the ID could be IDS_ALARM_PPG and the string "Alarm Property Page."

2. Use the string table editor to add an entry for the property page caption that will be displayed on the page's tab. For example, use IDS_ALARM_PPG_CAPTION and the string "Alarm."

3. Use the property page name to register the property page. In the **UpdateRegistry** function in your property page class, update the **AfxOleRegisterPropertyPage** function to use your property page name ID as the last parameter. This will update the registry so that the property page can be properly invoked when requested. The following example updates the registry for the **Clock** control:

```
BOOL CAlarmPropPage::CAlarmPropPageFactory::UpdateRegistry(BOOL bRegister)
{
    if (bRegister)
        return AfxOleRegisterPropertyPageClass(AfxGetInstanceHandle(),m_clsid,
    IDS_ALARM_PPG);
    else
        return AfxOleUnregisterClass(m_clsid, NULL);
}
```

4. Enable the caption by modifying the property page constructor to pass the caption ID to the base class, **COlePropertyPage**. The following example shows how to accomplish this:

```
CAlarmPropPage::CAlarmPropPage() : COlePropertyPage(IDD,
IDS_ALARM_PPG_CAPTION)
{
    //{{AFX_DATA_INIT(CAlarmPropPage)
    m_AlarmHour = 0;
    m_AlarmMinute = 0;
    m_bAlarmSet = -1;
    m_AlarmSound = _T("");
    m_AlarmCommand = _T("");
    //}}AFX_DATA_INIT
}
```

▶ **To add the property page to the control's property page list**

1. Update the macro block in the control class's property page to use the new property page.

2. Add a new PROPPAGEID entry for the new property page.

3. Increment the number of property pages in the BEGIN_PROPPAGEIDS macro.

The following example shows how to add the custom Alarm page to the **Clock** control.

```
BEGIN_PROPPAGEIDS(CClockCtrl, 2)
    PROPPAGEID(CClockPropPage::guid)
    PROPPAGEID(CAlarmPropPage::guid)
END_PROPPAGEIDS(CClockCtrl)
```

You can display the property page at run time by using the **COleControl::OnProperties** function as shown in the following example:

```
void CClockCtrl::OnRButtonUp(UINT nFlags, CPoint point)
{
  COleControl::OnRButtonUp(nFlags, point); // Call the base version.
  COleControl::OnProperties(NULL, this->GetSafeHwnd(), NULL);
}
```

Creating an Enumerated Property

Sometimes a property has several possible values. In such cases, the property page can easily display the valid selections in an appropriate manner, such as in a drop-down combo box.

A number of properties have their own property browsers, such as the Properties window in Visual Basic, which provides an alternate way to view the list of valid property values. MFC provides a mechanism to create these browsers with the necessary information so that they, too, display only the valid selections for a property. To limit the list of valid property values for a given property, you must create an enumerated property.

This section describes how to implement enumerated properties.

How Enumerated Properties Work

When a control container requests the possible values of a property, the framework asks the control for an array of strings that represents those values by calling **OnGetPredefinedStrings**. The control then supplies an array of strings, which is displayed to the user in the property viewer.

The framework then calls **OnGetPredefinedValue** to request the actual property value for one of the predefined strings. Finally, the framework calls **OnGetDisplayString** to attain a string that represents the current property value. This string is usually one of the strings provided in **OnGetPredefinedStrings**.

For example, the **Clock** sample control has a property called **AlarmType** that can take a discrete set of values, as described in the following table.

Property value	String	Resulting action(s)
0	Event Only	Fires alarm event.
1	Event and Sound	Fires alarm event and plays the alarm sound file.
2	Event and Command	Fires alarm event and runs the alarm's command line.
3	Event, Sound, and Command	Fires alarm event, plays the alarm sound file, and runs the alarm's command line.

Implementing an Enumerated Property

The following steps describe how to create an enumerated control property.

▶ **To create an enumerated control property**

1. If it is not already available, add the property.
2. Override **COleControl::OnGetPredefinedStrings**.
    a. Determine the dispatch identifier (DISPID) of the property.
    b. Fill the **CStringArray** array provided with the valid property strings.
    c. Fill the **CDWordArray** parameter with a value you choose to associate with each string. The value has no particular meaning except that it acts as a tag that will be passed to **OnGetPredefinedValue**, and it is **OnGetDisplayString** that will uniquely define a string.
3. Override **COleControl::OnGetPredefinedValue**.
    a. Validate that the DISPID is one of the enumerated properties.
    b. Given the value that represents a string, return the actual property value.

4. Override **COleControl::OnGetDisplayString**.

   a. Validate that the DISPID is one of the enumerated properties.

   b. Given the current value of the property, usually defined by its member variable, return the display string.

The following sample code implements an enumerated property. To copy this code for use in your own projects, see "Implementing an Enumerated Property" on the accompanying CD-ROM.

```
// SAMPLES\Ch06\CLOCK
// ClockCtl.cpp

BOOL CClockCtrl::OnGetPredefinedStrings( DISPID dispid,
                        CStringArray* pStringArray,
                        CDWordArray* pCookieArray )
{
  BOOL bResult = FALSE;

  if(dispidAlarmType == dispid)
  {
  // See if the the dispatch ID is for the AlarmType property
     try
     {
        // Fill in the values in pStringArray and pCookieArray
        // with the AlarmType info
        // ID_ALARMTYPE_BASE is the offset of the beginning
        // ALARMTYPE property value
        for (int i = 0; i < 4; i++)
        {
            CString Name;
            Name.LoadString(ID_ALARMTYPE_BASE + i);
            pStringArray->Add(Name);
            pCookieArray->Add(i);
        }

        bResult = TRUE;
     }
```

code continued on next page

code continued from previous page

```
        catch(CException* e)
        {
            pStringArray->RemoveAll();
            pCookieArray->RemoveAll();
            e->Delete();
            bResult = FALSE;
        }
    }

    if (!bResult)
        bResult = COleControl::OnGetPredefinedStrings(dispid,
            pStringArray, pCookieArray);

    return bResult;
}

BOOL CClockCtrl::OnGetPredefinedValue( DISPID dispid,
        DWORD dwCookie, VARIANT FAR* lpvarOut )
{
    if(dispidAlarmType == dispid)
    {
        VariantClear(lpvarOut);
        V_VT(lpvarOut) = VT_I2;
        V_I2(lpvarOut) = (short)dwCookie;

        return TRUE;
    }

    return COleControl::OnGetPredefinedValue(dispid, dwCookie,
            lpvarOut);
}
```

code continued on next page

```
code continued from previous page
BOOL CClockCtrl::OnGetDisplayString( DISPID dispid, CString&
strValue )
{
  if(dispidAlarmType == dispid)
  {
      switch(m_AlarmType)
      {
      case 0:
      case 1:
      case 2:
      case 3:
          strValue.LoadString(ID_ALARMTYPE_BASE + m_AlarmType);
          break;
      }
      return TRUE;
  }
    return COleControl::OnGetDisplayString(dispid, strValue);
}
```

Although not shown, the property strings have been stored in the string table resource.

Lab 6.1: Building an ActiveX Control Using an Existing Class

In this lab, you will create an ActiveX control from an existing device-independent bitmap (DIB) class, set properties for the control, and add a property page for the control.

To see the demonstration "Lab 6.1 Demonstration," see the accompanying CD-ROM.

Estimated time to complete this lab: **120 minutes**

To complete the exercises in this lab, you must have the required software. For detailed information about the labs and setup for the labs, see "Labs" in "About This Course."

Lab 6.1: Building an ActiveX Control Using an Existing Class

The code that forms the starting point for this lab is located in the folder *<install folder>*\Labs\Ch6\Lab6.1\Ex01.

The solution code for this lab is located in the folder *<install folder>*\Labs\Ch6\Lab6.1.

Objectives

After completing this lab, you will be able to:

- Package an existing class as an ActiveX control.
- Use the ActiveX Control Test Container.
- Add property pages to an ActiveX control.

Prerequisites

Before working on this lab, you should be familiar with the following:

- Using the ControlWizard to create an ActiveX control
- Setting ActiveX control properties
- Implementing property pages for ActiveX controls

Exercises

The following exercises provide practice working with the concepts and techniques covered in this chapter.

- Exercise 1: Building an ActiveX Control

    In this exercise, you will create an ActiveX control by encapsulating the existing device-independent bitmap (DIB) class. After you create the control, you will test the control using the ActiveX Control Test Container.

- Exercise 2: Setting Properties for an ActiveX Control

    In this exercise, you will set properties for the ActiveX control you created in Exercise 1.

- Exercise 3: Adding a Property Sheet Interface

    In this exercise, you will use a property sheet to create a design mode interface for the ActiveX control you implemented in Exercise 2.

Exercise 1: Building an ActiveX Control

The code that forms the basis for this exercise is in *<install folder>*\Labs\Ch06\Lab6.1\Ex01. After you have created your project, copy the files into your project folder.

In this exercise, you will create an ActiveX control. You will use an existing device-independent bitmap (DIB) class. After you create the control, you will test the control by using the ActiveX Control Test Container.

▶ **Build the framework control**

1. Start Microsoft Visual Studio 6.0.
2. On the **File** menu, click **New**.

   The **New** dialog box appears.
3. On the **Projects** tab, click **MFC ActiveX ControlWizard**, set the project name to PalView and click **OK** to start ControlWizard. The following illustration shows the **New** dialog box.

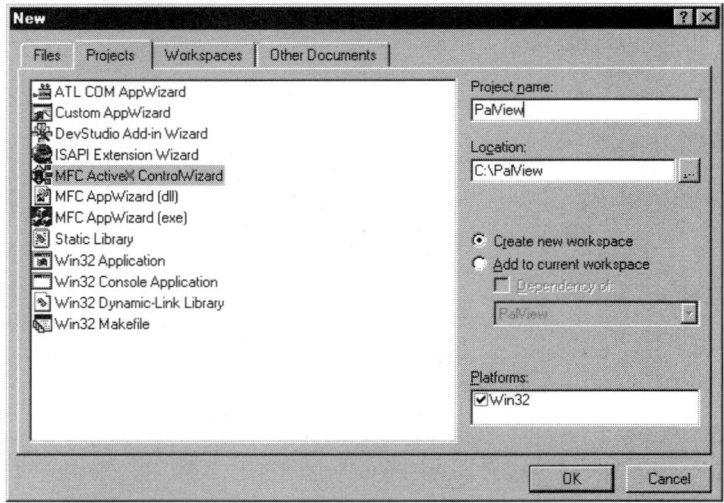

Lab 6.1: Building an ActiveX Control Using an Existing Class

4. In Step 1 of ControlWizard, create one control, leave the other options at their default settings, and click **Next**. The following illustration shows the **MFC ActiveX ControlWizard - Step 1** dialog box.

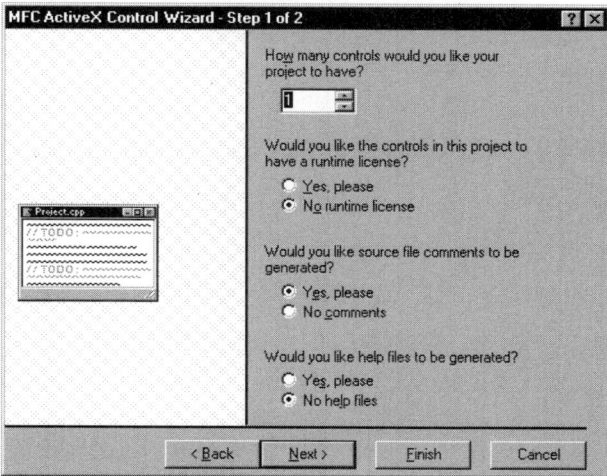

5. In Step 2 of ControlWizard, accept the default settings for all options and click **Finish**.

   The **New Project Information** dialog box appears.

   The following illustration shows the **MFC ActiveX ControlWizard - Step 2** dialog box.

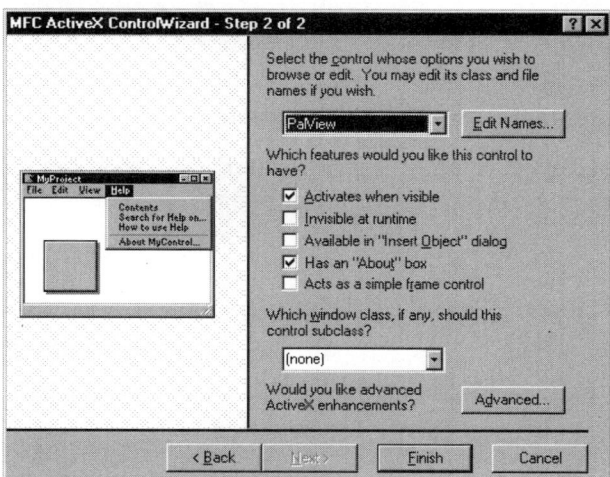

The following illustration shows the **New Project Information** dialog box.

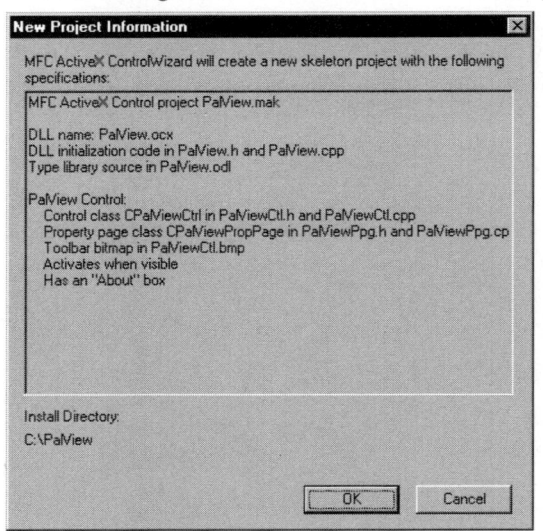

6. Click **OK** to create the project.
7. On the **Project** menu, click **Add to Project,** and click **Files.**

   Insert the files Dib.cpp and DibPal.cpp into the project. You do not need to insert their headers files; Visual Studio will resolve their dependencies.

The **CDIB** class creates a device-independent bitmap from an existing bitmap file, and the **CDIBPal** class uses this information to determine the colors used to create the bitmap.

▶ **Integrate CDIBPal into the CPalViewCtrl control**

1. Right-click **CPalViewCtrl** in ClassView and add a protected member variable. The protected member variable will be defined as follows:

   ```
   CDIBPal*    m_pDibPal;
   ```

   This pointer will be used to refer to the **CDIBPal** object.
2. Open the file PalViewCtl.cpp.
3. Include the files Dib.h and DibPal.h before the file PalViewCtl.h.

Lab 6.1: Building an ActiveX Control Using an Existing Class

4. Update the constructor to initialize the m_pDibPal message to **NULL**. The following sample code shows an example of how your code should look. To copy this code for use in your own projects, see "Lab 6.1.1 CPalViewCtrl Constructor" on the accompanying CD-ROM.

```
CPalViewCtrl::CPalViewCtrl()
{
  InitializeIIDs(&IID_DPalView, &IID_DPalViewEvents);
  m_pDibPal = NULL;
}
```

5. Update the destructor to delete m_pDibPal if it exists. The following sample code shows an example of how your code should look. To copy this code for use in your own projects, see "Lab 6.1.1 CPalViewCtrl Destructor" on the accompanying CD-ROM.

```
CPalViewCtrl::~CPalViewCtrl()
{
  if (NULL != m_pDibPal)
     delete m_pDibPal;
}
```

▶ Update the CPalViewCtrl::OnDraw function to use the CDibPal::Draw function

1. Modify **CPalViewCtrl::OnDraw** to use **CDIBPal::OnDraw** if **CDIBPal** has been instantiated, as follows:

   ```
   if(NULL != m_pDibPal)
       m_pDibPal->Draw(pdc, rcBounds, TRUE);
   ```

   Otherwise, fill the control with a white brush as shown in the following code:

   ```
   else
       pdc->FillRect(rcBounds,
           CBrush::FromHandle((HBRUSH)GetStockObject(WHITE_BRUSH)));
   ```

313

2. Save PalViewCtl.cpp. The following sample code shows an example of how your code should look. To copy this code for use in your own projects, see "Lab 6.1.1 OnDraw" on the accompanying CD-ROM.

```
void CPalViewCtrl::OnDraw(
CDC* pdc, const CRect& rcBounds, const CRect& rcInvalid)
{
  if(NULL != m_pDibPal)
      m_pDibPal->Draw(pdc, rcBounds, TRUE);
  else
      pdc->FillRect(rcBounds,
          CBrush::FromHandle((HBRUSH)GetStockObject(WHITE_BRUSH)));
}
```

▶ **Add a function to extract the palette from a DIB file**

1. Right-click **CPalViewCtl** in ClassView and add a protected member function as follows:

    ```
    void ExtractPalFromDIBFile(LPCTSTR lpszFileSpec)
    ```

    The function will be used to extract the color palette from the DIB file.

2. Add the following local variables to the implementation of the **ExtractPalFromDIBFile**:

    ```
    CDIB     Dib; //use to load Device Independent Bitmap
    CFile    DibFile; //used to open bitmap file
    ```

3. Open the bitmap file, using the path stored in lpszFileSpec as follows:

    ```
    if(DibFile.Open(lpszFileSpec, CFile::modeRead))
    ```

4. Copy the file into a **CDIB** instance as follows:

    ```
    if(Dib.Load(&DibFile))
    ```

5. Create a palette and extract the color table from the DIB into the palette as follows:

    ```
    CDIBPal* pTemp = new CDIBPal;
    ASSERT(pTemp != NULL);
    if(pTemp->Create(&Dib))
    ```

6. Add the following code to delete the instance of **CDIBPal**, if it exists.

   ```
   if(NULL != m_pDibPal)
   {
       delete m_pDibPal;
       m_pDibPal = NULL;
   }
   ```

7. Assign the palette you created to m_pDibPal as follows:

   ```
   m_pDibPal = pTemp;
   ```

8. Draw the palette in 3-D style as follows:

   ```
   m_pDibPal->SetDraw3D(TRUE);
   ```

9. Save PalViewCtl.cpp. The following sample code shows an example of how your code should look. To copy this code for use in your own projects, see "Lab 6.1.1 ExtractPalFromDIBFile" on the accompanying CD-ROM.

```
void CPalViewCtrl::ExtractPalFromDIBFile(LPCSTR lpszFileSpec)
{
  CDIB     Dib;
  CFile    DibFile;

  if(DibFile.Open(lpszFileSpec, CFile::modeRead))
  {
      // Load the bitmap file into a CDIB object
      if(Dib.Load(&DibFile))
      {
          CDIBPal* pTemp = new CDIBPal;
          ASSERT(pTemp != NULL);
          // This will extract the color table from the CDIB object
          if(pTemp->Create(&Dib))
          {
              // Get rid of any existing CDIBPal object
              if(NULL != m_pDibPal)
              {
                  delete m_pDibPal;
                  m_pDibPal = NULL;
              }
              // Ready to go
              m_pDibPal = pTemp;
```

code continued on next page

code continued from previous page
```
            // Make sure the new palette reflects our
            // current state
            m_pDibPal->SetDraw3D(TRUE);
        }
        else
        {
            delete pTemp;
        }
    }
}
```

 Tip The Microsoft Foundation Class Library provides two mechanisms for implementing a property:

- Member variables with notification
- **Get** and **Set** methods

In general member variables are used when the property is a simple stored value. Use **Get** and **Set** methods for those properties that update the user interface, or require other calculations to take place when their value changes.

▶ **Add DibFileName property**

1. In ClassWizard, click the **Automation** tab and click **Add Property**. The **Add Property** dialog box appears. The following illustration shows the **Add Property** dialog box.

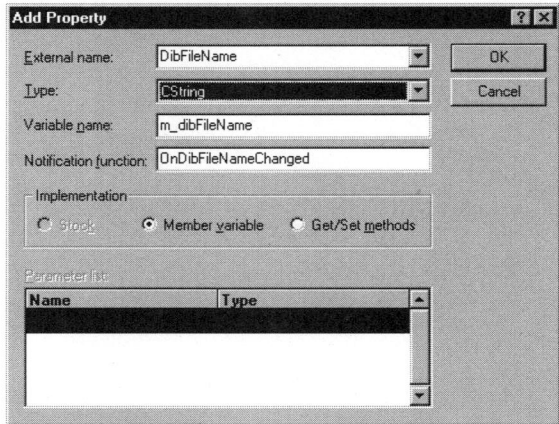

Lab 6.1: Building an ActiveX Control Using an Existing Class

2. With **CPalViewCtrl** as the class, create a new **DibFileName** property, using the following settings.

External name	Type	Variable name	Notification function
DibFileName	CString	m_dibFileName	OnDibFileNameChanged

3. In PalViewCtl.cpp, modify the new **OnDibFileNameChanged** function to extract the palette from **DibFileName** and repaint the control. The following sample code shows an example of how your code should look. To copy this code for use in your own projects, see "Lab 6.1.1 OnDibFileNameChanged" on the accompanying CD-ROM.

```
void CPalViewCtrl::OnDibFileNameChanged()
{
  ExtractPalFromDIBFile(m_dibFileName);
  InvalidateControl();
  SetModifiedFlag();
}
```

4. In the constructor, initialize m_dibFileName as follows:

   m_dibFileName = _T ("");

▶ Build and run the control using the ActiveX Control Test Container

1. Save all files and build the file PalView.ocx.
2. Visual Studio provides a test container for ActiveX controls. To run the test container, click **ActiveX Control Test Container** on the **Tools** menu.

317

The following illustration shows the ActiveX Control Test Container.

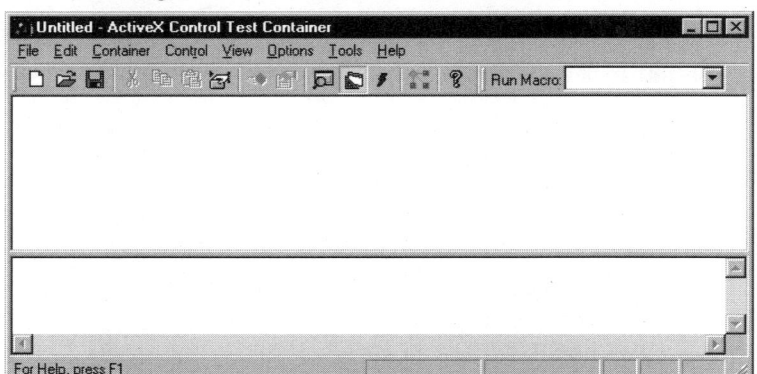

3. On the **Edit** menu, click **Insert New Control**, then click **PalView**. Resize the control to an appropriate size.
4. On the **Edit** menu, click **Properties**.

    The **Properties** dialog box appears. Because you have not implemented a property sheet for this control, invoking **Properties** displays only the blank default property sheet provided by ControlWizard.

The completed code for this exercise is in *<install folder>*\Labs\Ch06\Lab6.1\Ex01\Solution.

Exercise 2: Setting Properties for an ActiveX Control

Continue with the files you created in Exercise 1 or, if you do not have a starting point for this exercise, the code that forms the basis for this exercise is in *<install folder>*\Labs\Ch06\Lab6.1\Ex02.

In this exercise, you will set the properties for the ActiveX control you created in Exercise 1.

▶ **Implement the ShowColorSelection and Show3D properties**

1. The **ShowColorSelection** and **Show3D** properties are member variables of the **CPalViewCtrl** class. They are implemented in the same way as the **DibFileName** property in Exercise 1, as member variables with notification functions. Using ClassWizard, create the following properties.

External name	Type	Variable name	Notification function
ShowColorSelection	BOOL	m_showColorSelection	OnShowColorSelectionChanged
Show3D	BOOL	m_show3D	OnShow3DChanged

2. When **ShowColorSelection** is changed, redraw the control to show or hide the red outlining rectangle indicating the color tile selected. Invalidate the control in **OnShowColorSelectionChanged**:

    ```
    void CPalViewCtrl::OnShowColorSelectionChanged()
    {
        InvalidateControl();
        SetModifiedFlag();
    }
    ```

3. Call **SetDraw3D** in **OnShow3DChanged**. Pass m_show3D as a parameter to **SetDraw3D**.

    ```
    void CPalViewCtrl::OnShow3DChanged()
    {
        if (NULL != m_pDibPal)
        {
            m_pDibPal->SetDraw3D(m_show3D);
            InvalidateControl();
        }
        SetModifiedFlag();
    }
    ```

▶ **Implement the SelectionIndex property**

1. In **CPalViewCtrl**, implement the **SelectionIndex** property as a pair of **Get/Set** methods as follows:

External name	Type	Get	Set
SelectionIndex	short	GetSelectionIndex	SetSelectionIndex

2. To get the selection index, use **CDIBPal::GetSelectionIndex** to query the control. Return−1 if you do not have a **CDIBPal** instance:

   ```
   short CPalViewCtrl::GetSelectionIndex()
   {
       short nSelectionIndex = -1;
       if (NULL != m_pDibPal)
       {
           nSelectionIndex = m_pDibPal->GetSelectionIndex();
       }
       return nSelectionIndex;
   }
   ```

3. To set the selection index, use **CDIBPal::SetSelectionIndex**:

   ```
   void CPalViewCtrl::SetSelectionIndex(short nNewValue)
   {
       if(nNewValue >= 0 && nNewValue < 256)
       {
           if (NULL != m_pDibPal)
           {
               m_pDibPal->SetSelectionIndex(nNewValue);
               FireSelChange(nNewValue);
               InvalidateControl();
           }
       }
       SetModifiedFlag();
   }
   ```

In the previous example, the **FireSelectionChange** function fires the selection change event, which has not yet been added to the ActiveX control being created.

▶ **Add event handling for left-click and double-click**

1. Start ClassWizard.
2. On the **ActiveX Events** tab, click **Add Event**.

   The **Add Event** dialog box appears.

Lab 6.1: Building an ActiveX Control Using an Existing Class

3. Add a stock event for **DblClick,** as shown in the following illustration.

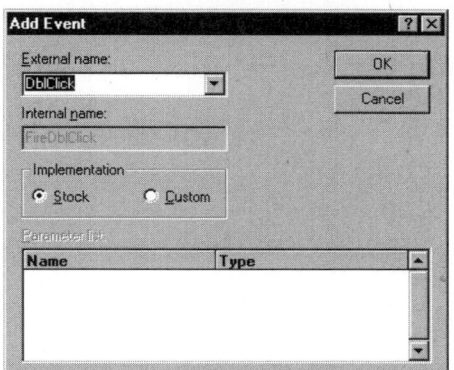

4. Add a custom event for **SelChange.** Add a short parameter, nSelectionIndex.

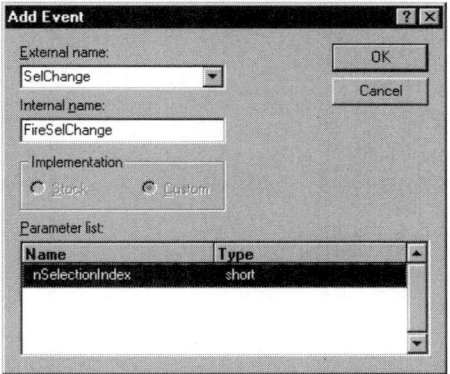

5. Open the **Message Maps** tab in ClassWizard and add a handler for the WM_LBUTTONDOWN message in the **CPalViewCtrl** class.

6. In the code for **OnLButtonDown,** validate that the ActiveX control has instantiated a **CDIBPal** object, and if so, get the size of the control:

```
if(NULL != m_pDibPal)
{
    int x, y;
    GetControlSize(&x, &y);
    CRect rcControl(0, 0, x, y);
```

7. Pass **CRect** and **CPoint** to **CDIBPal::HitTest** to get the cell that was clicked. Then, set the selection index:

   ```
   int nPalIndex = m_pDibPal->HitTest(rcControl, point);
   if(-1 != nPalIndex)
   {
       SetSelectionIndex(nPalIndex);
   }
   ```

8. Save PalViewCtl.cpp. The following sample code shows the completed function. To copy this code for use in your own projects, see "Lab 6.1.2 CPalViewCtrl::OnLButtonDown" on the accompanying CD-ROM.

```
void CPalViewCtrl::OnLButtonDown(UINT nFlags, CPoint point)
{
  if(NULL != m_pDibPal)
  {
      int x, y;
      GetControlSize(&x, &y);
      CRect rcControl(0, 0, x, y);

      // Ask the DibPal object which palette index would
      // be hit by the mouse click
      int nPalIndex = m_pDibPal->HitTest(rcControl, point);
      if(-1 != nPalIndex)
          //Change the selection property
          SetSelectionIndex(nPalIndex);
  }
  COleControl::OnLButtonDown(nFlags, point);
}
```

▶ **Implement a method to get the current color from the palette**

1. On the **Automation** tab in ClassWizard, add a method to get a color from the palette.

External name	Return type	Parameter name	Parameter type
GetColorFromPalette	long	nPalIndex	short

2. Edit the code for the **GetColorFromPalette** method as follows:

   a. Check that the palette index is between 0 and 255:

   ```
   COLORREF      crRet = 0; // Default to BLACK
   if(nPalIndex >= 0 && nPalIndex < 256)
   {
   ```

   b. Return CDIBPal::GetColorFromIndex if there is a CDIBPal object:

   ```
   if(NULL != m_pDibPal)
   {
      crRet = m_pDibPal->GetColorFromIndex(nPalIndex);
   }
   return crRet;
   }
   ```

3. Save PalViewCtl.cpp. The following sample code shows the complete function. To copy this code for use in your own projects, see "Lab 6.1.2 CPalViewCtrl::GetColorFromPalette" on the accompanying CD-ROM.

```
long CPalViewCtrl::GetColorFromPalette(short nPalIndex)
{
  COLORREF     crRet = 0; // Default to BLACK
  if(nPalIndex >= 0 && nPalIndex < 256)
  {
      if(NULL != m_pDibPal)
          crRet = m_pDibPal->GetColorFromIndex(nPalIndex);
  }
  return crRet;
}
```

▶ Modify the functions provided by ControlWizard

DoPropExchange is called by the framework when loading or storing a control from a persistent storage representation, such as a stream or property set. This function normally makes calls to the PX_ family of functions to load or store specific user-defined properties of an ActiveX control. Add PX_ calls for the properties you just implemented as follows:

```
PX_Bool(pPX, _T("ShowColorSelection"), m_showColorSelection, TRUE);
PX_Bool(pPX, _T("Show3D"), m_show3D, FALSE);
PX_String(pPX, _T("DibFileName"), m_dibFileName, _T(""));
```

1. After loading DibFileName, get the palette from that file:

   ```
   if (pPX->IsLoading())
   {
       ExtractPalFromDIBFile(m_dibFileName);
   }
   ```

2. Save PalViewCtl.cpp. The following sample code shows the complete function. To copy this code for use in your own projects, see "Lab 6.1.2 CPalViewCtrl::DoPropExchange" on the accompanying CD-ROM.

   ```
   void CPalViewCtrl::DoPropExchange(CPropExchange* pPX)
   {
     ExchangeVersion(pPX, MAKELONG(_wVerMinor, _wVerMajor));
     COleControl::DoPropExchange(pPX);

     PX_Bool(pPX, _T("ShowColorSelection"), m_showColorSelection, TRUE);
     PX_Bool(pPX, _T("Show3D"), m_show3D, FALSE);
     PX_String(pPX, _T("DibFileName"), m_dibFileName, _T(""));

     if (pPX->IsLoading())
     {
         ExtractPalFromDIBFile(m_dibFileName);
     }

   }
   ```

3. In the **CPalViewCtrl** constructor, initialize m_showColorSelection to **TRUE** and m_show3D to **FALSE**. The following sample code shows the complete constructor. To copy this code for use in your own projects, see "Lab 6.1.2 CPalViewCtrl Complete Constructor" on the accompanying CD-ROM.

   ```
   CPalViewCtrl::CPalViewCtrl()
   {
     InitializeIIDs(&IID_DPalView, &IID_DPalViewEvents);
     m_pDibPal = NULL;
     m_dibFileName = _T("");

     m_showColorSelection = TRUE;
     m_show3D = FALSE;

   }
   ```

4. In **ExtractPalFromDIBFile,** modify the call to **CDIBPal::SetDraw3D** to use m_show3D:

   ```
   m_pDibPal->SetDraw3D(m_show3D);
   ```

5. In **CPalViewCtrl::OnDraw,** modify the call to **CDIBPal::Draw** to use m_showColorSelection:

   ```
   m_pDibPal->Draw(pdc, rcBounds, m_showColorSelection);
   ```

6. Save PalViewCtl.cpp. Build and run PalView.ocx using the ActiveX Control Test Container.

The completed code for this exercise is in *<install folder>*\Labs\Ch06\Lab6.1\Ex02.

Exercise 3: Adding a Property Sheet Interface

Continue with the files you created in Exercise 2 or, if you do not have a starting point for this exercise, the code that forms the basis for this exercise is in *<install folder>*\Labs\Ch06\Lab6.1\Ex03.

In this exercise, you will use a property sheet to create a design mode interface for the ActiveX control you implemented in Exercise 2. ControlWizard provides a property sheet with one blank page.

▶ **Modify the property page provided by MFC AppWizard**

The first property page will have two check boxes: one for the **ShowColorSelection** property and the other for the **Show3D** property as shown in the following illustration.

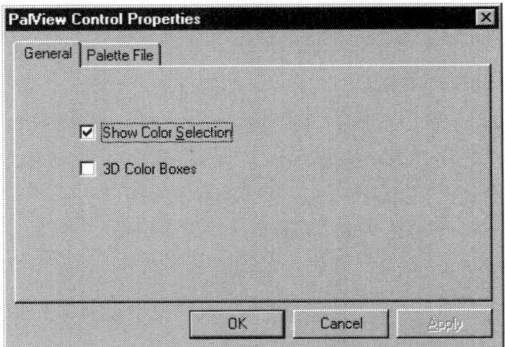

MFC Development Using Microsoft Visual C++ 6.0

1. Delete the static text control on the IDD_PROPPAGE_PALVIEW dialog box template. Add and position controls on this template according to the following table.

Type	ID	Caption
Check box	IDC_COLORSELECTION	Show Color &Selection
Check box	IDC_3D_BOXES	&3D Color Boxes

2. Create member variables and link them to their properties according to the following table. Press the CTRL key, and double-click **controls** to display their variables.

ID	Type	Variable name	Property name
IDC_COLORSELECTION	BOOL	m_bShowColorSelection	**ShowColorSelection**
ICD_3D_BOXES	BOOL	m_bShow3D	**Show3D**

▶ **Add a new property page**

The new property page will enable your users to set the palette to be displayed. The following illustration shows a sample palette property page.

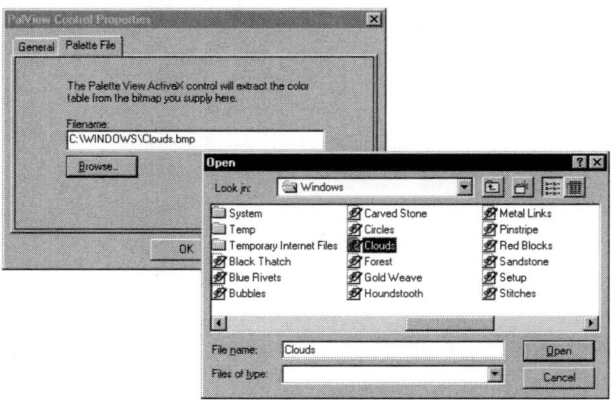

Lab 6.1: Building an ActiveX Control Using an Existing Class

1. Create a new dialog template. On the **Insert** menu, click **Resource** to display the properties resources. Expand the Dialog icon, click **IDD_OLE_PROPPAGE_SMALL**, and add this dialog box template with the following controls.

Type	ID	Caption
Dialog	IDD_PROPPAGE_DIBFILE	None
PushButton	IDC_BROWSE	&Browse
Edit control	IDC_DIB_FILENAME	None
Static	IDC_STATIC	Filename:
Static	IDC_STATIC	The Palette View ActiveX control will extract the color table from the bitmap file you supply here.

2. Use ClassWizard to create a new class based on the IDD_PROPPAGE_DIBFILE dialog box. Make the base class **COlePropertyPage**. Name the new class **CDibFilePropPage** and use DibPrpg.cpp and DibPrpg.h as file names.

3. Create a member variable for the edit control.

ID	Type	Variable name	Property name
IDC_DIB_FILENAME	**CString**	m_DibFileName	DibFileName

4. In **CDibFilePropPage**, create a command handler for the click event of the IDC_BROWSE message.

5. In the **CDibFilePropPage::OnBrowse** function, display a common file dialog box and set the text of the file name edit control with the results. The sample code on the following page shows the complete function. To copy this code for use in your own projects, see "Lab 6.1.3 CDibFilePropPage::OnBrowse" on the accompanying CD-ROM.

327

```
void CDibFilePropPage::OnBrowse()
{
  CFileDialog dlg(TRUE);
  if(dlg.DoModal() == IDOK)
  {
      CEdit * pEdit = (CEdit *)GetDlgItem(IDC_DIB_FILENAME);
      if(NULL != pEdit)
          pEdit->SetWindowText(dlg.GetPathName());
  }
}
```

6. In the string table resource, add two strings for captions.

ID	Caption
IDS_DIBPAGE	Palette File
IDS_DIBPAGE_CAPTION	Palette File

7. In the **UpdateRegistry** function of DibPrpg.cpp, modify the call to **AfxOleRegisterPropertyPageClass** to use IDS_DIBPAGE instead of 0. Note that ClassView does not display this member function, which is located in the .cpp file. The following sample code shows an example of how your code should look. To copy this code for use in your own projects, see "Lab 6.1.3 CDibFilePropPage::CDibFilePropPageFactory::UpdateRegistry" on the accompanying CD-ROM.

```
BOOL CDibFilePropPage::CDibFilePropPageFactory::UpdateRegistry(BOOL
bRegister)
{
  // TODO: Define string resource for page type;
  // replace '0' below with ID.
  if (bRegister)
      return AfxOleRegisterPropertyPageClass(AfxGetInstanceHandle(),
          m_clsid, IDS_DIBPAGE);
  else
      return AfxOleUnregisterClass(m_clsid, NULL);
}
```

8. In the **CDibFilePropPage::CDibFilePropPage** function, change the initialization to use IDS_DIBPAGE_CAPTION instead of 0. The following sample code shows the complete function. To copy this code for use in your own projects, see "Lab 6.1.3 CDibFilePropPage::CDibFilePropPage" on the accompanying CD-ROM.

```
CDibFilePropPage::CDibFilePropPage() :
  COlePropertyPage(IDD, IDS_DIBPAGE_CAPTION)
{
  //{{AFX_DATA_INIT(CDibFilePropPage)
  m_DibFileName = _T("");
  //}}AFX_DATA_INIT
}
```

9. Save this file.

▶ **Setup the new property page in CPalViewCtrl**

1. Include DibPrpg.H in PalViewCtl.cpp.
2. Change the BEGIN_PROPPAGEIDS macro to indicate that you will have two pages in the property sheet as follows:

   ```
   BEGIN_PROPPAGEIDS(CPalViewCtrl, 2)
   ```

3. Add an additional PROPPAGEID macro for **CDibFilePropPage** as follows:

   ```
   PROPPAGEID(CDibFilePropPage::guid)
   ```

4. Save PalViewCtl.cpp. The following code shows the complete macro block:

   ```
   BEGIN_PROPPAGEIDS(CPalViewCtrl, 2)
       PROPPAGEID(CPalViewPropPage::guid)
       PROPPAGEID(CDibFilePropPage::guid)
   END_PROPPAGEIDS(CPalViewCtrl)
   ```

5. Build and use the control.

The completed code for this exercise is in <install folder>\Labs\Ch06\Lab6.1\Ex03\Solution.

Data Binding in an ActiveX Control

A data-bound control is an ActiveX control that is "data aware." When you implement a data-bound control, you bind a property of the control to a data source. Doing so specifies what data to display in the control. The data source can be a specific field or column in a database, the value of another control property, a real-time data feed, and so on.

Introduction to Data Binding

Data binding is a negotiation between a control and a control container, whereby the control requests permission to change some property value, and subsequently informs the container that the data has changed. A common belief is that data binding refers to an ActiveX control that is database aware. Although a data-bound ActiveX control usually is database aware, the mechanism does not enforce this.

In a typical implementation of a data-bound control, controls are placed on a form where they can provide a visual interface to the current record of the database. The following illustration shows a form in Visual Basic that serves as a database front end. The form contains a data control and two data-bound edit boxes to view fields in a database.

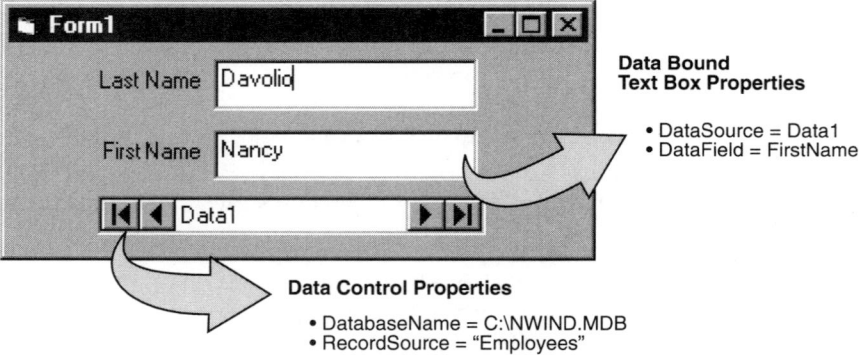

The control container must provide the interface between the control and the field in a database. This aspect of data binding is not discussed here. For an example of how a data-bound control is implemented from the control container, search for "DAOCTL: ActiveX Control Container with Data Bound Controls" in MSDN Library Visual Studio 6.0 and see the MFC sample project DAOCTL.

How Data Binding Works

A control with a property designated as bound cannot modify the value of the property without first getting permission from the control container. If permission is given and the value is changed, the control must then notify the control container that the change has occurred.

MFC provides two **COleControl** functions for modifying property values:

- **BoundPropertyRequestEdit**

    Provides the request to the control container to change the data value.

- **BoundPropertyChanged**

    Is called to inform the control container that the data has changed.

Both these functions require a DISPID parameter to identify which property is being addressed.

Each property has associated **Get** and **Set** functions that you must implement. While the **Get** function simply returns the property value as with a nonbound control, the **Set** function must first request permission to edit the property by calling **BoundPropertyRequestEdit**, and inform the control container that the value changed by calling **BoundPropertyChanged**.

Creating a Bindable Property

To create a property that can be bound, select the **Bindable Property** check box in ClassWizard, and provide the appropriate implementation in the property's access functions.

▶ **To create a bindable property**

1. Add a custom property to the ActiveX control using ClassWizard. You must have implemented the property using the **Get/Set** methods.
2. On the **Automation** tab in ClassWizard, click **Data Binding**.
3. Select the **Bindable Property** check box.
4. Select any other options that apply, and click **OK** to confirm your choices.
5. On the **Automation** tab, click **Edit Code**.
6. Edit the property's **Set** function.

The following sample code shows a common implementation of this code. To copy this code for use in your own projects, see "The Set Function for an Bindable Property" on the accompanying CD-ROM.

```
//Samples/Ch06/Clock
//Sets the bound property
void CBoundCtrl::SetDataBoundProperty(LPCTSTR lpszNewValue)
{
  // Request permission to change bound property
  // "dispidDataBoundProperty"
  if(BoundPropertyRequestEdit (dispidDataBoundProperty))
  {
      // Change the bound property
      m_strDBProp = lpszNewValue;
      SetModifiedFlag();
      // Notify container that bound property has changed
      BoundPropertyChanged(dispidDataBoundProperty);
      InvalidateControl();
  }
  else
  {
      // Permission to change the property was denied.
      // Use SetNotPermitted to throw an appropriate error to the container.
      SetNotPermitted();
  }
}
```

Data Binding Options

When you request data binding for a control, ClassWizard presents the following dialog box:

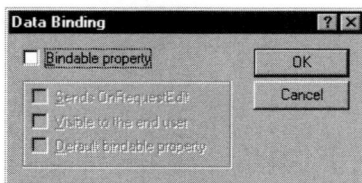

You must select the **Bindable Property** check box for the control to be automatically bound. The remaining options are not required, and are defined in the following table.

Binding option	Description
Sends OnRequestEdit	The property requests permission from the database before modifying the value.
Visible to the End User	The container displays the property in a property-binding dialog box.
Default Bindable Property	Makes the bindable property the control container's default choice.

Optimizing ActiveX Controls

Performance is a crucial factor to consider when creating ActiveX controls. You can use the advanced features of the MFC ActiveX ControlWizard to optimize the performance of controls.

Advanced Features for ActiveX Controls

The MFC ActiveX ControlWizard provides advanced features to help optimize the performance of your ActiveX controls. To select advanced features, click the **Advanced** button in Step 2 of the ActiveX ControlWizard, and then select the features you want in the **Advanced ActiveX Features** dialog box. Choosing any of these features adds a **GetControlFlags** function to the control class.

The following illustration shows the **Advanced ActiveX Features** dialog box.

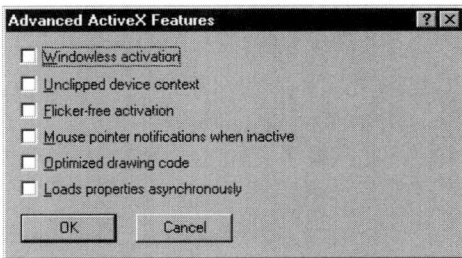

The base version of **COleControl::GetControlFlags** returns the value fastBeginPaint |clipPaintDC. The clipPaintDC value causes **COleControl** to make a call to **IntersectClipRect**. If you are certain that your control does not paint outside its client rectangle, you can improve performance by disabling the flag associated with clipPaintDC as follows:

```
DWORD CMyCtrl::GetControlFlags()
{
    return COleControl::GetControlFlags() & ~clipPaintDC;
}
```

The code to remove this flag can be automatically generated for your control. When creating your control with ControlWizard, select the **Unclipped device context** option in the **Advanced ActiveX Features** dialog box. The flag will be removed automatically.

The other flag, fastBeginPaint, is used by **COleControl::OnPaint** (which calls your control's **OnDraw** function) to create a DC optimized for use by controls.

Optimizing Drawing Code

The **OnDraw** function provides optimization through the rcInvalid parameter. This parameter defines the rectangular area of the control that needs redrawing. You can use this area, usually smaller than the entire control area, to speed the painting process.

You can also speed the redrawing of controls by using metafiles. For detailed instructions about how to use metafiles, search for "ActiveX Controls: Painting an ActiveX Control" and "OLE Controls: Top Tips" in the MSDN Library Visual Studio 6.0.

The first parameter of **COleControl::OnDraw** is a pointer to a DC. As the control is drawing itself, it will typically create Graphics Device Interface (GDI) objects (such as pens, brushes, and fonts), then select those GDI objects into the DC, perform its drawing operations, and restore the original GDI objects into the DC. This process can take a lot of time and system resources. Furthermore, other controls may be drawing themselves in the container using the same container-supplied DC.

You can improve the performance of a control that uses GDI objects by clicking the **Advanced** button in Step 2 of the ActiveX ControlWizard and selecting the **Optimized drawing code** option. For more information about this option, search for "Optimizing Control Drawing" in the MSDN Library Visual Studio 6.0.

Windowless Activation

The ActiveX Control specification provides windowless activation for ActiveX containers only. Windowless controls are compatible with containers that are not written to support windowless controls. In these containers, the windowless controls simply create a window when active.

When a control maintains an on-screen window, it also has to manage messages for that window. Therefore, windowless controls are faster than windowed controls.

Unlike windowed controls, windowless controls support transparent painting and nonrectangular screen regions. A common example of a transparent control is a text control with a transparent background. The control paints the text but not the background, so whatever is under the text shows through. Newer implementations of this type of control often use nonrectangular controls, such as arrows and round buttons.

For a complete discussion about how to create and use windowless controls, search for "Providing Windowless Activation" in the MSDN Library Visual Studio 6.0.

Debugging and Handling Errors in ActiveX Applications

This section describes methods of communicating errors to ActiveX containers and debugging ActiveX applications.

Communicating Errors in ActiveX Controls

When errors occur in your ActiveX control, you should communicate these errors to the control container. There are two methods of communicating errors:

- **COleControl::ThrowError**

  Call this function if the error occurs within a **Get** or **Set** function, or in the implementation of an Automation method as shown on the following page:

```
void CClockCtrl::SetAlarmMinute(short nNewValue)
{
    if (nNewValue < 0 || nNewValue >= 60)
    {
        ThrowError(CTL_E_INVALIDPROPERTYVALUE,
            "AlarmMinute must be between 0 and 59, inclusive");
    }
    m_AlarmMinute = nNewValue;
    SetModifiedFlag();
}
```

COleControl provides a set of convenient functions (**SetNotPermitted**, **SetNotSupported**, and **GetNotSupported**) that calls **ThrowError** with appropriate parameters for the type of error.

- **COleControl::FireError**

    Use this function for any other error condition. Calling this function fires the stock **Error** event.

Both functions are easy to use and have parameters that enable you to pass information to the control container about the type of error. For a complete list of ActiveX control error codes, search for "ActiveX Controls: Advanced Topics" in MSDN Library Visual Studio 6.0.

Debugging ActiveX Applications

ActiveX applications perform a number of tasks outside the programmer's direct control. Communication among DLLs, usage counts on objects, and Clipboard operations are just a few areas where you can encounter unexpected behavior. Usually, when unexpected behavior occurs, your first step is to track down the source. Frequently in ActiveX applications, how to debug a particular problem is not immediately obvious.

The MSDN Library Visual Studio 6.0 includes a series of topics explaining techniques that you can use to track down problems, some of which are unique to ActiveX applications. It also introduces you to special tools and testing aids to help you write solid ActiveX applications.

Debugging ActiveX applications begins with the same general debugging techniques you use in other kinds of applications. For more information about debugging ActiveX applications, search for "Debugging ActiveX Applications with MFC" in MSDN Library Visual Studio 6.0.

To debug an ActiveX server and container, start two instances of Visual C++. Load the container into one instance and load the server into the other, set appropriate breakpoints in each, and debug. When the container makes a call into the server that hits a breakpoint, the container will wait until the server code returns. You also can trace calls that exceed process boundaries. For more information on tracing these calls, search for "The Trace Macro" in MSDN Library Visual Studio 6.0.

Sample Applications

The following table describes the sample applications related to this chapter. These sample applications are located in the folder *<install folder>*\Samples\Ch06.

Sample application subfolder	Description of application
Clock	A full-featured ActiveX control built using ControlWizard.
UseClock	A **CFormView**-based SDI application that uses the **Clock** control. The **Clock** control must be installed and registered before you run this application.

Self-Check Questions

To see the answers to the Self-Check Questions, see Appendix A.

1. **Which dispatch map entry do you use to access a set of values through a single control property?**

    A. DISP_PROPERTY_NOTIFY

    B. DISP_PROPERTY

    C. DISP_PROPERTY_PARAM

    D. DISP_PROPERTY_EX

2. **Implementing an ActiveX control's default property page most closely resembles which other process?**

   A. Adding controls to a normal dialog box
   B. Adding data-bound controls to a **CDaoRecordView** form
   C. Reading and writing to the registry
   D. Associating a toolbar button with a menu item

3. **What is a data-bound ActiveX control?**

   A. An ActiveX control that is bound to a field in a database
   B. An ActiveX control whose **Get/Set** methods have RFX, DFX, or DDX entries to enable the exchange of information
   C. A negotiation between a control and its container, in which the container gives permission to the control to change a property value, and is informed when the control does so
   D. An ActiveX control with information overload

Chapter 7:
Using OLE DB Templates for Data Access

Multimedia

Universal Data Access 340

OLE DB Object Model 342

Creating an OLEDB Application by Using AppWizard 349

Lab 7.1 Demonstration 360

Lab 7.2 Demonstration 372

OLE DB is a set of COM interfaces that provide uniform access to data stored in diverse data sources. Using OLE DB, your application can access data stored in database management system (DBMS) and non-DBMS data sources.

DBMS data sources are traditional databases that store data in tabular format. Non-DBMS data sources are data containers that do not store data in tabular format. Some common examples of non-DBMS data sources are electronic mail boxes, text files, and spreadsheets.

In this chapter you will learn to use OLE DB consumer templates to build applications that access data stored in DBMS and non-DBMS data sources.

Objectives

After completing this chapter, you will be able to:

- List the benefits of using the OLE DB technology for data access.
- Describe the role of OLE DB components in data access.
- Explain the architecture of provider and consumer template classes.
- Build consumer applications by using OLE DB consumer templates.

Overview of OLE DB

This section discusses the need for a generic data access interface standard such as OLE DB and briefly describes the different types of OLE DB applications and OLE DB components.

Benefits of OLE DB

Open Database Connectivity (ODBC), which is the industry standard for data access interfaces, requires data to be stored in a tabular format. However, a vast amount of critical information necessary to conduct day-to-day business is found outside traditional databases. To take advantage of the benefits of database technology, such as queries, transactions, and security, organizations were compelled to move the data from its original containing system into a DBMS.

Over time, businesses realized that transferring data into a DBMS is an expensive and redundant operation. This realization led to the development of OLE DB, which is a more generalized and more efficient strategy for data access than ODBC.

To see the expert point-of-view "Universal Data Access," see the accompanying CD-ROM.

Some benefits of using OLE DB include:

- Access to component DBMSs

    Often, applications do not require or use all the functionality packaged in a commercial, monolithic DBMS. Yet, they are forced to pay additional resource overhead for functionality they do not need. OLE DB divides a DBMS into functional areas, such as data access and updates (rowsets), query processing, catalog information, notifications, transactions, security, and remote data access. By defining a DBMS as a set of well-defined components, OLE DB enables applications to use only the necessary DBMS functionality.

- Open, extensible collection of interfaces

    OLE DB interfaces define the boundaries of DBMS components, such as row containers and query processors, to enable uniform access to diverse information sources. This approach views a DBMS as a conglomerate of cooperating components that consume and produce data through a uniform set of interfaces.

- Support for diverse information sources

    OLE DB makes it easy for applications to access data stored in diverse DBMS and non-DBMS information sources. DBMS sources may include mainframe databases such as IMS and DB2, server databases such as Oracle and Microsoft SQL Server, and desktop databases such as Microsoft Access, Paradox, and Microsoft FoxPro. Non-DBMS sources can include information stored in file systems such as Microsoft Windows NT and UNIX, indexed sequential files, e-mail, spreadsheets, project management tools, and many other sources.

Types of OLE DB Applications

The two types of OLE DB applications are consumers and providers.

Consumers

A consumer application retrieves data from a data source for further processing. Examples of consumers are Microsoft Visual C++-based and Microsoft Visual Basic-based applications that access an Oracle or Microsoft Access database.

Providers

There are two types of provider applications:

- Data providers

    A data provider is any application that owns data. It can expose its data in a tabular format, regardless of the format in which it stores data. Examples of data providers are relational DBMSs, spreadsheets, indexed sequential access methods (ISAMs), and e-mail.

- Service providers

    A service provider does not have its own data, but it facilitates data access between a data provider and a consumer. Examples of service providers are query processors and cursor engines. Service providers act both as consumers and providers. In its role as a consumer, a service provider retrieves data from the base tables owned by the data provider. In its role as a provider, the query processor creates a rowset from the retrieved data and returns it to the consumer.

For more information about OLE DB providers, search for "Using the OLE DB Provider Templates" in the MSDN Library Visual Studio 6.0.

The following illustration shows the relationship between the consumer, data provider, and service provider.

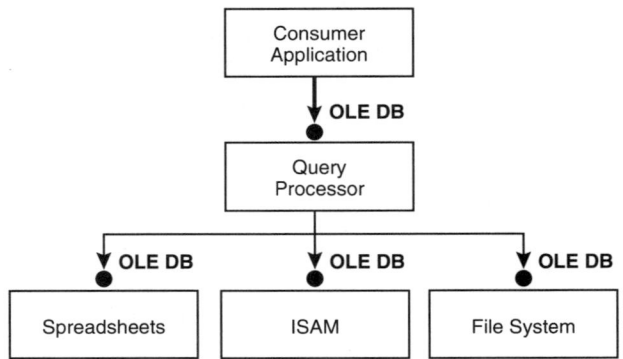

OLE DB Components

OLE DB consists of several components, each of which is a COM object. The following illustration shows OLE DB components.

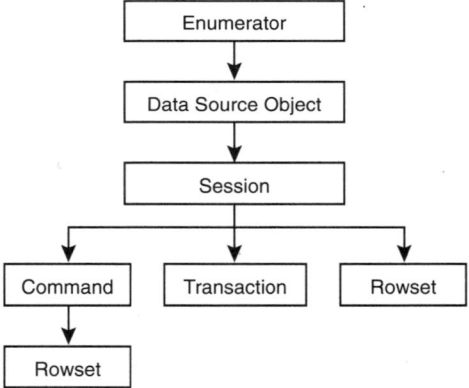

To see the animation "OLE DB Object Model," see the accompanying CD-ROM.

Enumerators

An enumerator is a COM object that can locate available data sources and other enumerators. Consumers that are not customized for a particular data source use enumerators to find a data source to use.

The OLE DB Software Development Kit (SDK) includes a root enumerator that traverses the registry looking for data sources and other enumerators. Other enumerators traverse the registry or search in a provider-specific manner. For example, the MSDASQL enumerator will search for ODBC data sources.

Data Source Objects

Data source objects contain the code to connect to a data source, such as a file or a DBMS. To access an OLE DB provider, a consumer must first create an instance of a data source object. The data source object exposes IDBInitialize, which the consumer uses to connect to the data source. Once a data source object has been successfully initialized, the consumer can call methods in IDBProperties to query the capabilities of a provider. These capabilities include rowset properties such as scrollability and transaction properties such as supported isolation levels.

Sessions

A data source object creates one or more sessions. The primary function of a session is to provide a context for transactions. A session can be in one of the following modes:

- Manual commit

    If you call the **CSession** member function **StartTransaction** to start an explicit transaction, the session is in manual commit mode. You must explicitly commit or abort any work done in the session. You can call **StartTransaction** only after the session has been successfully created.

- Auto-commit

    If transactions are not supported or if the call to **StartTransaction** is not made, the session is in auto-commit mode. Any work done in the session is automatically committed; it cannot be aborted.

Transactions

A transaction enables consumers to define units of work within a provider. These units of work have the atomicity, concurrency, isolation, and durability (ACID) properties. A transaction enables more flexible access to data among concurrent consumers.

For providers that support nested transactions, calling **StartTransaction** within an existing transaction begins a new nested transaction below the current transaction. Calling the **Commit** or **Abort** method commits or aborts the transaction at the lowest level, respectively.

Commands

In OLE DB, data definition language (DDL) and data manipulation language (DML) statements are referred to as text commands. A command object contains a text command and encapsulates the query processing services available in DBMSs.

Executing a command such as an SQL **SELECT** statement creates a rowset, while executing a command such as an SQL **UPDATE** or **CREATE TABLE** statement does not create a rowset.

Text commands are expressed in a provider-specific language, which is typically ANSI SQL92.

Rowsets

The rowset object enables OLE DB data providers to expose data in tabular form. A rowset is a set of rows in which each row has columns of data. Base table providers present their data in the form of rowsets. Query processors present the result of queries in the form of rowsets.

Rowsets can be created in one of the following ways:

- As a result of a query

    This method is supported by all providers.

- By calling **IOpenRowset::OpenRowset**

    Simple providers, such as those built over a base table, index, file, or in-memory structure, generally do not support this method.

Errors

Each OLE DB method provides a return code that indicates the success or failure of the method. There are two types of return codes.

- Success or warning

    Success or warning codes begin with S_ or DB_S_ and indicate that the method successfully completed.

- Error

    Error codes begin with E_ or DB_E_ and indicate that the method failed completely and was unable to do any useful work.

Introduction to OLE DB Templates

OLE DB Templates refers to a set of classes that help you develop OLE DB applications with minimum effort. You use these classes to implement many of the commonly used OLE DB object interfaces.

The OLE DB templates are provided in the form of a template library that is similar to the Active Template Library (ATL). The classes in this template library can be grouped into:

- Provider classes

    You use these classes to implement a database provider application.
- Consumer classes

    You use these classes to implement a database consumer application.

This section describes the provider and consumer templates and their architecture.

OLE DB Provider Templates

The OLE DB Provider Templates support the OLE DB version 1.1 specification. Using these templates, you can implement simple read-only provider applications. You can also implement read/write providers using these templates, but you need to add code manually. The provider applications may or may not support commands.

For example, you can build a provider that executes the DOS **DIR** command to query the file system. The provider will return the directory information in a rowset, which is the standard OLE DB mechanism for returning tabular data.

The OLE DB provider architecture includes a data source object and one or more session objects, as shown in the following illustration.

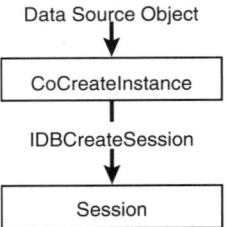

When a consumer application needs data, it calls the **CoCreateInstance** function to create a data source object, as shown in the following example:

```
int main()
{
   // Initialize OLE
   ...

   // Create an instance of a data source object for an email
   // data provider.
   CoCreateInstance(CLSID_MailProvider, 0, CLSCTX_LOCAL_SERVER,
IID_IDBInitialize, (void**) &pIDBInit);
   // Initialize the data source object for email data provider.
```

Each data provider is identified by a unique class identifier (CLSID) in the registry. The **CoCreateInstance** function creates an instance of the data source object through the object's class factory.

When a data source object is created, it is in an uninitialized state. For example, if the data source is a file, the data source object has not yet opened the file; if the data source is an SQL database, the data source object has not yet connected to the database.

The consumer can initialize the data source object by calling the **IDBInitialize::Initialize** function exposed by the data source object. After a data source object has been successfully initialized, the consumer calls the **IDBCreateSession::CreateSession** function to create a session.

The data source object creates one or more sessions. From a session, the consumer can do the following:

- Create a command by calling **IDBCreateCommand::CreateCommand,** if the provider supports commands. A single session can support multiple commands.
- Create a rowset by calling **IOpenRowset::OpenRowset.** This is similar to creating a rowset over a single table and is supported by all providers.

Building OLE DB provider applications is beyond the scope of this course. For information about building provider applications, search for "Creating an OLE DB Template Provider" in MSDN Library Visual C++ 6.0.

OLE DB Consumer Templates

The OLE DB Consumer Templates simplify the process of developing consumer applications. These templates provide the following features:

- Support for ATL and MFC developers to use the OLE DB interfaces
- Native C/C++ data types, such as **int** and **char,** for OLE DB programming
- An easy-to-use binding model for database parameters and columns

  For example, with the **CManualAccessor** class, you can use whatever data types you want as long as the provider can convert the type. It handles both result columns and command parameters.
- OLE DB features, such as provider-owned memory for improved performance and multiple accessors on a rowset

Using these templates, you can create applications that:

- Retrieve records from a data source for further processing.
- Execute parameterized queries to retrieve records selectively.

OLE DB Consumer Architecture

The classes in the top layer of OLE DB Consumer Templates conform to the OLE DB specification as closely as possible. Each class mirrors an existing OLE DB component. For example, the **CDataSource** class corresponds to the data source object in OLE DB.

The following illustration shows the OLE DB consumer classes.

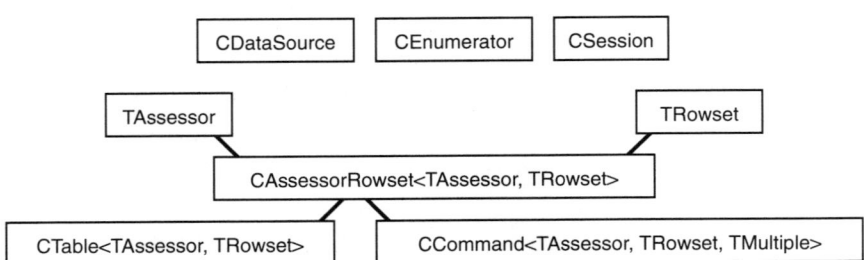

For more information about consumer classes, search for "OLE DB Consumer Templates Architecture" in MSDN Library Visual Studio 6.0.

The **CDataSource** class corresponds to an OLE DB data source object (DSO), which represents a connection through a provider to a data source.

The **CEnumerator** class calls an OLE DB enumerator object, which exposes the ISourcesRowset interface. ISourcesRowset returns a rowset describing all data sources and enumerators visible to the enumerator.

The **CSession** class represents a single database access session. One or more sessions can be associated with each provider connection (data source), which is represented by a **CDataSource** object.

TAccessor represents one of the following classes:

- **CAccessor**

    Supports multiple accessors on a rowset and is used when a record is statically bound to a data source.

- **CDynamicAccessor**

    Dynamically creates an accessor at run time based on the column information of the rowset. Use this class to retrieve data from a data source when you do not know the structure at compile time.

- **CManualAccessor**

    Represents an accessor type designed for advanced use. This class offers functions that can handle both columns and command parameters.

- **CDynamicParameterAccessor**

    Performs the same actions as **CDynamicAccessor**, but is used for handling unknown commands types. Use this class to get parameter information from the ICommandWithParameters interface.

TRowset represents one of the following classes:

- **CRowset**

    Encapsulates an OLE DB **IRowset** object and several related interfaces, and provides manipulation methods for rowset data.

- **CBulkRowset**

    Extends **CRowset** by overriding methods that retrieves and manipulates rows to work on data in bulk.

    Encapsulates a rowset and its associated accessors in a single class. This helps the consumer set and retrieve data.

    Provides a means to directly access a rowset that does not use parameters.

    Provides methods to set and run an OLE database command. Use this class when you need to perform a parameter-based operation.

Using CAccessor to Create a Consumer Application

You use MFC AppWizard to quickly create a base consumer application that uses **CAccessor**. You can then add code to the base application to include functionality, such as the addition and deletion of records in a data source.

This section describes how to use the **CAccessor** class to create a consumer application. You use the **CAccessor** class when you know at design time the structure and type of database you want to access.

Creating a Base Application Using MFC AppWizard

The first step in building a consumer application with **CAccessor** is to use MFC AppWizard to build a base application.

To see the demonstration "Creating an OLEDB Application by Using AppWizard," see the accompanying CD-ROM.

▶ **To create an application by using MFC AppWizard**

1. Invoke MFC AppWizard. Accept the default settings in the **Step 1 of 6** dialog box.
2. In the **Step 2 of 6** dialog box, click **Database view with file support** and then click **Data Source**.

    The **Database Options** dialog box appears.

The following illustration shows the **Database Options** dialog box.

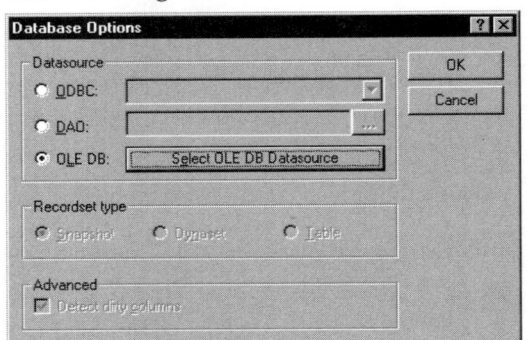

3. Select **OLE DB** and then click **Select OLE DB Datasource**.

   The **Data Link Properties** dialog box appears.

   The following illustration shows the **Data Link Properties** dialog box with the **Provider** tab selected.

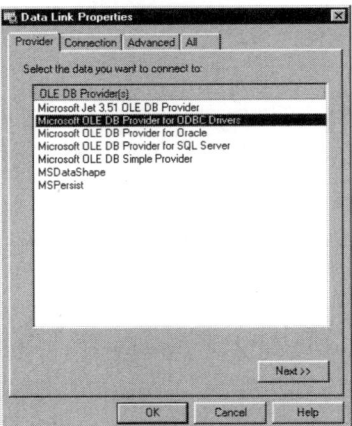

4. Select an OLE DB Provider from the list of providers that are displayed and click **Next**.

5. On the **Connection** tab, select or enter the location of the data source.

   If you choose a provider such as Microsoft Jet OLE DB Provider, specify the full path name of the database file. If you choose a provider such as Microsoft OLE DB Provider for ODBC Drivers, specify the data source name. If you choose Microsoft OLE DB Provider for Oracle, you must give the Oracle server name as the location.

The following illustration shows the **Data Link Properties** dialog box with the **Connection** tab selected.

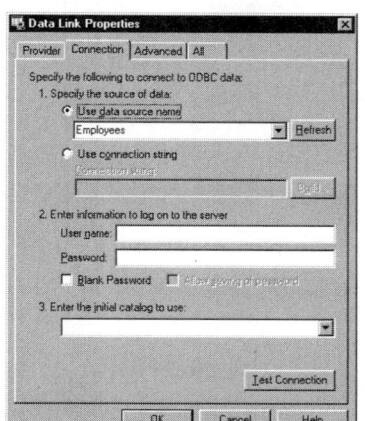

6. Enter the user name and password with which to connect to the data source.
7. Click **Test Connection** to test the connection to the provider.
8. To set advanced options, click the **Advanced** tab.

The following illustration shows the **Data Link Properties** dialog box with the **Advanced** tab selected.

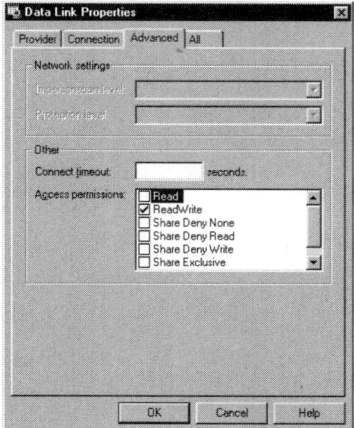

You can change the setting of any option. For example, in the **Access permissions** list box, you can select the **ReadWrite** check box.

9. Click **OK** to return to the **Database Options** dialog box and click **OK**.

The **Select Database Tables** dialog box appears. The following illustration shows this dialog box.

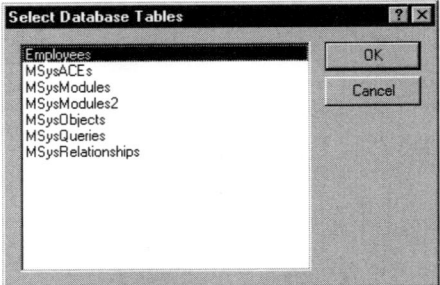

10. Select the table you want to access and click **OK**.
11. Click **Finish** to create the base application.

MFC AppWizard Implementation of CAccessor

MFC AppWizard uses the classes **CAccessor** and **CCommand** to access data from the data source. The wizard derives a class named **CXXXXSet** from **CCommand**, which inherits the **CAccessor** class. The **CAccessor** class in turn inherits **CEmployees**, which defines the structure of the records, as shown in the following example:

```
class CXXXXSet:    public CCommand<CAccessor<CEmployees>>
```

The following sample code shows the class definition of **CEmployees**. To copy this code for use in your own projects, see "CEmployees Class Definition" on the accompanying CD-ROM.

```
// Class Definition of CEmployees
// Samples\CH07\OleEmployee
class CEmployees
{
  public:
      int m_EmployeeID;
      char m_Name[51];
      char m_Address[51];
```

code continued on next page

Chapter 7: Using OLE DB Templates for Data Access

code continued from previous page

```
    BEGIN_COLUMN_MAP(CEmployees)
        COLUMN_ENTRY_TYPE(1,  DBTYPE_I4,  m_EmployeeID)
        COLUMN_ENTRY_TYPE(2,  DBTYPE_STR, m_Name)
        COLUMN_ENTRY_TYPE(3,  DBTYPE_STR, m_Address)
    END_COLUMN_MAP()

};
```

Note **CCommand** also inherits the **CRowset** class by default.

MFC AppWizard overrides the **Open** function of the **CCommand**-derived class. In the **Open** function, objects of **CDataSource** and **CSession** are defined, as shown in the following example:

```
public:

    HRESULT Open()
    {
        CDataSource  db;
        CSession     session;
        ...
    }
```

Note When MFC AppWizard generates the code for your application, the scope of the **CSession** object is limited to the **Open** function of the **CCommand<CAccessor<C***Tablename* **>>**-derived class.

MFC AppWizard defines an object of **CDBPropSet**, as shown in the following example:

```
    CDBPropSet    dbinit(DBPROPSET_DBINIT);
```

The **CDBPropSet** object is used to define the properties of the data source object. These properties are needed to open the data source object.

The following sample code shows the definition of data source properties. To copy this code for use in your own projects, see "Defining Data Source Properties" on the accompanying CD-ROM.

```
//Defining data source object properties
//  Samples\CH07\OleEmployee
...
HRESULT Open()
{
  ...
  CDBPropSet   dbinit(DBPROPSET_DBINIT);
  dbinit.AddProperty(DBPROP_INIT_DATASOURCE, "Employees");
  dbinit.AddProperty(DBPROP_INIT_MODE, (long)3);
  dbinit.AddProperty(DBPROP_INIT_PROMPT, (short)4);
  dbinit.AddProperty(DBPROP_INIT_LCID, (long)1033);
  ...
}
```

You use the **CDataSource** member function **Open** or **OpenWithServiceComponents**, to open the data source. The first argument of the **Open** function is the name of the data provider, and the second argument is the **CDBPropSet** object, which defines the properties of the data source. The following example opens a Microsoft Jet database by using the Microsoft OLE DB Provider for ODBC:

```
hr = db.Open("MSDASQL.1", &dbinit);
```

You use the **Open** function of the **CSession** class to open a session, as shown in the following example:

```
hr = session.Open(db);
```

After a session object is opened successfully and the properties of the rowset are defined, you can call the **Open** function of the **CCommand** class. The **Open** function takes as arguments the session object, the command text, which is an SQL statement, and the propertyset object.

The sample code on the following page sets rowset properties and calls the **Open** function. To copy this code for use in your own projects, see "Setting Rowset Properties" on the accompanying CD-ROM.

Chapter 7: Using OLE DB Templates for Data Access

```
// Setting properties of a rowset and opening it
// Samples\CH07\OleEmployee
...
HRESULT Open()
{
  ...
  CDBPropSet    propset(DBPROPSET_ROWSET);

  //The next 2 lines enable scrolling for the rowset
  propset.AddProperty(DBPROP_CANFETCHBACKWARDS, true);
  propset.AddProperty(DBPROP_IRowsetScroll, true);

  //The next 2 lines allow you to make changes to the rowset contents
  propset.AddProperty(DBPROP_IRowsetChange, true);
  propset.AddProperty(DBPROP_UPDATABILITY, DBPROPVAL_UP_CHANGE);

  hr = CCommand<CAccessor<CEmployees> >::Open(session,
      "SELECT * FROM Employees", &propset);
  ...
}
```

COleDBRecordView Class

When you create an OLE DB consumer application by using MFC AppWizard, the view class is derived from the **COleDBRecordView** class by default. **COleDBRecordView** displays database records in controls. **COleDBRecordView** is derived from **CFormView** and therefore is created using a dialog template. The view displays the fields of the **CRowset** object in the dialog box controls. You can implement functions that add and delete records and implement transaction processing.

A pointer to the **CCommand<CAccessor<C***Tablename***> >** class is declared within the definition of the view class, as shown in the following example:

```
class CXXXXView : public COleDBRecordView
{
  ...
public:
  CXXXXSet* m_pSet;
  ...
}
```

355

In the **OnInitialUpdate** function of the view class, use the **Open** function to open the recordset, as shown in the following example:

```
m_pSet->Open();
```

The following sample code shows the complete definition of **OnInitialUpdate**. To copy this code for use in your own projects, see "COLEDBSample2View::OnInitialUpdate" on the accompanying CD-ROM.

```
// Samples\CH07\OleEmployee
//The OnInitialUpdate function

void CXXXXView::OnInitialUpdate()
{
  m_pSet = &GetDocument()->m_oleEmployeeSet;
  {
      CWaitCursor wait;
      HRESULT hr = m_pSet->Open();
      if (hr != S_OK)
      {
          AfxMessageBox(_T("Record set failed to open."), MB_OK);
          // Disable the Next and Previous record commands,
          // since attempting to change the current record without an
          // open RecordSet will cause a crash.
          m_bOnFirstRecord = TRUE;
          m_bOnLastRecord = TRUE;
      }
  }
  COleDBRecordView::OnInitialUpdate();

}
```

In the previous example, m_bOnFirstRecord and m_bOnLastRecord are member variables of the **COleDBRecordView** class. Setting these variables to **TRUE** ensures that the navigation buttons on the toolbar and their corresponding menu command items are disabled.

Performing Database Operations

To display the contents of a recordset or to perform operations such as adding and deleting records, you need to add code to your application.

Displaying the Recordset

To display the contents of the recordset, complete the following steps:

1. Place controls on the dialog box created by MFC AppWizard.
2. Define member variables for the controls using ClassWizard.

    ClassWizard adds suitable DDX functions to handle the transfer of data from the controls to the member variables.

3. Alter the DDX functions to transfer data between the controls and the recordset variables, as shown in the following example:

    ```
    //{{AFX_DATA_MAP(COLEEmployeeView)
    //}}AFX_DATA_MAP
    DDX_Text(pDX, IDC_ADDRESS, m_pSet->m_Address,51);
    DDX_Text(pDX, IDC_EMPLOYEEID, m_pSet->m_ID);
    DDX_Text(pDX, IDC_NAME, m_pSet->m_Name,51);
    ```

In the previous example, the DDX functions have been placed outside AFX_DATA_MAP. This is because the example alters the DDX functions to use the rowset's member variables instead of those defined by ClassWizard. If the DDX functions were placed within AFX_DATA_MAP, the functionality of ClassWizard for the **COleDBRecordView**-derived class would be impaired.

The view has built-in functionality to scroll through the records in the recordset. You can also write your own handlers for the menu commands ID_RECORD_FIRST, ID_RECORD_NEXT, ID_RECORD_PREV and ID_RECORD_LAST generated by MFC AppWizard.

The following example implements a handler for ID_RECORD_LAST:

```
void CXXXXView::OnRecordLast()
{
  m_pSet->Update();
  m_pSet->MoveLast();
  UpdateData(FALSE);
}
```

You invoke the **Update** member function of **CRecordset** to update the database with any changes made to the current record. If you call **UpdateData** and pass **FALSE** as the argument, the controls on the form are updated with the data of the current record.

Adding Records to a Data Source

You add records to a data source by using the **Insert** member function of **CRecordset**. Before invoking the **Insert** function, you must invoke the **UpdateData** function, as shown in the following example:

```
void CXXXXView::OnRecordAdd()
{
  UpdateData(TRUE);
  m_pSet->Insert();
  .....
}
```

When you call **UpdateData** and pass **TRUE** as the argument, the current record is updated with the data of the controls.

Before you open the accessor, you must set the DBPROP_UPDATABILITY property to allow inserts, as shown in the following example:

```
propset.AddProperty(DBPROP_UPDATABILITY,
BPROPVAL_UP_CHANGE|DBPROPVAL_UP_INSERT|DBPROPVAL_UP_DELETE);
hr = CCommand<CAccessor<CEmployees> >::Open(session,
"SELECT * FROM Employees", &propset);
.....
```

In the previous example, DBPROP_UPDATABILITY has also been set to allow deletes and edits.

Deleting Records from a Data Source

You can delete records from a data source using the **Delete** member function of **CRecordSet**. This function deletes the record currently pointed to by the recordset pointer. After invoking the **Delete** function, you must invoke the **OnMove** function passing ID_RECORD_NEXT as the argument, to set the recordset pointer to the record next to the deleted record. You then invoke **UpdateData** to display the current record in the form.

The following example shows how to delete the current record:

```
void COLEEmployeeView::OnRecordDelete()
{
  m_pSet->Delete();
  //If the record that has just been deleted, is the last record
  //in the table, the form has to be cleared and the record
  //scrolling functionality of the view has to be turned off.
  if(!OnMove(ID_RECORD_NEXT))
  {
      if(!OnMove(ID_RECORD_LAST))
      {
          OnRecordClear(); //Clears the COleDBRecordView's controls
          m_bOnFirstRecord = TRUE;
          m_bOnLastRecord = TRUE;
      }
  }
  UpdateData(FALSE);
}
```

Editing Records in a Data Source

You do not need to write code to update existing records. You can simply edit the contents of the controls and scroll to the next or previous record. The **OnMove** function is called when you scroll to another record and ensures that the recordset is updated before the recordset pointer is moved.

Handling Transactions

OLE DB applications use the **CSession** object to implement transaction processing. The **CSession** object uses the ITransaction interface to commit, abort, and obtain status information about transactions. You use the **StartTransaction** member function of the **CSession** class to begin a transaction, as shown in the following example:

```
session.StartTransaction();
```

Changes are not written back to the data source until you invoke the **Commit** member function, as shown in the following example:

```
m_pSet->session.Commit()
```

Lab 7.1: Using CAccessor

In this lab, you will create a consumer application by using the **CAccessor** class. You will add, delete, and update records in a database table.

To see the demonstration "Lab 7.1 Demonstration," see the accompanying CD-ROM.

Estimated time to complete this lab: **30 minutes**

To complete the exercises in this lab, you must have the required software. For detailed information about the labs and setup for the labs, see "Labs" in "About This Course."

The solution code for this lab is located in the folder *<install folder>*\Labs\Ch07\Lab7.1\Ex01\Solution.

Objectives

After completing this lab, you will be able to:

- Create a consumer application by using the **CAccessor** class.
- Add, update, and delete records in a database table.

Prerequisites

There are no prerequisites for this lab.

Exercises

The following exercise provides practice working with the concepts and techniques covered in this chapter.

- Exercise 1: Performing Database Operations

    In this exercise, you will implement add, delete, and update functions to manipulate records in a database table.

Exercise 1: Performing Database Operations

In this exercise, you will implement add, delete, and update functions to manipulate records in a database table.

▶ Create an application by using MFC AppWizard

1. Copy the Employees database from *<install folder>*\Labs\Ch07\Lab7.1\Ex01 into your project folder. Ensure that the access permission is read-write.
2. Invoke MFC AppWizard.
3. Name the new project workspace **OledbApp**.
4. In Step 1 of MFC AppWizard, click **single document**, and then click **Next**.
5. In Step 2 of AppWizard, click **Database view with file support** and then click **Data Source**.

   The **Database Options** dialog box appears.
6. Select **OLE DB** and then click **Select OLE DB Datasource**.

   The **Data Link Properties** dialog box appears.
7. Select **Microsoft Jet 3.51 OLE DB Provider** from the list of providers and click **Next**.
8. Enter the name of the database file.
9. Enter the user name and password to connect to the data source.
10. Click **Test Connection** to test the connection to the provider and click **OK**.
11. Click **OK** to close the **Database Options** dialog box.
12. Select the **Employees** table and click **OK**.
13. In Step 4 of MFC AppWizard, clear the **Printing and print preview** option.
14. Click **Finish** to create the skeletal program for the application.

▶ Add controls to IDD_OLEDBAPP_FORM dialog box

In this procedure, you will create a form as shown in the following illustration.

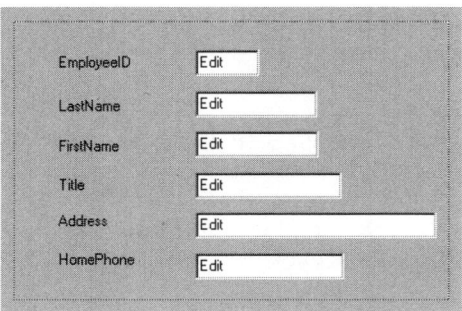

- In IDD_OLEDBAPP_FORM, add the following controls to the form.

Control type	ID	Caption
Static text	IDC_STATIC	EmployeeID
Edit box	ID_EMPID	None
Static text	IDC_STATIC	LastName
Edit box	ID_LNAME	None
Static text	IDC_STATIC	FirstName
Edit box	ID_FNAME	None
Static text	IDC_STATIC	Title
Edit box	ID_TITLE	None
Static text	IDC_STATIC	Address
Edit box	ID_ADDRESS	None
Static text	IDC_STATIC	HomePhone
Edit box	ID_PHONE	None

▶ Add DDX functions

In this procedure, you will add DDX functions to handle the transfer of data between the controls and the recordset variables.

- In the **DoDataExchange** function of the OledbAppView.cpp file, add DDX functions after the //{{AFX_DATA_MAP block as follows:

```
//{{AFX_DATA_MAP(COledbAppView)
//}}AFX_DATA_MAP
DDX_Text(pDX, ID_EMPID, m_pSet->m_EmployeeID);
DDX_Text(pDX, ID_LNAME, m_pSet->m_LastName,21);
DDX_Text(pDX, ID_FNAME, m_pSet->m_FirstName,11);
DDX_Text(pDX, ID_TITLE, m_pSet->m_Title,31);
DDX_Text(pDX, ID_ADDRESS, m_pSet->m_Address,61);
DDX_Text(pDX, ID_PHONE, m_pSet->m_HomePhone,25);
```

▶ Modify the IDR_MAINFRAME menu resource

1. Open the IDR_MAINFRAME menu resource.
2. Delete the **Edit** menu and all menu items under **Edit**.
3. Add the following menu items to the **Record** menu.

ID	Caption
ID_RECORD_CLEAR	Clear
ID_RECORD_ADD	Add Record
ID_RECORD_DELETE	Delete Record
ID_RECORD_COMMIT	Commit

▶ Modify the IDR_MAINFRAME toolbar resource

1. Open the IDR_MAINFRAME toolbar resource.
2. Add four toolbar items, giving them the IDs ID_RECORD_CLEAR, ID_RECORD_ADD, ID_RECORD_DELETE, and ID_RECORD_COMMIT, respectively.

   Your toolbar should look like the following toolbar.

▶ Create message map entries

In this procedure, you will create message map entries for the menu items on the **Record** menu.

1. Open OledbAppView.h and add the following entries after the //{{AFX_MSG message:

   ```
   afx_msg void OnRecordPrev();
   afx_msg void OnRecordNext();
   afx_msg void OnRecordClear();
   afx_msg void OnRecordAdd();
   afx_msg void OnRecordDelete();
   afx_msg void OnRecordCommit();
   ```

2. Insert message map entries for ON_COMMAND in the **COledbAppView** implementation file after the //{{AFX_MSG message as follows:

   ```
   ON_COMMAND(ID_RECORD_PREV,   OnRecordPrev)
   ON_COMMAND(ID_RECORD_NEXT,   OnRecordNext)
   ON_COMMAND(ID_RECORD_CLEAR,  OnRecordClear)
   ON_COMMAND(ID_RECORD_ADD,    OnRecordAdd)
   ON_COMMAND(ID_RECORD_DELETE, OnRecordDelete)
   ON_COMMAND(ID_RECORD_COMMIT, OnRecordCommit)
   ```

▶ Implement the OnRecordPrev and OnRecordNext handlers

1. In the OledbAppView.cpp file, write the code for the **OnRecordPrev** handler as follows:

   ```
   void COledbAppView::OnRecordPrev()
   {
       //Ensures that the user does not scroll ahead of BOF
       if(!OnMove(ID_RECORD_PREV))
           OnMove(ID_RECORD_FIRST);
   }
   ```

2. In the OledbAppView.cpp file, write the code for the **OnRecordNext** handler as follows:

   ```
   void COledbAppView::OnRecordNext()
   {
       //Ensures that the user does not scroll beyond EOF
       if(!OnMove(ID_RECORD_NEXT))
           OnMove(ID_RECORD_LAST);
   }
   ```

▶ Implement the Clear function

In this procedure, you will clear the values of the current record displayed on the form.

- In the OledbAppView.cpp file, write the code for the **OnRecordClear** handler as follows:

Lab 7.1: Using CAccessor

```
void COledbAppView::OnRecordClear()
{
  m_pSet->m_EmployeeID = 0;
  m_pSet->m_LastName[0] = '\0';
  m_pSet->m_FirstName[0]= '\0';
  m_pSet->m_Title[0]= '\0';
  m_pSet->m_Address[0]= '\0';
  m_pSet->m_HomePhone[0]= '\0';
  UpdateData(FALSE);
}
```

▶ Implement the Add and Delete functions

1. Open OledbAppSet.h.

2. In the **AddProperty** function of **propset**, change the second argument as follows to allow addition and deletion of records:

   ```
   propset.AddProperty(DBPROP_UPDATABILITY,
   DBPROPVAL_UP_CHANGE|DBPROPVAL_UP_INSERT|DBPROPVAL_UP_DELETE);
   ```

3. In the OledbAppView.cpp file, write the code for the **OnRecordAdd** handler as follows:

   ```
   void COledbAppView::OnRecordAdd()
   {
       UpdateData(TRUE);
       m_pSet->Insert();
       m_pSet->MoveLast();
       //If the record was added to a table which contained no records
       //the view's record scroll functionality, which would have been
       //turned off in OnInitialUpdate, has to be turned on

       if(m_bOnFirstRecord && m_bOnLastRecord)
       {
           m_bOnFirstRecord = FALSE;
           m_bOnLastRecord = FALSE;

       }
   }
   ```

4. Write the code for the **OnRecordDelete** handler as follows:

```
void COledbAppView::OnRecordDelete()
{
    m_pSet->Delete();
    //If the record that has just been deleted, is the last record
    //in the table, the form has to be cleared and the record
    //scrolling functionality of the view has to be turned off.

    if(!OnMove(ID_RECORD_NEXT))
    {
        if(!OnMove(ID_RECORD_LAST))
        {
            OnRecordClear();
            m_bOnFirstRecord = TRUE;
            m_bOnLastRecord = TRUE;
        }
    }
    UpdateData(FALSE);
}
```

▶ **Implement the Commit function**

In this procedure, you will use the **Commit** member of the session object to write the changes in the recordset to the data source.

1. Delete the local instance of the **CSession** object from the **Open** function of the **COledbAppSet** class.

2. Declare a public instance of the **CSession** object in the **COledbAppSet** class to make the session object available outside the class:

   ```
   CSession session;
   ```

3. In the **Open** function of OledbAppSet.h file, begin a transaction by invoking **StartTransaction** after the call to the CSession **Open** member function as follows:

   ```
   session.StartTransaction();
   ```

4. In the OledbAppView.cpp file, write the code for the **OnRecordCommit** handler as follows:

```
void COledbAppView::OnRecordCommit()
{
    m_pSet->session.Commit();
}
```

▶ **Add an update handler for the Delete menu command**

1. Using ClassWizard, add an update handler for the **Delete** menu command.
2. Write code for the update handler as follows:

```
void COledbAppView::OnUpdateRecordDelete(CCmdUI* pCmdUI)
{
    if(m_bOnFirstRecord && m_bOnLastRecord)
        pCmdUI->Enable(FALSE);
    else
        pCmdUI->Enable(TRUE);
}
```

The previous example code disables the **Delete** command if all the records in the table have been deleted.

▶ **Build and test your application**

- Run your application and test the options under the **Record** menu.

Note To add a record, click the Clear button on the toolbar, enter the new record in the form and then click Add.

The solution code for this exercise is located in the folder *<install folder>*\Labs\Ch07\Lab7.1\Ex01\Solution.

Using CDynamicAccessor to Create a Consumer Application

You can use the **CDynamicAccessor** class to retrieve data from a data source when you do not know the structure of the data source at design time. This class creates an accessor at run time based on the column information of the rowset. It also creates and manages a buffer for the data.

If you used MFC AppWizard to create a **CAccessor**-based application, you can modify the application to use **CDynamicAccessor**.

▶ **To modify a CAccessor-based application to use CDynamicAccessor**

1. Delete the XXXXSet.h and XXXXSet.cpp files from the project.

   These files define the recordset for the **CAccessor** class. Because the **CDynamicAccessor** class maintains its own buffer, these files are no longer required.

2. Delete all references to the XXXXSet.h file from all files in the project.
3. Delete all references to the CXXXXSet class from all files in the project.
4. Delete the **OnGetRowSet** function from the **CXXXXView** class.
5. Delete all references to the pointer m_pSet.
6. In the XXXXView.h and XXXXView.cpp files, replace all occurrences of **COleDBRecordView** with **CFormView**.

   MFC AppWizard derives the **CXXXXView** class from the **COleDBRecordView** class. **COleDBRecordView** is a form view that is directly connected to a **CRowset** object. The **COleDBRecordView** object uses the **CRowset** object to provide a default implementation for moving to the first, next, previous, or last record. However, because you are not making use of the scrolling functionality provided by the **COleDBRecordView**, you will derive the view from the **CFormView** class.

7. In the **CXXXXView** class, declare protected member variables of the **CDataSource** class, the **CSession** class, and the **CCommand<CDynamicAccessor>** class, as shown in the following example:

   ```
   CDataSource m_DataSource;
   CSession m_Session;
   CCommand<CDynamicAccessor> DynamicAccessor;
   ```

8. Declare a protected member variable of type **integer** and an array of void pointers, as shown in the following example:

   ```
   int m_ColCnt;
   void *m_pVoid[3];
   ```

   The integer variable is used to store the count of the number of columns in the table being accessed. The array of void pointers is used to access the data in the buffer defined by the **CDynamicAccessor** class. In the previous example, the size of the array is defined as 3. However, you can set the size at run time by using the **new** operator and the number of columns in the table.

9. For each field in the table, create a control on the **FormView** dialog box and define suitable member variables for each control, as shown in the following example:

   ```
   long      m_EmployeeID;
   char      m_Address[51];
   char      m_Name[51];
   ```

Note In the previous example, the controls have been created at design time. You can create them at run time using each control's **Create** member function.

10. In the **OnInitialUpdate** function of the view class, create an object of type **CDBPropSet** and use the **AddProperty** member function to add properties to the property set.

    The following sample code sets the properties of the property set. To copy this code for use in your own projects, see "Adding Properties to CDBPropSet" on the accompanying CD-ROM.

```
//Samples\Ch07\DynAcc01
//Adding properties to the CDBPropSet object

CDBPropSet    dbinit(DBPROPSET_DBINIT);
dbinit.AddProperty(DBPROP_AUTH_CACHE_AUTHINFO, true);
dbinit.AddProperty(DBPROP_AUTH_ENCRYPT_PASSWORD, false);
dbinit.AddProperty(DBPROP_AUTH_MASK_PASSWORD, false);
dbinit.AddProperty(DBPROP_AUTH_PASSWORD, "");
dbinit.AddProperty(DBPROP_AUTH_PERSIST_ENCRYPTED, false);
```

code continued on next page

code continued from previous page

```
dbinit.AddProperty(DBPROP_AUTH_PERSIST_SENSITIVE_AUTHINFO, false);
dbinit.AddProperty(DBPROP_AUTH_USERID, "Admin");
dbinit.AddProperty(DBPROP_INIT_DATASOURCE, ".\\employees.mdb");
dbinit.AddProperty(DBPROP_INIT_MODE, (long)3);
dbinit.AddProperty(DBPROP_INIT_PROMPT, (short)2);
dbinit.AddProperty(DBPROP_INIT_PROVIDERSTRING,
";COUNTRY=0;CP=1252;LANGID=0x0409");
dbinit.AddProperty(DBPROP_INIT_LCID, (long)1033);
```

Note In the previous example, the DBPROP_INIT_DATASOURCE property has been set to a specific data source. You can set this property to a data source at run time by allowing the user to choose from a list of data sources. For an example of how to implement this functionality, see the sample project DynAcc02 in *<install folder>*\Samples\Ch07.

11. Open the data source object by using the **Open** function, as shown in the following example:

    ```
    m_DataSource.Open("Microsoft.Jet.OLEDB.3.51", &dbinit);
    ```

Note In the previous example, the name of the provider, Microsoft.Jet.OLEDB.3.51, was passed to the **Open** function. You can display a list of providers and allow the user to select from this list at run time. For an example of how to implement this functionality, see the sample project DynAcc02 in Samples\Ch07.

12. Using the **Open** function, open a session on the data source, as shown in the following example:

    ```
    m_Session.Open(m_DataSource);
    ```

13. Set properties for the accessor by using a **CDBPropSet** object, as shown in the following example:

```
CDBPropSet  propset(DBPROPSET_ROWSET);
propset.AddProperty(DBPROP_CANFETCHBACKWARDS, true);
propset.AddProperty(DBPROP_IRowsetChange, true);
propset.AddProperty(DBPROP_UPDATABILITY, DBPROPVAL_UP_CHANGE);
```

14. Invoke the **CCommand<CDynamicAccessor>** member function **Open** to access the records in the data source table, as shown in the following example:

```
DynamicAccessor.Open(m_Session,"Select * from employees",&propset);
```

> **Note** The previous example sets the SQL statement to be used to open the accessor at design time. You can set the SQL statement at run time. You can display a list of tables available in the data source and allow the user to select the table to be opened. You can then read the schema of the table and display a list of columns for the user to choose from. Using the columns selected, you can generate an SQL statement and use it with the **Open** function to open the accessor. For an example of how to implement this functionality, see the sample project DynAcc02 in *<install folder>*\Samples\Ch07.

You can use the **CRowset** member functions **MoveFirst, MoveNext, MoveLast,** and **MovePrev** to scroll through the records in the recordset. The following table lists other functions that provide information about the data in the dynamic accessor's buffer.

Function	Description
GetColumnCount	Returns a count of the number of columns in the data source table.
GetColumnType	Returns the data type of a specific column in the data source table. For example, the code: `DynamicAccessor.GetColumnType(1, &mType);` stores the data type of column 1 in the variable mType, which is of type **DBTYPE**.
GetValue	Returns the data from a specific column in the current record. For example, the code: `pVoid = DynamicAccessor.GetValue(1);` returns a pointer to the value stored in column one. Column numbers start from 1. The pointer pVoid is a void pointer that can point to any data type.

Lab 7.2: Using CDynamicAccessor

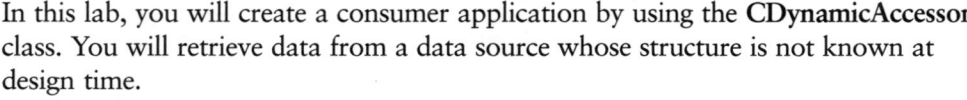

In this lab, you will create a consumer application by using the **CDynamicAccessor** class. You will retrieve data from a data source whose structure is not known at design time.

To see the demonstration "Lab 7.2 Demonstration," see the accompanying CD-ROM.

Estimated time to complete this lab: **30 minutes**

To complete the exercises in this lab, you must have the required software. For detailed information about the labs and setup for the labs, see "Labs" in "About This Course."

The code that forms the starting point for this lab is located in the folder *<install folder>*\Labs\Ch07\Lab7.2\Ex01.

The solution code for this lab is located in the folder *<install folder>*\Labs\Ch07\Lab7.2\Ex01\Solution.

Objectives

After completing this lab, you will be able to:

- Create a consumer application by using the **CDynamicAccessor** class.
- Retrieve data from a data source.

Prerequisites

There are no prerequisites for this lab.

Exercises

The following exercise provides practice working with the concepts and techniques covered in this chapter.

- Exercise 1: Retrieving Data from a Data Source

  In this exercise, you will retrieve data from a data source whose structure is not known at design time.

Exercise 1: Retrieving Data from a Data Source

The code that forms the basis for this exercise is in <install folder>\Labs\Ch07\ Lab7.2\Ex01.

In this exercise, you will retrieve data from a data source whose structure is not known at design time.

▶ **Use CDynamicAccessor to retrieve data from a data source**

1. Open the fileOLEDBDynAccAppView.h.
2. Declare a protected member function to retrieve data from a data source:

   ```
   void RetrieveRecords();
   ```

3. Open the file OLEDBDynAccAppView.cpp.
4. In the **RetrieveRecords** function, create an object of type **CDBPropSet** as follows:

   ```
   CDBPropSet  propset(DBPROPSET_ROWSET);
   ```

5. Declare two **char** arrays to store the field values as follows:

   ```
   char dispStr[500], tempStr[500];
   ```

6. Declare a pointer to the Field structure as follows:

   ```
   struct Field *pFieldData;
   ```

   The Field structure is defined in OLEDBDynAccAppView.h as follows:

   ```
   struct Field
   {
       void *pField;
       DBTYPE ColType;
   };
   ```

   *pField is a pointer to the location in the buffer where the field value is stored. ColType stores the field data type.

7. Obtain a pointer to the list box that will be used to display data from the database table as follows:

   ```
   m_plbData=(CListBox*)GetDlgItem(IDC_DATA);
   m_plbData->ResetContent();
   ```

373

8. Use the **AddProperty** member function of **CDBPropSet** object to set properties for the accessor as follows:

   ```
   propset.AddProperty(DBPROP_CANFETCHBACKWARDS, true);
   ```

   DBPROP_CANFETCHBACKWARDS allows backward fetching and scrolling in nonsequential rowsets.

9. Declare a variable of **CCommand<CDynamicAccessor>** class as follows:

   ```
   CCommand<CDynamicAccessor> dynamicAccessor;
   ```

10. Invoke the **CCommand<CDynamicAccessor>** member function **Open** to access the records in the data source table as follows:

    ```
    if (S_OK != dynamicAccessor.Open(m_session,m_cmd_str,&propset))
    {
        MessageBox("Failed to Open");
        return;
    }
    ```

11. Create instances of the Field structure based on the number of columns selected by the users from the Columns dialog box, as follows:

    ```
    pFieldData = new Field[m_columnsDlg.m_ColsSelected];
    ```

12. Invoke the **MoveFirst** function to position the rowset pointer at the first record, as follows:

    ```
    dynamicAccessor.MoveFirst();
    ```

13. Obtain the column type of each field in the table as follows:

    ```
    for(int i = 1; i <= m_columnsDlg.m_ColsSelected; i++)
    {
        dynamicAccessor.GetColumnType(i, &((pFieldData + (i - 1))->ColType));
    }
    ```

14. Initialize the character string tempStr, as follows:

    ```
    tempStr[0] = '\0';
    ```

15. Retrieve the value of each field and add the value to the list box after typecasting it to appropriate data type.

    The following sample code shows how the completed **RetrieveRecords** function should look. To copy this code for use in your own projects, see "Lab 7.2.1 RetrieveRecords" on the accompanying CD-ROM.

```
void COLEDBDynAccAppView::RetrieveRecords()
{
  CDBPropSet    propset(DBPROPSET_ROWSET);
  char dispStr[500], tempStr[500];
  struct Field *pFieldData;

  m_plbData=(CListBox*)GetDlgItem(IDC_DATA);
  m_plbData->ResetContent();

  propset.AddProperty(DBPROP_CANFETCHBACKWARDS, true);

  CCommand<CDynamicAccessor> dynamicAccessor;

  if (S_OK != dynamicAccessor.Open(m_session,m_cmd_str,&propset))
  {
      MessageBox("Failed to Open");
      return;
  }

  pFieldData = new Field[m_columnsDlg.m_ColsSelected];

  dynamicAccessor.MoveFirst();

  for(int i = 1; i <= m_columnsDlg.m_ColsSelected; i++)
  {
      dynamicAccessor.GetColumnType(i, &((pFieldData + (i - 1))->
          ColType));
  }

  tempStr[0] = '\0';
```

code continued on next page

code continued from previous page

```
    do
    {
        dispStr[0]='\0';
        for(int i =1 ; i <= m_columnsDlg.m_ColsSelected; i++)
        {
            switch ((pFieldData + (i - 1))->ColType)
            {
            case DBTYPE_I2: (pFieldData + (i - 1))->pField =
                dynamicAccessor.GetValue(i);
                        sprintf(tempStr," %d ",
                *((int*)((pFieldData + (i - 1))->pField)));
                        break;
            case DBTYPE_I4:  (pFieldData + (i - 1))->pField =
                dynamicAccessor.GetValue(i);
                        sprintf(tempStr," %d ",
                *((long*)((pFieldData + (i - 1))->pField)));
                        break;
            default:     (pFieldData + (i - 1))->pField =
                dynamicAccessor.GetValue(i);
                        sprintf(tempStr," %s ", (pFieldData +
                (i - 1))->pField);
                        break;
            }
            strcat(dispStr, tempStr);
        }

        m_plbData->AddString(dispStr);

    }while(dynamicAccessor.MoveNext()==S_OK);
    delete pFieldData;
}
```

16. Invoke **RetrieveRecords** function from **OnFileOpen**.

    The sample code on the following page shows an example of how your code should look. To copy this code for use in your own projects, see "Lab 7.2.1 OnFileOpen" on the accompanying CD-ROM.

Lab 7.2: Using CDynamicAccessor

```
void COLEDBDynAccAppView::OnFileOpen()
{

 if(enumDlg.DoModal()==IDOK)
 {
     datasourceDlg.m_RootEnum = &(enumDlg.RootEnum);
     if(datasourceDlg.DoModal()==IDOK)
     {
         tablesDlg.m_session = &(datasourceDlg.m_session);
         tablesDlg.m_source = &(datasourceDlg.m_source);
         if(tablesDlg.DoModal()==IDOK)
         {
             columnsDlg.m_session = tablesDlg.m_session;
             m_session = *(tablesDlg.m_session);
             columnsDlg.m_Tbl = &(tablesDlg.Tbl);
             columnsDlg.DoModal();
             m_cmd_str =    columnsDlg.m_cmd_str;
             RetrieveRecords();
         }

     }

 }
}
```

▶ **Build and test your application**

- Run your application. On the **File** menu, click **Open** to retrieve data from a data source.

The solution code for this exercise is located in the folder *<install folder>*\Labs\Ch07\Lab7.2\Ex01\Solution.

Using CManualAccessor to Create a Consumer Application

You use the **CManualAccessor** class when:

◆ The structure of the data source is not known, and
◆ You want to define custom binding specifications at run time.

CManualAccessor enables you to specify the binding information, whereas **CDynamicAccessor** generates the binding information for you.

If you used MFC AppWizard to create a **CAccessor**-based application, you can modify the application to use **CManualAccessor**. You need to delete the XXXXSet.h and XXXXSet.cpp files from the project and delete all references to the XXXXSet.h file. Delete all references to the class CXXXXSet and the pointer m_pSet across all project files. Delete the **OnGetRowSet** function from the **CXXXXView** class. In the XXXXView.h and XXXXView.cpp files, replace all occurrences of **COleDBRecordView** with **CFormView**.

To use a manual accessor to access records in a data source, you need to do the following:

1. Open the root enumerator and traverse the rowset describing the enumerators and data sources available.

    Enumerators have attributes m_szDescription, m_szName and m_nType. The attribute m_szDescription provides a short description of the enumerator, m_szName contains the name of the enumerator or data source, and m_nType stores the type of enumerator. If m_nType has a value of 1, then the enumerator is a data source and can be used directly. If m_nType has a value of 2, then it is an enumerator that is associated with underlying data sources. You open the root enumerator by using the **Open** function as shown in the following example:

    ```
    m_RootEnum.Open(&CLSID_OLEDB_ENUMERATOR);
    ```

    In the previous example, **m_RootEnum** is an object of the **CEnumerator** class. The **CEnumerator** class exposes the ISourcesRowset interface, which returns a rowset describing all data sources and enumerators.

    You can traverse the enumerators available with the root enumerator by using the **MoveNext, MoveFirst, MovePrev** and **MoveLast** functions, as shown in the following example:

    ```
    if(m_RootEnum.MoveFirst() == S_OK)
    {
    ...
        do
        {
        .....
        }while (m_RootEnum.MoveNext() == S_OK);
        .....
    }
    ```

The following sample code traverses the rowset of enumerators and displays their names in a list box. To copy this code for use in your own projects, see "Traversing the Root Enumerator" on the accompanying CD-ROM.

```
//Samples\Ch07\ManAcc01
//Traverses the list of enumerators and displays their names in a
// listbox

BOOL CEnumDlg::OnInitDialog()
{
  USES_CONVERSION;
  CDialog::OnInitDialog();

  m_plbEnum=(CListBox*)GetDlgItem(IDC_ENUMERATOR);
  if(m_RootEnum.m_spSourcesRowset==NULL)
  {
      m_pOK=(CButton*)GetDlgItem(IDOK);
      m_pOK->EnableWindow(FALSE);
      if (m_RootEnum.Open(&CLSID_OLEDB_ENUMERATOR) != S_OK)
      {
          ::AfxMessageBox("Failed to Open Enumerator");
          OnCancel();
      }
      else
      {
          m_pOK->EnableWindow(TRUE);
      }
  }
  if(m_RootEnum.MoveFirst() == S_OK)
  {
      int i=0;
      do
      {
          m_plbEnum->AddString(W2T(m_RootEnum.m_szDescription));
          m_listEnum[i]=W2T(m_RootEnum.m_szName);
          i++;
      }while (m_RootEnum.MoveNext() == S_OK);
      m_plbEnum->SetCurSel(0);
  }
  return TRUE;
}
```

To open an underlying data source for m_nType 2 root enumerators, complete the following steps:

- Declare a COM pointer, as shown in the following example:

```
CComPtr<IMoniker>  spMoniker;
```

- Use the pointer to get a moniker on the root enumerator, as shown in the following example:

```
m_pRootEnum->GetMoniker(&spMoniker,
   W2T(m_pRootEnum->m_szParseName));
```

- Use the moniker to gain access to the underlying data sources, as shown in the following example:

```
Enum.Open(spMoniker);
```

In the previous example, **Enum** is an object of **CEnumerator** type.

- Traverse the data sources available by using the **MoveFirst**, **MovePrev**, **MoveNext**, and **MoveLast** functions, as shown in the following example:

```
if(m_Enum.MoveFirst()==S_OK)
{
   do
   {
      ......
   }while (m_Enum.MoveNext() == S_OK);
   ........
}
```

The sample code on the following page displays a list of data sources in a dialog box. To copy this code for use in your own projects, see "Accessing the Underlying Data Sources" on the accompanying CD-ROM.

Chapter 7: Using OLE DB Templates for Data Access

```
//Samples\Ch07\ManAcc01
//Gets a moniker onthe root enumerator and accesses the underlying data
//sources. The function displays a list of available data sources.
BOOL CDataSourceDlg::OnInitDialog()
{
  USES_CONVERSION;

  CDialog::OnInitDialog();
  m_pDataSourcePath=(CEdit*)GetDlgItem(IDC_DATASOURCE_PATH);
  m_pDataSource=(CComboBox*)GetDlgItem(IDC_DATASOURCE_NAME);
  m_pOK=(CButton*)GetDlgItem(IDOK);

  if(m_pRootEnum->m_nType==1)
  {
      m_pDataSourcePath->EnableWindow(TRUE);
      m_pDataSource->EnableWindow(FALSE);
  }
  else
  {
      m_pDataSourcePath->EnableWindow(FALSE);
      m_pDataSource->EnableWindow(TRUE);

      CComPtr<IMoniker> spMoniker;

      if(m_pRootEnum->GetMoniker(&spMoniker,
             W2T(m_pRootEnum->m_szParseName))==S_OK)
      {
          if(m_Enum.m_spSourcesRowset==NULL)
          {
              if (m_Enum.Open(spMoniker) != S_OK)
              {
                  ::AfxMessageBox("Failed to Open Data Source");
                  m_pOK->EnableWindow(FALSE);
                  OnCancel();
                  return FALSE;
              }
              else
              {
                  m_pOK->EnableWindow(TRUE);
              }
          }
```

code continued on next page

```
code continued from previous page
            int i=0;
            if(m_Enum.MoveFirst()==S_OK)
            {
                do
                {
                    m_pDataSource->AddString(W2T(m_Enum.m_szName));
                    m_listDataSource[i]= W2T(m_Enum.m_szName);
                    i++;
                }while (m_Enum.MoveNext() == S_OK);
                m_pDataSource->SetCurSel(0);
            }
            else
            {
                m_pOK->EnableWindow(FALSE);
                OnCancel();
                return FALSE;
            }
        }
    }
    return TRUE;
}
```

2. Open the data source by using the **Open** function, as shown in the following example:

    ```
    m_source.Open(*m_pRootEnum,&dbinit)
    ```

    The previous example opens the data source by using the root enumerator. The **m_source** object is of type **CDataSource**, and **dbinit** is of type **CDBPropSet**. You use the **AddProperty** function of the **dbinit** object to define properties for the data source. The following example sets the **USERID** property to **Admin**:

    ```
    dbinit.AddProperty(DBPROP_AUTH_USERID, "Admin");
    ```

    The sample code on the following page sets properties and opens a data source. To copy this code for use in your own projects, see "Opening the Data Source" on the accompanying CD-ROM.

Chapter 7: Using OLE DB Templates for Data Access

```
//Samples\Ch07\ManAcc01
//Sets properties and opens a data source
void CDataSourceDlg::OnKillfocusDatasourcePath()
{
  USES_CONVERSION;
  UpdateData(TRUE);
  CDBPropSet   dbinit(DBPROPSET_DBINIT);
  dbinit.AddProperty(DBPROP_AUTH_CACHE_AUTHINFO, true);
  dbinit.AddProperty(DBPROP_AUTH_ENCRYPT_PASSWORD, false);
  dbinit.AddProperty(DBPROP_AUTH_MASK_PASSWORD, false);
  dbinit.AddProperty(DBPROP_AUTH_PASSWORD, "");
  dbinit.AddProperty(DBPROP_AUTH_PERSIST_ENCRYPTED, false);
  dbinit.AddProperty(DBPROP_AUTH_PERSIST_SENSITIVE_AUTHINFO, false);
  dbinit.AddProperty(DBPROP_AUTH_USERID, "Admin");
  dbinit.AddProperty(DBPROP_INIT_DATASOURCE, m_Path);
  dbinit.AddProperty(DBPROP_INIT_MODE, (long)16);
  dbinit.AddProperty(DBPROP_INIT_PROMPT, (short)2);
  dbinit.AddProperty(DBPROP_INIT_PROVIDERSTRING, ";
       COUNTRY=0;CP=1252;LANGID=0x0409");
  dbinit.AddProperty(DBPROP_INIT_LCID, (long)1033);
  if (m_source.Open(*m_RootEnum,&dbinit)!= S_OK)
  {
      ::AfxMessageBox("Failed to Open Data Source");
      m_pOK->EnableWindow(FALSE);
      OnCancel();
      return;
  }
}
```

3. Open a session on the data source by using a **CSession** object, as shown in the following example:

   ```
   m_pSession->Open(*m_pSource);
   ```

4. Open the tables within the data source by using a **CTables** object, as shown in the following example:

   ```
   m_Tbl.Open(*m_pSession,NULL,NULL,NULL,"TABLE")
   ```

   In the previous example, **m_Tbl** is a **CTables**-type object. The **Open** function takes five arguments; the first argument is the session object, and the remaining arguments are restrictions that can be applied when the **CTables** object is opened. The last argument to the **Open** function ensures that only user-defined tables are accessed.

You can traverse the tables available in the data source by using the **MoveFirst**, **MovePrev**, **MoveNext**, and **MoveLast** functions, as shown in the following example:

```
if(m_Tbl.MoveFirst()==S_OK)
{
    .....
    do
    {
        ....
    }while (m_Tbl.MoveNext() == S_OK);
    ....
}
```

5. Determine the schema of the table by using a **CColumns** object, as shown in the following example:

```
m_Col.Open(*m_pSession,NULL,NULL,m_Tbl->m_szName);
```

The object **m_Col** is of type **CColumns**. The last argument to the **Open** function is an attribute of the **CTables** object, which contains the name of the table whose column information is to be accessed. The schema can be used to construct the SQL statement that is required to retrieve that data from the data source. The following sample code constructs an SQL statement using the fields selected by the user. To copy this code for use in your own projects, see "Generating the SQL Statement" on the accompanying CD-ROM.

```
//Samples\Ch07\ManAcc01
//Generates an SQL statement form the list of columns the
//user selects

void CColumnsDlg::OnKillFocus(CWnd* pNewWnd)
{
  int nLbSelItems[100];
  CDialog::OnKillFocus(pNewWnd);

  m_plbColumns->GetSelItems(m_fld_cnt,nLbSelItems);
  m_ColsSelected=m_plbColumns->GetSelCount();
  m_cmd_str="Select";
```

code continued on next page

code continued from previous page

```
    for(int j = 0 ; j < m_ColsSelected; j++)
    {
        if(j==0)
        {
            m_cmd_str=m_cmd_str+ "  " + m_listColumns[nLbSelItems[j]];
        }
        else
        {
            m_cmd_str=m_cmd_str+ " , " + m_listColumns[nLbSelItems[j]];
        }
    }
    if(m_ColsSelected==0)
    {
        m_ColsSelected=m_fld_cnt;
        m_cmd_str="Select * ";
    }
    m_cmd_str=m_cmd_str + " FROM ";
    m_cmd_str=m_cmd_str + m_pTbl->m_szName;

}
```

6. Declare an object of type **CCommand<CManualAccessor>**, as shown in the following example:

    ```
    CCommand<CManualAccessor> manAcc;
    ```

7. Invoke the **CreateAccessor** function to create the manual accessor, as shown in the following example:

    ```
    manAcc.CreateAccessor(m_ColsSelected, pBind,
            sizeof(MyBind)*m_ColsSelected);
    ```

    In the previous example, the first argument defines the number of columns to be accessed, the second argument is a pointer to the buffer where the data that is retrieved is to be stored, and the third argument defines the size of the buffer. The sample code on the following page defines the buffer. To copy this code for use in your own projects, see "Defining the Dynamic Accessor Buffer" on the accompanying CD-ROM.

```
//Samples\Ch07\ManAcc01
//Defines a buffer for the manual accessor

struct MyBind
{
  MyBind()
  {
      memset(this, 0, sizeof(*this));
  }

  TCHAR    szValue[40];
  DWORD    dwStatus;
};
```

8. Open the manual accessor by using the **Open** function, as shown in the following example:

   ```
   manAcc.Open(m_session,m_cmd_str);
   ```

   In the previous example, **m_session** is the session that was opened earlier on the data source, and **m_cmd_str** contains the SQL statement to be used to access the data.

9. Traverse the records in the table by using the **MoveFirst, MovePrev, MoveNext,** and **MoveLast** functions.

Sample Applications

The following table describes the sample applications related to this chapter. These sample applications are located in the folder <install folder>\Samples\Ch07.

Sample application subfolder	Description of application
OLEEmployee	An OLE DB Templates-based application that makes use of the **CAccessor** class to access data from a specific data source using a specific provider. Before you run this application, you need to create an ODBC data source called Employees, by using the ODBC Data Source Administrator. Ensure that the database file has read-write permissions.

table continued on next page

table continued from previous page

Sample application subfolder	Description of application
DynAcc01	An OLE DB Templates-based application that makes use of the **CDynamicAccessor** class to access data from a specific data source using a specific provider. Ensure that the database file has read-write permissions.
DynAcc02	An OLE DB Templates-based application that makes use of the **CDynamicAccessor** class to access data from any data source. The user can choose from a list of providers, select a data source, select a table, select columns from the table, and then display that data stored in the table. When prompted to specify the path to the data source, in the **Data Source** dialog box, specify the complete path to the data source. Ensure that the data source has read-write permissions.
ManAcc01	An OLE DB Templates-based application that makes use of the **CManualAccessor** class to access data from any data source. The user can choose from a list of providers, select a data source, select a table, select columns from the table, and then display that data stored in the table. When prompted to specify the path to the data source, in the **Data Source** dialog box, specify the complete path to the data source. Ensure that the data source has read-write permissions.

Self-Check Questions

To see the answers to the Self-Check Questions, see Appendix A.

1. What is the role of a data provider?

   A. Expose the data in a tabular format.
   B. Facilitate data access by a consumer.
   C. Retrieve data from a data source.
   D. Store data in a tabular format.

2. **Which OLE DB component helps you search for data sources?**
   A. Data source objects
   B. Sessions
   C. Commands
   D. Enumerators

3. **Which base class of the consumer template classes encapsulates a rowset and its accessors?**
   A. CTable
   B. CCommand
   C. CAccessorRowset
   D. CDataSource

4. **Which function creates a data source object?**
   A. OpenRowset
   B. CoCreateInstance
   C. Initialize
   D. CreateSession

5. **Which is the default base view class for consumer applications that use CAccessor?**
   A. CFormView
   B. CView
   C. COleDBRecordView
   D. CListView

Chapter 8:
Creating ADO Database Applications

Multimedia

ADO Object Model 391

Using Data Controls 397

Using Data Bound
  Dialog Wizard 402

Lab 8.1 Demonstration 432

ActiveX Data Objects (ADO) acts as the bridge between OLE DB and your applications. OLE DB has a programming interface that is designed for optimal functionality in a wide variety of applications, but it does not meet the requirement for a simple programming interface. ADO is an application programming interface (API) that simplifies OLE DB.

The ADO programming model defines the sequence of activities necessary to gain access to and update a data source. The model is based on a set of objects where each object simplifies a specific database operation, such as connecting to a database or retrieving data. Objects possess methods and properties. Methods perform some operation on data. Properties either represent some attribute of the data, or control the behavior of some object method. Associated with objects are events, which are notifications that some operation has occurred, or is about to occur.

In this chapter, you will learn to use the ADO programming model to create applications that use data controls and data-bound dialog boxes to access databases. You will also learn to perform queries and find records in a database table.

Objectives

After completing this chapter, you will be able to:

- Describe the role of ADO in applications that require database access.
- Describe the ADO programming model.
- Implement ADO in Microsoft Foundation Class (MFC)-based applications by using data controls.
- Implement ADO in MFC-based applications by using the data-bound dialog box.
- Perform queries and searches on databases and rowsets.

Introduction to ADO

ADO helps you develop applications that access and manipulate data through an OLE DB provider. ADO provides a set of objects that simplify database-related operations, such as connecting to a database and retrieving rowsets.

This section begins with an introduction to ADO. You will learn about the features of ADO and benefits of using ADO to access data. You will also look at the ADO object model and see what objects, properties, and methods are available.

This section also introduces you to the two approaches to implementing ADO technology in MFC-based applications.

Benefits of Using ADO

ADO is designed as an easy-to-use application-level interface to OLE DB. OLE DB provides high-performance access to any data source. A data source includes relational and nonrelational databases, e-mail, and file systems. ADO provides a minimal number of layers between your application and data source to provide a lightweight, high-performance interface.

ADO is easy to use because it is based on the generic Automation interface, which is supported by several tools and languages. ADO combines the best features of Remote Data Objects (RDO) and Data Access Objects (DAO), using similar conventions with simplified semantics that make it easy to learn.

In addition, ADO provides high speed and low memory overhead for improved performance.

- De-emphasizes the object hierarchy

    You need not navigate through a hierarchy to create objects, because objects are independent. This model results in fewer objects and a smaller working set. You track and create only the relevant objects.

- Supports free-threaded objects for efficient Web server applications
- Supports batch processing and stored procedures with in/out parameters and return values

    ADO also supports retrieval of multiple recordsets by stored procedures and batch statements.

- Provides advanced rowset cache management for better performance

 To see the animation "ADO Object Model," see the accompanying CD-ROM.

ADO Object Model

The ADO 2.0 object model consists of the following:

- Objects and properties
- Collections
- Methods

Objects and Properties

The following illustration shows the ADO objects and how they are related.

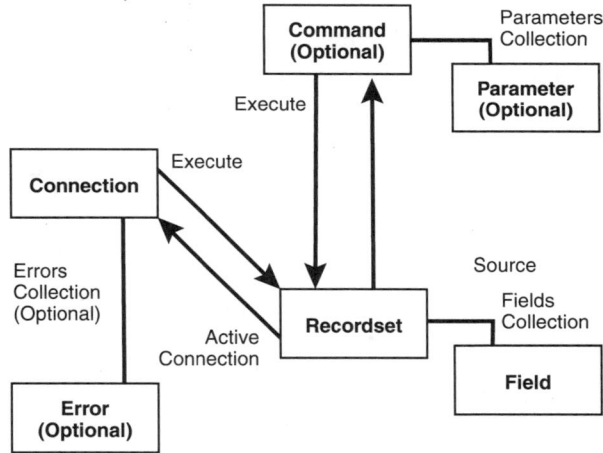

Each ADO object has a set of properties associated with it. You can customize data access operations by modifying the values of these properties.

The properties of an ADO object can be classified into two categories:

- Dynamic properties

    These properties are defined by the underlying data provider. Each such property is represented as a **Property** object.

- Built-in properties

    These are native ADO properties and are automatically available to any newly created object.

For a complete list of ADO object properties, see "ADO Properties" in ADO Documentation, OLE DB SDK 1.5.

Collections

A collection refers to a group of similar objects owned by another object. For example a **Rowset** object owns a collection of **Field** objects, where each **Field** object represents a column in the rowset.

The ADO object model has the following collections:

- **Errors** collection

    A **Connection** object contains an **Errors** collection, which contains all the **Error** objects created in response to a single failure involving the data provider.

- **Parameters** collection

    A **Command** object contains a **Parameters** collection made up of **Parameter** objects. Each **Parameter** object represents a parameter of the specific command.

- **Properties** collection

    Each ADO object has a **Properties** collection, which contains a set of **Property** objects. Each **Property** object represents a dynamic property of the specific instance of an object.

- **Fields** collection

    A **Recordset** object has a **Fields** collection made up of **Field** objects. Each **Field** object represents a column in the recordset.

Methods

The following table lists some ADO methods that you can use to implement ADO in your applications.

Method	Description	Applies to
MoveFirst, MoveLast, MoveNext, MovePrevious	Moves to the first, last, next, or previous record in a specified **Recordset** object and makes that record the current record.	**Recordset** object
Open	Opens a connection to a data source.	**Connection** object
GetRows	Retrieves multiple records of a recordset into an array.	**Recordset** object

For a complete list of ADO methods, see "ADO Methods" in ADO Documentation, OLE DB SDK 1.5.

Using ADO in MFC-based Applications

You can create an ADO application in two ways: by using data controls and by using the data-bound dialog box.

Using the Data Controls

You can use the data controls to access a data source. The following illustration shows an application that uses this approach to implement ADO.

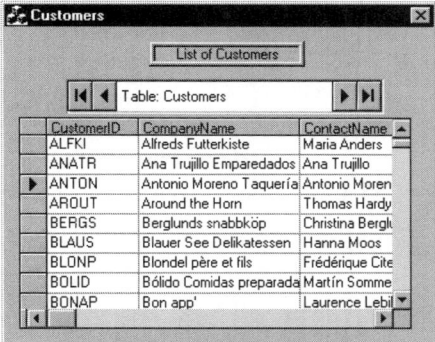

The ADO data control connects to the database and retrieves recordsets. A data-bound control binds to the data control and displays the records retrieved from a database.

For information about how to implement ADO in an MFC-based application by using this technique, see "Implementing ADO Using Data Controls" on page 397 in this chapter.

Using the Data-bound Dialog Box

In addition to using data controls, you can create a data-bound dialog box to implement ADO.

Note If you are using the Enterprise Edition of Microsoft Visual C++, you can use the ADO Data Bound Dialog Wizard to create the dialog box. If you are using the Professional or Standard Edition, you need to create the dialog box manually.

The data-bound dialog box contains controls, such as edit boxes and check boxes, that are bound to the fields of a recordset.

The following illustration shows an application with a data-bound dialog box.

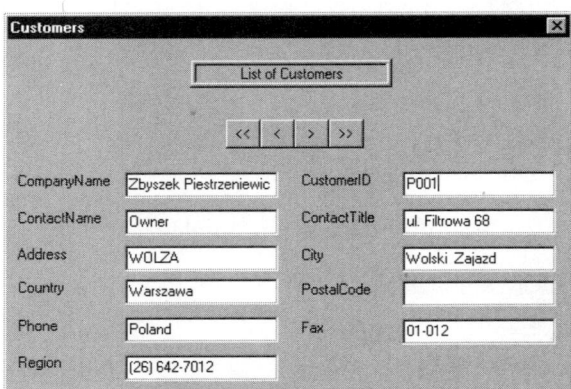

The data-bound dialog box provides you record-level access to your data. You can perform database operations, such as adding new records and modifying existing records.

For information about how to create a data-bound dialog box, see "Using the Data-bound Dialog Box" on page 401 in this chapter.

Using Data Controls

In this section, you will learn to use the data controls — the ADO data control and the data-bound controls — to create an ADO application.

The ADO data control connects to the database and retrieves rowsets. A data-bound control binds to the ADO data control and displays recordsets retrieved from a database.

The ADO Data Control

The ADO data control is a graphic control that provides an easy-to-use interface to help you develop applications with minimum code. Instead of using ADO objects, such as **Connection** and **Recordset**, you can use the ADO data control to quickly create a connection to a database and retrieve records.

The following illustration shows an ADO data control.

```
|◄|◄| ADODC1    |►|►|
```

The ADO data control establishes a connection between a data provider and a data-bound control. A data-bound control is any Windows control that has a **DataSource** property. For more information about data-bound controls, see "Data-bound Controls" on page 396 in this chapter.

The ADO data control performs the following functions:

- Connects to a local or remote database
- Opens a specified database table or defines a set of records based on an SQL query or stored procedure
- Supplies field values to data-bound controls
- Enables addition or modification of field values displayed in data-bound controls, depending on the functionality supported by the provider and the data source

For a step-by-step procedure of how to use an ADO data control to implement a client application, see "Implementing ADO Using Data Controls" on page 397 in this chapter.

Properties of an ADO Data Control

The following table lists some important properties of the ADO data control that you can set to define a connection to a database.

Property	Description
Provider	Specifies the data provider.
DataSourceName	Specifies the name of the data source.
UserName and Password	Specifies the name of the user and password, if the database is password-protected.
RecordSource	Defines the recordset. Could either be a table name or an SQL statement.

table continued on next page

table continued from previous page

Property	Description
ConnectionString	Specifies the settings necessary to make a connection. For example, the connection string for Microsoft.Jet.OLEDB.3.51 provider is as follows: `"Provider=Microsoft.Jet.OLEDB.3.51; Data source=d:\\databases\\db1.mdb; Mode=Read|Write|ReadWrite"`

Events Associated with an ADO Data Control

The following table lists some ADO data control events that you can implement in your applications.

Event	Occurs
WillMove	When a recordset is opened or the current record of a recordset is changed.
MoveComplete	After the **WillMove** event.
WillChangeField	Before the **Value** property changes.
InfoMessage	When the data provider returns a result.

For a complete list of ADO data control properties and methods, search for "ADO Reference" in MSDN Library Visual Studio 6.0.

Data-bound Controls

Data-bound controls are ActiveX controls that have two important characteristics:

- They have a **DataSource** property.
  You can set this property to the ID of an ADO data control.
- They can display data retrieved by the ADO data control to which they are bound.

ActiveX data controls include:

- **DataList, DataCombo,** and **DataGrid.**
- Lightweight controls, such as lightweight **CheckBox** and lightweight **ComboBox.**
- Microsoft FlexGrid and Hierarchical FlexGrid.

The following illustration shows a **DataGrid** control bound to an ADO data control.

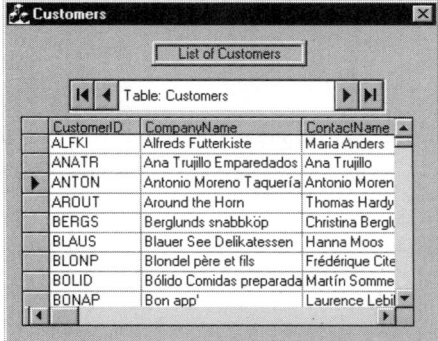

Implementing ADO Using Data Controls

To implement an ADO application that uses data controls, complete the following steps.

1. Create a dialog-based application.
2. Insert the ADO data control and set its properties.
3. Insert a data-bound control and set its properties.
4. Compile and run the program.

Each step is explained in more detail below.

To see the demonstration "Using Data Controls," see the accompanying CD-ROM.

▶ **To create a dialog-based application**

1. Invoke MFC AppWizard.
2. In Step 1 of MFC AppWizard, select **Dialog based,** and then click **Finish.**
3. Click **OK** to confirm the selection.

MFC Development Using Microsoft Visual C++ 6.0

▶ **To insert the ADO data control and set its properties**

1. Invoke the Components and Controls Gallery and select **Registered ActiveX Controls**.

   A list of ActiveX controls appears.

2. Select **Microsoft ADO Data Control Version 6.0 (OLEDB)** and click **Insert**. Click **OK** to confirm the insertion.

   The **Confirm Classes** dialog box appears.

3. Click **OK**, and then **Close** to close the Gallery.

4. Invoke Resource Editor.

   Note the Microsoft ADO Data Control button on the **Controls** toolbar.

5. Delete the static control from the dialog box. Add an ADO data control to the dialog box.

   The following illustration shows the dialog box.

   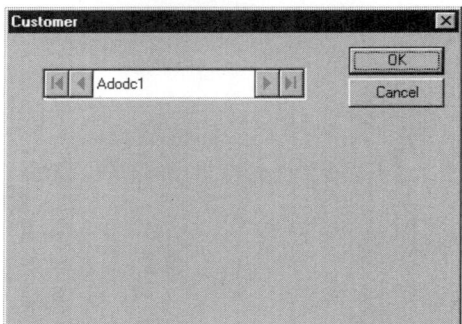

6. Right-click the data control and click **Properties** on the shortcut menu.

   The **Properties** dialog box appears. The following illustration shows the **Properties** dialog box.

   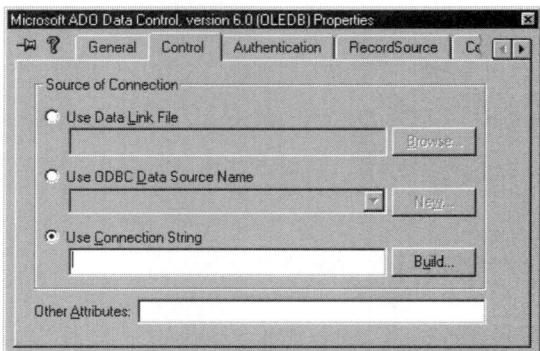

7. On the **General** tab, set a caption for the control; for example, **Table: Customer**.
8. On the **Control** tab, set the source of connection by selecting **Use Connection String**.
9. Click **Build** to construct the connection string.

    The **Data Link Properties** dialog box appears. The following illustration shows the **Data Link Properties** dialog box with the **Provider** tab selected.

    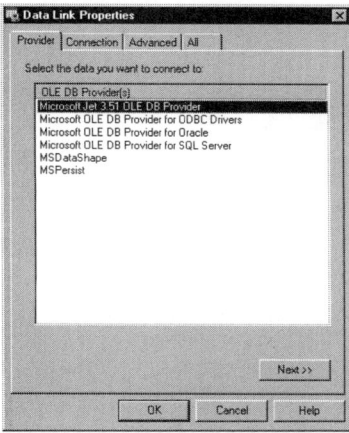

10. On the **Provider** tab, select a provider from the list (for example, **Microsoft Jet 3.51 OLE DB Provider**), and then click the **Connection** tab.

    The following illustration shows the **Data Link Properties** dialog box with the **Connection** tab selected.

    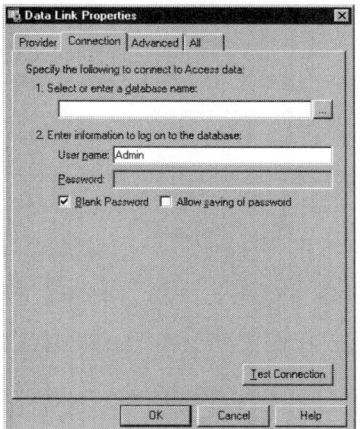

11. Specify the full path of the data source file name.
12. If the data source is password-protected, specify a user name and password to log on to the data source.
13. Click **Test Connection** to test the connection.

    The following illustration shows the results of testing a connection.

    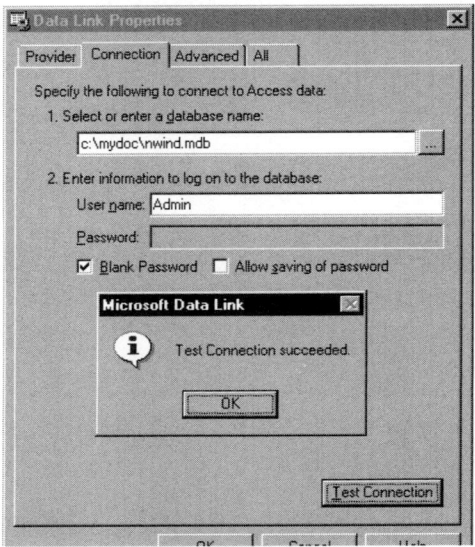

14. Click **OK** to return to the Resource Editor.

    The complete connection string is displayed in the **Properties** dialog box. For example:

    ```
    Provider=Microsoft.Jet.OLEDB.3.51;Data Source=C:\mydoc\nwind.mdb
    ```

15. On the **RecordSource** tab, in the **Command Text** field, specify an SQL statement. For example:

    ```
    SELECT * FROM CUSTOMERS
    ```

▶ **To insert a data-bound ActiveX control and set its properties**

1. Invoke the Components and Controls Gallery and select **Registered ActiveX Controls**.

    A list of ActiveX controls appears.

2. Select **Microsoft Data Grid Control, version 6.0** and click **Insert**. Click **OK** to confirm the insertion.

    The **Confirm Classes** dialog box appears.

3. Click **OK** to accept the default.
4. Click **Close** to close the Gallery.
5. Invoke Resource Editor.

    Note the **Microsoft Data Grid Control** button on the **Controls** toolbar.

6. Add the data grid control below the ADO data control.

    The following illustration shows the dialog box.

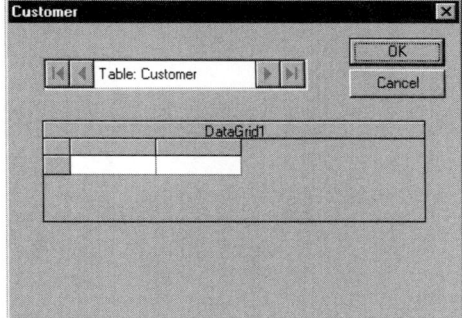

7. Right-click the data-bound control and click **Properties** on the shortcut menu.
8. On the **All** tab, set the **DataSource** property to the ID of the ADO data control.

Compile and run the application. The recordset is displayed in the data grid control. Use the ADO data control to navigate through the recordset.

Using the Data-bound Dialog Box

In this section, you will learn how to implement ADO by creating a data-bound dialog box. The dialog box will contain intrinsic controls, such as edit boxes and check boxes, which are bound to the columns of a recordset.

You will learn to create resources, classes, and the Component Object Model (COM) initialization code necessary to implement the data-bound dialog box. The dialog box will allow record-level access to your data.

Building an Application Using the Wizard

The Enterprise Edition of Visual C++ 6.0 provides the ADO Data Bound Dialog Wizard to create skeletal code for a data-bound dialog box-based ADO application. However, if you are using the Professional Edition, this wizard is not available, and you will have to write the MFC AppWizard – generated code yourself. For information about how to do this, see "Building an Application Without the Wizard" on page 416 in this chapter.

To implement an ADO application using the ADO Data Bound Dialog Wizard, complete the following steps.

1. Create a dialog-based application by using MFC AppWizard.
2. Invoke the ADO Data Bound Dialog Wizard to create the data-bound dialog box.
3. Add code to display the data-bound dialog box.

Each step is explained in more detail below.

To see the demonstration "Using Data Bound Dialog Wizard," see the accompanying CD-ROM.

▶ **To create a dialog-based application by using MFC AppWizard**

1. Invoke MFC AppWizard. In Step 1 of MFC AppWizard, select **Dialog based**, and then click **Finish**.
2. Click **OK** to confirm the selection.

▶ **To invoke the Data Bound Dialog Wizard**

1. On the **Project** menu, click **Add To Project**, and then select **Components and Controls**.

   The **Components and Controls Gallery** dialog box appears.
2. Double-click **Visual C++ Components**.
3. In the list of Visual C++ components, select **ADO Data Bound Dialog**.

Chapter 8: Creating ADO Database Applications

The following illustration shows the **Components and Controls Gallery** dialog box with the wizard selected.

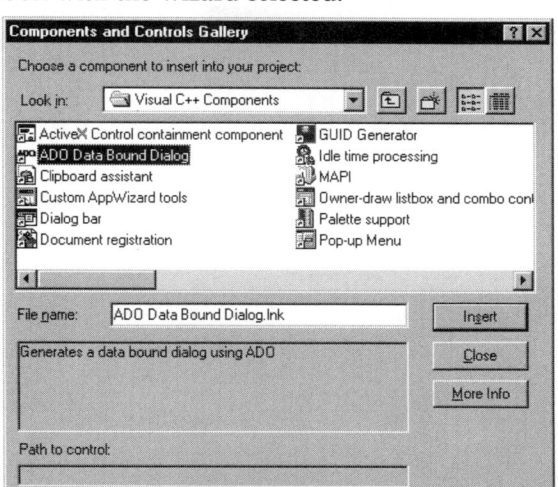

4. Click **Insert**, and then click **OK** to confirm the insertion.

   The **ADO Data Bound Dialog Wizard - Step 1 of 4** dialog box appears. The following illustration shows the **Step 1 of 4** dialog box.

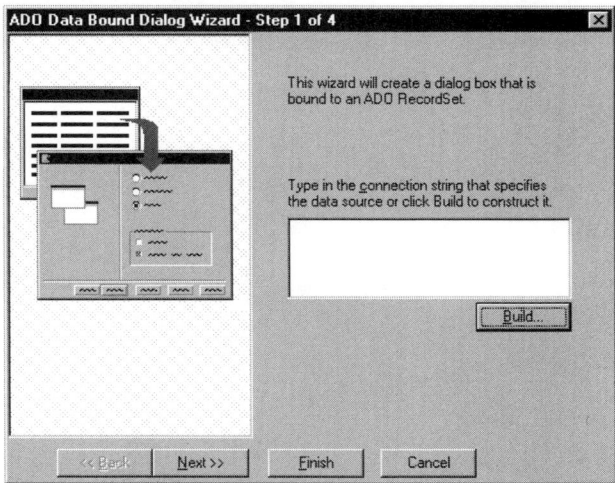

   You can type the connection string to specify the data source or click **Build** to build the string.

5. Click **Build** to build the connection string.

The **Data Link Properties** dialog box appears. The following illustration shows the dialog box.

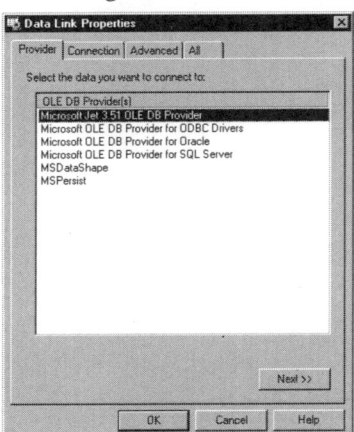

6. On the **Provider** tab, choose a provider; for example, **Microsoft Jet 3.51 OLE DB Provider**.

7. On the **Connection** tab, specify the path to the data source and the user name and password to log on to the data source. Click **OK** to return to the wizard.

    The connection string will be similar to the following:

    ```
    Provider=Microsoft.Jet.OLEDB.3.51;Data Source=c:\databases\db1
    ```

8. Click **Next** to display the **ADO Data Bound Dialog Wizard - Step 2 of 4** dialog box.

    The following illustration shows the **Step 2 of 4** dialog box.

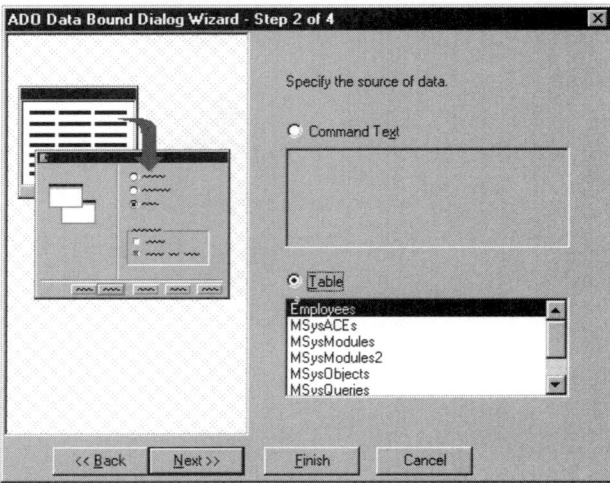

9. You can either select **Command Text** and type the SQL statement to retrieve the data or select **Table** and select the table name from the list that is displayed. Click **Table** and select a table from the list.

10. Click on **Next** to display the **ADO Data Bound Dialog Wizard - Step 3 of 4** dialog box.

    The following illustration shows the **Step 3 of 4** dialog box.

    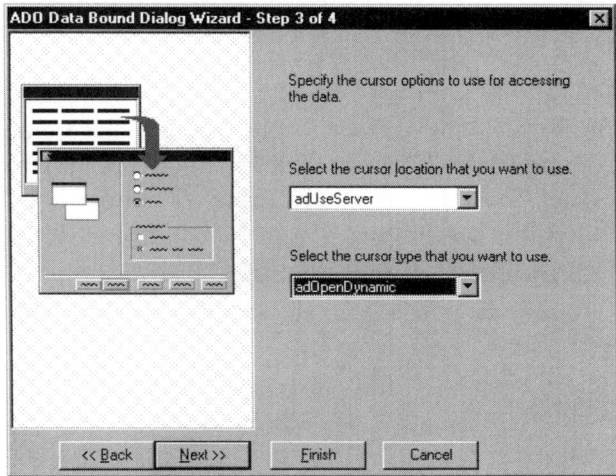

11. Select a cursor location. The following options are available:

    - **adUseClient**

      Select **adUseClient** to use the MS Client Cursor Engine, which provides static, batch-updateable results.

    - **adUseServer**

      Select **adUseServer** to use cursors provided by the OLE DB provider.

12. Select a cursor type. The following options are available:

    - **adOpenStatic**

      Creates a static cursor. This cursor type provides you with a static copy of data that you can use to search or generate reports. Additions, changes, or deletions by other users are not visible.

    - **adOpenForwardOnly**

      Creates a forward-only cursor. This cursor type is similar to a static cursor except that you can only scroll forward through records. Improves performance in situations when you only need to make a single pass through a recordset.

- **adOpenDynamic**

  Creates a dynamic cursor. Additions, changes, and deletions by other users are visible, and all types of movement through the recordset are allowed, except bookmarks if the provider doesn't support them.

- **adOpenKeyset**

  Creates a keyset cursor. This cursor type is similar to a dynamic cursor, except that you cannot see records that other users add, although records that other users delete are inaccessible from your recordset. Data changes by other users are made visible.

13. Click **Next** to display a list of changes that will be made to your project in **ADO Data Bound Dialog Wizard - Step 4 of 4**, or click **Finish** to return to the **Components and Controls Gallery** dialog box. The following illustration shows the **Step 4 of 4** dialog box.

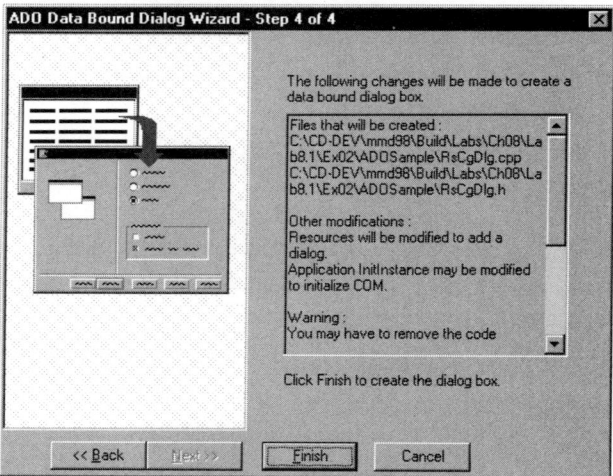

14. Click **Close** to close the Component and Controls Gallery.

▶ To add code to display the data-bound dialog box

You need to integrate the dialog box, **CG_IDD_RECORDSET**, with the dialog box created by MFC AppWizard. For example, you may add a button to the default dialog box that, when clicked, displays the data-bound dialog box.

The ADO Data Bound Dialog Wizard makes the following changes to your project:

◆ Adds the following classes:

- **CCustomRs**

    This class is derived from **CADORecordBinding**. It binds the member variables to columns in the database. The following sample code shows the definition and members of this class. To copy this code for use in your own projects, see "Definition of CCustomRs" on the accompanying CD-ROM.

```
// Samples\CH08\ADOSample2
// RsCgDlg.h
class CCustomRs :
  public CADORecordBinding
{
BEGIN_ADO_BINDING(CCustomRs)
  ADO_VARIABLE_LENGTH_ENTRY2(1, adVarChar, m_szAddress,
sizeof(m_szAddress), lAddressStatus, FALSE)
  ADO_VARIABLE_LENGTH_ENTRY2(2, adVarChar, m_szCity,
sizeof(m_szCity), lCityStatus, FALSE)
  ADO_VARIABLE_LENGTH_ENTRY2(3, adVarChar, m_szCompanyName,
sizeof(m_szCompanyName), lCompanyNameStatus, FALSE)
  ADO_VARIABLE_LENGTH_ENTRY2(4, adVarChar, m_szContactName,
sizeof(m_szContactName), lContactNameStatus, FALSE)
  ADO_VARIABLE_LENGTH_ENTRY2(5, adVarChar, m_szContactTitle,
sizeof(m_szContactTitle), lContactTitleStatus, FALSE)
  ADO_VARIABLE_LENGTH_ENTRY2(6, adVarChar, m_szCountry,
sizeof(m_szCountry), lCountryStatus, FALSE)
  ADO_VARIABLE_LENGTH_ENTRY2(7, adVarChar, m_szCustomerID,
sizeof(m_szCustomerID), lCustomerIDStatus, FALSE)
  ADO_VARIABLE_LENGTH_ENTRY2(8, adVarChar, m_szFax,
sizeof(m_szFax), lFaxStatus, FALSE)
  ADO_VARIABLE_LENGTH_ENTRY2(9, adVarChar, m_szPhone,
sizeof(m_szPhone), lPhoneStatus, FALSE)
  ADO_VARIABLE_LENGTH_ENTRY2(10, adVarChar, m_szPostalCode,
sizeof(m_szPostalCode), lPostalCodeStatus, FALSE)
  ADO_VARIABLE_LENGTH_ENTRY2(11, adVarChar, m_szRegion,
sizeof(m_szRegion), lRegionStatus, FALSE)
END_ADO_BINDING()
```

code continued on next page

code continued from previous page

```cpp
  protected:
    CHAR  m_szAddress[61];
    ULONG lAddressStatus;
    CHAR  m_szCity[16];
    ULONG lCityStatus;
    CHAR  m_szCompanyName[41];
    ULONG lCompanyNameStatus;
    CHAR  m_szContactName[31];
    ULONG lContactNameStatus;
    CHAR  m_szContactTitle[31];
    ULONG lContactTitleStatus;
    CHAR  m_szCountry[16];
    ULONG lCountryStatus;
    CHAR  m_szCustomerID[6];
    ULONG lCustomerIDStatus;
    CHAR  m_szFax[25];
    ULONG lFaxStatus;
    CHAR  m_szPhone[25];
    ULONG lPhoneStatus;
    CHAR  m_szPostalCode[11];
    ULONG lPostalCodeStatus;
    CHAR  m_szRegion[16];
    ULONG lRegionStatus;
};

//
// TODO : These definitions should be moved to the resource header.
//
#define ID_BTN_MOVEPREVIOUS           201
#define ID_BTN_MOVENEXT               202
#define ID_BTN_MOVELAST               203
#define ID_BTN_MOVEFIRST              204
#define IDC_STATIC_ADDRESS       1001
#define IDC_EDIT_ADDRESS         2001
#define IDC_STATIC_CITY          1002
#define IDC_EDIT_CITY        2002
#define IDC_STATIC_COMPANYNAME       1003
#define IDC_EDIT_COMPANYNAME         2003
#define IDC_STATIC_CONTACTNAME       1004
#define IDC_EDIT_CONTACTNAME         2004
#define IDC_STATIC_CONTACTTITLE      1005
```

code continued on next page

code continued from previous page

```
#define  IDC_EDIT_CONTACTTITLE       2005
#define  IDC_STATIC_COUNTRY    1006
#define  IDC_EDIT_COUNTRY      2006
#define  IDC_STATIC_CUSTOMERID       1007
#define  IDC_EDIT_CUSTOMERID         2007
#define  IDC_STATIC_FAX        1008
#define  IDC_EDIT_FAX          2008
#define  IDC_STATIC_PHONE      1009
#define  IDC_EDIT_PHONE        2009
#define  IDC_STATIC_POSTALCODE       1010
#define  IDC_EDIT_POSTALCODE         2010
#define  IDC_STATIC_REGION     1011
#define  IDC_EDIT_REGION       2011
```

Note the BEGIN_ADO_BINDING macro, which binds the columns in the database to variables declared in the class. The wizard declares variables using data types that provide the closest match to the data types of the columns in the database.

- **CRsCgDlg**

    This class is derived from **CCustomRs** and **CDialog**. The following sample code shows the definition and members of this class. To copy this code for use in your own projects, see "Definition of CRsCgDlg" on the accompanying CD-ROM.

```
//  Samples\CH08\ADOSample2
//  RsCgDlg.h
class CRsCgDlg :
  public CDialog,
  public CCustomRs
{
// Construction
public:
  CRsCgDlg(CWnd* pParent = NULL);
  ~CRsCgDlg();

  BOOL OnInitDialog();
```

code continued on next page

code continued from previous page

```cpp
// Dialog Data
  //{{AFX_DATA(CRsCgDlg)
  enum { IDD = CG_IDD_RECORDSET };
  CString m_strDlgAddress;
  CString m_strDlgCity;
  CString m_strDlgCompanyName;
  CString m_strDlgContactName;
  CString m_strDlgContactTitle;
  CString m_strDlgCountry;
  CString m_strDlgCustomerID;
  CString m_strDlgFax;
  CString m_strDlgPhone;
  CString m_strDlgPostalCode;
  CString m_strDlgRegion;
  //}}AFX_DATA

// Overrides
  // ClassWizard generated virtual function overrides
  //{{AFX_VIRTUAL(CRsCgDlg)
  protected:
  virtual void DoDataExchange(CDataExchange* pDX);    // DDX/DDV support
  //}}AFX_VIRTUAL

// Implementation
protected:

  void RefreshBoundData();
  void GenerateError(HRESULT hr, PWSTR pwszDescription);

  _RecordsetPtr m_pRs;

  CString m_strConnection;
  CString m_strCmdText;

  // Generated message map functions
  //{{AFX_MSG(CRsCgDlg)
  afx_msg void OnBtnMoveFirst();
  afx_msg void OnBtnMoveLast();
  afx_msg void OnBtnMoveNext();
  afx_msg void OnBtnMovePrevious();
  //}}AFX_MSG
  DECLARE_MESSAGE_MAP()
};
```

- Adds the following files:
  - RsCgDlg.h
  - RsCgDlg.cpp

  If your project contains multiple data-bound dialog boxes, these file names are appended with a number starting with 1. For example, the files corresponding to the second data-bound dialog box in your project would be named RsCgDlg1.cpp and RsCgDlg1.h.
- Adds a dialog box named **CG_IDD_RECORDSET** with controls to display the data values.
- Adds code to the project's application **InitInstance** to initialize COM. If you added COM initialization code to your application manually, then you may need to remove the code added by the ADO Data Bound Dialog Wizard.

Default Implementation of Data-bound Dialog Box

The RsCgDlg.cpp file implements the functionality of the data-bound dialog box.

The constructor of the dialog box initializes two strings—the connection string and the command text.

Connection String

The connection string stores information about the type of provider being used, the data source, and the mode in which the data source is to be opened. If the provider is Microsoft.Jet.OLEDB.3.51, then the data source is specified as the path to the database file. If the provider is ODBC, the data source is the name of the ODBC data source.

The following code shows the connection string for an ODBC provider:

```
m_strConnection = _T("Provider=MSDASQL.1;User ID=admin;
Data source=ado3; Mode=Read|Write|ReadWrite");
```

The following code shows the connection string for the Microsoft.Jet.OLEDB.3.51 provider:

```
m_strConnection = _T("Provider=Microsoft.Jet.OLEDB.3.51; Data
source=d:\\databases\\db1.mdb; Mode=Read|Write|ReadWrite");
```

Command Text

The command text can either be the name of a table or an SQL statement as shown in the following example:

```
m_strCmdText = _T("Employees");
m_strCmdText = _T("Select * from Employees");
```

In the **OnInitDialog** function, **CreateInstance** function is invoked to create a pointer of type _RecordsetPtr, as shown in the following example:

```
\\ m_pRs is declared as _RecordsetPtr m_pRs;
m_pRs.CreateInstance(_uuidof(Recordset));
```

The CursorLocation attribute is set to specify the location of the cursor. For example:

```
m_pRs->CursorLocation = adUseServer;
```

The Open Function

The **Open** function is called to open a cursor for the recordset, as shown in the following example:

```
m_pRs->Open((LPCTSTR)m_strCmdText, (LPCTSTR)m_strConnection,
adOpenStatic, adLockOptimistic, adCmdTableDirect);
```

The **Open** function takes the following arguments:

- Command text

    Specifies the command text.

- Connection string

    Specifies the connection string.

- Cursor type

    Defines the type of cursor to be created.

- Locking type to be used with the cursor

You can choose one of the following values for this argument.

Lock type	Description
adLockReadOnly	Read-only—you cannot alter the data.
adLockPessimistic	Pessimistic locking (by record or by page depending on the provider)—the provider does what is necessary to ensure successful editing of the records, usually by locking records at the data source immediately upon editing.
adLockOptimistic	Optimistic locking (by record or by page depending on the provider)—the provider uses optimistic locking, locking records only when you call the **Update** method.
adLockBatchOptimistic	Optimistic batch updates—required for batch update mode as opposed to immediate update mode.

- Type of command object

You can choose one of the following values for this argument.

Command type option	Description
adCmdText	Evaluates **CommandText** as a textual definition of a command.
adCmdTable	Evaluates **CommandText** as a table name in a generated SQL query returning all columns.
adCmdTableDirect	Evaluates **CommandText** as a table name whose columns are all returned.
adCmdStoredProc	Evaluates **CommandText** as a stored procedure.
adCmdUnknown	Default. The type of command in the **CommandText** property is not known.
adCommandFile	Evaluates **CommandText** as the file name of a persisted recordset.

The QueryInterface Function

The call to **Open** is followed by a call to the **QueryInterface** function. This function returns a pointer to the IADORecordBinding interface. It returns S_OK if the interface is supported, or S_FALSE if the interface is not supported.

The following example shows the **QueryInterface** function initializing the **piAdoRecordBinding** pointer:

```
m_pRs->QueryInterface(__uuidof(IADORecordBinding),
    (LPVOID *)&piAdoRecordBinding);
```

The keyword **__uuidof** retrieves the GUID attached to the expression IADORecordBinding. The pointer piAdoRecordBinding is of type IADORecordBinding and receives the pointer to the interface, if it is supported.

The member function **BindToRecordset** of the IADORecordBinding interface is called to associate the fields in the rowset with variables as shown in the following sample code:

```
piAdoRecordBinding->BindToRecordset(this);
```

The following sample code shows the complete code for the **InitDialog** function. To copy this code for use in your own projects, see "CRsCgDlg::OnInitDialog Function" on the accompanying CD-ROM.

```
//Samples\CH08\ADOSample2
BOOL CRsCgDlg::OnInitDialog()
{
  IADORecordBinding *piAdoRecordBinding = NULL;

  CDialog::OnInitDialog();

  try
  {
      m_pRs.CreateInstance(__uuidof(Recordset));

      m_pRs->CursorLocation = adUseServer;
      m_pRs->Open((LPCTSTR)m_strCmdText, (LPCTSTR)m_strConnection,
          adOpenStatic, adLockOptimistic, adCmdTableDirect);
```

code continued on next page

code continued from previous page

```
        if (FAILED(m_pRs->QueryInterface(__uuidof(IADORecordBinding),
        (LPVOID *)&piAdoRecordBinding)))
            _com_issue_error(E_NOINTERFACE);
        piAdoRecordBinding->BindToRecordset(this);
        RefreshBoundData();
    }

    catch (_com_error &e)
    {
        GenerateError(e.Error(), e.Description());
    }

    if (piAdoRecordBinding)
        piAdoRecordBinding->Release();

    return TRUE;
}
```

Message Handlers

The ADO Data Bound Dialog Wizard defines message handlers to navigate through the records. The following table lists these message handlers and describes the functions they invoke.

Message handler	Function invoked	Recordset pointer moves to
OnBtnMoveFirst	**MoveFirst**	First record
OnBtnMovePrevious	**MovePrevious**	Previous record
OnBtnMoveNext	**MoveNext**	Next record
OnBtnMoveLast	**MoveLast**	Last record

These handlers also invoke a function named **RefreshBoundData**, which transfers the data from the recordset to the dialog box controls. The code on the following page shows an example of a **RefreshBoundData** function:

```
void CRsCgDlg::RefreshBoundData()
{
  if (adFldOK == lEmployeeIDStatus)
      m_lDlgEmployeeID = m_lEmployeeID;
  else
      m_lDlgEmployeeID = _T("");
  if (adFldOK == lFirstNameStatus)
      m_strDlgFirstName = m_szFirstName;
  else
      m_strDlgFirstName = _T("");
  if (adFldOK == lLastNameStatus)
      m_strDlgLastName = m_szLastName;
  else
      m_strDlgLastName = _T("");

  UpdateData(FALSE);
}
```

If the data source returns no records, the provider sets both the **BOF** and **EndOfFile** properties to **TRUE**, and the current record position is undefined. If you selected an updateable cursor type, you can still add new data to this empty recordset object.

Building an Application Without the Wizard

With the Enterprise Edition of Visual C++ 6.0, you can use the Data Bound Dialog Wizard to create skeletal code that displays the records in a database table. However, if you are using the Professional edition of Visual C++ 6.0, you have to write code to implement the same functionality. To create a data-bound dialog box without using the wizard, you follow these steps:

1. Create a dialog-based application using MFC AppWizard.
2. Add controls to the default dialog box.
3. Modify your application to initialize OLE DLLs.
4. Modify the dialog header file to ensure that the application works with newer versions of ADO.
5. Create a **CADORecordBinding**-derived class to store the records that are accessed from the database table.
6. Modify the default dialog class, which is created by MFC AppWizard, to implement access to the database.
7. Add handlers to implement scrolling through the records in the recordset.

Chapter 8: Creating ADO Database Applications

These steps are described in more detail below.

▶ To create a dialog-based application using MFC AppWizard

- Create a new project using MFC AppWizard and in the **Step 2 of 6** dialog box, click **Dialog** and click **Finish**.

▶ To add controls to the default dialog box

1. From the **Controls** toolbar, drag suitable controls onto the dialog box for each field in the database table being accessed.
2. Add suitable prompts for each field.
3. Add controls to the dialog box to implement scrolling through the database table.

The following illustration shows a sample dialog box.

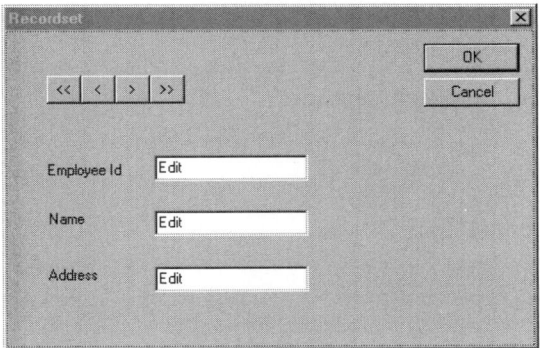

▶ To modify your application to initialize OLE DLLs

1. Open the **CWinApp** implementation file.
2. In the **InitInstance** function, call the **AfxOleInit** function to initialize OLE libraries, as shown in the following example:

```
if (!AfxOleInit())
{
    AfxMessageBox(_T("OLE initialization failed."));
    return FALSE;
}
```

417

▶ **To modify the dialog header file to ensure that the application works with newer versions of ADO**

- Import the ADO library file MSADO15.DLL and include the header file icrsint.h, as shown in the following example:

```
#import "C:\PROGRAM FILES\COMMON
FILES\SYSTEM\ADO\MSADO15.DLL" rename_namespace("ADOCG")
rename("EOF", "EndOfFile")
using namespace ADOCG;
#include "icrsint.h"
```

This ensures that the code can be used with different versions of ADO.

▶ **To create a CADORecordBinding-derived class to store the records that are accessed from the database table**

1. In the header file of the dialog class, create a **CADORecordBinding**-derived class.

2. Add protected member variables to the class for each field in the database table, as shown in the following example:

```
protected:
    LONG m_lID;
    CHAR m_szName[51];
    CHAR m_szAddress[51];
```

The data types of the protected member variables should match the data types of the fields in the database table.

3. Bind the member variables defined in the previous step to the fields in the database table by using the preprocessor macro BEGIN_ADO_BINDING. The sample code on the following page shows a sample **CADORecordBinding**-derived class. To copy this code for use in your own projects, see "The CADORecordBinding derived Class" on the accompanying CD-ROM.

Chapter 8: Creating ADO Database Applications

```
//Samples\CH08\ADOSample3
//Stores the records that are retrieved from a table
class CCustomRs :
  public CADORecordBinding
{
BEGIN_ADO_BINDING(CCustomRs)
  ADO_FIXED_LENGTH_ENTRY(1, adInteger, m_lID, lIDStatus, FALSE)
  ADO_VARIABLE_LENGTH_ENTRY2(2, adVarChar, m_szName,
sizeof(m_szName), lNameStatus, FALSE)
  ADO_VARIABLE_LENGTH_ENTRY2(3, adVarChar, m_szAddress,
sizeof(m_szAddress), lAddressStatus, FALSE)
END_ADO_BINDING()

protected:
  LONG m_lID;
  ULONG lIDStatus;
  CHAR m_szName[51];
  ULONG lNameStatus;
  CHAR m_szAddress[51];
  ULONG lAddressStatus;
};
```

In the previous sample code, the macro invokes the ADO_FIXED_LENGTH_ENTRY and ADO_VARIABLE_LENGTH_ENTRY2 macro functions.

The ADO_FIXED_LENGTH_ENTRY macro function sets up the binding between the fixed-length entry columns, such as integers and the member variables.

The ADO_VARIABLE_LENGTH_ENTRY2 macro function is invoked to set up the binding between the variable-length entry columns, such as character strings and the member variables.

Both ADO_FIXED_LENGTH_ENTRY and ADO_VARIABLE_LENGTH_ENTRY2 take the following arguments:

- Column to bind to
- Data type of the variable where the converted field will be stored
- Buffer used to convert the field to a variable

  With ADO_VARIABLE_LENGTH_ENTRY2, you also have to specify the size of the buffer as the fourth argument.

- Return value that indicates success of the field conversion

  The value returned is stored in a variable of type **ULONG** that must be declared within the class for each field. With ADO_VARIABLE_LENGTH_ENTRY2, this is the fifth argument.

- Boolean flag

  A value of **TRUE** indicates that ADO can update the associated field. With ADO_VARIABLE_LENGTH_ENTRY2, this is the sixth argument.

▶ **To implement the default dialog class generated by MFC AppWizard**

1. Modify the dialog class declaration to derive from the **CDialog** and the **CCustomRs** classes, as shown in the following example:

   ```
   class CADOSample1Dlg : public CDialog, public CCustomRs
   {
       .....
       .....
   }
   ```

2. Add two protected member variables of type **CString** to the dialog class, as shown in the following example:

   ```
   CString m_strConnection;
   CString m_strCmdText;
   ```

   The variable m_strConnection is for storing the connection string, and the variable strCmdText is for storing the name of the table to be opened or the SQL statement to be used to access the database table.

3. Using ClassWizard, declare member variables for each control. The controls will be used to display data from the database table.

4. Modify the constructor of the dialog class to set the connection string and command text variables, as shown in the following example:

   ```
   CADOSample1Dlg::CADOSample1Dlg(CWnd* pParent /*=NULL*/)
       : CDialog(CADOSample1Dlg::IDD, pParent)
   {
       m_strConnection = _T("Provider=MSDASQL.1;Data Source=OLEDBSample");
       m_strCmdText = _T("Employees");
       ........
   }
   ```

   The connection string is a semicolondelimited (;) string that specifies the provider and the data source to be used.

5. Add a protected _RecordsetPtr type variable to the dialog class, as shown in the following example:

```
class CADOSample1Dlg :
    public CDialog,
    public CCustomRs
{
.....
protected:

    _RecordsetPtr m_pRs;
.....
}
```

6. Set the _RecordsetPtr type object to **NULL** in the dialog constructor and the destructor.

7. Create a member function named **RefreshBoundData** to transfer the contents of the bound member variables of the **CCustomRs** class to the member variables associated with the controls on the dialog box. The following sample code shows the **RefreshBoundData** function. To copy this code for use in your own projects, see "The RefreshBoundData Function" on the accompanying CD-ROM.

```
//Samples\CH08\ADOSample3
//Transfers data from the recordset to the dialog member variables
void CADOSample1Dlg::RefreshBoundData()
{
  if (adFldOK == lIDStatus)
      m_lDlgID = m_lID;
  else
      m_lDlgID = 0;
  if (adFldOK == lNameStatus)
      m_strDlgName = m_szName;
  else
      m_strDlgName = _T("");
  if (adFldOK == lAddressStatus)
      m_strDlgAddress = m_szAddress;
  else
      m_strDlgAddress = _T("");

  UpdateData(FALSE);
}
```

8. In the **OnInitDialog**-derived function, declare a pointer of type IADORecordBinding and set it to **NULL**, as shown in the following example:

   ```
   BOOL CADOSample1Dlg::OnInitDialog()
   {
       IADORecordBinding *piAdoRecordBinding = NULL;
       .....
       .....
   }
   ```

9. Create an instance of the **_RecordsetPtr** object using the **CreateInstance** member function, as shown in the following example:

   ```
   m_pRs.CreateInstance(__uuidof(Recordset));
   ```

10. Set the cursor location using the _RecordsetPtr member variable CursorLocation, as shown in the following example:

    ```
    m_pRs->CursorLocation = adUseServer;
    ```

11. Open _RecordsetPtr using the **Open** member function, as shown in the following example:

    ```
    m_pRs->Open((LPCTSTR)m_strCmdText, (LPCTSTR)m_strConnection,
    adOpenDynamic, adLockOptimistic, adCmdTableDirect);
    ```

    The **Open** function takes the following arguments:
    - Command text

      This could either be an SQL statement or the name of the table to be opened.
    - Connection string

      This specifies the provider and the data source to be used.
    - Type of cursor to be used
    - Type of locking
    - Type of command object

12. Bind the recordset to the dialog box by completing the following steps:
    - Invoke the **QueryInterface** function to get a pointer to the IADORecordBinding interface, as shown in the following example:

      ```
      if (FAILED(m_pRs->QueryInterface(__uuidof(IADORecordBinding),
      (LPVOID *)&piAdoRecordBinding)))
        _com_issue_error(E_NOINTERFACE);
      ```

    - Invoke the **BindToRecordset** function to bind the recordset to the dialog box as follows:

      ```
      piAdoRecordBinding->BindToRecordset(this);
      ```

13. Invoke the **RefreshBoundData** function to transfer the data from the recordset to the controls on the dialog box.

The functions that are used to create an instance of the _RecordsetPtr object, open the _RecordsetPtr object, and bind the recordset to the dialog box can be placed within a **try** block. A suitable error handler can be invoked in the **catch** block to handle any error that may occur.

The following sample code shows the complete code for the **OnInitDialog** function. To copy this code for use in your own projects, see "The OnInitDialog Function" on the accompanying CD-ROM.

```
//Samples\CH08\ADOSample3
//Opens the recordset and binds the recordset to the columns of the
//data source
BOOL CADOSample1Dlg::OnInitDialog()
{
    IADORecordBinding *piAdoRecordBinding = NULL;

    CDialog::OnInitDialog();

    try
    {
        m_pRs.CreateInstance(__uuidof(Recordset));

        m_pRs->CursorLocation = adUseClient;
```

code continued on next page

code continued from previous page

```
        m_pRs->Open((LPCTSTR)m_strCmdText, (LPCTSTR)m_strConnection,
            adOpenStatic, adLockReadOnly, adCmdTableDirect);

        if (FAILED(m_pRs->QueryInterface(__uuidof(IADORecordBinding),
            (LPVOID *)&piAdoRecordBinding)))
            _com_issue_error(E_NOINTERFACE);
        piAdoRecordBinding->BindToRecordset(this);

        RefreshBoundData();
    }
    catch (_com_error &e)
    {
        GenerateError(e.Error(), e.Description());
    }

    if (piAdoRecordBinding)
        piAdoRecordBinding->Release();

    return TRUE;
}
```

▶ **To implement scrolling through the records in the recordset**

- Create handlers to implement move-first, move-next, move-previous, and move-last functionality. The following sample code shows the **OnBtnMoveFirst** function. To copy this code for use in your own projects, see "Handler for MoveFirst" on the accompanying CD-ROM.

```
//Samples\CH08\ADOSample3
//Displays the next record in the recordset.
void CADOSample1Dlg::OnBtnMoveFirst()
{
  try
  {
      m_pRs->MoveFirst();
      RefreshBoundData();
  }
  catch (_com_error &e)
  {
      GenerateError(e.Error(), e.Description());
  }
}
```

In the previous sample code, the _RecordsetPtr member function **MoveFirst** was invoked to scroll to the first record. You can also invoke **MoveNext**, **MovePrevious**, and **MoveLast** to reposition the current record pointer. After scrolling to a new record, you invoke the **RefreshBoundData** function to refresh the controls of the dialog box. The statements are placed within a **try** block to avoid scrolling beyond end of file or beginning of file.

Adding Records

You can add records to an updateable recordset by calling the **AddNew** function of the **_Recordset** class. The **AddNew** function creates and initializes a new record. The function takes two arguments, both of which are safearrays of variants. The first argument contains the names of the columns in the database. The second argument contains the data values for each column.

The following sample code invokes the **AddNew** function to add a new record to the database. To copy this code for use in your own projects, see "Adding a New Record" on the accompanying CD-ROM.

```
// Adds a new record to a recordset
// Samples\CH08\ADOSample3
void CADOSample3Dlg::OnAddRecord()
{
  long rgIndices[1];
  VARIANT rgf; //Stores field names
  VARIANT rgv; //Stores field values
  COleVariant fld[3], val[3];
  SAFEARRAYBOUND bound;
  try
  {
      UpdateData(TRUE);
      fld[0]="EmployeeID";
      val[0]=m_lDlgID;
      fld[1]="Name";
      val[1]=m_strDlgName;
      fld[2]="Address";
      val[2]=m_strDlgAddress;

      rgf.vt=VT_ARRAY|VT_VARIANT;
      rgv.vt=VT_ARRAY|VT_VARIANT;
```

code continued on next page

code continued from previous page

```
        bound.cElements=3;
        bound.lLbound=0;
        //Create a safe array of VARIANTs to store the field values
        rgv.parray=::SafeArrayCreate(VT_VARIANT,1,&bound);
        if(rgv.parray==NULL)
            AfxThrowMemoryException();
        //Create a safe array of VARIANTs to store the field names
        rgf.parray=::SafeArrayCreate(VT_VARIANT,1,&bound);
        if(rgf.parray==NULL)
            AfxThrowMemoryException();
        //Store the field names and values in the safearray of VARIANTs
        for ( int i = 0; i < 3; i++)
        {
            rgIndices[0]=i;
            ::SafeArrayPutElement(rgf.parray, rgIndices, &fld[i]);
            ::SafeArrayPutElement(rgv.parray, rgIndices, &val[i]);
        }

        m_pRs->AddNew(&rgf,&rgv);
    }
    catch (_com_error &e)
    {
        GenerateError(e.Error(), e.Description());
    }
}
```

Editing Records

You use the **Update** function to edit the current record of an updateable recordset. You pass the names of the fields to be updated and the new values to the **Update** function.

The sample code on the following page invokes the **Update** function to update the current record of the recordset. To copy this code for use in your own projects, see "Editing the Current Record of a Recordset" on the accompanying CD-ROM.

```cpp
// Updating the current record of a recordset
// Samples\CH08\ADOSample3
void CADOSample3Dlg::OnEditRecord()
{
  long rgIndices[1];
  VARIANT rgf; //Stores field names
  VARIANT rgv; //Stores field values
  COleVariant fld[3], val[3];
  SAFEARRAYBOUND bound;

  try
  {
      UpdateData(TRUE);
      fld[0]="EmployeeID";
      val[0]=m_lDlgID;
      fld[1]="Name";
      val[1]=m_strDlgName;
      fld[2]="Address";
      val[2]=m_strDlgAddress;

      rgf.vt=VT_ARRAY|VT_VARIANT;
      rgv.vt=VT_ARRAY|VT_VARIANT;

      bound.cElements=3;
      bound.lLbound=0;
      //Create a safe array of VARIANTs to store the field values
      rgv.parray=::SafeArrayCreate(VT_VARIANT,1,&bound);
      if(rgv.parray==NULL)
          AfxThrowMemoryException();
      //Create a safe array of VARIANTs to store the field names
      rgf.parray=::SafeArrayCreate(VT_VARIANT,1,&bound);
      if(rgf.parray==NULL)
          AfxThrowMemoryException();
      //Store the field names and values in the safearray of VARIANTs
      for ( int i = 0; i < 3; i++)
      {
          rgIndices[0]=i;
          ::SafeArrayPutElement(rgf.parray, rgIndices, &fld[i]);
          ::SafeArrayPutElement(rgv.parray, rgIndices, &val[i]);
      }
      m_pRs->Update(&rgf,&rgv);
  }
  catch (_com_error &e)
  {
      GenerateError(e.Error(), e.Description());
  }
```

Deleting Records

Use the **Delete** function to delete the current record of a recordset. You can also delete a group of records using this function.

The **Delete** function takes a single argument. The value of this argument can either be **adAffectCurrent** or **adAffectGroup**. The default, **adAffectCurrent,** deletes only the current record, while **adAffectGroup** deletes the records that satisfy the current filter property setting. To use **adAffectGroup,** you must set the filter property to one of the valid predefined constants.

The following sample code deletes the current record of the recordset. To copy this code for use in your own projects, see "Deleting a Record from a Recordset" on the accompanying CD-ROM.

```
//Deleting the current record of a recordset
//   Samples\CH08\ADOSample3
void CADOSample3Dlg::OnDelRecord()
{
    try
    {
        m_pRs->Delete(adAffectCurrent);
        m_pRs->MoveNext();
        if(m_pRs->EndOfFile)
            m_pRs->MoveLast();
        RefreshBoundData();

    }
    catch (_com_error &e)
    {
        if(m_pRs->EndOfFile && m_pRs->BOF)
        {
            BlankForm();
            UpdateData(FALSE);
        }
        else
            GenerateError(e.Error(), e.Description());
    }
}
```

Performing Queries

In this section, you will learn how to perform performing queries on data sources and rowsets. You will also learn how to search for specific records in a rowset.

Performing a Simple Query

You perform queries on a database by altering the WHERE clause associated with the recordset. To specify or change the selection criteria, complete the following steps:

1. Close the recordset object by invoking the **Close** member function. Closing the recordset object does not remove it from memory.
2. Change the property settings of the recordset.
3. Reopen the recordset.

The following example shows how to perform a simple query to retrieve those records whose Employee ID is greater than 3:

```
m_pRs->Close();
m_strCmdText = _T("Select * from employees where EmployeeID < 3");
m_pRs->Open((LPCTSTR)m_strCmdText, (LPCTSTR)m_strConnection,
   adOpenStatic, adLockReadOnly, adCmdUnknown);
if (FAILED(m_pRs->QueryInterface(__uuidof(IADORecordBinding),
   (LPVOID *)&piAdoRecordBinding)))
  _com_issue_error(E_NOINTERFACE);
piAdoRecordBinding->BindToRecordset(this);
```

Using Filters

You set the **Filter** property of the recordset to filter records in the recordset that satisfy a search criterion. When constructing the search criteria, you can use comparison operators such as ">" (greater than), "<" (less than), "=" (equal), or "like" (pattern matching). The comparison operator **like** can be used in conjunction with the asterisk (*) wildcard, which represents zero or more characters.

The following example selects all records whose **LastName** starts with "M."

```
m_pRs->Filter = "LastName like 'M*'";
```

You can also use logical operators such as **AND** and **OR** in the filter criteria, as shown in the following example:

```
m_pRs->Filter = "LastName like 'M*' OR LastName like 'S*'";
```

There is no precedence between **AND** and **OR**. Clauses can be grouped within parentheses. However, you cannot group clauses joined by **OR** with another clause by using **AND**. For example, you cannot group clauses as follows:

```
m_pRs->Filter = "(LastName like 'S*' OR LastName like 'M*') AND
FirstName like 'D*'";
```

Instead, you would construct this filter as:

```
m_pRs->Filter = "(LastName Like 'S*' AND FirstName like 'D*') OR
(LastName like 'M*' AND FirstName like 'D*')";
```

Searching for Records

You use the **Find** member function to search a recordset for records that satisfy the specified criteria. When a record that satisfies the search criteria is found, it becomes the current record. If none of the records in the recordset satisfy the search criteria, the current position is set to end of the recordset.

The following example shows how you can search for records within a recordset:

```
m_pRs->Find("LastName like 'M*'",3,adSearchForward);
```

The **Find** function takes the following arguments:

- A string containing the search criteria
- An optional long value that defines the starting point of the search operation
  You specify the starting location relative to the current record. For example, if you specify 3, the search skips three records from the current record.
- The search direction, which can be either **adSearchForward** or **adSearchBackward**
- An optional bookmark
  If you specify a bookmark, it will be used as the starting position for the search.

Lab 8.1: Using the Data-Bound Dialog Box

In this lab, you will add, delete, and update records in a database table. You will also filter records in a recordset to display only records that meet criteria entered by the user.

To see the demonstration "Lab 8.1 Demonstration," see the accompanying CD-ROM.

Estimated time to complete this lab: **40 minutes**

To complete the exercises in this lab, you must have the required software. For detailed information about the labs and setup for the labs, see "Labs" in "About This Course."

The code that forms the starting point for this lab is located in the folder <*install folder*>\Labs\Ch08\Lab8.1\Ex01.

The solution code for this lab is located in the folder <*install folder*>\Labs\Ch08\Lab8.1\Ex01\Solution.

Objectives

After completing this lab, you will be able to:

- Add, update, and delete records in a database table.
- Filter records in a recordset.

Prerequisites

There are no prerequisites for this lab.

Exercises

The following exercises provide practice working with the concepts and techniques covered in this chapter.

- Exercise 1: Adding, Deleting, and Updating Records

    In this exercise, you will implement the **add**, **delete**, and **update** functions to manipulate records in a database table.

- Exercise 2: Filtering Records

    In this exercise, you will use the **Filter** property of the recordset to filter records that satisfy the specified criteria.

Exercise 1: Adding, Deleting, and Updating Records

The code that forms the basis for this exercise is in *<install folder>*\Labs\Ch08\Lab8.1\Ex01.

In this exercise, you will implement the **add, update,** and **delete** functions to manipulate records in a database table.

The base application has been generated by the Data Bound Dialog Box Wizard and already has handlers that enable the user to navigate through the records in a database table.

▶ **Add controls to the CG_IDD_RECORDSET dialog box**

- In the **CG_IDD_RECORDSET** dialog box, add three buttons to implement adding, deleting and updating records as shown in the following illustration.

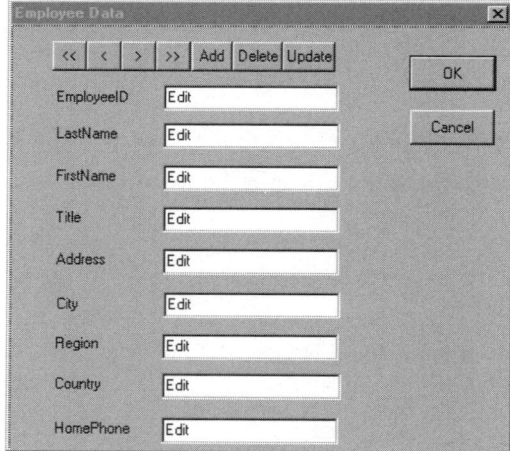

Give the **Add, Delete,** and **Update** controls the IDs **ID_ADD, ID_DELETE,** and **ID_UPDATE** respectively.

▶ **Create message map entries for the Add, Delete, and Update buttons**

1. Open the CRsCgDlg.h file and add the following entries after the // {{AFX_MSG message:

```
afx_msg void OnAdd();
afx_msg void OnDelete();
afx_msg void OnUpdate();
```

2. Insert the following message map entries for ON_BN_CLICKED in the **CRsCgDlg** implementation file:

   ```
   ON_BN_CLICKED(ID_ADD,OnAdd)
   ON_BN_CLICKED(ID_DELETE,OnDelete)
   ON_BN_CLICKED(ID_UPDATE,OnUpdate)
   ```

▶ **Implement the OnAdd button handler**

In this procedure, you will add records to a recordset by calling the **AddNew** function of the **_Recordset** class.

1. In RsCgDlg.cpp file, insert a handler for **OnAdd** as follows:

   ```
   void CRsCgDlg::OnAdd()
   {
   ```

2. Start a **try** block.
3. Invoke the **UpdateData** function with the argument **TRUE** to transfer the values from controls on the dialog box into the member variables corresponding to each column in the database table.
4. Declare two arrays of type **COleVariant** to store the names of columns in the table and the member variable values corresponding to each column in the table as follows:

   ```
   COleVariant fld[9],val[9];
   ```

5. Store the names of columns in the table and member variable values in the arrays fld and val, respectively:

   ```
   fld[0]="EmployeeID";
   val[0]=m_lDlgEmployeeID;
   fld[1]="LastName";
   val[1]=m_strDlgLastName;
   fld[2]="FirstName";
   val[2]=m_strDlgFirstName;
   fld[3]="Title";
   val[3]=m_strDlgTitle;
   fld[4]="Address";
   val[4]=m_strDlgAddress;
   fld[5]="City";
   val[5]=m_strDlgCity;
   ```

code continued on next page

code continued from previous page

```
fld[6]="Region";
val[6]=m_strDlgRegion;
fld[7]="Country";
val[7]=m_strDlgCountry;
fld[8]="HomePhone";
val[8]=m_strDlgHomePhone;
```

6. Declare and create two SafeArrays of variants as follows:

   ```
   VARIANT rgf,rgv;
   rgf.vt=VT_ARRAY|VT_VARIANT;
   rgv.vt=VT_ARRAY|VT_VARIANT;
   SAFEARRAYBOUND bound;
   bound.cElements=9;
   bound.lLbound=0;

   rgv.parray=::SafeArrayCreate(VT_VARIANT,1,&bound);
   if(rgv.parray==NULL)
       AfxThrowMemoryException();
   rgf.parray=::SafeArrayCreate(VT_VARIANT,1,&bound);
   if(rgf.parray==NULL)
       AfxThrowMemoryException();
   ```

7. Declare a variable of type **long** to store indexes for each dimension of the SafeArray as follows:

   ```
   long rgIndices[1];
   ```

8. Assign the values stored in the arrays fld and val to SafeArray as follows:

   ```
   for(int i=0; i<9;i++)
   {
       rgIndices[0]=i;
       ::SafeArrayPutElement(rgf.parray, rgIndices, &fld[i]);
       ::SafeArrayPutElement(rgv.parray, rgIndices, &val[i]);
   }
   ```

9. Invoke the **AddNew** function to add the record to the database table as follows:

   ```
   m_pRs->AddNew(&rgf,&rgv);
   ```

Lab 8.1: Using the Data-Bound Dialog Box

10. Write the code for the **catch** handler as follows:

    ```
    catch (_com_error &e)
    {
        GenerateError(e.Error(), e.Description());
    }
    ```

The following sample code shows an example of how your code should look. To copy this code for use in your own projects, see "Lab 8.1.1 OnAdd" on the accompanying CD-ROM.

```
void CRsCgDlg::OnAdd()
{

  try
  {
      UpdateData(TRUE);

      COleVariant fld[9],val[9];
      fld[0]="EmployeeID";
      val[0]=m_lDlgEmployeeID;
      fld[1]="LastName";
      val[1]=m_strDlgLastName;
      fld[2]="FirstName";
      val[2]=m_strDlgFirstName;
      fld[3]="Title";
      val[3]=m_strDlgTitle;
      fld[4]="Address";
      val[4]=m_strDlgAddress;
      fld[5]="City";
      val[5]=m_strDlgCity;
      fld[6]="Region";
      val[6]=m_strDlgRegion;
      fld[7]="Country";
      val[7]=m_strDlgCountry;
      fld[8]="HomePhone";
      val[8]=m_strDlgHomePhone;
```

code continued on next page

```
code continued from previous page
            VARIANT rgf,rgv;
            rgf.vt=VT_ARRAY|VT_VARIANT;
            rgv.vt=VT_ARRAY|VT_VARIANT;
            SAFEARRAYBOUND bound;
            bound.cElements=9;
            bound.lLbound=0;

            rgv.parray=::SafeArrayCreate(VT_VARIANT,1,&bound);
            if(rgv.parray==NULL)
                AfxThrowMemoryException();
            rgf.parray=::SafeArrayCreate(VT_VARIANT,1,&bound);
            if(rgf.parray==NULL)
                AfxThrowMemoryException();

            long rgIndices[1];
            for(int i=0; i<9;i++)
            {
            rgIndices[0]=i;
            ::SafeArrayPutElement(rgf.parray, rgIndices, &fld[i]);
            ::SafeArrayPutElement(rgv.parray, rgIndices, &val[i]);
            }
            m_pRs->AddNew(&rgf,&rgv);
    }
    catch (_com_error &e)
    {
        GenerateError(e.Error(), e.Description());
    }
}
```

▶ Implement the OnDelete button handler

In this procedure, you will use the **Delete** function to delete the current record of a recordset.

1. In RsCgDlg.cpp file, insert a handler for **OnDelete** as follows:

```
void CRsCgDlg::OnDelete()
{
```

Lab 8.1: Using the Data-Bound Dialog Box

2. Start a **try** block.
3. Invoke the **Delete** function to delete the record in the database table as follows:

    ```
    m_pRs->Delete(adAffectCurrent);
    ```

4. Move to the next record because the record that you deleted is now invalid:

    ```
    m_pRs->MoveNext();
    if(m_pRs->EndOfFile)
        m_pRs->MoveLast();
    RefreshBoundData();
    ```

5. Write the code for the **catch** handler as follows:

    ```
    catch (_com_error &e)
    {
        if(m_pRs->EndOfFile && m_pRs->BOF)
            BlankForm();
        else
            GenerateError(e.Error(), e.Description());
    }
    ```

The following sample code shows an example of how your code should look. To copy this code for use in your own projects, see "Lab 8.1.1 OnDelete" on the accompanying CD-ROM.

```
void CRsCgDlg::OnDelete()
{
  try
    {
        m_pRs->Delete(adAffectCurrent);
        m_pRs->MoveNext();
        if(m_pRs->EndOfFile)
            m_pRs->MoveLast();
        RefreshBoundData();
    }
    catch (_com_error &e)
    {
        if(m_pRs->EndOfFile && m_pRs->BOF)
            BlankForm();
        else
            GenerateError(e.Error(), e.Description());
    }

}
```

▶ **Implement the OnUpdate button handler**

In this procedure, you will use the **Update** function to edit the current record of a recordset. The code for the **OnUpdate** handler is similar to that for the **OnAdd** button handler. You will pass the names of the fields to be updated and the new values to the **Update** function.

- Invoke the **Update** function as follows:

    ```
    m_pRs->Update(&rgf,&rgv);
    ```

The following sample code shows an example of how your code should look. To copy this code for use in your own projects, see "Lab 8.1.1 OnUpdate" on the accompanying CD-ROM.

```
void CRsCgDlg::OnUpdate()
{

  try
  {
      UpdateData(TRUE);

      COleVariant fld[9],val[9];
      fld[0]="EmployeeID";
      val[0]=m_lDlgEmployeeID;
      fld[1]="LastName";
      val[1]=m_strDlgLastName;
      fld[2]="FirstName";
      val[2]=m_strDlgFirstName;
      fld[3]="Title";
      val[3]=m_strDlgTitle;
      fld[4]="Address";
      val[4]=m_strDlgAddress;
      fld[5]="City";
      val[5]=m_strDlgCity;
      fld[6]="Region";
      val[6]=m_strDlgRegion;
      fld[7]="Country";
      val[7]=m_strDlgCountry;
      fld[8]="HomePhone";
      val[8]=m_strDlgHomePhone;
```

code continued on next page

code continued from previous page

```
        VARIANT rgf,rgv;
        rgf.vt=VT_ARRAY|VT_VARIANT;
        rgv.vt=VT_ARRAY|VT_VARIANT;
        SAFEARRAYBOUND bound;
        bound.cElements=9;
        bound.lLbound=0;

        rgv.parray=::SafeArrayCreate(VT_VARIANT,1,&bound);
        if(rgv.parray==NULL)
            AfxThrowMemoryException();
        rgf.parray=::SafeArrayCreate(VT_VARIANT,1,&bound);
        if(rgf.parray==NULL)
            AfxThrowMemoryException();

        long rgIndices[1];
        for(int i=0; i<9;i++)
        {
        rgIndices[0]=i;
        ::SafeArrayPutElement(rgf.parray, rgIndices, &fld[i]);
        ::SafeArrayPutElement(rgv.parray, rgIndices, &val[i]);
        }
            m_pRs->Update(&rgf,&rgv);

    }
    catch (_com_error &e)
    {
        GenerateError(e.Error(), e.Description());
    }
}
```

▶ **Build and test your application**

- Run your application and test the add, delete, and update buttons.

The solution code for this exercise is located in the folder *<install folder>*\Labs\Ch08\Lab8.1\Ex01\Solution.

Exercise 2: Filtering Records

Continue with the files you created in Exercise 1 or, if you do not have a starting point for this exercise, the code that forms the basis for this exercise is in *<install folder>*\Labs\Ch08\Lab8.1\Ex02.

In this exercise, you will use the **Filter** property of the recordset to filter records that satisfy criteria entered by the user.

▶ **Add controls to CG_IDD_RECORDSET dialog box**

- In the **CG_IDD_RECORDSET** dialog box, add buttons to implement filtering of records as shown in the following illustration.

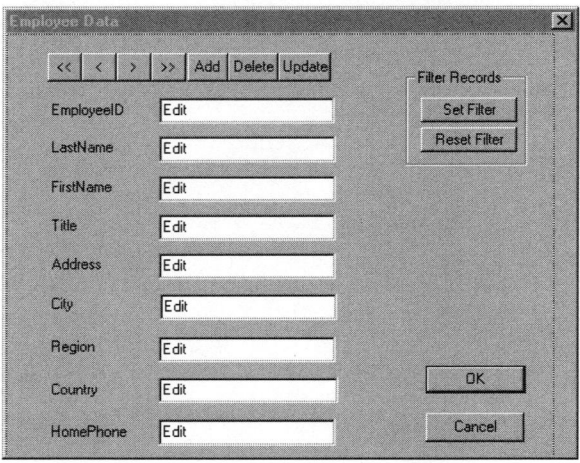

Give the filter and reset filter controls the IDs **ID_FILTER** and **ID_RESETFILTER**, respectively.

▶ **Create message map entries for the SetFilter and ResetFilter buttons**

1. Open the RsCgDlg.h file and add the following entries after the //{{AFX_MSG message:

    ```
    afx_msg void OnFilter();
    afx_msg void OnResetFilter();
    ```

2. Insert message map entries for the ON_BN_CLICKED message in the RsCgDlg.cpp implementation file as follows:

    ```
    ON_BN_CLICKED(ID_FILTER,OnFilter)
    ON_BN_CLICKED(ID_RESETFILTER,OnResetFilter)
    ```

Lab 8.1: Using the Data-Bound Dialog Box

▶ **Create a dialog box resource**

In this procedure, you will create a dialog box that enables the user to specify criteria. The following illustration shows the dialog box you will create.

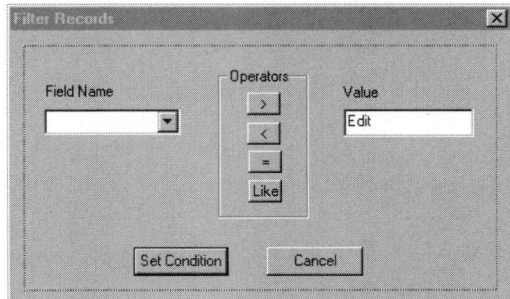

1. Use ResourceView to insert a new dialog box resource.
2. Set the **ID** and **Caption** properties of the dialog box as follows.

Property	Value
Caption	Filter Records
ID	IDD_QUERY

3. Add the following controls to the dialog box to create a dialog box as shown in the preceding illustration.

Control type	ID	Caption
Default command button	IDOK	Set Condition
Command button	IDCANCEL	Cancel
Static text	IDC_STATIC	Field Name
Combo box	ID_FIELD	None
Group box	IDC_STATIC	Operators
Command button	ID_GREATER	>
Command button	ID_LESSER	<
Command button	ID_EQUAL	=

table continued on next page

table continued from previous page

Control type	ID	Caption
Command button	ID_LIK	Like
Static text	IDC_STATIC	Value
Edit box	ID_VALUE	None

4. Open the **Combo Box Properties** dialog box, and click the **Data** tab.
5. In the **Enter listbox items** list box, enter the field names EmployeeID, FirstName, LastName, Title, Address, City, Region, Country and HomePhone.

▶ Create a dialog class by using ClassWizard

1. Invoke ClassWizard.
2. Select the **Create a new class** option, to create a new class for the **IDD_QUERY** dialog box and click **OK**.
3. In the **Name** box, type **CQuery** for the name of the associated C++ dialog class.
4. In the **Base** class box, select **CDialog**.
5. Click **OK**.

▶ Add member variables to the dialog class

In this procedure, you will create member variables for the new **CQuery** class.

1. Invoke ClassWizard.
2. On the **Member Variables** tab, set the class name to **CQuery** and add the following variables.

Control IDs	Type	Member
ID_FIELD	CString	m_Field
ID_VALUE	CString	m_Value

3. Open the Query.h file.

4. Create member variables to store the operator and criteria entered by the user as follows:

```
public:
char m_operator[7];
char cmd_str[51];
```

▶ Create message map entries for command buttons on the IDD_QUERY dialog box

1. Open Query.h and add the following entries after the //{{AFX_MSG message:

```
afx_msg void OnGreater();
afx_msg void OnLesser();
afx_msg void OnEqual();
afx_msg void OnLike();
afx_msg void OnSetCondition();
```

2. Insert message map entries for the ON_BN_CLICKED message in the **CQuery** implementation file as follows:

```
ON_BN_CLICKED(ID_GREATER,OnGreater)
ON_BN_CLICKED(ID_LESSER,OnLesser)
ON_BN_CLICKED(ID_EQUAL,OnEqual)
ON_BN_CLICKED(ID_LIK,OnLike)
ON_BN_CLICKED(IDOK,OnSetCondition)
```

▶ Implement the OnGreater button handler

- In the Query.cpp file, write the code for the **OnGreater** button handler as follows:

```
void CQuery::OnGreater()
{
   strcpy(m_operator, " > ");
}
```

Repeat the procedure to implement the **OnLesser, OnEqual,** and **OnLike** button handlers.

The sample code on the following page shows an example of how your code should look. To copy this code for use in your own projects, see "Lab 8.1.2 Operators" on the accompanying CD-ROM.

MFC Development Using Microsoft Visual C++ 6.0

```
void CQuery::OnGreater()
{
  strcpy(m_operator, " > ");
}

void CQuery::OnLesser()
{
  strcpy(m_operator, " < ");
}

void CQuery::OnEqual()
{
  strcpy(m_operator, " = ");
}

void CQuery::OnLike()
{
  strcpy(m_operator, " like ");
}
```

▶ **Implement the OnSetCondition button handler**

In this procedure, you will construct a criteria based on the field, operator, and the value entered by the user.

1. In the Query.cpp file, add the **OnSetCondition** button handler as follows:

   ```
   void CQuery::OnSetCondition()
   {
   ```

2. Invoke **UpdateData** with the argument **TRUE**.

3. Construct the criteria as follows:

   ```
   if(m_Field != _T("") && m_Value != _T(""))
   {
       strcpy(cmd_str,m_Field);
       strcat(cmd_str,m_operator);
       strcat(cmd_str,"'");
       strcat(cmd_str,m_Value);
       if(strcmp(m_operator," like ")==0)
           strcat(cmd_str, "*'");
       else
           strcat(cmd_str, "'");
   }
   CDialog::OnOK();
   ```

▶ Implement the OnFilter button handler

In this procedure, you will invoke a dialog box to accept criteria from the user and then filter records that satisfy the specified criteria.

1. In the RsCgDlg.cpp file, add the **OnFilter** handler as follows:

   ```
   void CRsCgDlg::OnFilter()
   {
   ```

2. Clear the values of the current record displayed on the form as follows:

   ```
   m_strDlgAddress = _T("");
   m_strDlgCity = _T("");
   m_strDlgCountry = _T("");
   m_lDlgEmployeeID = 0;
   m_strDlgFirstName = _T("");
   m_strDlgHomePhone = _T("");
   m_strDlgLastName = _T("");
   m_strDlgRegion = _T("");
   m_strDlgTitle = _T("");

   UpdateData(FALSE);
   ```

3. In ClassView, right click **CRsCgDlg**, and create a protected member variable m_qDlg of type **CQuery**.

4. Invoke the dialog box to accept the criteria as follows:

   ```
   int nRes = m_qDlg.DoModal();
   ```

5. Filter records that satisfy the specified criteria as follows:

   ```
   try
   {
       m_pRs->Filter = m_qDlg.cmd_str;
       if(m_pRs->BOF || m_pRs->EndOfFile)
       {
           MessageBox("No Matching Records");
           m_pRs->Filter="";
       }
       else
           OnBtnMoveFirst();
   }
   ```

6. Write the code for the **catch** handler.

The following sample code shows an example of how your code should look. To copy this code for use in your own projects, see "Lab 8.1.2 OnFilter" on the accompanying CD-ROM.

```
void CRsCgDlg::OnFilter()
{
  m_strDlgAddress = _T("");
  m_strDlgCity = _T("");
  m_strDlgCountry = _T("");
  m_lDlgEmployeeID = 0;
  m_strDlgFirstName = _T("");
  m_strDlgHomePhone = _T("");
  m_strDlgLastName = _T("");
  m_strDlgRegion = _T("");
  m_strDlgTitle = _T("");
  UpdateData(FALSE);
  int nRes = m_qDlg.DoModal();

  try
  {
      m_pRs->Filter = m_qDlg.cmd_str;
      if(m_pRs->BOF | m_pRs->EndOfFile)
      {
          MessageBox("No Matching Records");
          m_pRs->Filter="";

      }
      else
      OnBtnMoveFirst();


  }
  catch (_com_error &e)
  {
      GenerateError(e.Error(), e.Description());
  }
}
```

▶ Implement the OnResetFilter button handler

In this procedure, you will clear the **Filter** property so that all the records in the recordset will appear.

- Write the code for the **OnResetFilter** handler as follows:

```
void CRsCgDlg::OnResetFilter()
{
   m_pRs->Filter="";

}
```

▶ Build and test your application

- Run your application and test the **Filter** and **ResetFilter** buttons.

The solution code for this exercise is located in the folder *<install folder>*\Labs\Ch08\Lab8.1\Ex02\Solution.

Sample Applications

The following table describes the sample applications related to this chapter. These sample applications are located in the folder *<install folder>*\Samples\Ch08.

Sample application subfolder	Description of application
\ADOSample1	An application that uses the ADO data control with a data-bound control to access data in a database table. Ensure that the database file emp.mdb exists in the directory from which the application is executed, and has read-write permissions.
\ADOSample2	An application that uses the ADO data-bound dialog box to access data in a database table. The application has been created using the Data Bound Dialog Wizard available with the Enterprise edition of Visual C++ 6.0. Ensure that the database file emp.mdb exists in the directory from which the application is executed, and has read-write permissions.

table continued on next page

table continued from previous page

Sample application subfolder	Description of application
\ADOSample3	An application that uses the ADO data-bound dialog box to access data in a database table. The application has been created without using the Data Bound Dialog Wizard. Ensure that the database file emp.mdb exists in the directory from which the application is executed, and has read-write permissions.

Self-Check Questions

To see the answers to the Self-Check Questions, see Appendix A.

1. **Which object contains information on the data provider and the underlying schema?**

   A. Connection
   B. Recordset
   C. Command
   D. Field

2. **Which object contains an Errors collection created in response to a failure involving the provider?**

   A. Connection
   B. Command
   C. Recordset
   D. Parameters

3. **Which edition of Visual C++ provides the ADO Data Bound Dialog Wizard?**

   A. Professional only
   B. Enterprise only
   C. Both Professional and Enterprise
   D. Both Standard and Enterprise

4. Which event occurs after the WillMove event?
   A. MoveComplete
   B. WillChangeField
   C. MoveNext
   D. MoveLast

5. Which property of a data-bound control needs to be set in order to bind it to an ADO data control?
   A. RecordSource
   B. ConnectionString
   C. DataSourceName
   D. DataSource

Student Notes:

Chapter 9:
Building Internet Applications

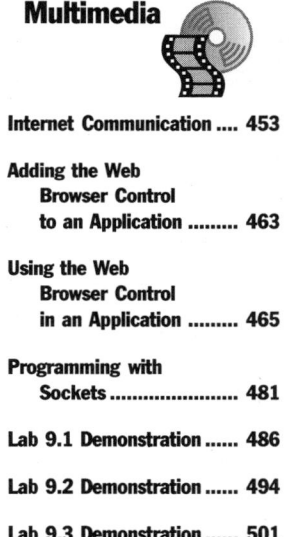

Multimedia

Internet Communication 453

Adding the Web
  Browser Control
  to an Application 463

Using the Web
  Browser Control
  in an Application 465

Programming with
  Sockets 481

Lab 9.1 Demonstration 486

Lab 9.2 Demonstration 494

Lab 9.3 Demonstration 501

In this chapter, you will learn to build applications that access the Internet.

The chapter begins with an overview of Internet concepts and terminology. It then describes how to use the Microsoft Internet Explorer control and the Microsoft ActiveX Web Browser control in your applications. The later sections discuss the different categories of classes provided by Microsoft Foundation Class (MFC) and explain how to build custom applications with these classes.

Objectives

After completing this chapter, you will be able to:

♦ Describe the Internet framework.

♦ Describe the different types of Internet applications.

♦ Create MFC-based applications that invoke Internet Explorer.

♦ Use the Web Browser control in MFC-based applications.

♦ Create MFC-based applications that use the WinInet classes to communicate across the Internet.

♦ Create MFC-based applications that use the synchronous and asynchronous WinSock classes.

Basic Internet Concepts

This section introduces the basic Internet concepts and terminology that you will need to successfully complete this chapter. It also describes the range of Internet capabilities an application can offer, and the MFC support available for implementing Internet applications.

The Internet Framework

A network is a collection of computers that are connected by a data-link medium, such as Ethernet or Token Ring. The Internet is a global network of such computer networks. An intranet is an organization-level internet.

While each network has its own method of communicating among its host computers, there is a need to standardize communication among all networks on the Internet. The TCP/IP protocol suite is the standard protocol that enables communication on the Internet.

The following illustration shows how different networks communicate with each other.

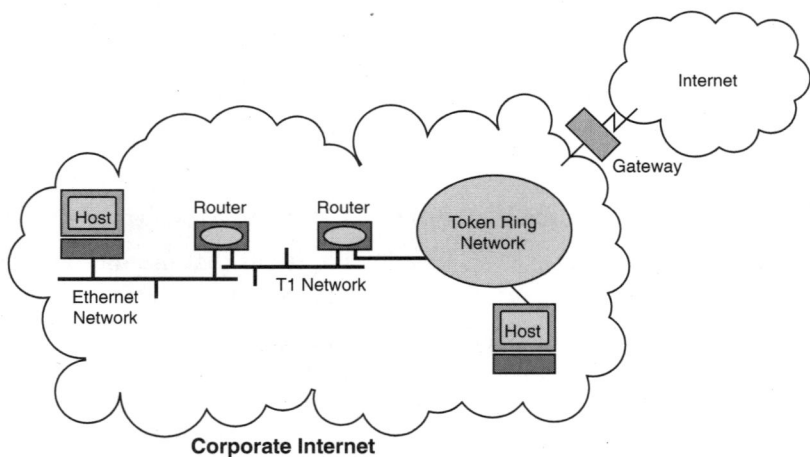

The purpose of any network is to transfer data between host computers. The data is meaningful only to the applications residing on the hosts; the network itself sees it only as data. The TCP/IP protocols package the host computer's data and add header information to enable routing of the data.

You can think of a program's interaction with a network as the activation of a series of layers, starting at the application layer and ending at the network's physical layer, where the data is sent as a stream of bits over the network. To see the animation "Internet Communication," see the accompanying CD-ROM.

Types of Internet Applications

The Internet and intranets are becoming more and more important to application developers. Not only are developers using the Internet to retrieve resources and to communicate with peers, but they are also finding it necessary to connect their applications to the Internet.

An application can connect to or communicate with the Internet in various ways. In the simplest case, an "Internet-aware" application recognizes a reference to an Internet resource and calls another application, such as Microsoft Internet Explorer, to handle all Internet access. "Internet-enabled" applications interact directly with the Internet using low-level techniques.

Internet-Aware Applications

An Internet-aware application accesses the Internet indirectly, through a software proxy. The application invokes this proxy, often a browser such as Internet Explorer, or a utility such as Telnet, as a separate process. After completing the task associated with the Internet resource, the user closes the proxy and continues with the main application. From a developer's perspective, this solution provides a great deal of functionality and is easy to implement. On the other hand, the application has very little control over the proxy utility; it starts the utility, and has no more association with it.

Internet-Enabled Applications

An Internet-enabled application interacts directly with the Internet. The application can interact with the network software at a high level, through an embedded control such as the Web Browser control, or through application-level services such as File Transfer Protocol (FTP) and Hypertext Transfer Protocol (HTTP). If the application's requirements call for a closer interaction with the TCP/IP protocol suite, you can make calls to the WinSock API functions.

MFC Support for Internet Applications

In the Microsoft Visual C++ and MFC environment, you can use the Web Browser control and the MFC Internet classes to build Internet applications.

MFC Development Using Microsoft Visual C++ 6.0

The browser object is available as a control that you can embed within the application. You also can control Internet Explorer through Automation. Both these methods use the HTTP protocol for viewing HTML pages, which provide the basis for the World Wide Web.

Alternatively, you can use the **CHTMLView** class to implement the functionality of the browser control in your applications. The **CHTMLView** class is derived from **CView** and is a wrapper class for the **Web Browser** control.

MFC also provides some control classes, such as **CIPAddressControl** and **CProgressCtrl**, that you can use to build Internet-enabled applications. For more information about these control classes, see "Internet Explorer 4.0 Common Controls" on page 225 in Chapter 5, "Using Controls."

At a lower level, MFC includes Win32 Internet (WinInet) class support for the HTTP protocol through the **CInternetSession** and **CHttpConnection** classes.

At the same level as HTTP support, classes are also available to implement custom FTP and Gopher services.

Below the level of HTTP support, several classes are available to interact with the WinSock API. These classes can be used to create custom service applications, such as an application that offers features that the FTP, HTTP, or Gopher classes do not have.

The following illustration shows the Internet classes provided by MFC.

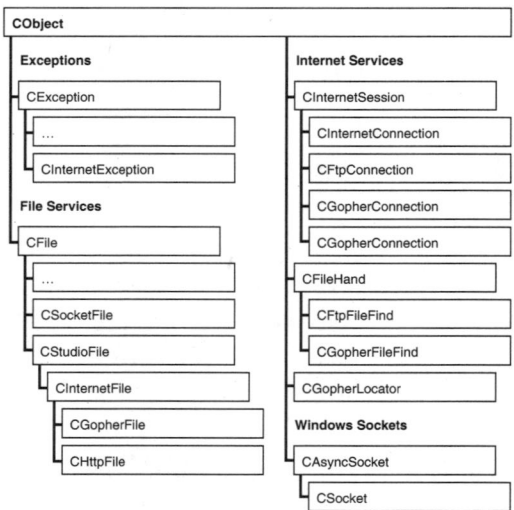

Using the Internet Explorer Object

The Internet Explorer object is an Automation object that you can use to control Internet Explorer from within an application. This section introduces the object model and describes how to use it in your application.

Properties and Methods

The Internet Explorer object has a predefined set of properties and methods. It does not support events.

Properties

Properties are settings or values that are maintained by an object. An object exposes its **Get** member functions to enable your application to retrieve the value of properties. For writable properties, the object exposes the **Set** member functions.

The following table lists some of the properties exposed by the Internet Explorer object.

Function	Description
BOOL GetBusy()	Returns **TRUE** if the object is engaged in a navigation or downloading operation.
void SetVisible(BOOL val)	Accepts a BOOL value and controls whether the object is visible.
void SetFullScreen(BOOL val)	If the value is **TRUE**, Internet Explorer will be placed in full-screen mode. In full-screen mode, the Internet Explorer main window is maximized, and the status bar, menu bar, and title bar are hidden.

Methods

A method enables your application to request an action of the object. The table on the following page lists some of the methods available for the Internet Explorer object.

Method	Description
void GoBack()	Tells the object to navigate backward one item in the history list.
void GoForward()	Tells the object to navigate forward one item in the history list.
void GoHome()	Tells the object to navigate to the home page specified in the **Internet Explorer Options** dialog box.
void GoSearch()	Tells the object to navigate to the search page as specified in the **Internet Explorer Options** dialog box.

For a complete listing of properties and methods, search for "CHTMLView class members" in MSDN Library Visual Studio 6.0.

For more information about the Internet Explorer object model specification, go to the Win32 Internet Programmer's Reference page at http://www.microsoft.com/msdn/sdk/mactivex/docs/wininet/inetref.htm.

Controlling Internet Explorer

There are two ways you can invoke the Internet Explorer: use the **ShellExecute** function or use Automation.

Using the ShellExecute Function

If your application needs only to start Internet Explorer (or your default browser) and has no need to interact with it, you can invoke the browser directly by calling the **ShellExecute** function. To invoke **ShellExecute**, implement a simple command handler like the one shown in the following example:

```
void CMyView::OnUtilityLaunchBrowser()
{
  ShellExecute(MyWin,"open","c:\\ie\\iexplore.exe", NULL, NULL,
  SW_SHOW);
}
```

Using Automation

If your application needs to control Internet Explorer after starting it, you can use Automation to set properties and invoke methods of the **Internet Explorer** object. Using Automation gives your application a much greater degree of control over Internet Explorer than does invoking it as an independent process through the **ShellExecute** function.

▶ **To use Automation with the Internet Explorer object**

1. Add Automation support for clients to your application.
2. Use ClassWizard to define a new class based on the Internet Explorer object model.
3. Create an instance of the class within your code.
4. Attach a dispatch object to the class.

    A dispatch object exposes the IDispatch interface. Through the IDispatch interface, a client application sets and gets properties of an object and calls methods of an object.

5. Manipulate the object through its properties and methods, using member functions of the created class.

Using Automation

The steps in implementing Automation are described below.

Adding Automation Support for Clients

You can add Automation support to clients by using either of the following two methods:

- Select the **Automation** check box in Step 3 of MFC AppWizard.

    This will automatically include the code required for automation support in a new application.

- Manually add code to provide automation support for clients.

    Use this method to upgrade an existing application.

▶ **To manually add Automation support for clients to an existing application**

1. Add the include directive for the file afxdisp.h to Stdafx.h as follows:

   ```
   #include <afxdisp.h>
   ```

2. Add the following line of code to the **InitInstance** function of your **CWinApp**-derived class. This function initializes the OLE dynamic libraries.

   ```
   AfxOleInit();
   ```

Using ClassWizard to Create the Internet Explorer Object Class

Using the information contained in type library files, ClassWizard generates a wrapper class containing member functions for each method and property.

▶ **To create a wrapper class for the Internet Explorer object**

1. Start ClassWizard.
2. In the **ClassWizard** dialog box, click **Add Class**, and then click **From a type library**.
3. In the **Import from Type Library** dialog box, navigate to the \Windows\System (or System32) folder and select **Shdocvw.dll**.
4. From the list that appears, select **CWebBrowserApp**, and then click **OK**.

   ClassWizard will create a new class for your project called **CWebBrowserApp**.

Creating an Instance of Internet Explorer

After adding the class definition for the **Internet Explorer** object, create an instance of the **Internet Explorer** object. First, make sure that you have included the header file Shdocvw.h in all the implementation files that access the object's properties and methods. Then add code as follows to create an instance of the object:

```
CWebBrowserApp* m_pIE = new CWebBrowserApp;
```

Attaching a Dispatch Interface

When ClassWizard creates a new class by importing a type library, it derives the new class from **COleDispatchDriver**. The **COleDispatchDriver** class implements the client-side support for applications that support Automation. Member functions of this class provide access to attach, detach, create, and release a dispatch connection of type **IDispatch**.

To attach an **IDispatch** connection to your class, call the **CreateDispatch** member function. There are two variations of this function: One requires a class identifier (CLSID) of the Automation object; the other requires the programmatic identifier (ProgID), an easy-to-remember string used to identify the object. The following example uses the ProgID to attach a connection to your class:

```
m_pIE->CreateDispatch("InternetExplorer.Application");
```

Using the Object

Once the object is created and has an **IDispatch** connection to your code, your application can set properties and invoke methods of that object. The following example code causes Internet Explorer to navigate to a specific URL site, and makes the browser visible:

```
COleVariant noArg; //  declare a VT_EMPTY variant.
m_pIE->Navigate("www.microsoft.com", &noArg, &noArg, &noArg, &noArg);
m_pIE->SetVisible(TRUE);
```

The empty **COleVariant** arguments can be set to further customize the **Navigate** method.

For more information about **COleVariant** arguments, search for "COleVariant::COleVariant" in MSDN Library Visual Studio 6.0.

Using the Web Browser Control

The **Web Browser** control is an ActiveX component available in Microsoft Visual Studio. This control encapsulates the browsing capabilities of Internet Explorer, enabling you to create sophisticated HTTP browsing applications with little effort.

The **Web Browser** control supports Web browsing through both point-and-click hyperlinking and Uniform Resource Locator (URL) navigation. The control maintains a history list that enables the user to browse forward and backward through previously browsed sites, folders, and documents. The **Web Browser** control directly handles the navigation, hyperlinking, history lists, favorites, and security.

In this section, you will learn how to use the **Web Browser** control in MFC-based applications.

Properties, Methods, and Events

The **Internet Explorer** object and the **Web Browser** control share a common object model. Most of the properties and methods are common to both the objects.

For more information about the properties and methods of the **Web Browser** control, see "Properties and Methods" on page 455 in this chapter.

The main difference between the **Internet Explorer** object and the **Web Browser** control is that the browser control also supports events. You can override these events to implement the browsing requirements of your applications.

Events

Events are notifications that a control can send to a control container in response to user interaction.

The following table lists some **Web Browser** functions that you can override to take appropriate action for your application.

Function	Description
void ProgressChange(long Progress, long ProgressMax)	Occurs when the progress of a download operation is updated. The first parameter specifies the amount of total progress or – 1 when the download is complete. The second parameter specifies the maximum progress value.
void StatusTextChange (LPCTSTR text)	Occurs when the status bar text has changed.
void TitleChange(LPCTSTR text)	Occurs when the title of the current document becomes available or changes.

For a complete list of properties, methods, and events, search for "CHTMLView class members" in MSDN Library Visual Studio 6.0.

Adding the Web Browser Control

The first step in creating an application with a Web Browser control is to create an application that can act as an ActiveX control container. You can do this using one of the following methods:

- In Step 3 of AppWizard, select the **ActiveX Controls** check box.

    The following illustration shows the **MFC AppWizard - Step 3** dialog box with the check box selected.

    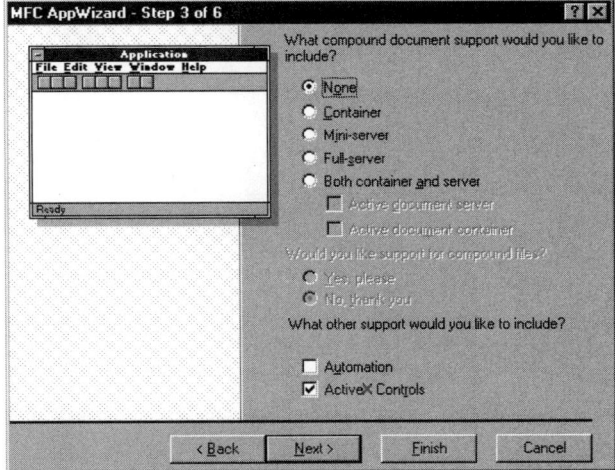

- Use the Components and Controls Gallery to insert the ActiveX Control containment component into your project.

The following illustration shows the **Components and Controls Gallery** dialog box.

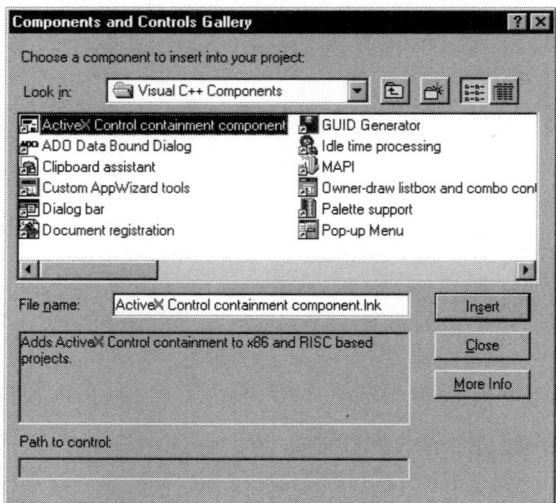

- Manually add the following lines of code to your application.

    1. Add this line to the Stdafx.h header file.

       ```
       #include <afxdisp.h>
       ```

    2. Add the following line to the **InitInstance** member function of the **CWinApp**-derived class.

       ```
       AfxEnableControlContainer();
       ```

       The **AfxEnableControlContainer** function enables support for OLE controls.

Once you have added control container support to your application, you can add the **Web Browser** control to your project.

▶ **To add the Web Browser control to your project**

   1. On the Visual Studio **Project** menu, click **Add To Project**, and then click **Components and Controls**.
   2. Double-click the **Registered ActiveX Controls** folder.
   3. Select **Microsoft Web Browser** and click **Insert**, and then click **OK** to confirm the selection.

In the ClassView pane, you see a class named **CWebBrowser2**. Expand this class to examine the properties and methods exposed by this control.

To see the demonstration "Adding the Web Browser Control to an Application," see the accompanying CD-ROM.

If you want your application to respond to events, you must manually add event handlers. For more information about how to add event handlers, see "Implementing the Web Browser Control" on page 465 in this chapter.

Creating the Web Browser Control

After installing the **Web Browser** control into your project as a wrapper class, you need to construct an instance of the class and then create the control. To do this, you complete the following three steps:

1. Add include directives for the **Web Browser** control's header file to the appropriate source files.
2. Create a member variable that will point to the **Web Browser** control object in the view class.
3. Add the code to create the control.

These steps are described in more detail below.

▶ **To create an instance of the Web Browser control**

1. In the header file of the view class, add the following line after the include directive for Stdafx.h:

   ```
   #include "webbrowser2.h"
   ```

2. In the Visual Studio ClassView pane, right-click the view class and click **Add Member Variable**.

   The **Add Member Variable** dialog box appears.

3. In the **Variable Type** field, type **CWebBrowser2***.
4. In the **Variable Name** field, type **m_pBrowse**. Accept the default setting of public access and click **OK**.
5. It is good practice to initialize the member variable to NULL. Add the following line to the view constructor:

   ```
   m_pBrowse = NULL;
   ```

MFC Development Using Microsoft Visual C++ 6.0

6. Create a resource symbol named IDC_WBC. You need this resource ID to create the Browser control.
7. Use ClassWizard to add a message handler for WM_CREATE to the view class.
8. In the **OnCreate** member function of the view class, after the call to the base class's **OnCreate** function, add code to create the control. The following sample code shows the complete **OnCreate** function. To copy this code for use in your own projects, see "Creating the Web Browser Control" on the accompanying CD-ROM.

```
// Creating the Web Browser Control using a dummy menu ID
// Samples\CH09\Browse
int CBrowseView::OnCreate(LPCREATESTRUCT lpCreateStruct)
{
  if (CView::OnCreate(lpCreateStruct) == -1)
      return -1;

  // Define the area where the control will reside.
  CRect rect;
  GetClientRect(&rect);
  //
  // Create the control.
  // IDC_WBC is a unique identifier for the control and was defined
  // using a dummy menu item.
  m_pBrowse= new CWebBrowser2;
  ASSERT(m_pBrowse);
  if (!m_pBrowse->Create(NULL,NULL, WS_VISIBLE,rect,this, IDC_WBC)) {
      TRACE("failed to create browser\n");
      return 0;
  }
  // Initialize the first URL.
  COleVariant noArg;
  m_pBrowse->Navigate("www.microsoft.com",&noArg,&noArg,&noArg,&noArg);

  return 0;
}
```

Note Although you can successfully build the project with this code in it, you will not see the **Web Browser** control until you add code to implement it.

464

Implementing the Web Browser Control

Implementing a Web Browser control involves three main steps:

- Set properties
- Call methods
- Handle events

To see the demonstration "Using the Web Browser Control in an Application," see the accompanying CD-ROM.

Setting Properties

The following example sets the properties of the **Web Browser** control to adjust the control's size when handling a WM_SIZE message from Windows:

```
void CBrowseView::OnSize(UINT nType, int cx, int cy)
{
    // the base class handler is called.
    CView::OnSize(nType, cx, cy);

    // m_pBrowse is a member variable of the view class
    if (m_pBrowse)
    {
        m_pBrowse->SetWidth(cx);
        m_pBrowse->SetHeight(cy);
    }
}
```

Invoking Methods

Invoking a method of the **Web Browser** control is similar to invoking an ActiveX control method. You begin by identifying the methods that you need to implement based on the requirements of your application.

The following example shows how to use the **Navigate** method of the **CWebBrowser** class.

```
COleVariant noArg;
// navigate to a specific home page.
m_pBrowse->Navigate("www.microsoft.com", noArg, noArg, noArg, noArg);
```

You can then build and run your application. You will see that the **Web Browser** control displays the Web site specified in the **Navigate** method.

Handling Events

Events are not automatically included in the **Wrapper** class when you add the class by using the Visual Studio Components and Controls Gallery. To support events, you need to add code manually.

▶ **To handle an event**

1. Determine the function prototype and ID of the event.
2. Add the event function handler to the **Wrapper** class.
3. Link the event to the handler.

The following procedures describe the steps for adding the **TitleChange** event to the **Wrapper** class in the sample application Browse, which is located in the folder \Samples\CH09.

▶ **To determine the prototype and id for the TitleChange event handler**

1. On the Visual Studio **Tools** menu, click **OLE/COM Object Viewer**.
2. In the left pane of the **OLE/COM Object Viewer** dialog box, double-click the **Controls** folder and right-click **Microsoft Web Browser**.
3. On the shortcut menu, click **View Type Information**. The following illustration shows this step.

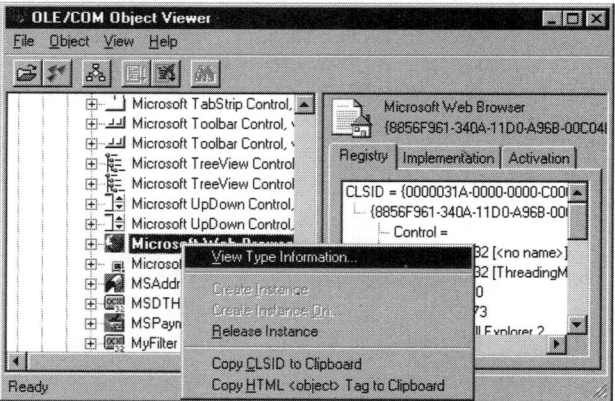

The **ITypelib Viewer** dialog box appears.

4. In the **ITypeLib Viewer** dialog box, double-click **dispinterface DWebBrowserEvents**. Double-click the **Methods** folder to display the events for the **Web Browser** control.

5. In the **Methods** folder, click **TitleChange**.

   The information you require about the prototype and ID for the event handler is displayed in the right of the **ITypeLib Viewer** dialog box. The following illustration shows the **ITypeLib Viewer** dialog box.

   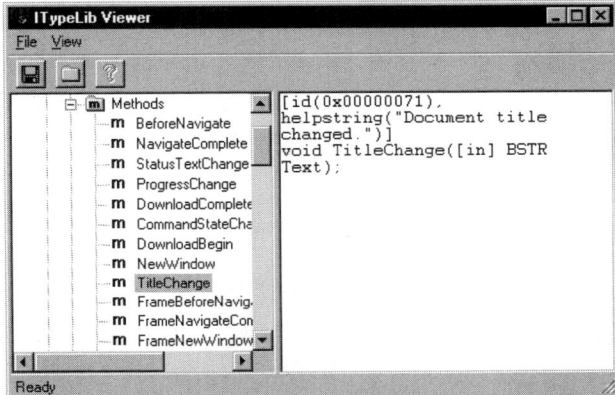

Adding the Event Handler

The prototype of the **TitleChange** event, which is written in Microsoft Interface Definition Language (MIDL), is as follows:

```
void TitleChange([in] BSTR Text)
```

The following code shows the MIDL syntax translated to C++:

```
void ClassName::OnTitleChange(LPCTSTR Text)
```

Once you know the prototype, you add the event handler as you would add any other function. In the Visual Studio ClassView pane, right-click the class name that you want to handle the event. Then click **Add Member Function** on the shortcut menu and provide the prototype information.

Here is an example of the code for the event **OnTitleChange**:

```
void CBrowseView::OnTitleChange(LPCTSTR Text)
{
// Format a string and set the mainframe window's title
CString strTitle;
strTitle.Format("MyBrowser - %s", Text);
AfxGetMainWnd()->SetWindowText(strTitle);
}
```

Linking the Event to the Handler

Finally, you must link the event to the event handler by adding an event map entry.

▶ **To make an event map entry**

1. Add a DECLARE_EVENTSINK_MAP() macro call to the header file of the class that handles the event.
2. Add an include directive for Afxdisp.h in the implementation file of the class that handles the event.
3. Add an event sink map in the implementation file of the class that handles the event.

The following procedure describes these steps for the sample application Browse.

▶ **To add a DECLARE_EVENTSINK_MAP() macro call in BrowseView.h**

1. In the file BrowseView.h, add the following line after the call to DECLARE_MESSAGE_MAP():

   ```
   DECLARE_EVENTSINK_MAP()
   ```

2. In the implementation file of the class that handles the event, add the following line after the directive #include "Stdafx.h":

   ```
   #include "afxdisp.h"
   ```

3. Add an event sink map after the line END_MESSAGE_MAP as follows:

   ```
   BEGIN_EVENTSINK_MAP(CBrowseView, CView)
       ON_EVENT(CBrowseView, IDC_WBC, 0x71, OnTitleChange, VTS_BSTR)
   END_EVENTSINK_MAP()
   ```

   The value 0x71 is the ID value you retrieved when you determined the prototype and ID for the **TitleChange** event handler.

   Compile and run the application to see the effect of implementing the **TitleChange** event.

Implementing HTML Views

The **CHTMLView** class is derived from **CView** and provides specialized functionality for designing applications that are dependent on the Web. **CHTMLView** provides the functionality of the **Web Browser** control within the context of the MFC document/view architecture.

The following illustration shows an application with an HTML view.

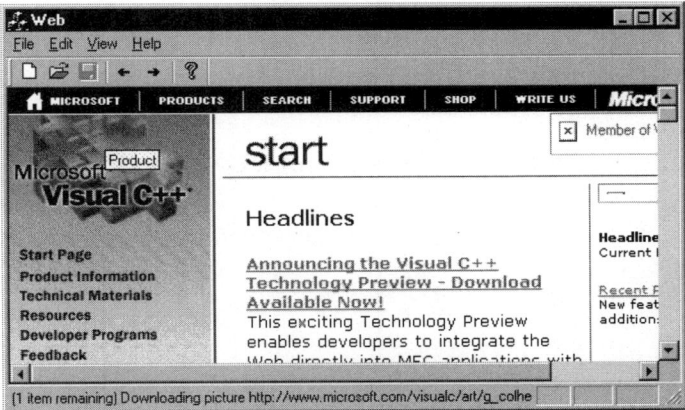

The HTML view is available only to applications running under Microsoft Windows 95 and Windows NT versions 3.51 and later in which Internet Explorer 4.0 (or later) has been installed.

▶ **To create an application (either SDI- or MDI-based) with an HTML view**

- Invoke MFC AppWizard. In Step 6 of 6, set the application's base view class to **CHTMLView**.

▶ **To convert an existing application to support an HTML view**

- Open the implementation file of the view class, and replace all instances of your current view class (usually **CView**) with **CHTMLView**.

- Repeat the same substitution in your view's header file, replacing your current view class with **CHTMLView**.

- In your application's StdAfx.h file, append the following line of code:

    ```
    #include <afxhtml.h>
    ```

▶ To implement an application with an HTML view

When you create an HTML view application using MFC AppWizard, AppWizard automatically adds the code to implement the view.

To implement HTML view manually, you need to override the **OnInitialUpdate** member function of your application's view class. In the function body of **OnInitialUpdate**, add a call to the **CHTMLView::Navigate** function to cause the contained **Web Browser** control to load the specified HTML page.

For example, the following line of code causes your application to start with Microsoft's home page displayed in its view (assuming you are connected to the Internet when you start the application).

```
Navigate( _T("http://www.microsoft.com"),0,0,0);
```

For more information about HTML view, search for "CHTMLView" in MSDN Library Visual Studio 6.0.

Using the WinInet Classes

This section provides an overview of the three important Internet protocols: HTTP, FTP, and Gopher. It also describes the MFC classes that support these protocols.

Connecting to the Internet

An Internet session is your link with a service, such as HTTP, FTP, or Gopher. You can have multiple connections with any of the services. The MFC classes **CInternetSession**, **CInternetConnection**, and **CInternetFile** provide support for HTTP, FTP, and Gopher connections.

CInternetSession

Use the **CInternetSession** class to create and initialize one or more simultaneous Internet sessions. The first step in creating an Internet link is to construct a **CInternetSession** object as follows:

```
CInternetSession session;
```

Then, call **CInternetSession::OpenUrl** to retrieve a file handle to an FTP, HTTP, Gopher, or FILE resource. The type of handle retrieved depends on the URL type.

The following table lists the valid types.

URL type	File handle type
file://	CStdioFile*
http://	CHttpFile*
ftp://	CInternetFile*
gopher://	CGopherFile*

If you require a specific service, you can retrieve the handle using one of the following functions:

- **CInternetSession::GetHttpConnection**
- **CInternetSession::GetFtpConnection**
- **CInternetSession::GetGopherConnection**

CInternetConnection

The **CInternetConnection** class manages your connection to an Internet server. **CInternetConnection** is the base class of the classes that provide functionality for communicating with an FTP, HTTP, or Gopher server.

The following illustration shows the classes derived from **CInternetConnection**.

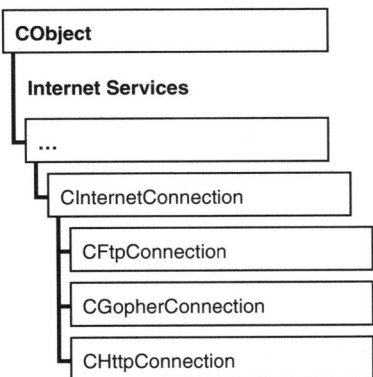

If the client computer is directly connected to the Internet, call *GetXxxConnection* with a single argument specifying the server name. For example, the following code retrieves an FTP connection:

```
CInternetSession session;
CFtpConnection* m_pFtp= session.GetFtpConnection("ftp.microsoft.com");
```

If the client computer is connected to the Internet through a proxy server, you need to specify the proxy server name, your log-on name, and your log-on password when making a connection.

The following example makes a request as "anonymous" through a proxy server called "ftp-gw." The user's e-mail name is specified as password.

```
CInternetSession session;
CFtpConnection* m_pFtp= session.GetFtpConnection("ftp-gw",
"anonymous@servername, myname@mycompany.com");
```

You must get the details about the proxy name from your network administrator.

CInternetFile

CInternetFile is the base class for the **CHttpFile** and **CGopherFile** file classes. It enables remote access to servers that use the HTTP and Gopher protocols. **CInternetFile** also is used when opening an FTP file.

CInternetFile objects are never created directly, but instead are created indirectly using **CGopherConnection::OpenFile**, **CHttpConnection::OpenRequest**, or **CFtpConnection::OpenFile**. For example:

```
// m_pFtp is a pointer to a CFtpConnection object.
CInternetFile* pFile = m_pFtp->OpenFile("readme.txt");
```

Getting Status Information about a Session

You can override the member function **CInternetSession::OnStatusCallback** to get status of your Internet session. Getting the status of the session is useful for lengthy operations, such as downloading a large file or searching the Web.

To get status of your session, you complete the following steps:

1. Derive a new class from **CInternetSession**.
2. Override the **CInternetSession::OnStatusCallback** member function.

Chapter 9: Building Internet Applications

3. Call **CInternetSession::EnableStatusCallback(TRUE)** to register the callback function.

The following sample code shows how to implement **CInternetSession::OnStatusCallback**. To copy this code for use in your own projects, see "An Implementation of CInternetSession::OnStatusCallback" on the accompanying CD-ROM.

```
// Sample OnStatusCallback code for debugging.
void CInetSession::OnStatusCallback(
  DWORD dwContext, DWORD wInternetStatus,
  LPVOID lpvStatusInformation, DWORD dwStatusInformationLength)
{
switch (wInternetStatus)
{
case INTERNET_STATUS_RESOLVING_NAME:
    TRACE("Looking up the IP address.\n");
    break;
case INTERNET_STATUS_REQUEST_COMPLETE:
    TRACE("Asynchronous operation completed\n");
    break;
case INTERNET_STATUS_HANDLE_CLOSING:
    TRACE("Handle closed.\n");
    break;
case INTERNET_STATUS_HANDLE_CREATED:
    TRACE("New handle created.\n");
    break;
case INTERNET_STATUS_NAME_RESOLVED:
    TRACE("IP address found.\n");
    break;
case INTERNET_STATUS_CONNECTING_TO_SERVER:
    TRACE("Connecting to the socket address.\n");
    break;
case INTERNET_STATUS_CONNECTED_TO_SERVER:
    TRACE("Successfully connected to the socket address.\n");
    break;
case INTERNET_STATUS_SENDING_REQUEST:
    TRACE("Sending request to the server.\n");
    break;
case INTERNET_STATUS_REQUEST_SENT:
    TRACE("Request sent to server.\n");
    break;
```

code continued on next page

```
code continued from previous page
    case INTERNET_STATUS_RECEIVING_RESPONSE:
        TRACE("Waiting for server to respond.\n");
        break;
    case INTERNET_STATUS_RESPONSE_RECEIVED:
        TRACE("Response received from server\n");
        break;
    case INTERNET_STATUS_CLOSING_CONNECTION:
        TRACE("Closing connection to server.\n");
        break;
    case INTERNET_STATUS_CONNECTION_CLOSED:
        TRACE("Connection to server closed.\n");
        break;
    default :
        TRACE("OnStatusCallback: Unknown status message\n");
        break;
    }
}
```

Writing HTTP Applications

Hypertext Transfer Protocol (HTTP) is an Internet protocol that has the following characteristics:

- Distributive

    One hypertext document may have links to many servers.

- Collaborative

    The client and server work together through the protocol to present the best possible presentation of the data to the user.

- Hypermedia

    The protocol is independent of the content being transferred.

HTTP sits on top of the TCP/IP layer, or another reliable transport layer, and is based on the request/response paradigm.

The Request/Respond Paradigm

HTTP clients and servers interact through messages. HTTP messages consist of client-to-server requests and server-to-client responses.

A request message consists of a request line, zero or more headers, and an optional entity-body. The request line has three parts: the request verb, the target URL, and the client's HTTP version number.

The following is a sample request message. It uses the GET verb to retrieve the desired target URL from the server.

```
GET http://www.microsoft.com/intdev/sdk/docs/wininet/ HTTP/1.0
Accept: text/*
User-Agent: MyClientProgram.exe
If-Modified-Since: Thu Oct24 10:07:04 1996
```

A response message consists of a status line, zero or more headers, and an optional entity-body. A status line consists of the server's HTTP version, a response code, and a short textual description of the code. The following is a sample response message:

```
HTTP/1.0 200 OK
Content-Type: text/html
Content-Length: 1277
Last-Modified: Tue, 15 Oct 1996 23:52:00 GMT
```

Processing a Hyperlink

When a user clicks a hyperlink within a hypertext document, the following sequence of events occurs:

1. The embedded hyperlink string is parsed for the server name, the path on the server, and the file name.
2. The client establishes a connection to a server.
3. The client sends a request, usually asking for a file.
4. The server responds with the data of that file.
5. The server closes the connection.

Establishing the Connection

To create an HTTP application, you must first create an Internet session by using the **CInternetSession** class. Once you create the session, you can use **CInternetSession::GetHttpConnection** to establish a connection.

The following example creates a session and establishes an HTTP connection to the microsoft.com Web site:

```
CInternetSession session;
CHttpConnection* pCon= session.GetHttpConnection("microsoft.com");
```

The **CHttpConnection** object manages an HTTP connection to a server.

Formulating a Request

Once you have established a connection, you can use **CHttpConnection::OpenRequest** to formulate a request to the Web server.

The **CHttpConnection** class has a single member function, **CHttpConnection::OpenRequest,** which retrieves a pointer to a **CHttpFile** object. You pass a verb and a resource to the **OpenRequest** function as shown in the following example:

```
CHttpFile* pFile=pCon->OpenRequest("GET","/intdev/sdk/docs/wininet/");
```

You can add headers to the message by using **CHttpFile::AddRequestHeaders**. You can add multiple headers by separating the headers using a carriage return/line feed (CR/LF) in the string parameter. For example, the following code adds two headers to the message:

```
CString strHeaders("Accept: text/*\r\nUser-Agent: MyClientProgram.exe\r\n");
pFile->AddRequestHeaders(strHeaders);
```

Sending a Request

Once you establish a connection and formulate a request, you can call **SendRequest** to send the request to the server as follows:

```
pFile->SendRequest();
```

Receiving a Response

You can use **CHttpFile::ReadString** to read the resultant data from the server, one line at a time, as shown in this example:

```
CString line;
while (pFile->ReadString(line)!=FALSE)
{
    //process a line of data from server.
}
```

To examine the response headers from the server, call **CHttpFile::QueryInfo**. You can extract individual header values, or you can extract all of the headers, as shown in this example:

```
CString strHeader;
if (pFile->QueryInfo(HTTP_QUERY_RAW_HEADERS_CRLF, strHeader))
{
  TRACE("%s\n", strHeader);
}
```

Writing FTP Applications

The File Transfer Protocol (FTP) enables transfer of files between incompatible computers, operating systems, and file systems. FTP also provides clients with general file management capabilities, such as retrieving directory listings, file attribute examination, directory navigation, and creation and deletion of directories on FTP servers.

MFC supports FTP mainly through the following classes:

- **CInternetSession**

    Manages your Internet session.

- **CFtpConnection**

    Manages your FTP connection and supports the directory-level FTP services.

- **CFtpFileFind**

    Enables you to work with file listings by examining file attributes.

The CFtpConnection Class

CFtpConnection manages your connection to the FTP server. You need to obtain a pointer to an instance of this class by using the function **CInternetSession::GetFtpConnection**.

Once you obtain this pointer, you can read and write files, move through the directory structure, and create and delete directories.

For a complete listing of **CFtpConnection** class members, search for "CFtpConnection" in MSDN Library Visual Studio 6.0.

The CFtpFileFind Class

CFtpFileFind is an MFC class derived from the **CFileFind** class. The **CFileFind** class supports wildcard characters and provides functions to retrieve file attributes. **CFtpFileFind** extends this base class by enabling searches and queries on files located on FTP servers.

CFtpFileFind supports UNIX-style searches using the wildcard characters asterisk (*) and question mark (?). The asterisk wildcard specifies zero or more of any character, while the question mark specifies a single character.

For example, searching for files with the string **?rain*.?x?** will return matches on files such as "Drain.exe," "Train.txt," and "BrainMatter.wxy," but will not return a match on files such as "Rain.exe" and "Strain.exe."

CFtpFileFind also provides a rich selection of attribute functions, such as **GetCreationTime**, **IsDirectory**, and **IsHidden**.

To use the **CFtpFileFind** class, construct an instance of it. Then use **CFtpFileFind::FindFile** to initialize the search specifying a search criteria for the string parameter, with or without wildcard characters. You must call **CFtpFileFind::FindNextFile** before querying the attributes of the file found.

The search is performed in the FTP file server's current working directory. You can perform additional searches on other directories by using the same instance of **CFtpFileFind**, but you must reset the object by calling the **CFtpFileFind::Close** member function, changing the current remote directory, and then calling **CFtpFileFind::FindFile** again.

The following sample code shows how to specify the search criteria and then iterates through each found file in one directory on the FTP server. To copy this code for use in your own projects, see "Using the CFtpFileFind Class" on the accompanying CD-ROM.

```
//Sample code showing how to specify a search condition and process
//the resultant data
CFtpFileFind ff(m_pFtp);    // m_pFtp is a CFtpConnection* object.
BOOL success;
success= ff.FindFile("*"); // searching for all files, including
directories, in the current directory
while (TRUE ==success) {
// Need to call FindNextFile before doing any attribute queries.
    success =ff.FindNextFile();// return value is for next file
//   ... perform any required file enquiry AFTER FindNextFile
    if (ff.IsDirectory())
//       ... do something with directories
    else
//       ... do something with files
}
ff.Close();    // close this search
```

Public FTP Servers

Generally, a client FTP application provides a user name and password to the FTP server. Often, though, public FTP servers are established to act as file servers to anyone connecting to them. To accomplish this, a convention has been established to use the string "anonymous" as the user name and the user's e-mail name as the password. Typically, the FTP server discards the password value.

To see the specifications of FTP, go to the FTP Specification page on the Network Working Group's Web site at ftp://nic.merit.edu/documents/rfc/rfc0959.txt.

Writing Gopher Applications

The Gopher protocol supports distributed document search and retrieval. It is based on a menu-driven paradigm where the client is provided a list of menu items. Menu items can be a variety of resources, such as documents, directories, search engines, FTP sites, and sound files. When a user selects one of the menu items, the Gopher client retrieves the requested resource as a document, or accesses another Gopher server that then presents another list of menu items.

Using the Gopher protocol is like using HTTP. The client makes a connection with a Gopher server and sends a request. The server sends the information and then closes the connection.

For more information about the Gopher protocol, go to the Internet Gopher Protocol page on the following Network Working Group Web site at ftp://ds.internic.net/rfc/rfc1436.txt.

MFC Support for Gopher

MFC provides general Internet support for the Gopher protocol through the **CInternetSession** class. In addition, the classes listed in the following table provide specific support for Gopher.

Class name	Description
CGopherConnection	This class manages the connection to the Gopher server. You use **CInternetSession::GetGopherConnection** to retrieve a pointer to an object.
CGopherLocatorType	This object type represents a token to a Gopher item. It is used by an application to retrieve the item.
CGopherFileFind	Similar to **CFtpFileFind**, this class responds to application requests to find specific documents.
CGopherFile	This class finds and reads files on a Gopher server.

Using the WinSock Classes

This section covers MFC support for low-level network programming. The section begins with a discussion of sockets and the TCP/IP protocol suite. This discussion is followed by an overview of the Windows Socket (WinSock) API, which is the standard API for network programming on Windows-based computers. The last topic in the section shows you how to use the **CAsyncSocket** and **CSocket** classes to create powerful Internet applications.

Introduction to Sockets

The term socket is used to describe an endpoint of communication on a computer network. A socket is associated with a process on the computer. A process needs a socket at its end, as well as at the other end of the network, to perform any communication. Most network interaction involves two sockets for peer-to-peer or client/server communication. Other configurations involve multicast or broadcast communication, such as the ones found in multiuser conferencing, radio broadcasting connections, and network management tasks.

The Socket API provides an abstraction layer to developers, helping you complete tasks that otherwise would require knowledge and manipulation of network card details and TCP/IP protocol details.

To use sockets for network communication, complete the following steps:

1. Create a local socket.
2. Connect with a remote computer.
3. Transfer data back and forth.
4. Close the connection.

Although using sockets eliminates some of the device- and protocol-specific programming work, network applications using sockets still must understand, and in some cases define, the format used for transferring the raw data. Therefore, writing applications using the WinSock classes requires more work than writing applications using the WinInet classes.

Types of Sockets

There are three types of sockets:

◆ Connection-oriented sockets

   A high-level socket that acts like a phone connection. Once a connection is established, it remains open until one of the parties explicitly ends it.

◆ Connectionless sockets

   A high-level socket that acts like a mail courier. It does not maintain a connection to the destination.

◆ Raw sockets

   A low-level socket that lets an application manipulate the individual fields of the protocol headers. For example, you can use raw sockets to create a network application that determines which routers a datagram passes through.

To see the animation "Programming with Sockets," see the accompanying CD-ROM.

The Roles of Clients and Servers in WinSock Programming

Clients and servers can be connection-oriented or connectionless. Connection-oriented servers require connection-oriented clients. Likewise, connectionless servers require connectionless clients.

- Role of a client application

    Initializes its socket and then initiates communication with a server. It is an active participant. A client application typically does not specify a local port number, but lets WinSock assign one for it.

- Role of a server application

    Initializes its socket with a specific port number, and then waits passively for a client message. When a request comes in, the server application will respond by either creating a connection at a new port (if a streaming socket), or by accepting the datagram (if a datagram socket). A new port usually is created for connection-oriented sockets, so that the original port is kept open for other clients seeking connections.

Using TCP/IP for Socket Communication

The TCP/IP protocol suite is a set of protocols used to send data through the Internet. While the sockets paradigm is independent of the protocol suite used, TCP/IP is usually the underlying transport layer used for socket communication. Other protocols, such as FTP and HTTP, also use the TCP protocol as its underlying transport layer.

The TCP/IP suite is hierarchically structured. The following illustration shows the hierarchy of protocols in the suite.

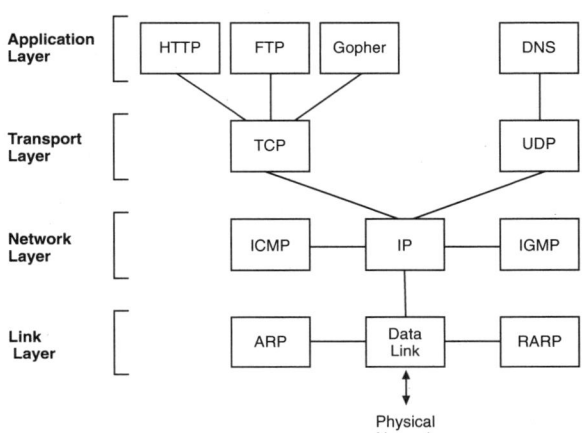

Protocols that provide sophisticated services depend on simpler protocols lower in the hierarchy. For instance, the Transmission Control Protocol (TCP) relies on a simpler network layer protocol, the Internet Protocol (IP) layer, which only attempts to deliver data to a destination computer. IP is an unreliable protocol. There is no guarantee provided at the IP layer.

The more sophisticated TCP layer provides a reliable communication connection between computers, guaranteeing that data will be successfully transferred. TCP guarantees the transfer of data by using techniques, such as handshaking, timeouts, retries, and checksum calculations.

The WinSock API

The Windows Socket API is a standard set of functions used on Windows-based computers to perform process-to-process communications across networks. It is based on the University of California, Berkeley, UNIX implementation BSD (Berkeley Software Distribution) version 4.3.

Windows Socket API Version 1.1

Windows Socket API version 1.1 consists of functions that can be divided into three functional groups: sockets, database, and Windows-specific.

Socket Functions

Some functions pertain to all socket types, while others pertain to only some types.

The following table lists some socket functions.

Function name	Description
accept	Acknowledges an incoming connection and associates it with an immediately created socket. The original socket returns to the listening state.
bind	Assigns a local name to an unnamed socket.
closesocket	Removes a socket from the per-process object reference table.
connect	Initiates a connection on the specified socket.

Database Functions

The following table lists some database functions.

Name	Description
gethostbyaddr	Retrieves the name(s) and address corresponding to a network address.
gethostbyname	Retrieves the name(s) and address corresponding to a host name.
gethostname	Retrieves the name of the local host.

Windows-Specific Functions

The following table lists some Windows-specific functions.

Name	Description
WSACancelBlockingCall	Cancels an outstanding blocking API call.
WSACleanup	Signs off from the underlying Windows Sockets DLL.

table continued on next page

table continued from previous page

Name	Description
WSAGetLastError	Obtains details of the last Windows Sockets API error.
WSAIsBlocking	Determines whether the underlying Windows Sockets DLL is already blocking an existing call for this thread.

Windows Socket API Version 2

Windows Sockets version 2 provides many new features while maintaining backward compatibility with version 1.1. Architecturally, WinSock 2 is a layer separate from the transport layer (TCP, for example). In this respect, the WinSock 2 API has become more of an operating system component. Features of WinSock 2 include the following:

- Transport layer independence

    Windows Sockets 1.1 is TCP/IP-centric. WinSock 2.x uses the familiar sockets interface to provide access to protocols other than TCP/IP.

- Conventions for negotiating quality of service (QOS) levels for attributes like bandwidth and latency

- Protocol-independent multicast and broadcast

    Applications can discover what capabilities a transport layer provides.

To view the latest WinSocket 2.x specification go to http://www.stardust.com/wsresource/winsock2/readme.html.

MFC Support for WinSock

MFC provides support for the Windows Socket API through two classes:

- **CSocket**

    This class encapsulates the API at a higher level and takes advantage of **CSocketFile** and **CArchive** to facilitate the sending and receiving of data.

- **CAsyncSocket**

    This class encapsulates the Windows Socket API at a lower level than **CSocket**. Use **CAsyncSocket** if you know network programming and want to program close to the API level.

For more information about these classes, search for "CSocket" and "ASyncSocket" in MSDN Library Visual Studio 6.0.

AfxSocketInit()

The Visual Studio Gallery provides a WinSock component that you can insert into your project so that your application can take advantage of the WinSock API. When you add the WinSock component to your project, a statement to call **AfxSocketInit** is placed in the **InitInstance** function of your application class.

By default, **AfxSocketInit** passes no parameter; however, you can pass a pointer to a WSADATA data structure to retrieve useful information about the Windows Socket API implementation on which your application is running. Information returned in this data structure includes the Windows Socket API version, the maximum number of sockets that it supports, and the maximum User Datagram Protocol (UDP) datagram size that your application can send.

Lab 9.1: Using the Web Browser Control

In this lab, you will implement the **Web Browser ActiveX** control in an application.

To see the demonstration "Lab 9.1 Demonstration," see the accompanying CD-ROM.

Estimated time to complete this lab: **40 minutes**

To complete the exercises in this lab, you must have the required software. For detailed information about the labs and setup for the labs, see "Labs" in "About This Course."

The code that forms the starting point for this lab is located in the folder *<install folder>*\Labs\Ch09\Lab9.1.

The solution code for this lab is located in the folder *<install folder>*\Labs\Ch09\Lab9.1.

Objectives

After completing this lab, you will be able to:

- Create an MFC-based application that is a control container.
- Use the Components and Controls Gallery to include the **Web Browser** control in your project.

- Programmatically create a **Web Browser** control and set properties and invoke methods of the **Web Browser** control.
- Handle events of the **Web Browser** control in your application.

Prerequisites

There are no prerequisites for this lab.

Exercises

The following exercises provide practice working with the concepts and techniques covered in this chapter.

- Exercise 1: Using the Web Browser Control

    In this exercise, you will create a simple control container application and use the Components and Controls Gallery to add the **Web Browser** control to the project. You also will add code to create an instance of the **Web Browser** control and to invoke a method and set properties of the control.

- Exercise 2: Handling Web Browser Control Events

    In this exercise, you will modify the application created in Exercise 1 of this lab to handle a Web Browser control event.

Exercise 1: Using the Web Browser Control

In this exercise, you will create a simple a control container application and use the Components and Controls Gallery to add the **Web Browser** control to the project. You also will add code to create an instance of the **Web Browser** control and to invoke a method and set properties of the control.

▶ **Create a control container application**

1. Start Visual Studio and then on the **File** menu, click **New**.
2. In the **New** dialog box, click the **Projects** tab, and select **MFC AppWizard (EXE)**.
3. In the **Location** field, type the directory path under which you want to create the project. Type **Browse** in the **Project Name** field, accept the default option **Create new workspace**, then click **OK**.
4. In Step 1 of MFC AppWizard, select **Single Document** for the type of application to create, and then click **Next**.

5. In Step 2 of MFC AppWizard, accept the default settings and click **Next**.
6. In Step 3 of MFC AppWizard, accept the default of **None** for compound document support and under other support, make sure that the **ActiveX Controls** check box is checked. You can accept defaults for the remaining steps, so click **Finish**.

▶ **Add the Web Browser control to your project**

1. On the **Project** menu, click **Add To Project,** and then click **Components and Controls**. In the **Gallery** dialog box, double-click the **Registered ActiveX Controls** folder.
2. Select the **Microsoft Web Browser Control** component, click **Insert,** and then click **OK**.
3. In the **Confirm Classes** dialog box, click **OK**.
4. In the **Gallery** dialog box, click **Close**.

    Note that the **CWebBrowser2** class has been added to the list of classes in the Browse application.

5. In the ClassView pane, expand the **CWebBrowser2** class to view properties and methods of the class.

▶ **Create an instance of the Web Browser control**

1. Before you create an instance of the **Web Browser** control, you will need to include the header file for the **CWebBrowser2** class in the header file of the view class.
2. You also need to add a member variable for a pointer to a **Web Browser** control to the class in which you will create the control. In this case, you will embed the control in the view class.

    a. In the ClassView pane, right-click **CBrowseView**, then click **Add Member Variable**.

    b. In the **Add Member Variable** dialog box, type **CWebBrowser2*** in the **Variable Type** field.

    c. Type **m_pBrowse** in the **Variable Name** field.

    d. Accept the default value of **Public access,** and click **OK**.

    e. In BrowseView.cpp, add the following line to the constructor **CBrowseView::CBrowseView**:

    ```
    m_pBrowse = NULL;
    ```

3. Create a control ID to use as a parameter for the **Web Browser** control **Create** function.

   a. In the ResourceView pane, right-click the **Menu** folder and select **Insert menu**.

   b. In the Menu editor pane, double-click the empty top-level menu item provided and in the **Menu Item Properties** dialog box, set the **Caption** property to **IDs**.

   c. In the Menu editor pane, double-click the empty menu item under IDs. In the **Menu Item Properties** dialog box, set the **ID** property to **IDC_WBC**. This is the control ID you will provide as a parameter to the **Web Browser** control's **Create** function in the next step.

   You can add caption and prompt information to help you remember what this resource is for.

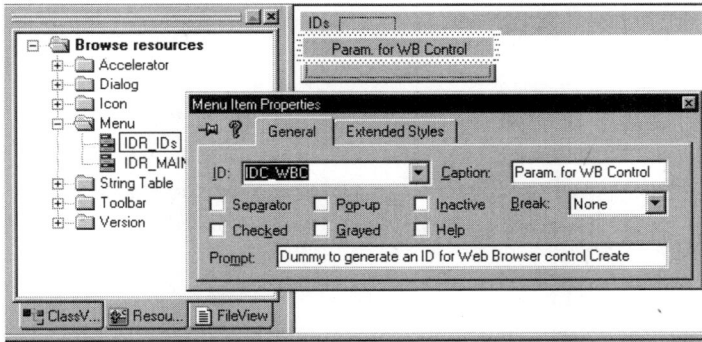

4. To embed the control in the view, add a message handler for the WM_CREATE message to the view class, and place the code to create an instance of the **Web Browser** control in the message handler.

   a. In the ClassView pane, right-click **CBrowseView**, and then click **Add Windows Message Handler**.

   b. From the list of handlers, select **WM_CREATE**, then click **Add and Edit**.

   c. In the **CBrowseView::OnCreate** function, add the following code before the return statement:

   ```
   // Define the area where the control will reside.
   CRect rect;
   GetClientRect(&rect);
   ```

   code continued on next page

code continued from previous page

```
// Create the control.
// IDC_WBC is a unique identifier for the control and was defined
// in Step 3 using a dummy menu item.
m_pBrowse = new CWebBrowser2;
ASSERT(m_pBrowse);
if (!m_pBrowse->Create(NULL,NULL,WS_VISIBLE,rect,this,IDC_WBC))
{
   TRACE("failed to create browser\n");
   delete m_pBrowse;
   m_pBrowse = NULL;
   return 0;
}
```

You will not be able to see any results from the code you have added until you have completed the next two steps of invoking a method and setting properties of the control.

▶ **Invoke a method of the Web Browser control**

- Following the lines added to the **CBrowseView::OnCreate** function in the previous procedure, add the code shown below to invoke the **Web Browser** control's **Navigate** method:

```
// Initialize the first URL.
COleVariant noArg;
m_pBrowse->Navigate("www.microsoft.com", &noArg, &noArg,
                    &noArg, &noArg);
```

Replace the string "www.microsoft.com" with the Web site name created by the Personal Web Server.

Note The empty **COleVariant** arguments can be set to further customize the **Navigate** method. For more information about **COleVariant** arguments, search for "COleVariant::COleVariant" in MSDN Library Visual Studio 6.0.

▶ Set properties of the Web Browser control

To set properties of the control, add a message handler for the WM_SIZE message to the view class, and place the code to set the height and width properties of the **Web Browser** control in the message handler.

1. In the ClassView pane, right-click **CBrowseView**, and then click **Add Windows Message Handler**.
2. From the list of handlers, select **WM_SIZE**, then click **Add and Edit**.
3. In the **CBrowseView::OnSize** function, add the following code after the call to the base class's **OnSize** function:

   ```
   if (m_pBrowse)
   {
       m_pBrowse->SetWidth(cx);
       m_pBrowse->SetHeight(cy);
   }
   ```

   This code causes the **Web Browser** control to resize when a user resizes the application's mainframe window.

▶ Build and test your application

- If you have an active connection to the Internet, you should see the default page for the Microsoft Corporation's Web site displayed in the **Web Browser** control in your application's view class.

The solution code for this exercise is located in the folder *<install folder>*\Labs\Ch09\Lab9.1\Ex01\Solution.

Exercise 2: Handling Web Browser Control Events

Continue with the files you created in Exercise 1 or, if you do not have a starting point for this exercise, the code that forms the basis for this exercise is in *<install folder>*\Labs\Ch09\Lab9.1\Ex02.

In this exercise, you will modify the application from Exercise 1 of this lab to handle a **Web Browser** control event.

There are three main steps to handle events:

- Determine the function prototype and ID of the event.
- Add the event function handler to the **Wrapper** class.
- Link the event to the handler.

▶ **Determine the function prototype and ID of the event**

1. On the Visual Studio **Tools** menu, click **OLE/COM Object Viewer**.
2. In the left pane of the **OLE/COM Object Viewer** dialog box, double-click the **Controls** folder. Scroll down the list and right-click **Microsoft Web Browser Control**.
3. On the menu that appears, click **View Type Information**.
4. In the **ITypeLib Viewer** dialog box that appears, double-click **dispInterface DWebBrowserEvents2**, and then double-click the **Methods** folder.

   This displays the event methods for the **Web Browser** control.

> **Tip** If you do not see the dispInterfaceDWebBrowserEvents node in the left-hand pane of the ITypeLib Viewer dialog box, on the View menu, see whether "Group by type kind" is checked. If so, click Group by type kind to uncheck it and the dispInterfaceDWebBrowserEvents node will appear.

5. In the **Methods** folder, click **StatusTextChange**. The information you require about the ID for the event and the prototype for the event handler appears in the right pane of the **ITypeLib Viewer** dialog box:

   ```
   [id(0x00000066)
   void StatusTextChange([in] BSTR Text);
   ```

▶ **Add the event function handler to the control's Wrapper class**

1. Before you create the **OnStatusTextChange** event handler, create a public member function, **Status**, in the **CMainFrame** class. This helper function, which enables the view class to access the status bar object, will be called in the **OnStatusTextChange** event handler.

    a. In the ClassView pane, right-click **CMainFrame**, and then click **Add Member Function**.

b. In the **Add Member Function** dialog box, type **void** in the **Function Type** field, type **Status(LPCTSTR text)** in the **Function Declaration** field, then click **OK**.

c. Add the following line to the **Status** function:

```
m_wndStatusBar.SetPaneText(0,text,TRUE);
```

2. You can now add the **OnStatusTextChange** event handler function. In the ClassView pane, right-click **CBrowseView**, then click **Add Member Function**.

3. In the **Add Member Function** dialog box, type **void** in the **Function Type** field, type **OnStatusTextChange(LPCTSTR text)** in the **Function Declaration** field, then click **OK**.

4. Add the following lines to the **OnStatusTextChange** function:

```
// Only write to status line if there is a non-zero string.
// (lstrlen works on either ANSI or UNICODE strings.)
if (lstrlen(text))
    ((CMainFrame*)AfxGetMainWnd())->Status(text);
```

Tip **AfxGetMainWnd** returns a **CFrameWnd** pointer. You must cast the return value to a **CMainFrame** pointer because **Status** is a member function of the **CMainFrame** class.

5. Because the **Status** function called in the previous step is a member of the **CMainFrame** class, add the following line to BrowseView.cpp file to include the header file for the **CMainFrame** class:

```
#include "mainfrm.h"
```

▶ Link the event to the handler

In this application, the view class handles the **OnStatusTextChange** event, so the changes outlined below are made in each case to the appropriate view class file(s).

1. Add a DECLARE_EVENTSINK_MAP() macro call to the header file for the class that handles the event.

    a. Open the BrowseView.h file.

    b. Add the following line after the call to DECLARE_MESSAGE_MAP():

    ```
    DECLARE_EVENTSINK_MAP()
    ```

2. Add an event sink map to the source file for the class that handles the event. Recall that the event ID displayed in the OLE/COM Object Viewer for the **StatusTextChange** event was 0x66.

   a. Open BrowseView.cpp.

   b. After the line END_MESSAGE_MAP(), add the following lines to add an event sink map to the view class:

   ```
   BEGIN_EVENTSINK_MAP(CBrowseView, CView)
      ON_EVENT(CBrowseView, IDC_WBC, 0x66, OnStatusTextChange,
   VTS_BSTR)
   END_EVENTSINK_MAP()
   ```

▶ **Build and test your application**

- You will see that the text in the status bar changes as the **Web Browser** control navigation takes place.

The solution code for this exercise is located in the folder *<install folder>*\Labs\Ch09\Lab9.1\Ex02\Solution.

Lab 9.2: Using the HTTP WinInet Classes

In this lab, you will create an HTTP application.

To see the demonstration "Lab 9.2 Demonstration," see the accompanying CD-ROM.

Estimated time to complete this lab: **30 minutes**

To complete the exercises in this lab, you must have the required software. For detailed information about the labs and setup for the labs, see "Labs" in "About This Course."

The code that forms the starting point for this lab is located in the folder *<install folder>*\Labs\Ch09\Lab9.2\Ex01.

The solution code for this lab is located in the folder *<install folder>*\Labs\Ch09\Lab9.2\Ex01\Solution.

Objectives

After completing this lab, you will be able to:

- Create an Internet session.
- Get an HTTP connection.
- Open a request to an HTTP server.
- Send a request to an HTTP server.
- Read and display the data retrieved from the HTTP server.

Prerequisites

There are no prerequisites for this lab.

Exercises

The following exercise provides practice working with the concepts and techniques covered in this chapter.

- Exercise 1: Creating an HTTP Application

   In this exercise, you will create an application that accepts a URL from a user and then sequentially executes each part of a client HTTP transaction. Once the data is received from the HTTP server, the client application displays the data in the application view.

Exercise 1: Creating an HTTP Application

The code that forms the starting point for this exercise is in *<install folder>*\Labs\Ch09\Lab9.2\Ex01.

In this exercise, you will create an application that accepts a URL from a user and then sequentially executes each part of a client HTTP transaction. Once the data is received from the HTTP server, the client application displays the data in the application view.

In this exercise, you will add the code to:

- Create an Internet session.
- Obtain an HTTP connection.
- Open a request to retrieve a file.
- Send the request to the HTTP server.
- Read the header and data received from the server and display it in the application view.

The baseline application's view class already has menu command handlers for executing each part of a client HTTP transaction:

- **CIC_2View::OnInternetObtainUrl**
- **CIC_2View::OnInternetCreateSession**
- **CIC_2View::OnInternetGetConnection**
- **CIC_2View::OnInternetOpenRequest**
- **CIC_2View::OnInternetSendRequest**
- **CIC_2View::OnInternetReadInformation**

Only **OnInternetObtainUrl** contains implementation code. This handler invokes a dialog box that accepts the URL entered by the user. You will implement the remaining handlers in this lab.

The application is designed so that when the user enters a URL, the first menu item is enabled. The remaining menu items are enabled, in top-down order of their appearance on the menu, only after the previous menu item has been selected. To control the enabling of menu items, the application uses a state variable, m_processState. Each handler simply increments the value of this variable before exiting. Each menu item, using command updating, checks the value of m_processState to determine whether it is enabled.

Alternatively, a user can select the menu command **Obtain URL** followed by the menu command **All The Above** to complete all parts of a client HTTP transaction for the requested URL.

When the HTTP data is received, the headers and the body are added to a **CStringArray** object that is embedded in the application's **CDocument** object. The string array is then displayed to the application's view by forcing an update of the view.

Lab 9.2: Using the HTTP WinInet Classes

▶ **Create an Internet session**

1. Open the IC_2View.cpp file.

2. Add the following code to the body of the menu command handler **CIC_2View::OnInternetCreateSession**:

```
// Member function to close any previous session.
CloseSession();

// Create a new session.
m_pInternetSession = new CInternetSession;
ASSERT(m_pInternetSession != 0);

// Update the state of the menu items.
m_processState++;
```

▶ **Obtain an HTTP connection to the target HTTP server**

In this procedure, you will use the session's member function, **CInternetSession::GetHttpConnection**, to obtain an HTTP connection to the target HTTP server.

- Add the following code to the body of the menu item handler **CIC_2View::OnInternetGetConnection**:

```
CIC_2Doc* pDoc = GetDocument();

// Attempt to get an HTTP connection.
try {
  m_pHttpConnection =
      m_pInternetSession->GetHttpConnection(pDoc->m_Server,
      pDoc->m_Port);
}
catch (CInternetException *e)
{
  char buff[256];
  e->GetErrorMessage(buff,256);
  MessageBox(buff);
  e->Delete();
  return;
}
ASSERT(m_pHttpConnection != NULL);

// Update the state of the menu items.
m_processState++;
```

497

▶ Open an HTTP request

In this procedure, you will open an HTTP request specifying a **GET** command, which is used to retrieve a file. The **CDocument** object, **m_Object**, is a string containing the name of the file to retrieve from the server. If a file name was not specified in the URL the user entered, a default file will be returned.

- Add the following code to the body of the menu command handler **CIC_2View::OnInternetOpenRequest**:

```
// Set some request flags.
DWORD dwHttpRequestFlags = INTERNET_FLAG_EXISTING_CONNECT |
                           INTERNET_FLAG_NO_AUTO_REDIRECT;

CIC_2Doc* pDoc = GetDocument();

// Open a GET request and get an Internet File handle to
// communicate through.
m_pHttpFile = m_pHttpConnection->OpenRequest
                (CHttpConnection::HTTP_VERB_GET,pDoc->m_Object,
                 NULL, 1, NULL, NULL, dwHttpRequestFlags);

if (NULL == m_pHttpFile)
{
  CString s;
  s.Format ("An error occurred opening the request");
  MessageBox(s);
  return;
}

// Update the state of the menu items.
m_processState++;
```

Lab 9.2: Using the HTTP WinInet Classes

▶ Send an HTTP request

In this procedure, you will add additional header information to the HTTP header and send the request to the server.

- Add the following code to the body of the menu item handler **CIC_2View::OnInternetSendRequest**:

```
// Initialize our request header.
const TCHAR szHeaders[] =
   _T("Accept: text/*\r\nUser-Agent: IC_2\r\n");

BOOL rc;

// Send the request.
try {
   rc = m_pHttpFile->AddRequestHeaders(szHeaders);
   rc = m_pHttpFile->SendRequest();
}
catch (CInternetException * e)
{
   char buff[256];
   e->GetErrorMessage(buff,256);
   MessageBox(buff);
   e->Delete();
   return;
}

// Update the state of the menu items.
m_processState++;
```

You are now ready to receive, process, and display the data received from the HTTP server.

▶ Receive, process, and display the data received from the HTTP server

In this procedure, you will implement these steps in the **OnInternetReadInformation** handler:

- Extract the header information from the server's message.
- Add to the document object.
- Extract the body of the message that is the targeted HTML file.
- Add the body contents to the document.
- Update the view to display the header and body contents.

- Add the following code to the body of the menu item handler **CIC_2View::OnInternetReadInformation:**

```
char s[1024];
CIC_2Doc* pDoc = GetDocument();

//
// Get the received header and prepend to view output.
//
DWORD bufsiz= 1024;
if (m_pHttpFile->QueryInfo(HTTP_QUERY_RAW_HEADERS_CRLF, s,
                            &bufsiz))
{
   char * p = strtok(s, "\n\r");
   // Extract line at a time.
   while (p)
   {
       pDoc->m_WebPage.AddTail(p);
       p = strtok(NULL, "\n\r");
   }
   // Delimiter between header and body.
   pDoc->m_WebPage.AddTail(
       "+=+=+=+=+=+ End of Header +=+=+=+=+=+=+=+");
}

//
// Read body.
//
m_pHttpFile->SetReadBufferSize(4096);

while(m_pHttpFile->ReadString(s, 1023))
{
  // Extract a line at a time.
  char * p = strtok(s, "\n\r");
  while (p)
  {
      pDoc->m_WebPage.AddTail(p);
      p = strtok(NULL, "\n\r");
  }
}

// Have view repaint itself.
pDoc->UpdateAllViews(NULL);

// Update state of the menu items.
m_processState++;
```

▶ **Build and test your application**

- If you have an active connection to the Internet or an intranet, you will see the contents of the URL you requested displayed in the **Web Browser** control in your application's view class.

The solution code for this exercise is located in the folder *<install folder>*\Labs\Ch09\Lab9.2\Ex01\Solution.

Lab 9.3: Adding an HTML View

In this lab, you will create an application with an HTML view.

To see the demonstration "Lab 9.3 Demonstration," see the accompanying CD-ROM.

Estimated time to complete this lab: **15 minutes**

To complete the exercise in this lab, you must have the required software. For detailed information about the labs and setup for the labs, see "Labs" in "About This Course."

The solution code for this lab is located in the folder *<install folder>*\Labs\Ch09\Lab9.3\Ex01\Solution.

Objectives

After completing this lab, you will be able to:

- Use an HTML view in an application.

Prerequisites

There are no prerequisites for this lab.

Exercises

The following exercise provides practice working with the concepts and techniques covered in this chapter.

- Exercise 1: Adding an HTML View

  In this exercise, you will use the HTML view to add the functionality of the **Web Browser** control. You will add handlers to browse forward and backward through the previously browsed sites on the World Wide Web.

Exercise 1: Adding an HTML View

In this exercise, you will use the HTML view to add the functionality of the **Web Browser** control. You will add handlers to browse forward and backward through the previously browsed sites on the World Wide Web.

▶ **Create an SDI-based application by using MFC AppWizard**

- Name the new project workspace **Web**.
- In Step 6, derive **CWebView** from **CHtmlView**, rather than **CView**.
- Finish and create the new project.

▶ **Add toolbar items**

1. Open the IDR_MAINFRAME toolbar resource.
2. Add two toolbar items, giving them the IDs ID_GOBACK and ID_GOFORWARD, respectively.

   Your toolbar should look like the toolbar in the following illustration.

3. Save the Web.rc file.

▶ **Add command handlers for the toolbar items**

1. Invoke ClassWizard.
2. Add a handler for the ID_GOBACK message to **CWebView**, and accept the default **OnGoback** function name. Similarly, add a handler for the ID_GOFORWARD message.

▶ **Implement the command handlers for ID_GOBACK and ID_GOFORWARD toolbar items**

1. In the **OnGoback** function of the WebView.cpp file, invoke the following function to allow navigation to the previous item in the history list:

   ```
   CHtmlView::GoBack();
   ```

2. In the **OnGoforward** function of WebView.cpp, invoke the following function to allow navigation to the next item in the history list:

   ```
   CHtmlView::GoForward();
   ```

3. Save WebView.cpp.

▶ **Implement navigation**

1. Open WebView.cpp.
2. In the call to **Navigate2** function of **OnInitialUpdate**, replace the string "www.microsoft.com" with the Web site name created by Personal Web Server.

▶ **Build and run your application**

- Run your application and navigate the Web using the toolbar buttons you created.

The solution code for this exercise is located in the folder *<install folder>*\Labs\Ch09\Lab9.3\Ex01\Solution.

Sample Applications

The following table provides a description of the sample application related to this chapter. The sample application is located in the folder *<install folder>*\Samples\Ch09.

Sample application subfolder	Description of application
Browse	Implements an application with a **Web Browser** control.

For additional examples of Internet applications, refer to the MFC sample applications FTPTREE and TEAR, which are included in MSDN Library Visual Studio 6.0.

Self-Check Questions

To see the answers to the Self-Check Questions, see Appendix A.

1. **The primary purpose of the CFtpFileFind class is to find which files?**

    A. The first file that matches a search string on an FTP server

    B. All files in the current FTP directory that match the search string

    C. All files in the entire FTP server that match the search string

    D. All files on all active FTP servers that match the search string

2. **Which classes are used by CSocket to simplify sending and receiving data using a socket?**

    A. CHttpConnection and CHtmlStream

    B. CAsyncSocket and COleStream

    C. CInternetFile and CInternetSession

    D. CSocketFile and CArchive

3. **Which type of socket should be established by the application to make communication between two computers reliable?**

    A. Raw

    B. Connection-oriented (streaming)

    C. Datagram

    D. Connectionless

4. **Which wrapper class does ClassWizard create for Internet Explorer object?**

    A. CWebBrowser2

    B. IWebBrowserApp

    C. CWinInet

    D. CWebBrowserApp

Chapter 10:
Printing and Print Preview

Multimedia

Overriding CView
Functions to Enhance
Printer Support 510

Lab 10.1 Demonstration 520

This chapter explains how the printing process works by exploring the relationship between screen output and printer output, and the similarities and differences of these two output options. It also covers how you can add print support to your application by using Microsoft Foundation Class (MFC) AppWizard. The later topics of this chapter cover obtaining printer information and using this information to control the printed document.

Objectives

After completing this chapter, you will be able to:

- Describe the printing process and the default printing capabilities provided by MFC for an MFC AppWizard-generated application.
- Add default printer support to your application.
- Retrieve information relating to printers and print jobs at run time.
- Enhance default printer support to implement custom requirements.

Adding Default Printer Support

Adding default printer support to your application is a simple task when you use MFC AppWizard.

This section describes the printing process and the printer support that MFC provides to implement printing. It also explains how you can enable default printer support for your applications.

The last topic outlines some printing-related issues you must handle in your application.

Introduction to the Printing Process

The printing process involves three phases:

1. The request phase

   In this phase, the application receives a print request from the user.

2. The preparation phase

   In this phase, the application displays the **Print** dialog box, in which the user can specify the settings for the print job.

3. The printing phase

   In this phase, the application divides the document into a set of pages based on user settings. The application then prints each page along with its header and footer.

The following illustration shows the three phases of the printing process.

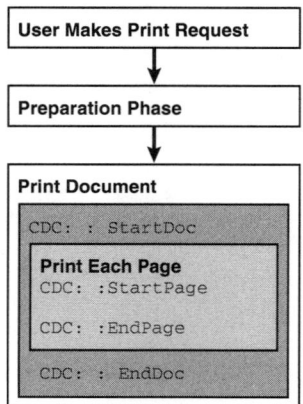

Enabling Default Printer Support

When you use MFC AppWizard to create an application, the wizard offers you the option of adding default printer support. To add this support to your application, select the **Printing and Print Preview** check box in Step 4 of MFC AppWizard.

The following illustration shows the **MFC AppWizard - Step 4** dialog box with the printer support option enabled.

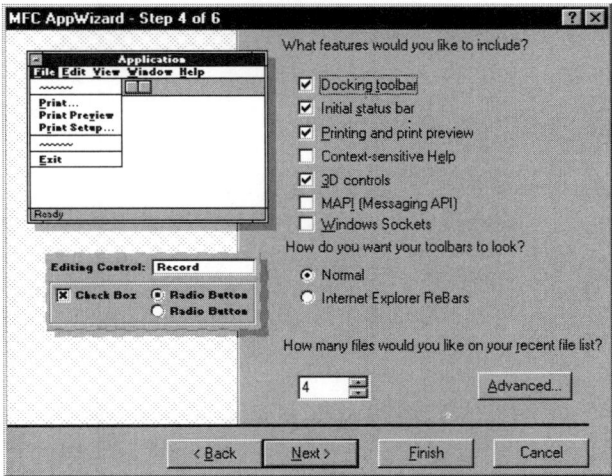

When you select this option, MFC adds the following commands to the **File** menu of your application:

- Print
- Print Preview
- Print Setup

MFC also adds the code to implement these commands in the implementation file of the view class.

MFC Support for Printing

MFC provides printer support in the following ways:

- By adding **CView** member functions to your view class
- By implementing device-independent display of data

CView Member Functions for Printing

When you enable printing for an application in MFC AppWizard, MFC automatically adds the required **CView** member functions to the view class of the application. The framework calls these functions during the three phases of printing (request, preparation, and printing) to implement a print job.

The following table lists the **CView** functions that are called for printing a document.

Name	Related printing phase	Result
OnPreparePrinting	Request	Inserts default values in the **Print** dialog box and displays it; also creates the device context for the printer.
OnBeginPrinting	Preparation	Allocates fonts or other Graphic Device Interface (GDI) resources; also sets the length of the document that needs to be printed.
OnPrepareDC	Preparation	Adjusts the attributes of the device context for a given page; also performs print-time pagination.
OnPrint	Printing	Prints each page, including header and footer.
OnEndPrinting	Printing	Releases GDI resources or reestablishes default settings.

Device-Independent Display

In MFC-based applications, the **OnDraw** member function of the **CView** class handles the drawing operation, regardless of whether the device is the screen or a printer. MFC implements this feature by passing a pointer to a **CDC** object as a parameter, as shown in this example:

```
virtual void OnDraw(CDC* pDC);
```

The **CDC** object represents the device context that should receive the image produced by **OnDraw**.

When the window displaying the document receives a WM_PAINT message, the framework calls **OnDraw** and passes it a device context for the screen. Accordingly, the **OnDraw** function sends its output to the screen.

When the window displaying the document receives a print command from the user, the framework calls the **OnPrint** function. The **OnPrint** function in turn calls the **OnDraw** function with a device context for a printer. The **OnDraw** function then sends its output to the printer.

The following illustration shows how MFC-based applications can perform simple printing without requiring extra effort on your part.

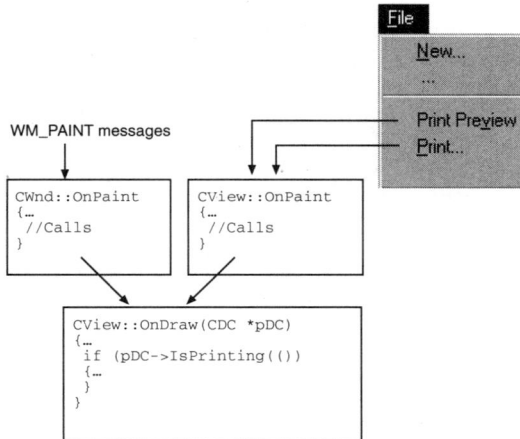

Screen Display vs. Printing

While there are many similarities between printing and screen display, there are also some significant differences between the two that your application must anticipate and handle. For example, when you print a document from your application, the application must divide the document into distinct pages and print them one at a time, rather than display whatever portion is visible in a window as with screen output.

When you develop your application, you must consider some characteristics of printed pages, including:

- Size of the paper used for printing

    The user may use standard letter-size paper, an envelope, or some other size paper.

- Page orientation

    The user may choose landscape or portrait orientation for the print job.

The MFC Library cannot predict how your application will handle these types of issues, so it provides a protocol for you to add these capabilities. The protocol is a set of overrideable **CView** class member functions that return information on print settings selected by the user.

Enhancing Printer Support

You can enhance printer support by overriding the **CView** member functions. For example, if the printed version of your document needs headers and footers, you may need to override the **OnPrint** function to add code to include headers and footers in the printout.

To see the animation "Overriding CView Functions to Enhance Printer Support," see the accompanying CD-ROM.

To enhance printer support, you need information related to the following:

- Settings of the default printer
- Settings chosen by the user for the current print job
- Attributes of the printer device context

This section begins by explaining how you can retrieve information related to printing and then describes how you can use this information in the **CView** functions.

Determining Printer Characteristics

You can obtain information about default printer settings in two ways:

◆ On application startup

If your application needs information about the characteristics of the Windows default printer on startup, override the **InitInstance** member function of the **CWinApp**-derived class.

The following sample code queries for printer information at application initialization. To copy this code for use in your own projects, see "Determining Printer Characteristics" on the accompanying CD-ROM.

```
// Getting printer information on application startup
// Samples\CH10\Prprevue
// Prprevue.cpp
BOOL CMyApp::InitInstance()
{
    ...

    // These 2 statements are needed to give the app the
    // default printer information. Without them, the call
    // to CreatePrinterDC fails.
    PRINTDLG dlg;
    GetPrinterDeviceDefaults(&dlg);

    CDC dc;
    if (0 != CreatePrinterDC(dc))
    {
        TEXTMETRIC tm;
        dc.GetTextMetrics(&tm);
        int x = dc.GetDeviceCaps(HORZRES);
        int y = dc.GetDeviceCaps(VERTRES);
        ...
    }

    ...
}
```

- Subsequent to application startup

   The default printer setting may be changed either by the user or by another application while your application is running. To track changes to the default printer, implement the **OnWinIniChange** member function of the **CWnd**-derived class. The framework calls this function to allow your application to handle a Windows message.

Retrieving Information About the Current Print Job

You use the pInfo parameter that is passed to the **CView**-derived functions to obtain information about the current print job. The pInfo parameter of the **CView::***OnXxxx* functions is a pointer to an object named **CPrintInfo**. The **CPrintInfo** object stores information about the print job.

CPrintInfo Class Members

The following table describes some **CPrintInfo** class members.

Data member	Description
m_pPD	Contains a pointer to the **CPrintDialog** object that is used for the **Print** dialog box.
m_bDirect	Contains a flag indicating whether the document is being printed directly (without displaying the **Print** dialog box).
m_bContinuePrinting	Contains a flag indicating whether the framework should continue the print loop.
m_nCurPage	Identifies the number of the page that is currently being printed.
SetMaxPage	Sets the number of the last page of the document.

Tip For a complete list of **CPrintInfo** class members, search for "CPrintInfo" in MSDN Library Visual Studio 6.0.

Using the CPrintDialog Object

The **CPrintDialog** object is a member of the **CPrintInfo** class and encapsulates the services provided by the Windows common dialog box for printing. For example, by using **CPrintDialog**, you can determine the print range and the name of the selected print driver. The **CPrintDialog** object is created by using the **CPrintInfo** constructor **m_pPD**. The following table describes some **CPrintDialog** class members.

Data member	Description
m_pd	A structure used to customize a **CPrintDialog** object. A member of this structure, **Flags**, specifies the dialog box initialization flags. For example, PD_DISABLEPRINTTOFILE disables the **Print to File** check box, and PD_ALLPAGES indicates that the **All** option button was selected when the user closed the dialog box.
GetDefaults	Stores the current printer defaults without displaying a dialog box.
GetCopies	Retrieves the number of copies requested.
GetDeviceName	Retrieves the name of the currently selected printer device.

Tip For a complete list of the **CPrintDialog** class members, search for "CPrintDialog" in MSDN Library Visual Studio 6.0.

The following example code shows how to access a member of the **CPrintDialog** object through the pointer to the **CPrintInfo** object:

```
pInfo->m_pPD->m_pd.Flags  |= PD_DISABLEPRINTTOFILE;
```

The following illustration shows how the pInfo argument is used to access the **CPrintInfo** and **CPrintDialog** objects, and shows the relationships between these two objects.

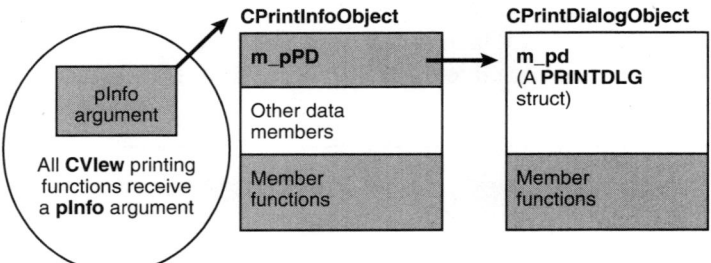

Retrieving Information About the Printer Device Context

The pDC parameter that is passed to all **CView::***OnXxxx* functions, except **OnPreparePrinting**, points to the device context object on which the image will be rendered. Use the member functions of the **CDC** class to obtain information related to the device context.

Tip For more information about the printer device context, search for "CDC Class Members" in MSDN Library Visual Studio 6.0.

Getting Information on Display Resolution

Use the **GetDeviceCaps** member function to get information about the display resolution. The following example code shows how you can retrieve the resolution settings as numeric values:

```
int x = dc.GetDeviceCaps(HORZRES);
int y = dc.GetDeviceCaps(VERTRES);
```

For more information about this function, search for "GetDeviceCaps" in MSDN Library Visual Studio 6.0.

Sending Escape Codes to the Printer

You can call the **Escape** member function of the pDC parameter from the **OnPrepareDC** member function to send escape codes to the printer on a page-by-page basis.

Getting the Current Status of a Device Context

You use the **IsPrinting** member function of the pDC parameter to determine whether the device context is used for printing.

Overriding CView-Derived Functions

This topic lists some overridable **CView**-derived functions and describes the reasons for overriding them. It also gives an example of each of the overridden functions.

The code samples discussed in this topic appear in the sample application Prprevue, which is located in the folder *<install folder>*\Samples\Ch10.

OnPreparePrinting

In the **OnPreparePrinting** function, you can customize the **Print** dialog box before it is displayed to the user. The following sample code disables the **Print to File** check box and displays the **Print** dialog box to the user. To copy this code for use in your own projects, see "Overriding OnPreparePrinting" on the accompanying CD-ROM.

```
// Customizing and Displaying the Print dialog box
// Samples\CH10\Prprevue
// Prinview.cpp
BOOL CPrintView::OnPreparePrinting(CPrintInfo* pInfo)
{
    // In this function, we can modify the behavior of the printer
    // dialog box before it's displayed. It's best to determine the
    // number of pages in the print job AFTER the dialog box has been
    // displayed.
    pInfo->m_pPD->m_pd.Flags |= PD_DISABLEPRINTTOFILE;

    return DoPreparePrinting(pInfo);
}
```

OnBeginPrinting

In the **OnBeginPrinting** function, you can examine changes made to the **Print** dialog box. The following sample code determines how many lines to print on each page based on the orientation selected by the user. To copy this code for use in your own projects, see "Overriding OnBeginPrinting" on the accompanying CD-ROM.

```
// Determining the number of pages to be printed based on user's
// selection
// Samples\CH10\Prprevue
// Prinview.cpp
void CPrintView::OnBeginPrinting(CDC* pDC, CPrintInfo* pInfo)
{
  TEXTMETRIC tm;
  pDC->GetTextMetrics(&tm);
  int y = pDC->GetDeviceCaps(VERTRES);

  // Allow for 3 lines at the top and 2 at the bottom
  int lines = (y / tm.tmHeight) - 5;

  // It's possible that the user has changed the printer
  // such that the number of lines it supports is less than
  // what the user currently wants. If so, both the desired
  // lines per page (stored in the view object) and the maximum
  // number of lines the current printer mode supports
  // (stored in the app object) will have to be changed.
  if (lines < GetPageLength())
  {
      SetPageLength(lines);
      CPrintApp * cpa = (CPrintApp *)::AfxGetApp();
      cpa->SetMaxPageLength(lines);
  }

  // The max page needs to be rounded up if the number of
  // lines to be printed isn't exactly divisible by
  // the lines per page.
  CPrintDoc* pDoc = GetDocument();
  ASSERT_VALID(pDoc);
  int pagecount = pDoc->LinesOnDocument() / GetPageLength();
  if ( 0 != (pDoc->LinesOnDocument() % GetPageLength()) )
      pagecount++;

  pInfo->SetMaxPage(pagecount);

  CScrollView::OnBeginPrinting(pDC, pInfo);
}
```

The previous example uses the **SetMaxPage** function to establish how many pages will be processed by the printing loop.

OnPrepareDC

You can override the **OnPrepareDC** function to set per page properties. The following sample code positions the pages based on page number. To copy this code for use in your own projects, see "Overriding OnPrepareDC" on the accompanying CD-ROM.

```
// Setting page properties
// Samples\CH10\Prprevue
// Prinview.cpp
void CPrintView::OnPrepareDC(CDC* pDC, CPrintInfo* pInfo)
{
  CScrollView::OnPrepareDC(pDC, pInfo);

  // On a scroll view, if you want to modify the DC, do it AFTER
  // the call to the base class version.
  // Just for demo purposes, this program prints odd-numbered
  // pages shifted 500 printer units to the right.
  if (pDC->IsPrinting())
      if (0 == (pInfo->m_nCurPage & 1))
          pDC->SetViewportOrg(0, 0);
      else
          pDC->SetViewportOrg(500, 0);
}
```

In the previous example, if the page number is even, the printed page is shifted to the left. If the page number is odd, the printed page is shifted to the right.

OnPrint

The actual printing of each page occurs in the **OnPrint** function. The sample code on the following page prints a header, the page content, and the footer for each page. To copy this code for use in your own projects, see "Overriding OnPrint" on the accompanying CD-ROM.

MFC Development Using Microsoft Visual C++ 6.0

```cpp
// Handling the actual printing
// Samples\CH10\Prprevue
// PrinView.cpp
void CPrintView::OnPrint(CDC* pDC, CPrintInfo* pInfo)
{
  int BeginningRow, EndingRow, i, x, y;
  TEXTMETRIC tm;
  CSize cs;
  CString s;

  CPrintDoc* pDoc = GetDocument();
  ASSERT_VALID(pDoc);

  pDC->GetTextMetrics(&tm);

  // From the page currently being printed, determine the
  // starting row of this simulated text document.
  BeginningRow = (pInfo->m_nCurPage - 1) * GetPageLength();

  // From that determine the ending row, which can't be
  // greater than the number of lines in the document.
  EndingRow = BeginningRow + GetPageLength();
  if (EndingRow > pDoc->LinesOnDocument())
      EndingRow = pDoc->LinesOnDocument();

  // Load the page header from the string table, then print it
  // centered at the top of the page.
  s.LoadString(IDS_COMPANY_LOGO);
  cs = pDC->GetTextExtent(s);
  x = pDC->GetDeviceCaps(HORZRES);
  pDC->TextOut((x - cs.cx) / 2, 0, s);

  // Print the requested number of lines on the current page.
  y = 3 * tm.tmHeight;
  for (i = BeginningRow; i < EndingRow; i++, y += tm.tmHeight)
      pDC->TextOut(0, y, pDoc->GetLine(i + 1));

  // Print the page footer, centered on the bottom line.
  s.Format(IDS_PAGE, pInfo->m_nCurPage);
  cs = pDC->GetTextExtent(s);
  y = pDC->GetDeviceCaps(VERTRES);
  pDC->TextOut((x - cs.cx) / 2, y - cs.cy, s);
```

code continued on next page

code continued from previous page

```
    // Since this isn't a WYSIWYG application, the base class's function
    // should not be called, since it would then call OnDraw, which in
    // this application is intended ONLY for screen display.
    //CScrollView::OnPrint(pDC, pInfo);
}
```

OnEndPrintPreview

You can alter the behavior of Print Preview in a number of ways, such as:

- Display the Print Preview window with a scroll bar so that the user can view other pages in the document.
- Cause Print Preview to maintain the user's position in the document by beginning its display at the current page.
- Alter the appearance of information that is displayed in Print Preview, such as page numbers.

The following sample code overrides the **OnEndPrintPreview** function to cause the document view to display the last page displayed by Print Preview. To copy this code for use in your own projects, see "Overriding OnEndPrintPreview" on the accompanying CD-ROM.

```
// Setting the current page of the document view based on the page
// previewed last
// Samples\CH10\Prprevue
// Prinview.cpp
void CPrintView::OnEndPrintPreview(CDC* pDC, CPrintInfo* pInfo,
                                    POINT point, CPreviewView* pView)
{
    // We want to be able to scroll in the view to the page corresponding
    // to where the user scrolled during print preview.

    // The pDC argument points to a printer DC. We need a DC for the view.

    CClientDC dc(this);
```

code continued on next page

```
code continued from previous page

    // We'll need to know a character's height.
    TEXTMETRIC tm;
    dc.GetTextMetrics(&tm);

    CPoint pt;
    // Simple multiplication determines the point.
    pt.y = (pInfo->m_nCurPage - 1) * tm.tmHeight * GetPageLength();
    pt.x = 0;
    ScrollToPosition(pt);

    CScrollView::OnEndPrintPreview(pDC, pInfo, point, pView);
}
```

Lab 10.1: Adding Print and Print Preview to TextView

In this lab, you will implement the printing override functions and provide a way to calculate printer metrics.

To see the demonstration "Lab 10.1 Demonstration," see the accompanying CD-ROM.

Estimated time to complete this lab: **30 minutes**

To complete the exercises in this lab, you must have the required software. For detailed information about the labs and setup for the labs, see "Labs" in "About This Course."

The code that forms the starting point for this lab is located in the folder *<install folder>*\Labs\Ch10\Lab10.1\Ex01.

The solution code for this lab is located in the folder *<install folder>*\Labs\Ch10\Lab10.1\Ex01\Solution.

Objectives

After completing this lab, you will be able to:

◆ Prepare the **Print** dialog box.
◆ Display a print preview.

Lab 10.1: Adding Print and Print Preview to TextView

- Respond to the user's selection in the **Print** dialog box.
- Print data from a non-document class.

Prerequisites

Before working on this lab, you should be familiar with the following:

- Member functions of the **CDC** class

You may find it helpful to review the MSDN Library Visual Studio 98 Help topics on graphics before attempting this lab.

Exercises

The following exercise provides practice working with the concepts and techniques covered in this chapter.

- Exercise 1: Adding Printing to the Text Viewer

    In Lab 4.3 (Optional), Exercise 1, "Implementing a Basic Text Viewer," you implemented code to create a multiple document interface (MDI) text viewer with file selection, display, and scrolling capabilities. In this exercise, you will implement the additional support needed to print documents. You will also implement the printing override functions and provide a way to calculate printer metrics.

Exercise 1: Adding Printing to the Text Viewer

The code that forms the starting point for this exercise is in *<install folder>*\Labs\Ch10\Lab10.1\Ex01.

In Lab 4.3 (Optional), Exercise 1, "Implementing a Basic Text Viewer," you implemented code to create a multiple document interface (MDI) text viewer with file selection, display, and scrolling capabilities. In this exercise, you will implement the additional support needed to print documents. You will implement the printing override functions and provide a way to calculate printer metrics.

▶ **Prepare the interface file for printing**

1. In the file TextView.h, declare instance variables for the following key printer characteristics:

    - Size of a character cell
    - Number of printable lines per page
    - Number of pages that are to be printed

    These declarations are all part of the protected implementation section:

    ```
    //print properties
    CSize   m_PrintCharSize;
    int     m_nLinesPerPrintPage;
    int     m_nPrintPages;
    ```

2. Create public accessor methods for lines and pages as shown:

    ```
    int GetLinesPerPrintPage() const
        { return m_nLinesPerPrintPage; }
    int GetPrintPageCount() const
        {   return m_nPrintPages; }
    ```

3. Save TextView.h.

▶ **Modify the constructor to initialize the new instance variables**

1. In the file TextView.cpp, initialize both the lines per page and the number of pages to 0. The complete constructor code is as follows:

    ```
    CTextView::CTextView()
            :   m_ViewCharSize(0,0),
                m_DocSize(0,0)

    {
        m_pFont = NULL;
        //print
        m_nLinesPerPrintPage= 0;
        m_nPrintPages       = 0;
    }
    ```

2. Save TextView.cpp.

Lab 10.1: Adding Print and Print Preview to TextView

▶ **Implement OnPreparePrinting**

In this procedure, you will override the **OnPreparePrinting** function to display the **Print** dialog box.

1. Calculate the printer's metrics as follows:

    ```
    ComputePrintMetrics();
    ```

2. Set the number of the last page as follows:

    ```
    pInfo->SetMaxPage(GetPrintPageCount());
    ```

3. Disable the **Print To File** button as follows:

    ```
    pInfo->m_pPD->m_pd.Flags |= PD_DISABLEPRINTTOFILE;
    ```

4. Display the **Print and Print Preview** dialog box as follows:

    ```
    BOOL bRet = DoPreparePrinting(pInfo);
    ```

5. Set the number of preview pages to 1 as follows:

    ```
    pInfo->m_nNumPreviewPages = 1;
    ```

6. Return from the dialog box as follows:

    ```
    return (bRet);
    ```

7. Save TextView.cpp.

The sample code on the following page shows an example of how your code should look. To copy this code for use in your own projects, see "Lab 10.1.1 OnPreparePrinting" on the accompanying CD-ROM.

```
BOOL CTextView::OnPreparePrinting(CPrintInfo* pInfo)
{
  ComputePrintMetrics();
  pInfo->SetMaxPage(GetPrintPageCount());
  pInfo->m_pPD->m_pd.Flags |= PD_DISABLEPRINTTOFILE;

  BOOL bRet = DoPreparePrinting(pInfo);

  pInfo->m_nNumPreviewPages = 1;
  return bRet;
}
```

▶ Implement ComputePrintMetrics

In this procedure, you will implement a function named **ComputePrintMetrics** that calculates the basic metrics for the printer device context (DC).

1. Declare a protected function in TextView.h as follows:

   ```
   void ComputePrintMetrics();
   ```

2. Define the function in TextView.cpp as follows:

   ```
   void CTextView::ComputePrintMetrics()
   ```

3. Get a pointer to the document object as follows:

   ```
   CTextDoc* pDoc = GetDocument();
   ```

4. Create the printer DC and set its mapping mode as follows:

   ```
   CDC* pDC = CreatePrinterDC();
   pDC->SetMapMode(MM_LOENGLISH);
   ```

5. Select the font into the DC, and retrieve its text metrics as follows:

   ```
   CFont* pPreviousFont = pDC->SelectObject(GetFont());
   TEXTMETRIC tm;
   pDC->GetTextMetrics(&tm);
   ```

6. Calculate the size of the character cells in device metrics as follows:

    ```
    m_PrintCharSize.cy = tm.tmHeight + tm.tmExternalLeading;
    m_PrintCharSize.cx = tm.tmAveCharWidth;
    pDC->LPtoDP(&m_PrintCharSize);
    ```

7. Retrieve the height of a page and calculate the number of lines per page as follows:

    ```
    int nPhysDevHeight = pDC->GetDeviceCaps(PHYSICALHEIGHT);
    int nPhysOffsetY  = pDC->GetDeviceCaps(PHYSICALOFFSETY);
    nPhysDevHeight -= nPhysOffsetY * 2;
    m_nLinesPerPrintPage = abs(nPhysDevHeight/m_PrintCharSize.cy );
    ```

8. Set the margin to 8 lines as follows:

    ```
    m_nLinesPerPrintPage -= 8;
    ```

9. From the lines per page, calculate the number of pages that will be printed as follows:

    ```
    m_nPrintPages = pDoc->GetLineList()->GetCount() /
                                        m_nLinesPerPrintPage;
    if (pDoc->GetLineList()->GetCount() % m_nLinesPerPrintPage)
    {
        m_nPrintPages++;
    }
    ```

10. Replace the old font in the DC before you destroy the DC as follows:

    ```
    if(pPreviousFont)
    {
        pDC->SelectObject(pPreviousFont);
    }
    ::DeleteDC(pDC->GetSafeHdc());
    ```

11. Save TextView.cpp.

The following sample code shows an example of how your code should look. To copy this code for use in your own projects, see "Lab 10.1.1 ComputePrintMetrics" on the accompanying CD-ROM.

```cpp
void CTextView::ComputePrintMetrics()
{
    CTextDoc* pDoc = GetDocument();

    CDC* pDC = CreatePrinterDC();
    pDC->SetMapMode(MM_LOENGLISH);

    CFont* pPreviousFont = pDC->SelectObject(GetFont());
    TEXTMETRIC tm;
    pDC->GetTextMetrics(&tm);

    m_PrintCharSize.cy = tm.tmHeight + tm.tmExternalLeading;
    m_PrintCharSize.cx = tm.tmAveCharWidth;
    pDC->LPtoDP(&m_PrintCharSize);

    int nPhysDevHeight = pDC->GetDeviceCaps(PHYSICALHEIGHT);
    int nPhysOffsetY = pDC->GetDeviceCaps(PHYSICALOFFSETY);
    nPhysDevHeight -= nPhysOffsetY * 2;

    m_nLinesPerPrintPage = abs(nPhysDevHeight/m_PrintCharSize.cy );
    m_nLinesPerPrintPage -= 8;

    m_nPrintPages = pDoc->GetLineList()->GetCount() /
                                        m_nLinesPerPrintPage;
    if (pDoc->GetLineList()->GetCount() % m_nLinesPerPrintPage)
    {
        m_nPrintPages++;
    }

    if(pPreviousFont)
    {
        pDC->SelectObject(pPreviousFont);
    }
    ::DeleteDC(pDC->GetSafeHdc());
}
```

Lab 10.1: Adding Print and Print Preview to TextView

▶ **Implement the CreatePrinterDC function**

1. Declare a protected function in TextView.h as follows:

   ```
   CDC* CreatePrinterDC();
   ```

2. Save TextView.h.

3. In TextView.cpp, define **CreatePrinterDC** as follows:

   ```
   CDC* CTextView::CreatePrinterDC()
   {
       PRINTDLG PrtDlg;
       HDC      hDC;
   ```

4. Determine whether or not you have a printer installed as follows:

   ```
   if (!AfxGetApp()->GetPrinterDeviceDefaults(&PrtDlg))
   ```

5. If you don't have a printer, display text on the screen DC:

   ```
   hDC = ::CreateDC("display",NULL,NULL,NULL);
   ```

6. If you do have a printer, show the **Print** dialog box as follows:

   ```
   CPrintDialog dlg(FALSE);
   dlg.m_pd.hDevMode = PrtDlg.hDevMode;
   dlg.m_pd.hDevNames = PrtDlg.hDevNames;
   hDC = dlg.CreatePrinterDC();
   ```

7. Create a pointer to a **CDC** instance from the handle to the DC that you have been using as follows:

   ```
   CDC* pDC = CDC::FromHandle(hDC);
   ```

8. Mark this DC as printing, so **CScrollView::OnPrepareDC** won't modify the viewport:

   ```
   pDC->m_bPrinting = TRUE;
   ```

9. Return the pointer to the CDC:

   ```
   return pDC;
   ```

10. Save TextView.cpp.

527

The following sample code shows an example of how your code should look. To copy this code for use in your own projects, see "Lab 10.1.1 CreatePrinterDC" on the accompanying CD-ROM.

```
CDC* CTextView::CreatePrinterDC()
{
  PRINTDLG PrtDlg;
  HDC      hDC;

  if (!AfxGetApp()->GetPrinterDeviceDefaults(&PrtDlg))
  {
      hDC = ::CreateDC("display",NULL,NULL,NULL);
  }
  else
  {
      CPrintDialog dlg(FALSE);
      dlg.m_pd.hDevMode = PrtDlg.hDevMode;
      dlg.m_pd.hDevNames = PrtDlg.hDevNames;
      hDC = dlg.CreatePrinterDC();
  }

  CDC* pDC = CDC::FromHandle(hDC);
  pDC->m_bPrinting = TRUE;
  return pDC;
}
```

▶ **Implement OnBeginPrinting**

In this procedure, you will invoke the **ComputePrintMetrics** function.

1. In the **CTextView::OnBeginPrinting**, make a call to **ComputePrintMetrics** that calculates the basic metrics for the printer DC:

    ComputePrintMetrics();

2. Save TextView.cpp.

For more information about the **OnBeginPrinting** function, see "Overriding CView-Derived Functions" on page 515 in this chapter.

Lab 10.1: Adding Print and Print Preview to TextView

▶ Implement OnPrint

In this procedure, you will override the function **OnPrint** to start actual printing.

1. Use ClassWizard or WizardBar to create **CTextView::OnPrint**.
2. Calculate which lines to print, using **ComputePrintableLines**:

   ```
   int nFirstLn, nLastLn;
   ComputePrintableLines(pDC, pInfo, nFirstLn, nLastLn);
   ```

3. Call the core **OnDraw** handler that you developed in Lab 4.3, Exercise 1, "Implementing a Basic Text Viewer:"

   ```
   OnDraw(pDC, nFirstLn, nLastLn);
   ```

4. Save TextView.cpp.

The following sample code shows an example of how your code should look. To copy this code for use in your own projects, see "Lab 10.1.1 OnPrint" on the accompanying CD-ROM.

```
void CTextView::OnPrint(CDC* pDC, CPrintInfo* pInfo)
{
    int nFirstLn, nLastLn;
    ComputePrintableLines(pDC, pInfo, nFirstLn, nLastLn);
    OnDraw(pDC, nFirstLn, nLastLn);
}
```

▶ Implement the ComputePrintableLines function

1. Declare a protected function in TextView.h as follows:

   ```
   void ComputePrintableLines( CDC* pDC, CPrintInfo* pInfo,
                               int& nFirst, int& nLast);
   ```

2. Save TextView.h.
3. In TextView.cpp, define **ComputePrintableLines** as follows:

   ```
   void CTextView::ComputePrintableLines( CDC*       pDC,
                                          CPrintInfo* pInfo,
                                          int&        nFirst,
                                          int&        nLast)
   ```

4. Get the document so that you will know how many lines are available to print as follows:

   ```
   CTextDoc* pDoc = GetDocument();
   ```

5. Set the first line equal to the number of lines per page multiplied by the zero-based page number:

   ```
   nFirst = GetLinesPerPrintPage() * (pInfo->m_nCurPage-1);
   ```

6. Set the last line equal to the first line plus the number of lines per page (or the last line in the document) as follows:

   ```
   nLast  = min( nFirst + GetLinesPerPrintPage() - 1,
                 pDoc->GetLineList()->GetCount() - 1);
   ```

7. Save TextView.cpp.

The following sample code shows an example of how your code should look. To copy this code for use in your own projects, see "Lab 10.1.1 ComputePrintableLines" on the accompanying CD-ROM.

```
void CTextView::ComputePrintableLines( CDC*        pDC,
                                       CPrintInfo* pInfo,
                                       int&        nFirst,
                                       int&        nLast)
{
  CTextDoc* pDoc = GetDocument();

  nFirst = GetLinesPerPrintPage() * (pInfo->m_nCurPage-1);
  nLast  = min( nFirst + GetLinesPerPrintPage() - 1,
                pDoc->GetLineList()->GetCount() - 1);
}
```

▶ **Build and test your application**

- Run your application. Open a file and try printing using the **Print** option. Use Print Preview to preview the file.

 **Note** Before you test your application, ensure that a printer is installed on your machine.

The solution code for this exercise is located in the folder *<install folder>*\Labs\Ch10\Lab10.1\Ex01\Solution.

Sample Applications

Here is the description of the sample application related to this chapter. The sample application is located in the folder \Samples\Ch10.

Sample application subfolder	Description of application
Prprevue	Implements default print and print preview functionality in an MFC application. Shows how to enhance printing capability by overriding **CView** printing functions.

Self-Check Questions

To see the answers to the Self-Check Questions, see Appendix A.

1. **Which statement determines where to redirect the output of the OnDraw function?**

    A. **CDC*** *pDC*

    B. **const CRect&** *rcBounds*

    C. **const CRect&** *rcInvalid*

    D. **CPrintInfo*** *pInfo*

2. **If you do not know the number of pages to print at the start of the process, which function will you override to provide print-time pagination?**

    A. **CView::OnPreparePrinting**

    B. **CView::DoPreparePrinting**

    C. **CView::OnPrepareDC**

    D. **CView::OnPrint**

3. What are the three major steps in the printing process?
   A. Displaying the **Print** dialog box, customizing it, and printing the document
   B. Customizing the **Print** dialog box, displaying it, and printing the document based on the settings selected by the user
   C. Showing a preview of the document, displaying the **Print** dialog box, and printing the document
   D. Overriding the **CView** member functions, displaying the **Print** dialog box, and printing the document.

Appendix A: Self-Check Answers

Chapter 2

1. **Which type of edit is supported by Edit and Continue?**
   - A. Editing header files

     Incorrect

     The Edit and Continue feature does not allow you to edit header files.
   - B. Editing function prototypes

     Incorrect

     The Edit and Continue feature does not allow you to edit function prototypes.
   - C. Editing functions on the call stack

     Correct

     You can edit functions on the call stack.
   - D. Editing C++ class definitions

     Incorrect

     The Edit and Continue feature does not allow you to edit C++ class definitions.

   For more information, see *Using the Edit and Continue Feature*, page 21.

2. **Which keyword transfers control to the matching exception handler?**
   - A. abort

     Incorrect

     The **abort** keyword terminates an application when no matching handler can be found.

B. try

   Incorrect

   The **try** keyword identifies a guard block.

C. throw

   Correct

   The **throw** keyword transfers control to the matching exception handler.

D. catch

   Incorrect

   The **catch** keyword is used to identify an exception handler.

For more information, see *Handling Exceptions*, page 24.

3. What is the base class for exception types in MFC?

A. CMemoryException

   Incorrect

   This is an extension of the base class meaning out of memory.

B. CResourceException

   Incorrect

   This is an extension of the base class designating a Windows resource-allocation exception.

C. CUserException

   Incorrect

   This is an extension of the base class that alerts the user with a message box, then throws a generic **CException**.

D. CException

   Correct

   The base class, **CException**, provides two member functions, **ReportError** and **GetErrorMessage**, to assist in handling exceptions.

For more information, see *MFC Exception Classes*, page 28.

4. What is the purpose of the stack unwinding process?

- A. Delivery of the exception object to the matching **catch** handler.

  Incorrect

  The stack unwinding process begins after the exception object is delivered to the **catch** handler.

- B. Destruction of automatic objects in the order in which they were created.

  Incorrect

  The stack unwinding process involves destruction of automatic objects in the reverse order.

- C. A call to the predefined **terminate** function.

  Incorrect

  The terminate function is called only when a matching **catch** handler is not found. When a matching **catch** handler is found, the stack unwinding process takes place to handle the exception.

- D. Destruction of local objects in the affected part of the stack in the reverse order.

  Correct

  Stack unwinding involves destruction of local objects in the reverse order.

For more information, see *Exception-Handling Process*, page 27.

Chapter 3

1. Which function adds menu items to a cascading menu?

- A. AppendMenuItems

  Incorrect

  This is not a valid member function of the **CMenu** class.

- B. AddPopupItems

  Incorrect

  This is not a valid member function of the **CMenu** class.

- C. AppendMenu

  Correct

  You use the **AppendMenu** function to add menu items to a cascading menu at run time.

D. **AddMenu**

   Incorrect

   This is not a valid member function of the **CMenu** class.

For more information, see *Implementing Cascading Menus*, page 45.

2. To create a dockable toolbar, which steps must you complete?

A. You only need to enable docking for the frame window.

   Incorrect

   You must complete all three steps: enable docking for the frame, enable docking for each toolbar you want to be dockable, and dock the toolbar to the frame.

B. You only need to enable docking for each toolbar you want to be dockable.

   Incorrect

   You must complete all three steps: enable docking for the frame, enable docking for each toolbar you want to be dockable, and dock the toolbar to the frame.

C. You only need to add code to dock the toolbar to a frame window.

   Incorrect

   You must complete all three steps: enable docking for the frame, enable docking for each toolbar you want to be dockable, and dock the toolbar to the frame.

D. You must complete all three steps: enable docking for the frame, enable docking for each toolbar you want to be dockable, and dock the toolbar to the frame.

   Correct

   You must complete all three steps: enable docking for the frame, enable docking for each toolbar you want to be dockable, and dock the toolbar to the frame.

For more information, see *Enabling Docking in a Frame Window*, page 50.

3. Which drawing type must you specify to include graphics in a status bar?

A. SBT_IMAGES

   Incorrect

   This is not a valid drawing type.

B. SBT_OWNERDRAW

   Correct

   You must specify **SBT_OWNERDRAW** in the **SetText()** function to include graphics in a status bar.

C. SBT_NOBORDERS
   Incorrect
   This property does not add graphics to a status bar.

D. SBT_POPOUT
   Incorrect
   This property does not add graphics to a status bar.

For more information, see *Enhancing Status Bars*, page 54.

4. How do you invoke modal and modeless dialog boxes?

A. Invoke modal dialog boxes with **CDialog::DoModal**. Invoke modeless dialog boxes with **CDialog::Create**.
   Correct

B. Invoke modal dialog boxes with **CDialog::DoModal**. Invoke modeless dialog boxes with **CDialog::DoModeless**.
   Incorrect
   DoModeless is not a member of the **CDialog** class.

C. Invoke modal dialog boxes with **CModal::Create**. Invoke modeless dialog boxes with **CModeless::Create**.
   Incorrect
   CModeless is not a valid MFC class.

D. Invoke modal dialog boxes with **CDialog::Create**. Invoke modeless dialog boxes with **CDialog::DoModal**.
   Incorrect
   The reverse is true.

For more information, see *Using Modeless Dialog Boxes*, page 83.

5. What is the advantage of using common dialog boxes?

A. Makes your code portable across operating systems.
   Incorrect
   Common dialog boxes are system dialog boxes that you can use for implementing operations that are common to many applications.

B. Improves run-time performance of your applications.
   Incorrect
   Common dialog boxes are system dialog boxes that you can use for implementing operations that are common to many applications.
C. Reduces time needed to build property sheets and tabbed dialog boxes.
   Incorrect
   Property sheets and tabbed dialog boxes are derived from **CPropertyPage** and not from common dialog boxes.
D. Makes the user interface of your applications consistent with other Windows-based applications.
   Correct
   Using common dialog boxes makes your application consistent with other Windows-based applications.

For more information, see *Customizing Common Dialog Boxes*, page 60.

6. Which is the base class of a dialog bar control?

A. **CDlgCtrl**
   Incorrect
   This is not a valid MFC class.
B. **CReBar**
   Incorrect
   CReBar is the base class for rebar controls.
C. **CDialog**
   Incorrect
   CDialog is the base class for dialog boxes.
D. **CDialogBar**
   Correct
   CDialogBar forms the base class for dialog bars.

For more information, see *Using Dialog Bars*, page 90.

Appendix A: Self-Check Answers

7. Which function adds controls to a rebar?

- A. SetReBarCtrl()

  Incorrect

  This is not a member function of the **CReBar** class.

- B. AddReBar()

  Incorrect

  This is not a member function of the **CReBar** class.

- C. AddBar()

  Correct

  You use the **CReBar::AddBar()** member function to add controls to a rebar.

- D. GetReBarCtrl()

  Incorrect

  This function provides direct access to the underlying rebar control. It does not add controls to a rebar.

For more information, see *Adding Child Windows to a Rebar*, page 96.

Chapter 4

1. What is the relationship between views and other framework classes?

- A. A view is owned by the mainframe object.

  Incorrect

  A view is the child of a main frame window.

- B. A view is embedded in its corresponding document object.

  Incorrect

  Although these classes contain pointers to each other.

- C. A view is refreshed by the mainframe object.

  Incorrect

  The document object is responsible for refreshing its views.

- D. A view displays the contents of a document object.

  Correct

  This is the primary concept behind the document/view architecture.

For more information, see *The CView Class*, page 131.

539

2. How do you enhance an existing application to support a scrolling view?

A. By adding code to the **OnInitialUpdate** function
   Incorrect
   Replace the name of the base class of the view with **CScrollView**.

B. By setting the base class of the view to **CScrollView**
   Correct
   Scrolling capability is implemented in the class **CScrollView**.

C. By calling CView::SetScrollSizes
   Incorrect
   Replace the name of the base class of the view with **CScrollView**.

D. By adding a scrollbar object to the view
   Incorrect
   Replace the name of the base class of the view with **CScrollView**.

For more information, see *Adding Scrolling Views*, page 147.

3. What differentiates a dynamic splitter window from a static splitter window?

A. Static splitters cannot have different views associated with each pane, whereas dynamic splitters can.
   Incorrect
   The reverse is true.

B. Dynamic splitters have no maximum number of panes, but static splitters are limited to 256 panes.
   Incorrect
   Dynamic splitters are limited to only four panes, whereas static splitters are limited to 256 panes.

C. You must declare a **CDynSplitterWnd** object for a dynamic splitter and a **CSplitterWnd** object for static splitters.
   Incorrect
   You declare a **CSplitterWnd** object for both types of splitters.

D. Dynamic splitter windows can be destroyed at run time, whereas static splitter windows cannot.

Correct

Dynamic splitter windows can be created and destroyed at run time, whereas static splitter windows cannot be created or destroyed at run time.

For more information, see *Implementing Splitter Windows*, page 151.

4. Which property name-value pairs is set by AppWizard for a form view?

A. Style: Popup
Incorrect
MFC AppWizard sets **Style** to **Child**.

B. Border: None
Correct
MFC AppWizard sets **Border** to **None**.

C. Titlebar: On
Incorrect
MFC AppWizard sets **Titlebar** to **Off**.

D. System Modal: On
Incorrect
MFC AppWizard does not set the **System Modal** property for a form view.

For more information, see *User-Defined Form Views*, page 162.

5. Which class is used as the base class for control views?

A. CControlView
Incorrect
This is not a valid MFC class.

B. CCtrlView
Correct
All control views are derived from **CCtrlView**.

C. CListView
Incorrect
CListView is the base class for list views, and not for all control views.

D. CView

Incorrect

CView is not the base class for creating views with embedded controls.

For more information, see *Implementing Control Views*, page 166.

Chapter 5

1. What are events?

A. The actions that the ActiveX control can perform at the request of the container

Incorrect

Methods are the actions that the control can perform at the request of the container.

B. The settings that change the appearance or behavior of an ActiveX control

Incorrect

Properties are settings that change the appearance or behavior of an ActiveX control.

C. The notifications that an ActiveX control container sends to an ActiveX control in response to user interaction or some other occurrence

Incorrect

Events are not the notifications that a container sends to an ActiveX control, but the notifications that the ActiveX control sends to the control container in response to user interaction or some other occurrence.

D. The notifications that an ActiveX control sends to an ActiveX control container in response to user interaction or some other occurrence

Correct

Events are notification messages that a control sends to its container. These are very similar to notification messages that a common control sends to its parent dialog box.

For more information, see *Using Automation*, page 232.

2. What does a .odl file contain?

A. The specification for the interface that an object supports, including its properties, methods, and events, in text format

Correct

An .odl (Object Description Language) file is a text file that provides the specification for the interface that an object supports, including its properties, methods, and events.

B. Information to provide a common interface for the control with many different kinds of applications, in binary format

Incorrect

The binary file that contains information to provide a common interface for the control with many different kinds of applications is the type-library (.tlb) file.

C. Executable code for the ActiveX control

Incorrect

The executable code for the ActiveX control is contained in the .ocx file.

D. Dynamic-link library routines that are loaded with the ActiveX control

Incorrect

No correlation exists.

For more information, see *Using Automation*, page 232.

3. Which notification message is sent if the progress control cannot complete an operation because there is not enough memory available?

A. MCN_GETDAYSTATE

Incorrect

MCN_GETDAYSTATE is a **CMonthCalCtrl** notification message.

For more information, see *Processing Notification Messages from Controls Supplied by MFC*, page 245.

B. IPN_FIELDCHANGED

Incorrect

IPN_FIELDCHANGED is a **CIPAddressCtrl** notification message.

For more information, see *Processing Notification Messages from Controls Supplied by MFC*, page 245.

MFC Development Using Microsoft Visual C++ 6.0

C. NM_OUTOFMEMORY

Correct

NM_OUTOFMEMORY is the notification message that is sent if the progress control cannot complete an operation because there is not enough memory available.

For more information, see *Processing Notification Messages from Controls Supplied by MFC*, page 245.

D. CMemoryException

Incorrect

CMemoryException is an object that represents an out-of-memory exception condition and is not an event. Memory exceptions are thrown automatically by **new**.

For more information, see *Handling Errors and Exceptions*, page 22.

Chapter 6

1. **Which dispatch map entry do you use to access a set of values through a single control property?**

    A. DISP_PROPERTY_NOTIFY

    Incorrect

    Used when you need to be notified that a property value has changed.

    B. DISP_PROPERTY

    Incorrect

    Used when it is not important to know when the property value changes.

    C. DISP_PROPERTY_PARAM

    Correct

    Used when you want to access a set of values through a single control property.

    D. DISP_PROPERTY_EX

    Incorrect

    Used when you need to compute the value of a property at run time, perform validation, or implement read-only or write-only properties.

    For more information, see *Custom Properties*, page 285.

Appendix A: Self-Check Answers

2. Implementing an ActiveX control's default property page most closely resembles which other process?

   A. Adding controls to a normal dialog box
      Correct

      Except that there is an extra string that you must enter when you add the associated member variable: the name of the OLE property.

   B. Adding data-bound controls to a **CDaoRecordView** form
      Incorrect

      There is no backing database for an ActiveX control property.

   C. Reading and writing to the registry
      Incorrect

      Although it might be desirable to store a property's value in the registry, there is no connection between the registry and the ActiveX control's property page.

   D. Associating a toolbar button with a menu item
      Incorrect

      There is no correlation here.

For more information, see *Implementing ActiveX Control Property Pages*, page 296.

3. What is a data-bound ActiveX control?

   A. An ActiveX control that is bound to a field in a database
      Incorrect

      Although this is a common implementation of the concept, it is not a requirement.

   B. An ActiveX control whose **Get/Set** methods have RFX, DFX, or DDX entries to enable the exchange of information
      Incorrect

      These information exchange techniques have little to do with an ActiveX control.

C. A negotiation between a control and its container, in which the container gives permission to the control to change a property value, and is informed when the control does so
Correct
It is up to the container to provide the interface between the control and the actual data item to be changed.

D. An ActiveX control with information overload
Incorrect

For more information, see *Data Binding in an ActiveX Control*, page 330.

Chapter 7

1. What is the role of a data provider?

A. Expose the data in a tabular format.
Correct
A data provider exposes its data in a tabular format.

B. Facilitate data access by a consumer.
Incorrect
A service provider facilitates data access by a consumer.

C. Retrieve data from a data source.
Incorrect
A data provider exposes its data in a tabular format.

D. Store data in a tabular format.
Incorrect
A data provider exposes its data in a tabular format.

For more information, see *Types of OLE DB Applications*, page 341.

2. Which OLE DB component helps you search for data sources?

A. Data source objects
Incorrect
A data source object helps you access a data source.

B. Sessions

   Incorrect

   A session object helps you define transactions.

C. Commands

   Incorrect

   A command object helps you execute commands.

D. Enumerators

   Correct

For more information, see *OLE DB Components*, page 342.

3. Which base class of the consumer template classes encapsulates a rowset and its accessors?

A. CTable

   Incorrect

   This class is derived from **CAccessorRowset,** which encapsulates the functionality of a rowset and its accessors.

B. CCommand

   Incorrect

   This class is derived from **CAccessorRowset,** which encapsulates the functionality of a rowset and its accessors.

C. CAccessorRowset

   Correct

D. CDataSource

   Incorrect

   CDataSource represents a connection to a data source.

For more information, see *OLE DB Consumer Templates*, page 347.

4. Which function creates a data source object?

A. OpenRowset

   Incorrect

   This function creates a rowset.

B. CoCreateInstance

   Correct

C. Initialize

   Incorrect

   This function initializes a data source object.

D. CreateSession

   Incorrect

   This function creates a session object.

For more information, see *OLE DB Provider Templates*, page 345.

5. Which is the default base view class for consumer applications that use CAccessor?

A. CFormView

   Incorrect

   COleDBRecordView is the base class for OLE DB consumer applications that use **CAccessor** to retrieve data.

B. CView

   Incorrect

   COleDBRecordView is the base class for OLE DB consumer applications that use **CAccessor** to retrieve data.

C. COleDBRecordView

   Correct

D. CListView

   Incorrect

   COleDBRecordView is the base class for OLE DB consumer applications that use **CAccessor** to retrieve data.

For more information, see *COleDBRecordView Class*, page 355.

Chapter 8

1. Which object contains information on the data provider and the underlying schema?

   A. Connection

      Correct

      The **Connection** object contains information about the data source and the underlying schema.

   B. Recordset

      Incorrect

      The **Recordset** object represents the set of records retrieved from the database.

   C. Command

      Incorrect

      The **Command** object defines a specific command that you intend to execute on a data source.

   D. Field

      Incorrect

      The **Field** object represents a column of data.

For more information, see *ADO Object Model*, page 391.

2. Which object contains an Errors collection created in response to a failure involving the provider?

   A. Connection

      Correct

      A **Connection** object contains an **Errors** collection, which consists of all the **Error** objects created in response to a single failure involving the provider.

   B. Command

      Incorrect

      A **Command** object contains a **Parameters** collection made up of **Parameter** objects.

   C. Recordset

      Incorrect

      A **Recordset** object has a **Fields** collection made up of **Field** objects.

D. Parameters

   Incorrect

   A **Parameter** object represents a parameter of the specific command. A **Command** object contains a **Parameters** collection made up of **Parameter** objects.

For more information, see *ADO Object Model*, page 391.

3. Which edition of Visual C++ provides the ADO Data Bound Dialog Wizard?

A. Professional only

   Incorrect

   The ADO Data Bound Dialog Wizard is not available in the Professional edition.

B. Enterprise only

   Correct

C. Both Professional and Enterprise

   Incorrect

   The ADO Data Bound Dialog Wizard is not available in the Professional edition.

D. Both Standard and Enterprise

   Incorrect

   The ADO Data Bound Dialog Wizard is not available in the Standard edition.

For more information, see *Using ADO in MFC Applications*, page 393.

4. Which event occurs after the WillMove event?

A. MoveComplete

   Correct

   The **MoveComplete** event occurs after the **WillMove** event.

   For more information, see *ADO Data Control*, page 394.

B. WillChangeField

   Incorrect

   The **WillChangeField** event occurs before a pending operation changes the value of one or more Field objects in the **Recordset**.

   For more information, see *ADO Data Control*, page 394.

C. MoveNext

   Incorrect

   The **MoveNext** method moves to the next record in a displayed recordset and makes that record the current record.

   For more information, see *ADO Object Model*, page 391.

D. MoveLast

   Incorrect

   The **MoveLast** method moves to the last record in a displayed recordset and makes that record the current record.

   For more information, see *ADO Object Model*, page 391.

5. Which property of a data-bound control needs to be set in order to bind it to an ADO data control?

A. RecordSource

   Incorrect

   The **RecordSource** property of an ADO data control defines the recordset.

   For more information, see *ADO Data Control*, page 394.

B. ConnectionString

   Incorrect

   The **ConnectionString** property of an ADO data control contains the information used to establish a connection to a data source.

   For more information, see *ADO Data Control*, page 394.

C. DataSourceName

   Incorrect

   The **DataSourceName** property of an ADO data control specifies the name of the data source.

   For more information, see *ADO Data Control*, page 394.

D. DataSource
    Correct
    The **DataSource** property of a data-bound control is set to bind it to an ADO data control.

    For more information, see *Data-bound Controls*, page 396.

Chapter 9

1. The primary purpose of the CFtpFileFind class is to find which files?

A. The first file that matches a search string on an FTP server
   Incorrect
   The class can find all files on a server, or across multiple servers, but the search needs to be reset after each directory/server change.

B. All files in the current FTP directory that match the search string
   Correct
   The class can find all files on a server, or across multiple servers, but the search needs to be reset after each directory/server change.

C. All files in the entire FTP server that match the search string
   Incorrect
   The class can find all files on a server, or across multiple servers, but the search needs to be reset after each directory/server change.

D. All files on all active FTP servers that match the search string
   Incorrect
   The class can find all files on a server, or across multiple servers, but the search needs to be reset after each directory/server change.

For more information, see *Writing FTP Applications*, page 477.

2. Which classes are used by CSocket to simplify sending and receiving data using a socket?

A. CHttpConnection and CHtmlStream
   Incorrect
   The **CSocketFile** and **CArchive** classes simplify sending and receiving data by enabling you to use serialization to read and write data.

B. **CAsyncSocket** and **COleStream**
   Incorrect

   The **CSocketFile** and **CArchive** classes simplify sending and receiving data by enabling you to use serialization to read and write data.

C. **CInternetFile** and **CInternetSession**
   Incorrect

   The **CSocketFile** and **CArchive** classes simplify sending and receiving data by enabling you to use serialization to read and write data.

D. **CSocketFile** and **CArchive**
   Correct

   The **CSocketFile** and **CArchive** classes simplify sending and receiving data by enabling you to use serialization to read and write data.

For more information, see *MFC Support for WinSock*, page 485.

3. Which type of socket should be established by the application to make communication between two computers reliable?

A. Raw
   Incorrect

   A connection-oriented (streaming) socket uses a reliable underlying protocol, such as TCP, to provide a connection between computers that guarantees data delivery. Raw sockets can be used, but the application must provide the reliability.

B. Connection-oriented (streaming)
   Correct

   A connection-oriented (streaming) socket uses a reliable underlying protocol, such as TCP, to provide a connection between computers that guarantees data delivery. Raw sockets can be used, but the application must provide the reliability.

C. Datagram
   Incorrect

   A connection-oriented (streaming) socket uses a reliable underlying protocol, such as TCP, to provide a connection between computers that guarantees data delivery. Raw sockets can be used, but the application must provide the reliability.

D. Connectionless

   Incorrect

   A connection-oriented (streaming) socket uses a reliable underlying protocol, such as TCP, to provide a connection between computers that guarantees data delivery. Raw sockets can be used, but the application must provide the reliability.

For more information, see *Introduction to Sockets*, page 480.

4. **Which wrapper class does ClassWizard create for Internet Explorer object?**

   A. CWebBrowser2

   Incorrect

   ClassWizard creates this class for a **Web Browser** control.

   B. IWebBrowserApp

   Correct

   ClassWizard creates this class as a wrapper for the **Internet Explorer** object.

   C. CWinInet

   Incorrect

   This is not a valid MFC class.

   D. CWebBrowserApp

   Incorrect

   This is not a valid MFC class.

For more information, see *Controlling Internet Explorer*, page 456.

Chapter 10

1. **Which statement determines where to redirect the output of the OnDraw function?**

   A. CDC* pDC

   Correct

   Depending on what the pDC parameter represents, the output is redirected appropriately.

B. **const CRect& *rcBounds***

   Incorrect

   This does not represent the destination of the output.

C. **const CRect& *rcInvalid***

   Incorrect

   This represents the rectangular area that needs repainting.

D. **CPrintInfo* pInfo**

   Incorrect

   This is not an argument of the **OnDraw** function.

For more information, see *MFC Support for Printing*, page 507.

2. If you do not know the number of pages to print at the start of the process, which function will you override to provide print-time pagination?

A. **CView::OnPreparePrinting**

   Incorrect

   This function is overridden only when you have prior knowledge of the total number of pages.

B. **CView::DoPreparePrinting**

   Incorrect

   This function is called by **OnPreparePrinting** to display the (common) print dialog box.

C. **CView::OnPrepareDC**

   Correct

   Called before each page is printed. You can use this function to dynamically adjust the DC attributes or page count.

D. **CView::OnPrint**

   Incorrect

   This function actually prints the current page, so it is too late to alter the current page count.

For more information, see *Introduction to the Printing Process*, page 506.

3. What are the three major steps in the printing process?

A. Displaying the **Print** dialog box, customizing it, and printing the document
   Incorrect
   The **Print** dialog box is customized before it is displayed to the user.

B. Customizing the **Print** dialog box, displaying it, and printing the document based on the settings selected by the user
   Correct

C. Showing a preview of the document, displaying the **Print** dialog box, and printing the document
   Incorrect
   Displaying a preview of the document is not part of the printing process.

D. Overriding the **CView** member functions, displaying the **Print** dialog box, and printing the document.
   Incorrect
   Overriding the **CView** member functions is not part of the printing process. It is done to implement the printing process.

For more information, see *Introduction to the Printing Process*, page 506.

Glossary

.APS
A binary version of the current resource file that is created by the Microsoft Visual Studio and used for quick loading of resources. Microsoft Visual Studio gives this file an .APS filename extension.

.BSC
A file created from source browser information (SBR) files, using the Microsoft Browse Information File Maintenance Utility (BSCMAKE). Browse information files can be examined in browse windows and usually have a .BSC extension.

.CLW
A file that ClassWizard generates, containing information needed to edit existing classes or add new classes to a project. ClassWizard also uses the ClassWizard file to store information needed to create and edit message maps and dialog data maps, and to create prototype member functions. ClassWizard files have a .CLW filename extension.

.CUR
A file that contains an image that defines the shape of a cursor on the screen. Cursor resource files usually have a .CUR filename extension.

.DSP
Formerly known as the .MAK file. The project build file that specifies how to build a particular project in a project workspace. The file contains source file names and locations, build settings, and debug settings, including breakpoints and watches. In terms of source control, .DSP files can be shared.

.DSW
A file created and maintained by Visual Studio that contains information formerly stored as part of the .MDP file. The file contains information about the project workspace such as a list of all the projects. This file is used by Visual Studio and should not be edited by the user. In terms of source control, the .DSW file can be shared.

.EXE
A program file created from one or more source code files translated into machine code and linked together. The MS-DOS, Windows, and Windows NT operating systems use the .EXE filename extension to indicate that the file is a runnable program.

.EXP

A file that contains information about exported functions and data items. The Microsoft 32-Bit Library Manager tool (LIB.EXE) generates the exports file from the module-definition (.DEF) file. The linker uses the exports file to build the dynamic-link library (.DLL) file. Exports files have a .EXP filename extension.

.H

An external source file, identified at the beginning of a program, that contains commonly used data types and variables used by functions in the program. The #include directive is used to tell the compiler to insert the contents of a header file into the program.

.HLP

A file that contains text and graphics needed to communicate online information about an application. Each help file contains one or more topics a user can select by clicking hot spots, using the keyword search, or browsing through topics. Help files have a .HLP filename extension. See also *Help topic*.

.HM

A file that defines Help context IDs corresponding to the IDs of dialog boxes, menu commands, and other resources in an application. The AppWizard file MAKEHELP.BAT calls the MAKEHM tool to generate this file from the contents of a RESOURCE.H file. The Help map file has a .HM filename extension.

.ICO

In Windows, a file that contains a bitmap of an icon. Icon files usually have a .ICO filename extension.

.ILK

A state file generated to hold status information for later incremental links of the program. The file has the same base name as the executable file or dynamic-link library and the filename extension .ILK. The incremental status file is created the first time the Incremental Linker (LINK.EXE) runs in incremental mode. LINK updates the file during subsequent incremental builds. LINK is the only tool that uses the .ILK file.

.ODL

In OLE Automation, text files containing a description of an application's interface. Object description language scripts are compiled into type libraries using the MkTypLib tool included with the OLE Software Development Kit.

.OGX

A C++ Component Gallery component that has been exported to a file so it can be shared. The resulting file contains classes and resources for the component.

.OPT

The workspace options file, which stores information about the physical layout and characterisitics you've determined for Visual Studio, such as window layout. In terms of source control, the .OPT file is not shareable.

.PBI

In a profiling operation, a file that provides condensed information to the Visual C++ profiler (PROFILE). The PREP program generates a profiler batch input file the first time the profiler is run on a program. The default filename extension for profiler batch input files is .PBI.

.PBO

An intermediate file generated by the Visual C++ profiler (PROFILE) and used to transfer information between profiling steps.

.PBT

In a profiling operation, the file generated by the PREP program and used as input to the PLIST program to generate a human-readable profile of the source code.

.PCH

A file containing compiled code for a portion of a project. Subsequent builds combine this file with the uncompiled code, thus shortening the overall compile time. The default filename extension for a precompiled header file is .PCH.

.PDB

A file used by the build tools to store information about a user's program. The program database file speeds linking during the debugging phase of development by keeping the debugging information separate from the object files.

.RC

Or resource script file. A text file containing descriptions of resources from which the resource compiler creates a binary resource file. For Microsoft Windows applications, resource-definition files usually have a .RC filename extension. For Apple Macintosh applications, such files are typically named with a .R extension and written with the Apple Rez script language.

.REG

In OLE applications, a text file description of the classes supported by a server application. When a server application is installed in a system, the contents of its registration entry file are merged with the system registry. Registration entry files usually have a .REG filename extension.

.RES

Or binary resource file. A binary file that contains a Windows-based application's resource data and is created by the resource compiler from the resource-definition (.RC) file. Compiled resource files usually have a .RES filename extension.

.RTF

A file that contains encoded, formatted text and graphics for easy transfer between applications. The rich-text encoding format is commonly used by document-processing programs such as Microsoft Word for Windows and for generating online Help files. Rich-text format files usually have a .RTF filename extension.

.SBR file
An intermediate file that the compiler creates for use by the Microsoft Browse Information Maintenance Utility (BSCMAKE). There is one .SBR file for each object (.OBJ) file. BSCMAKE uses the .SBR files to create a browse information (.BSC) file.

.TLB
Or OLE library. An OLE compound document file containing standard descriptions of data types, modules, and interfaces that can be used to fully expose objects for OLE Automation. The type library file usually has a .TLB filename extension and can be used by other applications to get information about the automation server.

.TXT
A human-readable file composed of text characters. A text file is usually identified by a file extension of .TXT.

accelerator key
Or keyboard accelerator, shortcut key, keyboard shortcut. A keystroke or combination of keystrokes that invokes a particular command. See also *accelerator table*.

accelerator resource
Or accelerator table. A data structure that contains a list of accelerator keys and the command identifiers associated with them.

accelerator table
Or accelerator resource. A data structure that contains a list of accelerator keys and the command identifiers associated with them.

accessor
A collection of information that describes how data is stored in the consumer's buffer. The provider uses this information to determine how to transfer data to and from this buffer.

active content
Generic term for active documents, active scripts, and active objects.

active document
Generic term for documents that include active content. Examples of active documents are an HTML page, a Java applet, an OLE document-object, and a document that contains ActiveX controls.

active HTML document
A Web page that contains ActiveX controls, active scripts, or Java applets.

active script
Executable scripts embedded in HTML, such as JScript or VBScript.

active state
1. In OLE, the state of an OLE object in a compound document when the user can edit the embedded object without leaving the container document's window.

Glossary

2. In general, the state of a program, document, device, or portion of the screen that is currently operational.

Active Template Library (ATL)
A set of compact, template-based C++ classes that simplify the programming of Component Object Model objects. ATL provides the mechanism to use and create COM objects.

ActiveX
All component technologies built on Microsoft's Component Object Model (COM), other than Object Linking and Embedding.

ActiveX control
The new name for programmable elements formerly known variously as OLE Controls, OCXs, or OLE Custom Controls. Controls previously built with the MFC Control Developer's Kit meet the ActiveX control specification.

ActiveX document
A document that contains ActiveX controls, Java applets, or ActiveX document objects. Also called active object or active script.

ActiveX scripting
Microsoft technology for connecting third-party script engines to applications.

ActiveX server extension
A dynamic-link library (DLL) that creates server extensions on any ISAPI-compliant Web server.

ActiveX server filter
A dynamic-link library (DLL) that intercepts and processes notifications directed to any ISAPI-compliant Web server.

ActiveX Server framework
Server-side technology extensions, including ISAPI, ActiveX server controls, ActiveX server applications, ActiveX server filters, and ActiveX server scripts.

address space
1. Or memory space. The portion of memory allocated to a given process. See also *heap*.
2. Or memory space. More generally, the range of memory locations to which a microprocessor can refer. Effectively, a computer's address space is the amount of memory a microprocessor could use if all the memory was available.

advise sink
An interface of a COM object that can receive notifications of changes in an embedded object or linked object. Containers that need to be notified of changes in objects implement an advise sink. Notifications originate in the server, which uses an advisory holder object to cache and manage notifications to containers. See also *container application*.

aggregate object
In the Component Object Model, an object whose implementation of certain interfaces is provided by one or more of its contained objects.

aggregation
A composition technique for implementing COM objects. With aggregation, a new object can reuse one or more existing objects. This reuse is achieved by exposing one or more of the interfaces in the original object.

ambient property
A run-time property that is managed and exposed by the container. Typically, an ambient property represents a characteristic of a form, such as background color, that is communicated to a control so the control can assume the look and feel of its surrounding environment.

apartment model threading
A threading model that can be used only on the thread that created it. Compare *free threading model*, *single threading model*.

application class
The class, derived from the MFC class **CWinApp**, that encapsulates the initialization, running, and termination of a Windows-based application. An application must have exactly one object of an application class. See also *application object*.

application framework
Or framework. A group of C++ classes in the Microsoft Foundation Class Library that provides the essential components of an application for Windows. The application framework defines the skeleton, or framework, of an application and supplies standard user-interface implementations that can be placed onto the skeleton. See also *class library*.

application object
The single instance of the application class. The application object controls documents, views, frame windows, and templates, and specifies application behavior such as initialization and cleanup for every instance of the application.

application programming interface (API)
A set of routines that an application uses to request and carry out lower-level services performed by a computer's operating system. For computers running a graphical user interface, an API manages an application's windows, icons, menus, and dialog boxes.

aspect ratio
The ratio of a pixel's width to height on a particular device. Information about a device's aspect ratio is used in the creation, selection, and display of fonts.

assertion
A Boolean statement in the debug version of a program that tests a condition that should, if the program is operating correctly, evaluate as true. If the condition is false, an error has occurred and the program will typically issue an error message that gives the user the option to abort the program, activate the debugger, or ignore the error.

asynchronous call

A call to a function that is executed separately so that the caller can continue processing instructions without waiting for the function to return. Contrast with *synchronous call*.

asynchronous moniker

A protocol for Internet-enabled applications and ActiveX controls that retains responsiveness of the user interface during file downloads.

asynchronous operation

1. Or overlapped I/O. In programming for Windows, a task that proceeds in the background, allowing the thread that requested the task to continue to perform other tasks. See also *synchronous operation*.

2. ore generally, an operation that proceeds independently of any timing mechanism such as a clock.

asynchronous processing

In ODBC, a method of processing transactions in which the database driver returns control to an application before a function call completes; the application can continue nondatabase processing while the driver completes the function in progress.

automatic storage class

In C++, the storage class for objects and variables that are local to the block of code where they are declared. The automatic storage class can be declared explicitly, by using the keywords auto or register, or implicitly, by default.

automatic variable

See *automatic storage class*.

automation client

In OLE Automation, an application that can manipulate exposed objects belonging to another application (called the OLE Automation server). The client drives the server application by accessing the objects' properties and functions. Microsoft Visual Basic is an example of an OLE Automation client application. See also *automation server*.

automation server

An application that exposes programmable objects to other applications, which are called "automation clients." Exposing programmable objects enables clients to "automate" certain functions by directly accessing those objects and using the services they make available. For example, a word processor might expose its spell-checking functionality so that other programs can use it. See also *automation client*.

background color

The color of the client area of an empty window or display screen, on which all drawing and color display take place.

backward compatibility
1. Ensuring that existing applications will continue to work in the new environment.
2. Ensuring that the new release of an application will be able to handle files created by a previous version of the product.

base name
The portion of the filename that precedes the extension. For example, SAMPLE is the base name of the file SAMPLE.ASM.

binding
1. The association of two pieces of information with one another, most often used in terms of a symbol (such as the name of a variable) with some descriptive information (such as a memory address, a data type, or an actual value).
2. In networking, a process that establishes the initial communication channel between the protocol driver and the network adapter card driver.
3. In OLE, the process of getting a compound-document object into a running state so that it can be activated.
4. A Windows Sockets keyword that identifies the bind socket library routine. The bind routine associates a local address with a socket.

bitmap
1. Or pixel image, pixel map. An array of bits that contains data describing the colors found in a rectangular region on the screen (or the rectangular region found on a page of printed paper).
2. Or bit image. A sequential collection of bits that represents, in memory, an image to be displayed on the screen or printed.

bookmark
A marker that uniquely identifies a specific record or row in a database, a specific line in source code, or an item or location in a word-processing file. The HTML equivalent of a bookmark is an anchor with the NAME attribute; this type of anchor is used as a destination for hyperlinks. When creating HTML documents in Word for Windows, for example, you use bookmarks to create anchors with the NAME attribute.

breakpoint
A location in a program where execution is stopped to allow the developer to examine the program's code, variables, and register values and, as necessary, to make changes, continue execution, or terminate execution.

build
1. (noun) The process of compiling and linking source code to generate an executable program, library, Help file, or other run-time file. The files produced from the build process are also sometimes referred to as a "build."

2. (verb) To compile and link source code in order to generate an executable program, Help file, or other run-time file.

bulk record field exchange (bulk RFX)
When bulk row fetching is implemented, the mechanism by which MFC ODBC classes transfer data between the field data members of a recordset object and the corresponding columns of an external data source. See also *record field exchange (RFX)*, *dialog data exchange (DDX)*.

bulk row fetching
In ODBC, the process of retrieving multiple rows from the data source in a single fetch operation. The number of rows retrieved depends on the recordset object's setting for the rowset size.

C++ exception handling
Built-in support provided by the C++ language for handling anomalous situations, known as "exceptions," that may occur during the execution of a program. With C++ exception handling, a program can communicate unexpected events to a higher execution context that is better able to recover from such abnormal events. These exceptions are handled by code that is outside the normal flow of control. See also *structured exception handling (SEH)*.

call stack
An ordered list of functions that have been called but have not returned, with the currently executing function listed first. Each call is optionally shown with the arguments and types passed to it. During a debug session, you can view the functions that have been called but have not returned.

catch block
Or catch handler. In C++, a block of exception-handling code preceded by the keyword **catch**. The code in the catch block is executed only if the code in the **try** block throws an exception of the type specified in the **catch** statement. See also C++ *exception handling*, *throw expression*.

child window
A window that has the WS_CHILD or WS_CHILDWINDOW style and is confined to the client area of its parent window, which initiates and defines the child window. Typically, an application uses child windows to divide the client area of a parent window into functional areas.

class identifier (CLSID)
A universally unique identifier (UUID) that identifies a type of OLE object. Each type of OLE object (item) has its CLSID in the registry so that it can be loaded and programmed by other applications. For example, a spreadsheet may create worksheet items, chart items, and macrosheet items. Each of these item types has its own CLSID that uniquely identifies it to the system. See also *registration entry file*.

class library
A set of related C++ classes that can be used in an application, either as originally defined or as the source for other derived classes. The Microsoft Foundation Class Library included in Visual C++ is an example of a class library that defines a framework for integrating the user interface of an application for Windows with the rest of the application.

client

An application or a process that requests a service from some other process, or from an in-process server. See also *client/server*.

client area

Or client rectangle. The portion of a window where the application displays output such as text or graphics.

client coordinates

An ordered pair (x,y) of numbers, relative to the origin (usually the upper-left corner of a window's client area), that designates a point in the client area.

client item

An object that provides an interface between an OLE item and the container application, and that is of a class derived from the MFC class **COleClientItem**. Client items are maintained by the container application and give the container application access to the presentation data and the native data. Client items also provide site(location) information to the server application for in-place activation.

client/server

1. The most commonly used model for distributed applications. Client applications request services from a server application. A server can have many clients at the same time, and a client can request data from multiple servers. An application can be both a client and a server. See also *client*.
2. In network architecture, a model for a local area network where clients initiate communication with the server, which carries out the requests in the form of replies. For example, the clients may be workstations communicating with a file server on which all of their data is stored. See also *client*.

collection class

In object-oriented programming, a class that can hold and process groups of class objects or groups of standard types. A collection class is characterized by its "shape" (the way the objects are organized and stored) and by the types of its elements. MFC provides three basic collection shapes: lists, arrays, and maps (also known as dictionaries).

color palette

An array containing the RGB values that identify the colors that can currently be displayed or drawn on the output device. Color palettes are used by devices that are capable of generating many colors but can only display or draw a subset of these at any given time.

command handler

In MFC, a member function of an object which handles a request. Command handler member functions take no parameters and return **void**.

command identifier

Or command ID. In MFC, an identifier that associates a command message with the user-interface object (such as a menu item, toolbar button, or accelerator key) that generated the command. Typically, command IDs are named for the functionality of the user-interface object they are assigned to. For example, a Clear All item in the Edit menu might be assigned an ID such as ID_EDIT_CLEAR_ALL.

command message

1. In Windows, a notification message from a user-interface object, such as a menu, toolbar button, or accelerator key. The framework processes command messages differently from other messages and such messages can be handled by a wider variety of object—documents, document templates, and the application object itself, in addition to windows and views.
2. In Media Control Interface (MCI), a symbolic constant that represents a unique command for an MCI device. Command messages have associated data structures that provide information a device requires to carry out a request.

common dialog box

A dialog box predefined in Windows that supports standard operations, such as the Open command on the File menu. An application displays a common dialog box by calling a single function rather than by supplying a dialog box procedure and using a resource file containing a dialog box template.

component object

An object that conforms to COM. Clients deal with a component object only through a pointer to an interface. See also *reference counting*, *marshaling*, *aggregation*.

Component Object Model (COM)

An open architecture for cross-platform development of client/server applications based on object-oriented technology as agreed upon by Digital Equipment Corporation and Microsoft Corporation. The Component Object Model defines an interface (similar to an abstract base class), **IUnknown**, from which all COM-compatible classes are derived.

connectable object

A COM object that supports event communication from the server to the client. The connectable object fires events by calling interfaces implemented on client objects. See also *advise sink*, *connection point*.

connection point

In OLE, a mechanism consisting of the object calling the interface, called the "source," and the object implementing the interface, called the "sink." The connection point implements an outgoing interface that is able to initiate actions, such as firing events and change notifications, on other objects. By exposing a connection point, a source allows sinks to establish connections to the source. See also *connectable object*.

connection string

Or connect string. In ODBC, a string expression used to open an external database.

consumer

A consumer is an OLE DB software component that needs to access data from a data source.

container application

Or OLE container. An application that can incorporate embedded or linked items into its own documents. The documents managed by a container application are able to store and display OLE Visual Editing items as well as data created by the application itself. A container application allows users to insert new items or edit existing items.

control bar

A window that can contain buttons, edit boxes, check boxes, or other kinds of Windows controls. A control bar is usually aligned with the top or bottom of a frame window and provides quick, one-step command actions. Control bars include toolbars, status bars, and dialog bars.

custom control

A special-format dynamic-link library (DLL) or object file that adds features and functionality to a Windows-based application user interface. A custom control can be a variation on an existing Windows dialog-box control (for example, a text box suitable for use with a pen and digitizing tablet) or an entirely new category of control. See also *ActiveX control*.

Data Access Objects (DAO)

A high-level set of objects that insulates developers from the physical details of reading and writing records. In a database application, for example, these objects include databases, table definitions, query definitions, fields, indexes, etc.

data definition language (DDL)

Or database design language, data design language. A language, usually a part of a database management system, that defines all attributes and properties of a database, especially record layouts, field definitions, key fields (and, sometimes, keying methodology), file locations, and storage strategy.

data file

A file consisting of data—text, numbers, or graphics, for example. Such a file is distinct from a program file of executable instructions.

data map

In MFC, a mechanism that automates the process of gathering values from a dialog box by providing functions to initialize the controls in the dialog box with the proper values, retrieve the data, and validate the data.

data source

In ODBC, a specific set of data, the information required to access that data, and the location of the data source, which can be described using a data source name. From a program's point of view, the data source includes the data, the DBMS, the network (if any), and ODBC.

database application

An application that manages files consisting of a number of records (or tables), each of which is constructed of fields (columns) of a particular type, together with a collection of operations that facilitate searching, sorting, recombination, and similar activities. See also *relational database*.

database form

A structured window, box, or other self-contained presentation element built into a database application that allows the user to perform a variety of data-access tasks, including data entry, read-only examination of data, and data updates. The form acts as a visual filter for the underlying data it is presenting, generally offering the advantages of better data organization and greater ease of viewing.

database management system

A layer of software between the physical database and the user. The DBMS manages all requests for database action (for example, queries or updates) from the user. Thus, the user is spared the necessity of keeping track of the physical details of file locations and formats, indexing schemes, and so on. In addition, a DBMS may permit centralized control of security and data-integrity requirements.

datagram

Describes a communications protocol or transport in which data packets are routed independently of each other and may follow different routes and arrive in a different order from which they were sent. UDP and IPX are examples of transport-layer datagram protocols.

datagram socket

A connectionless socket that provides a bidirectional flow of data. Datagram data may arrive out of order and possibly duplicated, but record boundaries in the data are preserved, as long as the records are smaller than the receiver's internal size limit. An example of a datagram socket is an application that keeps system clocks on the network synchronized. See also *stream socket*, *transport protocol*.

DC

A data structure defining the graphic objects, their associated attributes, and the graphic modes affecting output on a device.

data manipulation language

The subset of the SQL language used to retrieve and manipulate data.

debugger

A program designed to help find errors in another program by allowing the programmer to step through the program, examine data, and check conditions. There are two basic types of debuggers. Machine-level debuggers display the actual machine instructions (disassembled into assembly language) and allow the programmer to look at registers and memory locations. Source-level debuggers let programmers look at the original source code, examine variables and data structures by name, and so on.

default value

A value that the system or software assumes, unless the user makes an explicit choice.

derived types
Or user-defined types. Derived types are new types that can be used in a program, and can include directly derived types and composed derivative types.

Directly derived types are new types derived directly from existing types are types that point to, refer to, or (in the case of functions) transform type data to return a new type. Examples include: arrays of variables or objects, functions, pointers of a given type, references to objects, constants.

device-independent
A characteristic of software and files that generate the same output regardless of the hardware involved. A device-independent program could, for example, issue the same command to draw a rectangle regardless of whether the output device was a printer, a plotter, or a screen display.

DFX
The mechanism by which the MFC DAO classes transfer data between the field data members of a recordset object and the corresponding columns of an external data source. See also *record field exchange (RFX)*, *bulk record field exchange (Bulk RFX)*, *dialog data exchange (DDX)*.

dialog bar
A control bar that contains standard Windows controls. A dialog bar has dialog-box characteristics in that it contains controls and supports tabbing between them, and it uses a dialog template to represent the bar. Dialog bars can be aligned to the top, bottom, left, or right side of a frame window. See also *status bar*.

dialog box
In Windows, a child window used to retrieve user input. A dialog box usually contains one or more controls, such as buttons, list boxes, combo boxes, and edit boxes, with which the user enters text, chooses options, or directs the action of the command.

Dialog Data Exchange (DDX)
In MFC, a method for transferring data between the controls of a dialog box and their associated variables. DDX is an easy way to initialize the controls in a dialog box and to gather data input by the user. See also *dialog data validation (DDV)*.

Dialog Data Validation (DDV)
In MFC, a method for checking data as it is transferred from the controls in a dialog box. DDV is an easy way to validate data entry in a dialog box. See also *dialog data exchange (DDX)*.

dialog editor
A resource editor that allows you to place and arrange controls in a dialog-box template and to test the dialog box. The editor displays the dialog box exactly as the user will see it. While using the dialog editor, you can define message handlers and manage data gathering and validation with the ClassWizard.

dialog template
A template used by Windows to create a dialog window and display it. The template specifies the characteristics of the dialog box, including its overall size, initial location, and style, and the types and positions of its controls. A dialog template is usually stored as a resource, but templates can also be stored directly in memory. See also *dialog editor*.

dimmed

Or disabled, grayed, unavailable. The state and visual appearance of controls or menu items whose functionality is not presently available to a user.

dirty

Indicates that a file, object, or data item has been changed since the last time it was saved. Usually describes a flag or bit that is set to 1 when data changes and back to 0 when the data is saved to disk.

dispatch identifier (ID)

A 32-bit attribute value for identifying methods and properties in OLE Automation. All of the accessor functions for a single property have the same dispatch ID. The low-order 16 bits of the dispatch ID contain the distance from the top of the dispatch map; the high-order 16 bits contain the distance from the most derived class.

dispatch interface

In OLE Automation, the external programming interface of some grouping of functionality exposed by the automation server. For example, a dispatch interface might expose an application's mouse clicking and text data entry functions. See also *type library file*.

dispatch map

In MFC, a set of macros that expands into the declarations and calls needed to expose methods and properties for OLE Automation. The dispatch map designates the internal and external names of object functions and properties, as well as the data types of the function arguments and properties.

dockable toolbar

A toolbar that can be attached, or "docked," to any side of its parent window, or "floated" in its own mini-frame window. See also *floating toolbar*.

document object

An object that defines, stores, and manages an application's data. When the user opens an existing or new document, the application framework creates a document object to manage the data stored in the document.

document template

In MFC, a template used for the creation of documents, views, and frame windows. A single application object manages one or more document templates, each of which is used to create and manage one or more documents (depending on whether the application is SDI or MDI). Applications that support more than one type of document, such as spreadsheets as well as text, have multiple document template objects.

document/view architecture

A design methodology that focuses on what the user sees and needs rather than on the application or what the application requires. This design is implemented by a set of classes that manage, store and present application-specific data. These classes can manipulate disk-based data files (document objects), display a document's data (view objects), and automatically use a particular type of window (window objects).

drag-and-drop

A technique for moving or copying data between applications, between windows within an application, or within a single window in an application. The user selects the data to be transferred and drags the data to the desired destination.

driver

1. A hardware device that controls or regulates another device. A line driver, for example, boosts signals transmitted over a communications line, and a bus driver amplifies and regulates signals transmitted over a bus (data pathway).
2. A program that controls a device such as a printer or a mouse.

drop-down combo box

A combo box that contains a drop-down list and a selection field that the user can edit.

drop-down list

A list in a combo box that displays the current setting, but can be opened to display a list of choices. The user can select an item from the list to update the current setting.

drop-down menu

A menu that is displayed when the user selects a particular entry from a menu bar. See also *pop-up menu*.

drop-target

In a drag-and-drop operation, the destination window where the user drops the data being transferred.

DSN

The name of a data source that applications use to request a connection to the data source. For example, a data source name can be registered with ODBC through the ODBC Administrator program.

dual interface

An interface that derives from **IDispatch** and supports both late-binding via **IDispatch** and early-binding (VTBL binding) via direct COM methods for each of its automation methods.

dynamic-link library file

A file that contains one or more functions that are compiled, linked, and stored separately from the processes that use them. In Win32, the operating system maps the dynamic-link libraries (DLLs) into the address space of a process when the process is starting up or while it is running. The process then executes functions in the DLL. Dynamic-link library files usually have a .DLL filename extension.

dynaset

A recordset (or set of records) with dynamic properties that is the result of a query on a database document. A dynaset can be used to add, change, and delete records from the underlying database table or tables. See also *snapshot*.

edit buffer
In MFC database classes, a buffer that contains the current record during an update. Update operations may use this buffer to manage changes to the data source.

edit control
Or edit box, text box. A rectangular control window that a user can use to type and edit text. See also *static control*.

end of file
A value returned by an I/O routine when the end of a file (or, in some cases, an error) is encountered. The iostream library function **eof** returns TRUE on the end-of-file condition. When a file is opened in text mode, a logical end of file occurs whenever a CTRL+Z character is encountered.

error message
A message from the system or a program advising the user of a problem that requires human intervention in order to be solved.

event
1. In OLE, a notification message sent from one object to another (e.g. from a control to its container) in response to a state change or a user action.
2. More generally, any action or occurrence, often generated by the user, to which a program might respond. Typical events include keystrokes, mouse movements, and button clicks.

exception
An abnormal condition or error that occurs during the execution of a program and that requires the execution of software outside the normal flow of control. Examples of exceptions are running out of memory, resource allocation errors, and failure to find files. See also C++ *exception handling, structured exception handling (SEH)*.

exception handler
A block of code that reacts to a specific type of exception. If the exception is for an error from which the program can recover, the program can resume executing after the exception handler has executed. In this case, execution will resume where the exception was handled, not at the place where it was generated.

external name
1. In OLE Automation, an identifier that a class exposes to other applications. Automation clients use the external name to request an object of this class from an automation server.
2. In C/C++, an identifier declared with global scope or declared using the extern storage class.

File Transfer Protocol (FTP)
A method of retrieving files to your home directory or directly to your computer using TCP/IP. Many Internet sites have established publicly accessible repositories of materials that can be obtained using FTP with the account name "anonymous." Thus, these sites are called "anonymous ftp servers."

firewall

Or proxy server. A system or combination of systems that enforces a one-way barrier between two or more networks, usually used for security purposes. Firewalls accomplish all communication between the network and outside.

flag

Broadly, a marker of some type used by a computer in processing or interpreting information. Such a signal indicates the existence or status of a particular condition. Depending on its use, a flag can be code, embedded in data, that identifies some condition, such as the beginning or end of a word or a message, or it can be one or more bits set internally by hardware of software to indicate an event of some type, such as an error or the result of comparing two values.

floating toolbar

A toolbar that can appear anywhere on the user's display and is always on top of all other windows. Its size or position can be modified when floating. See also *dockable toolbar*.

focus

A temporary property of a user-interface object, such as a window, view, dialog box, or button, that permits the object to receive keyboard input from the user. The focus is usually conveyed through highlighting. See also *top-level window*.

form view

A program window whose client area contains dialog-box controls to permit entering, viewing, or altering data, generally in a form-based data-access application.

frame window

In MFC, the window that coordinates the interactions of the application with a document and its view. The frame window provides a visible frame around a view, with an optional status bar and standard window controls such as a control menu, buttons to minimize and maximize the window, and controls for resizing the window. The frame window is responsible for managing the layout of its child windows and other client-area elements such as control bars and views. The frame window also forwards commands to its views and can respond to notification messages from control windows. In OLE, a frame window is the outermost main window where the container application's main menu resides. See also *main frame window*.

framework

See *application framework*.

free threading model

A model in which an object that can be used on any thread at any time. Compare apartment-model threading, single threading model.

friend

A keyword used within a class declaration to specify that a function or another class has access to the private and protected members of the first class. The function or class specified with the **friend** keyword is considered a "friend" of the first class.

function

1. A block of code, consisting of a return type, function name, optional parameters, and statements, that performs one or more specific tasks within the source program and returns a value to the caller.

2. The purpose of or the action carried out by a program, routine, or other object.

Gopher

A client/server application that allows the user to browse large amounts of information. It presents the information to the user in a menu format. The original Gopher server was developed at the University of Minnesota.

graphics device interface

An executable program that processes graphical function calls from a Windows-based application and passes those calls to the appropriate device driver, which performs the hardware-specific functions that generate output. By acting as a buffer between applications and output devices, GDI presents a device-independent view of the world for the application while interacting in a device-dependent format with the device.

handler

1. In OLE, a DLL that resides in a client process and performs some tasks on behalf of the server, while delegating other tasks back to the server itself.

2. In general, a routine that manages a common and relatively simple condition or operation, such as error recovery or data movement. See also *message handler*.

heap

1. Or free store. A portion of memory reserved for a program to use for the temporary storage of data structures whose existence or size cannot be determined until the program is running. The program can request free memory from the heap to hold such elements, use it as necessary, and later free the memory.

2. In sorting, a partially ordered complete binary tree.

Help topic

The primary unit of information in a Help (.HLP) file. A topic is a self-contained body of text and graphics, similar to a page in a book. Unlike a page, however, a topic can hold as much information as you require. If there is more information in a topic than the Help window can display, scroll bars appear to let the user scroll through the information.

HTML

A markup language derived from SGML. Used to create a text document with formatting specifications that tells a software browser how to display the page or pages included in the document.

HTTP server

Or Web server. A server that runs a Hypertext Transfer Protocol service or application. This protocol defines the procedures used when connecting a Web browser to a Web server.

Hypertext Transfer Protocol (HTTP)
The Internet protocol used by World Wide Web browsers and servers to exchange information. The protocol makes it possible for a user to use a client program to enter a URL (or click a hyperlink) and retrieve text, graphics, sound, and other digital information from a Web server. HTTP defines a set of commands and uses ASCII text strings for a command language. An HTTP transaction consists of a connection, a request, a response, and a close.

idle state
The state of a modal dialog box or menu when it has finished processing a message and it has no more messages waiting in its active message queue.

idle time
The period during which the application has an empty message queue. Idle time permits the processing of background tasks.

IID
A globally unique identifier associated with an interface. Some functions take IIDs as parameters to allow the caller to specify which interface pointer should be returned.

image list
In MFC, a collection of same-sized images contained in a single, wide bitmap. Image lists are used to efficiently manage large sets of icons or bitmaps.

in-place activation
Or in-place editing, visual editing. The ability to activate an object within the context of its container document, as opposed to opening it in a separate window.

indexed sequential access method
Pronounced "EYE-sam." A scheme for decreasing the time necessary to locate a data record within a large database, given a unique key for the record. The key is the field in the record used to reference the record.

Interface Definition Language (IDL)
The OSF-DCE standard language for specifying the interface for remote procedure calls. See also *MIDL*.

Internet Server Application Programming Interface (ISAPI)
A set of functions for Internet servers, such as a Windows NT Server running Microsoft Internet Information Server (MIIS).

IP
The basic protocol of the Internet. It enables the delivery of individual packets from one host to another. It makes no guarantees about whether or not the packet will be delivered, how long it will take, or if multiple packets will arrive in the order they were sent. Protocols built on top of this add the notions of connection and reliability.

IP address
The Internet protocol address which is a 32-bit address assigned to a host. The IP address has a host component and a network component.

IP number

An Internet address that is a unique number consisting of 4 parts separated by dots, sometimes called a "dotted quad" (for example, 198.204.112.1). Every Internet computer has an IP number and most computers also have one or more domain names that are plain-language substitutes for the dotted quad.

ISAPI filter

An Internet server filter packaged as a dynamic-link library that runs on ISAPI-enabled servers.

join

A database operation that combines records from two or more tables, based on an exact match of key values in these tables. Once a recordset has been created based on a join, it functions as if the records were all in one table.

Just-in-Time (JIT) debugging

A technique that catches faults that occur while the program is running outside the development environment. You must set this option in the development environment before executing your program.

keyword

Or reserved word. A word that has special meaning to a program or in a programming language. Reserved words usually include those used for control statements, data declarations, and the like. A reserved word can be used only in certain predefined circumstances; it cannot be used in naming functions, variables, structures, labels, classes, or user-generated tools such as macros.

label

1. In a C or C++ function body, a unique name followed by a colon (:). Labels can denote statements to which a goto statement can branch. In a switch statement, the labels preceded by the keyword case list values to be compared to the expression at the top of the switch statement.

2. In user-interface design, application-defined text associated with a graphical element such as a button or check box.

3. In OLE, text describing an object that is linked or embedded as an icon.

Lightweight Remote Procedure Call

In OLE, a protocol for interprocess communication on a single machine. See also *Remote Procedure Call (RPC)*.

link

1. The Microsoft 32-Bit Incremental Linker (LINK.EXE).

2. To combine object files and libraries to form an executable file or dynamic-link library.

3. In OLE, a connection between two documents. A link has three properties: the name of its source data, its type (or class, as it is known internally), and its updating basis (either automatic or manual). Also, as a verb, it means to connect two documents with a link.

listserv
An Internet application that automatically "serves" mailing lists by sending electronic newsletters to a stored database of Internet user addresses. Although some listservs are moderated, users can often handle their own subscribe/unsubscribe actions without requiring anyone at the server location to personally handle the transaction.

literal
A value, used in a program statement, that is expressed directly rather than as a named constant or the contents of a variable. For example, in the statements

```
i = 25;
c = 'a';
cout << "Hello";
```

the values 25, 'a', and "Hello" are literals.

local remote procedure call
In RPC, a remote procedure call to another process on the same computer as the calling process.

local server
An OLE server object implemented as an executable file that runs on the same computer as the client application. Because the server application is an executable file, it runs in its own process.

lock
In COM and OLE, a pointer held to, and possibly a reference count incremented on, a running object. Two types of locks can be held on an object: strong and weak. To implement a strong lock, a server must maintain both a pointer and a reference count so that the object will remain "locked" in memory at least until the server releases it. To implement a weak lock, the server maintains only a pointer to the object so that the object can be destroyed by another process.

locking mode
A strategy for locking records in a recordset during update. A record is locked when it is read-only to all users but the one currently entering data in it. See also *optimistic locking*, *pessimistic locking*.

macro expansion
In C/C++, the process of replacing a macro name (defined with a **#define** directive) in the source code with the body of the macro during compilation.

main application window
Or main window. In an SDI application, the window that serves as the primary interface between the user and the application.

main frame window
The primary window responsible for coordinating the frame with its view. In an SDI application, the document frame window is also the main frame window. In an MDI application, document windows are child windows displayed in the main frame window. The styles and other characteristics of frame windows are inherited from the main frame-window class.

makefile
A file that contains all commands, macro definitions, options, and so on to specify how to build the projects in a project workspace. A makefile has the filename extension .MAK and usually has the same base name as the workspace configuration (.MDP) file.

marshaling
In OLE, the process of packaging and sending interface parameters across process boundaries. See also *Remote Procedure Call (RPC)*.

member function
In C++, a function declared inside a class definition. A class's member functions are used to get and set data members, display information to the user, and manipulate data according to the needs of the program.

member variable
Any item of data that is associated with a particular object. Each instance of a class has its own copy of the instance variables defined in the class. Called instance variables in Java.

message
A structure or set of parameters used for communicating information or a request. Messages can be passed between the operating system and an application, different applications, threads within an application, and windows within an application.

message cracker
A set of macros that extract useful information from the parameters of a message and hide the details of how information is packed.

message-driven
Or event-driven. A programming model in which the state of the running program changes in response to user actions and other events. These events cause the operating system to send messages to the part of the application that can handle the event.

message handler
In Windows, an object, such as a view or frame window, that provides handler functions to process messages.

message handler function
In MFC, a dedicated handler function processes each separate message. Message-handler functions are member functions of a class. Some kinds of message handlers are also called "command handlers."

In Windows, a function that responds to a message using parameters that have been translated from *wParam* and *lParam* and passed to the function. A message-handler function might track mouse activity or call member functions of the document to update its data.

message handling
The act of responding to messages received from the operating system. Applications use message-handling functions to process messages.

message loop

A program loop that retrieves messages from a thread's message queue and dispatches them to the appropriate window procedures. See also *message queue*.

message map

A mechanism to route Windows messages and commands to the windows, documents, views, and other objects in an MFC application. Message maps map Windows messages, commands from menus, toolbar buttons, accelerators and control-notification messages. A collection of macros in a class's source (.CPP) file specify which functions will handle various messages for the class.

message-map entry

An individual item in a message-map table that specifies the handler for a particular message. The framework searches the table for each incoming message and calls the handler for it automatically. See also *message map*.

message-map macro

One of the macros supplied by the Microsoft Foundation Class Library and used in a message map to specify which messages will be handled by which functions. Message-map macros are available to map Windows messages, command messages, and ranges of messages.

message pump

A program loop that retrieves messages from a thread's message queue, translates them, offers them to the dialog manager, informs the MDI manager about them, and dispatches them to the application. See also *message queue*.

message queue

A repository for window messages awaiting processing by a thread. The system message queue holds mouse and keyboard input waiting to be passed to a thread's message queue. A thread's message queue holds messages waiting to be retrieved by a thread's message loop.

message reflection

In MFC, a feature that allows notification messages to be handled in either a child control window or the parent window, or in both.

method

In object-oriented programming, a procedure that provides access to an object's data. In C++, public member functions are the equivalent of methods.

Microsoft Foundation Class Library (MFC)

A set of C++ classes that encapsulate much of the functionality of applications written for the Microsoft Windows operating systems.

Microsoft Interface Definition Language (MIDL)

Microsoft's implementation and extension of the OSF-DCE Interface Definition Language.

Microsoft Jet Database Engine

A database management system that retrieves data from and stores data in user and system databases. The Microsoft Jet database engine can be thought of as a data manager component with which other data access systems, such as Microsoft Access and Microsoft Visual Basic, are built.

modal

A restrictive or limiting interaction created by a given condition of operation. Modal often describes a secondary window that restricts a user's interaction with other windows. A secondary window can be modal with respect to its primary window or to the entire system. A modal dialog box must be closed by the user before the application continues. See also *modeless*.

modeless

Not restrictive or limiting interaction. "Modeless" often describes a secondary window that does not restrict a user's interaction with other windows. A modeless dialog box stays on the screen and is available for use at any time but also permits other user activities. See also *modal*.

moniker

An object that supports the **IMoniker** interface, which includes the **IPersistStream** interface; thus, monikers can be saved to and loaded from streams. Monikers can be saved to persistent storage, and they support binding.

multiple document interface (MDI)

The standard user-interface architecture for Windows-based applications. A multiple document interface application enables the user to work with more than one document at the same time. Each document is displayed within the client area of the application's main window. See also *child window, client area, single document interface (SDI)*.

multithreaded application

An application capable of carrying out multiple, independent paths of execution (or threads) at the same time. For example, an application may have additional threads to handle background or maintenance tasks so that the user doesn't have to wait for a task to complete before continuing to work with the application. See also *apartment-model threading, free threading model, single threading model*.

mutex object

In interprocess communication, a synchronization object whose state is signaled when it is not owned by a thread and nonsignaled when it is owned. Only one thread at a time can own a mutex.

native

1. An adjective describing a programming element that is specific to and supported by the particular platform on which it is running.
2. An adjective describing a programming element that is specific to a particular country.
3. In OLE, an adjective describing data that originated in the container document. See also *presentation data*.

notification message
A message that a control sends to its parent window when events, such as input from the user, occur.

object description language file
In OLE Automation, text files containing a description of an application's interface. Object description language scripts are compiled into type libraries using the MkTypLib tool included with the OLE Software Development Kit.

Open Database Connectivity (ODBC)
An open, vendor-neutral interface for database connectivity that provides access to a variety of personal computer, minicomputer, and mainframe systems, including Windows-based systems and the Apple Macintosh. The ODBC interface permits an application developer to develop, compile, and ship an application without targeting a specific database management system (DBMS). Users can add modules called database drivers that link the application to their choice of database management systems.

ODBC cursor library
A dynamic-link library that resides between the ODBC Driver Manager and the drivers and handles scrolling through data.

ODBC driver
A dynamic-link library file that implements ODBC function calls and interacts with a data source. A driver processes ODBC function calls, submits SQL requests to a specific data source, and returns results to the application. If necessary, the driver modifies an application's request so that the request conforms to syntax supported by the associated database management system.

OLE DB
OLE DB is a set of interfaces that provide applications with uniform access to data stored in diverse information sources.

optimistic locking
A recordset locking strategy in which records are left unlocked until explicitly updated. The page containing a record is locked only while the program updates the record, not while a user is editing a record. See also *pessimistic locking*.

owner window
A window that owns another window, thus affecting aspects of the owned window's appearance and behavior.

pane
One of the separate areas in a split window, or a rectangular area of the status bar that can be used to display information.

parent window
A window that generates one or more child windows.

parse map
Code that allows a **CHttpServer**-derived object in MFC to map client requests to its member functions. MFC provides parse map macros to help map form variables on a Web page to parameters in your function.

persistent
Lasting between program sessions, or renewed when a new program session is begun.

persistent property
Information that can be stored persistently as part of a storage object such as a file or directory. Persistent properties are grouped into property sets, which can be displayed and edited.

pessimistic locking
A recordset locking strategy in which a page is locked once a user begins editing a record on that page. While the page is locked, no other user can change a record on that page. The page remains locked until records are updated or the editing is canceled. See also *optimistic locking*.

platform
The hardware and operating system that support an application. "Platform" sometimes refers to the hardware alone, as in the Intel x86 platform.

pop-up menu
A menu that is hidden until the user performs an action (such as clicking the right mouse button) that causes Windows to display the menu. The pop-up menu contains commands that are relevant to the selection or the active window. See also *drop-down menu*.

pop-up window
An immovable, nonsizable window that remains on the screen until the user dismisses it. Pop-up windows typically contain definitions of terms or other parenthetical information. Good uses for pop-up windows include illustrations, examples, notes, tips, and lists of keyboard shortcuts.

predefined query
Or stored procedure. In SQL, a set of one or more SQL statements stored in a data source, available to be called from an application as needed. Predefined queries reduce the overhead of repeatedly specifying the same selection criteria.

presentation data
The data used by a container to display embedded or linked objects.

primary key
In a database program, a field or group of fields that uniquely identify a record in a table. No two records in a table can have the same primary key value.

private
In C++, describes a limited degree of access to class members, as specified using the **private** keyword. Access to the specified class member is restricted to member functions and friends of the member or class.

process
An executing application that consists of a private virtual address space, code, data, and other operating-system resouces, such as files, pipes, and synchronization objects that are visible to the process. A process also contains one or more threads that run in the context of the process.

property page
A grouping of properties presented as a tabbed page of a property sheet.

property set
In OLE structured storage, information describing a document, stored in a standard format so that other applications can locate and read that information. For example, a document created with a word processor can have a property set describing the author, title, and keywords.

property sheet
A special kind of dialog box that is generally used to modify the attributes of some external object, such as the current selection in a view. A property sheet has three main parts: the containing dialog box, one or more property pages shown one at a time, and a tab at the top of each page that the user clicks to select that page. An example of a property sheet is the Project Settings dialog box in the Microsoft Visual Studio.

protocol
1. In networking, a formal set of rules governing the format, timing, sequencing, and error control of exchanged messages on a data network; may also include facilities for managing a communications link and/or contention resolution; a protocol may be oriented toward data transfer over an interface, between two logical units directly connected, or on an end-to-end basis between two end users over a large and complex network

2. Rules and conventions of behavior for an action, such as argument passing, or an entity, such as the member functions of a class.

provider
A provider is an OLE DB software component that exposes data stored in a data source in a tabular format.

proxy
An interface-specific object that packages parameters for methods in preparation for a remote method call. A proxy runs in the address space of the sender and communicates with a corresponding stub in the receiver's address space. See also *marshaling, unmarshaling*.

proxy DLL
A file that contains the code to support the use of a custom OLE interface by both client applications and object servers. Compiling an OLE interface with the MIDL compiler generates the files needed to build a proxy DLL.

proxy server
Or firewall. A way to protect your local area network from being accessed by others on the Internet. The proxy server acts as a security barrier between your internal network and the

Internet, keeping others on the Internet from accessing confidential information on your internal network.

pseudo object
A portion of a document or embedded object, such as a range of cells in a spreadsheet, that can be the source for a COM object.

query
A request for records from a data source. For example, a query can be written that requests, essentially, "all invoices for Joe Smith," where all records in an invoice table with the customer name "Joe Smith" would be selected. See also *recordset*.

queue
A data structure in which elements are added to the end of a list and removed from the head of the list. A priority queue typically removes elements from the list according to some priority value assigned to each element. The system message queue, for example, holds mouse and keyboard input waiting to be processed.

radio button
Or option button. In graphical user interfaces, a round button operated by the user to toggle an option or choose from a set of related but mutually exclusive options. The radio button has two states, selected (or checked) and cleared (or unchecked). When selected, a black dot appears inside the button's circle.

Remote Data Objects (RDO)
A high-level set of objects that provide a framework for using code to manipulate components of a remote ODBC database system.

record
1. (noun) A collection of data about a single entity, such as an account or a customer, stored in a row of a table. A record consists of a group of contiguous columns (sometimes called "fields") that contain data of various types. See also *recordset*.

2. (verb) To retain information, usually in a file.

record field exchange (RFX)
When bulk row fetching is not implemented, the mechanism by which MFC ODBC classes transfer data between the field data members of a recordset object and the corresponding columns of an external data source. See also *bulk record field exchange (Bulk RFX)*, *dialog data exchange (DDX)*.

record view
In form-based data-access applications, a form view object whose controls are mapped directly to the field data members of a recordset object and indirectly to the corresponding columns in a query result or table on the data source. See also *form view*, *recordset*.

recordset

A set of records selected from a data source. The records can be from a table, a query, or a stored procedure that accesses one or more tables. A recordset can join two or more tables from the same data source, but not from different data sources. See also *dynaset, result set, snapshot*.

recordset object

In MFC, an instance of class **CRecordset** or class **CDaoRecordset**, or an instance of any class derived from these. See also *record field exchange (RFX)*.

reentrant

Code written so that it can be shared by several programs (or processes within a single program) at the same time. When code is reentrant, one program or process can safely interrupt the execution of another program or process, execute its own code, and then return control to the first program or process in such a way that the first program or process does not fail or behave in an unexpected way.

reference count

A count of the number of pointers that access, or make reference to, an object, allowing for multiple references to a single object. This number is decremented when a reference is removed; when the count reaches zero, the object's space in memory is freed.

reference counting

A running count of the number of clients of a resource. A reference count implements garbage collection, and also ensures that an object is not destroyed before all references to it are released.

referential integrity

In database management, a set of rules that preserves the defined relationships between tables when records are entered or deleted. Enforcing referential integrity would, for example, prevent a record from being added to a related table when there is no associated record in the primary table.

registration entry file

In OLE applications, a text file description of the classes supported by a server application. When a server application is installed in a system, the contents of its registration entry file are merged with the system registry. Registration entry files usually have a .REG filename extension.

registry

Or OLE system registry, Windows NT registry, system registration database. In 32-bit Windows, the database in which configuration information is registered. This database takes the place of most configuration and initialization files for Windows and new Windows-based applications. See also *registration entry file*.

registry key

A unique identifier assigned to each piece of information in the system registration database.

relational database

A type of database or database management system that stores information in tables–rows and columns of data–and conducts searches by using data in specified columns of one table to find additional data in another table.

Remote Procedure Call

A widely used standard defined by the Open Software Foundation (OSF) for distributed computing. RPC enables one process to make calls to functions that are part of another process. The other process can be on the same computer or on a different computer on the network.

resource

1. A program block, dialog box template, bitmap, font, or sound, for example, that can be used by more than one program or in more than one place in a program. The use of resources allows alteration of many features in a program without the necessity of recompiling the program from source code.
2. More generally, any part of a computer system or a network that can be allotted to a program or a process while it is running.

resource editor

A specialized utility program that can be used to add, edit and delete program resources.

result set

A collection of data returned by an SQL query on a database. A Known result set is when the database application knows the exact form of the SQL statements and, therefore, the form of the result set, at compile time. An Unknown result set is when the application does not know the exact form of the SQL statement at compile time and, therefore, cannot predict the format of these results prior to execution. See also *recordset*.

return code

Or result code, exit code. A predefined code used to report the outcome of a procedure or to influence subsequent events when a routine or process terminates (returns) and passes control of the system to another routine. The return code can indicate success or failure, or can even indicate a particular type of failure that is within the normal range of expectations. For example, the exception-handling functions in C++ generate return codes.

right outer join

A database term that describes the relationship between two tables on which a query is run. If two tables are connected with a right outer join, the resulting recordset contains all records from the table on the right but only those records from the table on the left where the joined fields are equal.

rollback

A database operation that allows recovery from changes made during a transaction that was canceled or failed. Rollback returns the records to the state they were in as of the last commit (saved transaction).

routers

A device that helps local area networks (LANs) and wide area networks (WANs) connect and interoperate. A router can connect LANs that have different network topologies, such as Ethernet and token ring.

run time
The point in time when a program is running, or the period of time needed to execute the program.

run-time class information
Information about an object's class accessed at run time. This information is useful for doing extra type-checking or creating dynamic objects at run time. Classes derived from the MFC class CObject can have this functionality. See also *run-time type information (RTTI)*.

run-time type information (RTTI)
A mechanism that allows the type of an object to be determined during program execution. Compare with type information.

running state
In OLE, the status of a compound document object (either a linked or embedded item) when the object's application is running and it is possible to edit the object, access its interfaces, and receive notification of changes.

schema number
In MFC serialization, the "version" of a class implementation, assigned to a class when the **IMPLEMENT_SERIAL** macro of the class is encountered. The schema number refers to the implementation of the class, not to the number of times a given object has been made persistent (usually referred to as the "object version"). Do not confuse this schema number with database terminology.

screen coordinates
A means of specifying the position of a point on the display screen in terms of vertical (y-coordinate) and horizontal (x-coordinate) displacement from the upper-left corner of the screen (origin). The position and size of a window can be described by one set of coordinates (x, y) that marks the point defining the upper-left corner of the window, and another set of coordinates (x', y') that marks the point defining the lower-right corner of the window.

scrolling
The process of moving a document in a window to permit viewing of any desired portion.

separator
1. In Windows, a special type of menu item that appears as a horizontal line. A separator can be used in a pop-up menu to divide a menu into groups of related items.
2. Or separator code. A Unicode value used to indicate line breaks (0x2028) or paragraph breaks (0x2029).
3. More generally, a keyword, character, or white space used to separate components of a name, a number, or a group of fields. For example, the decimal point (.) in 123.456 and the backslash (\) in ROOT\SUBDIR are separators.

serialization
1. Or object persistence. In MFC, the process of writing or reading an object to or from a persistent storage medium, such as a disk file. The basic idea of serialization is that an

object should be able to write its current state, usually indicated by the value of its member variables, to persistent storage. Later, the object can be re-created by reading, or deserializing, the object's state from storage.

2. In RPC, the process of marshaling data to and unmarshaling data from buffers that you control, in contrast to traditional RPC usage, where the stubs and the RPC runtime control the marshaling buffers.

3. Regarding procedures, use of MIDL-generated serialization stub to encode and decode one or more types with a single procedure call. Procedure serialization is accomplished by applying the encode and decode attributes to a function prototype in the ACF file.

4. Regarding types, use of MIDL-generated routines to size, encode, and decode objects of a specified type. The client application calls these routines to serialize the data. Type serialization is accomplished by applying the encode and decode attributes to a single data type, or to an interface, in the ACF file.

server

1. In a network, any device that can be shared by all users.

2. An application or a process that responds to a client request. See also *client/server*.

shell

A piece of software, usually a separate program, that provides communication between the user and the operating system. For example, the Windows Program Manager is a shell program that interacts with MS-DOS.

shortcut key

Or acclerator key, keyboard accelerator, keyboard shortcut. A keystroke or combination of keystrokes that invokes a particular command.

shortcut menu

A menu displayed within a window that provides quick access to frequently used commands that are also available from the main menu bar. The commands in a shortcut menu may change depending on the current state of the window.

single document interface (SDI)

A user interface architecture that allows a user to work with just one document at a time. Windows Notepad is an example of an SDI application. See also *multiple document interface (MDI)*.

single threading model

A model in which all objects are executed on a single thread. Contrast multithreaded application; compare free threading model, apartment-model threading.

skeleton application

Or starter application. A default application created by AppWizard that runs, opens and closes windows, and allows other operations on the windows. You add the necessary code to implement the functionality needed for your own application.

slider control

Or trackbar. A window containing a slider and optional tick marks. When the user moves the slider, using either the mouse or the direction keys, the control sends notification messages to indicate the change.

snapshot

1. In MFC, a recordset that reflects a static view of the data as it existed at the time the snapshot was created. See also *dynaset*, *recordset*.
2. Or screen dump. A copy of all or part of the display screen as it appears at a given instant.
3. More generally, a copy of an object's state or appearance at a given time.

socket

An object that represents an endpoint for communication between processes across a network transport (TCP/IP or AppleTalk, for example). Sockets have a type (datagram or stream) and can be bound to a specific network address. Windows Sockets provides an API for handling all types of socket connections in Windows. See also *datagram socket*, *stream socket*, *transport protocol*.

software development kit

A set of libraries, header files, tools, books, on-line help and sample programs designed to help a developer create software.

source code

Human-readable statements written in a high-level programming language, or assembly language.

source code editor

A text editor that may provide special formatting features which make it easier to generate readable, syntactically correct source code. For example, a source code editor may automatically indent blocks of code, check for balanced parentheses and brackets, or highlight keywords.

standard control

One of the controls provided by Microsoft Windows. These controls include buttons of several kinds, static- and editable-text controls, scroll bars, list boxes, and combo boxes. See also *custom control*.

starter files

In Visual C++, a set of files created by AppWizard that, when compiled, implement the basic features of a Windows application. The starter files consist of C++ source files, resource files, header files, and a project file. See also *skeleton application*.

static control

A control that enables an application to provide the user with certain types of text and graphics that require no response. Applications often use static controls to label other controls or to separate a group of controls.

status bar

A control bar at the bottom of a window, with a row of text output panes. The status bar is usually used as a message line (for example, the standard menu help message line) or as a status indicator (for example, the CAP, NUM and SCRL indicators). See also *dialog bar*.

stream socket

A connection-oriented socket that provides a bidirectional, sequenced, and unduplicated flow of data without record boundaries. Receipt of stream messages is guaranteed, and streams are well-suited to handling large amounts of data. Stream sockets are appropriate, for example, for implementations such as file transfer protocol (FTP), which facilitates transferring ASCII or binary files of arbitrary size. See also *datagram socket, transport protocol*.

string table

1. A Windows resource that contains a list of identifiers, values, and captions for the strings used in an application's framework. For example, the status bar prompts are located in the string table. When the resource compiler converts a string table specified in a resource-definition file, it separates it into blocks of 16 strings and stores them as individual resources.

2. More generally, any data structure used to store character strings. Typically, a string table is implemented as a hash table.

structured exception handling (SEH)

A mechanism for handling hardware- and software-generated exceptions that gives developers complete control over the handling of exceptions, provides support for debuggers, and is usable across all programming languages and computers. See also *C++ exception handling*.

Structured Query Language (SQL)

A database sublanguage used to query, update, and manage relational databases.

style

A value, or set of values, that defines the outward appearance and behavior of an object, such as a window, control, or document.

style bit

An individual bit of the 16-bit style parameter that pertains to a single style attribute. For example, the WS_VISIBLE style bit, when set, determines whether a particular window is visible to the user.

subclassing

In Windows programming, a technique that allows an application to intercept and process messages sent or posted to a particular window before the window has a chance to process them. By subclassing a window, an application can augment, modify, or monitor the behavior of the window.

symbol

1. A character other than the standard alphanumeric characters. It usually refers to algebraic, scientific, or linguistic characters not found on the keyboard.
2. In programming, a name that represents a register, an absolute value, or a memory address (relative or absolute).
3. To a compiler, a variable, function name, or other identifier.
4. In Visual C++, a resource identifier that consists of a text string (name) mapped to an integer value. A symbol provides a way to refer to resources and user-interface objects, both in source code and in the resource editors.

synchronous call

A function call that does not allow further instructions in the calling thread to be executed until the function returns. See also *asynchronous call*.

synchronous operation

1. In Windows programming, a task that requires the thread that initiated the operation to suspend activity until the task is completed. See also *asynchronous operation*.
2. In hardware, an operation that proceeds under control of a clock or timing mechanism.

tab control

A common control used to present multiple pages of information or controls to a user; only one page at a time can be displayed. A tab control is analogous to the dividers in a notebook or the labeled folders in a file cabinet. Tab controls imply a peer or logical relationship between each page of information. See also *property sheet*.

tab order

The order in which the TAB key moves the input focus from one control to the next within a dialog box. Usually, the tab order proceeds from left to right in a dialog box, and from top to bottom in a radio group.

target

The objective, or destination, of a computer command or operation. For example, the target machine in a remote debugging operation is the machine running the application that is being debugged.

template

1. In C++, a keyword that allows polymorphism with respect to different types, by passing the data type as a parameter to the code body.
2. More generally, a form or blueprint for an object that contains information about the default properties of that object. For example, a Microsoft Word document template may contain text, formatting, and graphics information as well as macros and AutoText entries.

template class
A C++ class that is instantiated by providing a specific data (or class) type to a template. The compiler builds a class to process data of that type according to the specifications of the template. The Microsoft Foundation Class Library uses template classes to implement the standard collection classes.

temporary object
An object that is created when needed and destroyed after the reference object to which it is bound is destroyed.

text editor
A program used to manage, edit, and print text files.

thread
The basic entity to which the operating system allocates CPU time. A thread can execute any part of the application's code, including a part currently being executed by another thread. All threads of a process share the virtual address space, global variables, and operating-system resources of the process.

thread local storage
A Win32 mechanism that allows multiple threads of a process to store data that is unique for each thread. For example, a spreadsheet application can create a new instance of the same thread each time the user opens a new spreadsheet. A dynamic-link library that provides the functions for various spreadsheet operations can use thread local storage to save information about the current state of each spreadsheet (row, column, and so on).

throw expression
In C++, a statement that transfers program control to a catch block in order to handle an exception. See also C++ *exception handling*, *catch block*, *try block*.

toolbar
A control bar based on a bitmap that contains a row of button images. These buttons can act like pushbuttons, check boxes, or radio buttons. See also *dialog bar*, *status bar*.

top-level window
A window that has no parent window, or whose parent is the desktop window.

transaction
In data management, a means of completing an "all or nothing" series of changes to a file. If one change fails, or if there is a system failure during the transaction, the file reverts back to its original state before the transaction began. See also *rollback*.

Transport Control Protocol/Internet Protocol (TCP/IP)
A set of transport protocols for the Internet that provides both connection-oriented (TCP) and connectionless (IP) data transfer. Commonly made up of four protocols: IP, TCP, UDP, and ICMP. See also *transport protocol*, *User Datagram Protocol (UDP)*.

transport layer

1. In remote debugging, a data link established between the host machine and the target machine.
2. The layer in the ISO/OSI communications model that is responsible for quality of service and accurate delivery of information. Among other services, the transport layer handles error detection and correction.

transport protocol

A set of conventions that govern how data is transported across networks. In a connection-oriented transport protocol, such as Transmission Control Protocol (TCP), applications are required to establish a virtual circuit before data transfer can take place. In a connectionless transport protocol, such as User Datagram Protocol (UDP), an established circuit is not required for data transfer and an application need only open and bind a socket in order to send and receive data.

try block

A guarded body of code in a **try-except** frame-based exception handler or **try-finally** termination handler. See also *catch block, throw expression*.

type information

In OLE, information about an object's class provided by a type library.

type library file

Or OLE library. An OLE compound document file containing standard descriptions of data types, modules, and interfaces that can be used to fully expose objects for OLE Automation. The type library file usually has a .TLB filename extension and can be used by other applications to get information about the automation server.

type safety

The assurance that a given function will be not presented, at run time, with data of a type it cannot handle. Type safety is assured through type checking and/or by the use of template classes that are designed to operate on data of many types. See also *run-time type information (RTTI)*.

Uniform Resource Locator (URL)

The address of a resource on the Internet. URL syntax is in the form `protocol://host/localinfo`, where `protocol` specifies the means of fetching the object (such as HTTP or FTP), `host` specifies the remote location where the object resides, and `localinfo` is a string (often a file name) passed to the protocol handler at the remote location. Also called Universal Resource Locator, Uniform Resource Identifier (URI).

Universal Naming Convention (UNC)

The standard format for paths that include a local area network file server, as in `\\server\share\path\filename`.

unmarshaling

In OLE, the process of unpacking parameters that have been sent across process boundaries.

update handler function

A function that administers changes made to an object or data file to make it more current.

updates

Actions or processes that make a system, object, or data file more current.

User Datagram Protocol (UDP)

A connectionless transport protocol that forms a user interface to the Internet Protocol (IP).

user-defined message

Any message that is not a standard Windows message.

user-defined types

See *derived types*.

user-interface object

In Windows, an object that provides functionality to the user-interface. For example, menu items, toolbar buttons, and accelerator keys are all user-interface objects.

variant

1. In OLE Automation, an instance of the VARIANT datatype, which can represent values of many different types, such as integers, floats, booleans, strings, pointers, etc.

2. In general, one of two or more data elements, functions, libraries, or whatever, exhibiting (usually slight) differences.

version information

An application's company and product identification, product release number, and copyright and trademark notification. Version information is held in a standard form in the executable (.EXE) file or dynamic-link library (DLL) file and is accessible by various tools and Windows functions.

view

1. (noun) A window object through which a user interacts with a document.

2. Or aspect. (noun) Generally, the manner in which data or a graphical image is displayed.

3. (verb) To display information on a computer screen, as in "to view a file."

viewport

A rectangle in device space that is used to specify a transformation between page and device space. The viewport extents (height and width) are always measured in pixels for a video display or in dots for printers.

viewport origin

The corner of the viewport from which the height and width of the viewport are measured.

virtual function

A member function of a base class, where the function is declared with the keyword `virtual`. If a base class contains a virtual function and a derived class defines the same function, the function from the derived class is invoked for objects of the derived class, even if it is called using a pointer or reference to the base class.

virtual function table (VTBL)

A table of function pointers, such as an implementation of a class in C++. The pointers in the VTBL point to the members of the interfaces that an object supports. See also *dual interface*.

window class

A set of attributes that Microsoft Windows uses as a template to create a window in an application. Windows requires that an application supply a class name, the window-procedure address, and an instance handle. Other elements may be used to define default attributes for windows of the class, such as the shape of the cursor and the content of the menu for the window.

window origin

1. The upper-left corner of a window's client area.

2. The corner of the window from which the extents are measured. See also *viewport origin*.

window procedure

A function, called by the operating system, that controls the appearance and behavior of its associated windows. The procedure receives and processes all messages to these windows.

WinInet

A set of functions contained in WININET.DLL that simplifies client access to the Internet via HTTP, FTP, and Gopher. This collection of functions is an extension to the Win32 API.

wizard

A special form of user assistance that guides the user through a difficult or complex task within an application. For example, a database program can use wizards to generate reports and forms. In Visual C++, the AppWizard generates a skeleton program for a new C++ application.

workspace

A directory containing zero or more source files, files that describe the workspace, and files that describe its contents.

wrapper class

A C++ class whose function is to provide an alternative interface for objects of another class. For example, C exceptions can be handled as typed exceptions, with the C++ catch handler, by using a C exception wrapper class.

wrapper function

A function whose purpose is to provide an interface to another function. Such an interface might create type safety where none existed in the original function.

Index

A

Active Template Library (ATL), 241
ActiveX applications, debugging, 336
ActiveX control property pages, 296
    custom, 301
    default, 297
    exchanging data, 298
    implementing, 296
    stock, 300
ActiveX controls, 231, 276
    advanced features, 333
    advantages, 276
    ambient properties, 289
    containers, 234, 235
    ControlWizard, 277
    creating, 277
    custom properties, 285
    data binding, 330, 331
    debugging, 335
    drawing code, 334
    enumerated properties, 304, 305
    events, 233, 293, 294
    features, 233
    implementing properties, 287
    Internet, 241
    methods, 233, 291, 292
    MFC-based applications, 236
    optimizing, 333
    painting, 281
    parameterized properties, 289
    properties, 233, 282–90
    registering, 280
    stock properties, 283
    type libraries, 233

ActiveX controls (continued)
    vs. custom controls, 232
    windowless activation, 335
ActiveX Data Objects (ADO), 13, 389, 390
    benefits, 390
    collections, 392
    data-bound controls, 396
    data controls, 393–97
    methods, 392
    MFC applications, 393
    object model, 391
    objects, 391
    properties, 391
    queries, 429, 430
adding
    bitmaps to applications, 243
    cascading menus, 45
    child windows, 96
    controls to projects, 237
    controls to property pages, 297
    custom events, 294
    custom methods, 292
    custom properties, 285
    custom property pages, 301
    dialog bars, 90
    dynamic menus, 40
    event handlers for controls, 240
    floating toolbars, 51
    ownerdraw menus, 48
    parameterized properties, 289
    records, 425
    records to data sources, 358
    scrolling views, 147
    stock events, 293

adding (continued)
   stock methods, 291
   stock properties, 283
   stock property pages, 300
   Web Browser control, 461
adjusting scrolling views, 149
ADO. *See* ActiveX Data Objects (ADO)
ADO Data Bound Dialog Wizard
   building applications, 402
   creating data-bound dialog boxes, 393
advantages
   ActiveX controls, 276
   ADO, 390
   MFC, 4
   OLE DB, 340
ambient properties. *See also* properties
   ActiveX controls, 289
anticipating errors, 23
application view, converting to scrolling view, 148
applications
   adding bitmaps to, 243
   adding controls to, 237
   ADO, 389
   building, 402, 416
   dialog boxes, communicating with, 86
   Explorer-style applications, 181
   Internet. *See* Internet applications
   MDI applications, 129
   MFC, creating, 5
   MFC-based applications, 236
   OLE DB, 341
   OLE DB consumer applications, 349, 352, 355, 356, 368, 377
   SDI applications, 129
   view classes, 129
   writing FTP applications, 477
   writing HTTP applications, 474
AppWizard
   building MDI applications, 239
   creating base applications, 349
   creating MFC applications, 5
   creating rebars, 95
   enhancements, 10
   implementing **CAccessor** class, 352

architecture
   document/view architecture, 4
   OLE DB consumer templates, 347
associating tree controls, 174
ATL. *See* Active Template Library (ATL)
ATL Object Wizard, 10
attributes, setting
   Internet Explorer 4.0 common controls, 230
   Windows common controls, 224
automatic text completion, 8
Automation
   adding support, 457
   invoking Internet Explorer, 456

B

benefits
   ActiveX controls, 276
   ADO, 390
   MFC, 4
   OLE DB, 340
bitmaps
   adding to applications, 243
   processing bitmap buttons, 245
building
   applications, 402, 416
   MDI applications, 139

C

CAccessor class
   creating base applications, 349
   implementation, 352
   OLE DB consumer applications, 347
cascading menus, implementing, 45
catch block, exception handling, 26
CDynamicAccessor class, 368
CEditView, 178, 179
child windows
   adding to rebars, 96
   setting titles, 145
   suppressing creation, 145
classes
   MFC, 4
   rebars, 95

Index

ClassView, invoking Dialog Editor, 9
ClassWizard, 5
   enhancements, 10
CListView, 168, 169
CManualAccessor class, 377
COleDBRecordView class, 355
collections, ADO, 392
command buttons, implementing, 85
command handlers
   consolidating into command ranges, 41
   implementing, 92
command text, data-bound dialog boxes, 412
commands, OLE DB components, 344
common dialog boxes. *See also* dialog boxes
   customizing, 60
communications
   ActiveX control errors, 335
   ActiveX controls, containers, 234
Componenet Manager, 11
Components and Controls Gallery, 6
components, OLE DB, 342
connection string, data-bound dialog boxes, 411
consolidating command handlers into
   command ranges, 41
consumers
   OLE DB applications, 341
   OLE DB consumer applications, 347–52, 355, 356, 368–71, 377
   OLE DB consumer templates, 347
containers
   ActiveX controls, 234
   implementing, 235
context-sensitive menus, 40
Continue feature, debugging, 21
control views, 166
   CEditView, 178
   CListView, 168, 169
   CRichEditView, 179
   CTreeView, 172, 173
controls, 219
   ActiveX controls, 231–42
   adding to property pages, 297
   disabling, 63

controls (continued)
   enabling, 63
   exchanging data, 298
   Internet Explorer 4.0 common controls, 225–31
   MFC, 242
   Windows common controls, 220–25
ControlWizard, 277
converting
   application view to scrolling view, 148
   coordinates, scrolling views, 150
coordinating multiple views, 183
creating
   ActiveX controls, 275
   ADO applications, 389
   custom property pages, 301
   data-bound dialog boxes, 393
   data binding, ActiveX controls, 331
   dynamic splitter windows, 152
   enumerated properties, ActiveX controls, 304–07
   Explorer-style applications, 181
   floating toolbars, 51
   Internet Explorer 4.0 common controls, 228
   MFC applications, 5
   OLE DB consumer applications, 347
   property sheets, 64
   rebars, 95
   static splitter windows, 154
   tabbed dialog boxes, 64
   user-defined form views, 162
   Web Browser control, 463
   Windows common controls, 222
CRichEditView, 179
CTreeView, 172, 173
custom controls vs. ActiveX controls, 232
custom events. *See also* events
   ActiveX controls, 294
custom methods. *See also* methods
   ActiveX controls, 292
custom properties. *See also* properties
   ActiveX controls, 285
custom property pages, adding, 301

599

customizing
    common dialog boxes, 60
    CTreeView, 174
    list controls, 169
    rebars, 97
CView class, 131

D

data-bound controls, ADO, 396
data-bound dialog boxes, 401
    adding records, 425
    building applications, 402, 416
    creating, 393
    default, 411
    deleting records, 428
    editing records, 426
data binding, ActiveX controls, 330, 331
data controls, ADO, 394
    accessing data sources, 393
    events, 396
    implementing, 397
    properties, 395
data source objects, OLE DB components, 342
data sources, adding records to, 358
database management system (DBMS), 340
database view classes, 166
DBMS. *See* database management system (DBMS)
DDV. *See* dialog data validation (DDV)
debugging, 19, 20. *See also* error handling
    ActiveX applications, 336
    ActiveX controls, 335
    Continue feature, 21
    Edit feature, 21
    Visual Studio debugger, 20
defaults
    ActiveX control property pages, 296
    data-bound dialog boxes, 411
    printers, 506, 507
    views, starting applications, 140
deleting
    dialog box objects, 86
    records, 428
    records from data sources, 358
design time, painting ActiveX controls, 281

development environment, Visual C++, 2
DHTML described, 13
dialog bars, 90
    adding, 90
    implementing command handlers, 92
dialog box objects, deleting, 86
dialog boxes
    common, customizing, 60
    coordinating controls, 62
    enhancements, 59
    extending DDV, 61
    modeless dialog boxes, 83–86
    property sheets, 64
    tabbed dialog boxes, 64
dialog data validation (DDV), extending, 62
disabling controls, 63
displaying
    modeless dialog boxes, 83
    recordsets, 357
dockable toolbars, 50
document/view architecture, 4
documents
    managing document/view interaction, 132
    views, relationships, 131
drag-and-drop, implementing, 181
drawing, optimizing, 334
dynamic menus, 40
dynamic parsing, 9
dynamic splitter windows. *See* splitter windows

E

Edit feature, debugging, 21
editing
    records, 426
    records in data sources, 359
editions, Visual C++, 3
Editor, 8
enabling
    Continue feature, 21
    controls, 63
    default printer support, 507
    docking toolbars, 50
    Edit feature, 21
    floating toolbars, 51

Index

enhancements
    dialog boxes, 59
    Editor, 8
    interfaces, 39
    Internet, 13
    menus, 40
    MFC, 12
    OLE DB Templates, 12
    projects, 9
    status bars, 54
    Test Container, 10
    toolbars, 50
    tools, 10
    Visual C++, 7
    Visual Studio debugger, 7
    wizards, 10
Enterprise Edition, Visual C++, 3
enumerated properties, ActiveX controls
    creating, 304
    implementing, 305
    process, 304
enumerators, OLE DB components, 342
environment, Visual C++, 2
error handling, 19, 22. *See also* debugging
    ActiveX applications, 336
    ActiveX controls, 335
    anticipating errors, 23
    exception handling, 24, 27
    MFC exception classes, 28
    OLE DB components, 342
    reporting errors, 23
events
    ActiveX controls, 233, 293–95
    adding handlers, controls, 240
    custom events, 295
    data controls, ADO, 396
    stock events, 293
    Web Browser control, 460, 465
exception handling. *See* error handling
exchanging data between controls,
    property pages, 298
Explorer-style applications, creating, 181
extending DDV, 61

F

features
    MFC, 3
    Visual C++, 2
filters, queries, 429
floating toolbars, 50, 51
form views
    database view classes, 166
    implementing, 162
    user-defined, 162
forms, **New Form** command, 9
FTP applications, writing, 477

G

graphic device interface (GDI) objects, optimizing, 334
Gopher applications, writing, 479

H

HTML views, implementing, 469
HTTP applications, writing, 474
hyperlinks, processing, 475

I

implementing
    ActiveX control containers, 235
    ActiveX control property pages, 296
    cascading menus, 45
    CEditView, 178
    CListView, 169
    command buttons, 85
    command handlers, 92
    CRichEditView, 179
    CTreeView, 173
    dynamic menus, 40
    enumerated properties, ActiveX controls, 305
    form views, 162
    HTML views, 469
    Ownerdraw menus, 48
    properties, 287
    splitter windows, 151
    Web Browser control, 465
instantiating
    Internet Explorer, 458
    Web Browser control, 463

IntelliSense features, 8
interfaces
    enhancements, 39
    Visual Studio debugger, 20
Internet
    ActiveX controls, 241
    MFC enhancements, 13
Internet applications, 451
    basic concepts, 452
    framework, 452
    Internet Explorer object, 455–59
    MFC support, 453
    types, 453
    Web Browser control, 459–70
    WinInet classes, 470, 474, 477, 479
    WinSock classes, 480, 483–86
    writing HTTP applications, 474
Internet Explorer, instantiating, 458
Internet Explorer 4.0 common controls, 225
    creating, 228
    MFC classes, 226
    processing notification messages, 230
    setting attributes, 229
Internet Explorer object, 455
    invoking Internet Explorer, 457
    properties, methods, 455
    using Automation, 457
intializing modeless dialog boxes, 83
invoking
    Internet Explorer, 456
    Dialog Editor, 9

L

last chance exception handling, 30
launching ControlWizard, 277
list controls
    customizing, 169
    populating, 171

M

MDI applications. *See* multiple-document interface (MDI) applications

menus
    cascading, 45
    dynamic, 40
    enhancements, 40
    ownerdraw, 48
message handlers, data-bound dialog boxes, 415
message maps, MFC, 5
methods
    ActiveX controls, 233, 291, 292
    ADO, 392
    custom, 292
    Internet Explorer object, 455
    stock, 291
    Web Browser control, 460, 465
MFC. *See* Microsoft Foundation Class (MFC)
MFC applications
    ActiveX controls, 236
    ADO, 393
    Internet applications. *See* Internet applications
MFC classes
    Internet Explorer 4.0 common controls, 226
    Windows common controls, 220
MFC exception classes, exception handling, 28
MFC functions, error handling, 23, 24
Microsoft Foundation Class (MFC), 1, 2
    applications, 5
    controls, 242
    database enhancements, 12
    enhancements, 12
    features, 3
    Internet enhancements, 13
    printer support, 507
modeless dialog boxes, 83
    communicating with applications, 86
    deleting dialog box objects, 86
    displaying, 83
    implementing command buttons, 85
    intializing, 83
multiple-document interface (MDI) applications, 129
    building, 139
    mulitple views, 139
    setting titles, child window frames, 145
    starting, default view, 140

Index

multiple-document interface (MDI) applications (continued)
    starting, selecting views, 142
    suppressing child window creation, 145
multiple views, 135
    coordinating, 183
    MDI applications, 139–45
    SDI applications, 135

N

new tools, Visual C++, 10
notification messages
    processing, 245
    processing, Internet Explorer 4.0 common controls, 230
    processing, Windows common controls, 225

O

object models, ADO, 391
objects, ADO, 391
OLE DB, 339, 340
    applications, 341
    benefits, 340
    components, 342
OLE DB applications, transactions, 355
OLE DB consumer applications
    CAccessor class, 349, 352
    CDynamicAccessor class, 368
    CManualAccessor class, 377
    COleDBRecordView class, 355
    creating, 349
    database operations, 356
OLE DB templates, 12, 345
    consumer templates, 347
    provider templates, 345
optimizing ActiveX controls, 333–35
ownerdraw menus, implementing, 48

P

painting, ActiveX controls, 281
parameterized properties, ActiveX controls, 289
parameters, pop-ups, 9
parsing, dynamic, 9

performance
    ActiveX controls, 333, 334
    Internet ActiveX controls, 241
populating
    list controls, 171
    tree controls, 175
printers, 505
    characteristics, 511
    default support, 506, 507
    enhanced support, 510
    MFC support, 507
    overriding **CView**-derived functions, 515
    process, 506
    retrieving device context information, 514
    retrieving information, 512
    screen display vs. printing, 509
printing, 505
    enhanced printer support, 510–18
    MFC support, 507
    process, 506
    screen display vs. printing, 509
processing
    hyperlinks, 475
    notification messages, 245
    notification messages, Internet Explorer 4.0 common controls, 230
    notification messages, Windows common controls, 225
Professional Edition, Visual C++, 3
projects
    adding controls to, 237
    enhancements, 9
properties
    ActiveX controls, 233, 282–90
    ADO, 391
    ambient properties, 289
    creating data binding, ActiveX controls, 331
    data controls, ADO, 395
    implementing, 287
    Internet Explorer object, 455
    parameterized properties, 289
    Web Browser control, 460, 465

property pages, ActiveX controls, 296
   custom, 301
   default, 297
   exchanging data, 298
   implementing, 296
   stock, 300
providers
   OLE DB applications, 341
   OLE DB provider templates, 345
public FTP servers, 479

Q

queries, 429
   filters, 429
   searching records, 430
   simple queries, 429

R

rebars, 94
   adding child windows, 96
   classes, 95
   creating, 95
   customizing, 97
records
   adding, 425
   adding to data sources, 358
   deleting, 428
   deleting from data sources, 358
   editing, 426
   editing in data sources, 359
   searching, 430
recordsets, displaying, 357
registering
   ActiveX controls, 280
   controls, 236
reporting errors, 23
request/respond paradigm, 474
Resource Editor, 9
rowsets, OLE DB components, 344
run-time menus, 40
run-time, painting ActiveX controls, 281

S

screen display vs. printing, 509
scrolling views, 148
   adding, 147
   adjusting, 149
   converting application view to, 148
   converting coordinates, 150
SDI applications. *See* single-document interface (SDI) applications
searching records, 430
selecting views, starting applications, 142
sessions, OLE DB components, 343
setting attributes
   Internet Explorer 4.0 common controls, 229
   Windows common controls, 224
setup, ControlWizard, 277
single-document interface (SDI) applications, 129
   mulitple views, 135
sockets, 480
   TCP/IP, 482
splitter windows, 152
   dynamic splitter windows, 152
   implementing, 151
   static splitter windows, 154
Standard Edition, Visual C++, 3
starting applications
   default view, 140
   selecting view, 142
static splitter windows. *See* splitter windows
status bars, enhancements, 54
stock events. *See also* events
   ActiveX controls, 293
stock methods. *See also* methods
   ActiveX controls, 291
stock properties. *See also* properties
   ActiveX controls, 283
suppressing child window creation, 145

T

tabbed dialog boxes, creating, 64
TCP/IP, socket communication, 482
Test Container, 12
text, automatic completion, 8
throw statement, exception handling, 26

Index

throwing MFC exceptions, 30
toolbars
   docking, 50
   enhancements, 50
   floating toolbars, 51
   status bars, enhancements, 54
tools, Visual C++, new, 10
transactions
   OLE DB applications, 359
   OLE DB components, 342
tree controls, customizing, 174
try block, exception handling, 25
type libraries, ActiveX controls, 233

U

UpdateAllViews function, 183
user-defined form views, 162. *See also* form views

V

variants, Visual Studio debugger, handling, 7
view classes, 129, 130
   CView class, 131
   managing document/view interaction, 132
views
   coordinating multiple views, 183
   documents, relationship, 131
   form views, 162, 166
   managing document/view interaction, 132
views, multiple, 135
   MDI applications, 135–47
   SDI applications, 135
views, scrolling, 148
   adding, 147
   adjusting, 149
   converting application view to, 148
   converting coordinates, 150
Visual C++, 1, 2
   building projects, 9
   Editor, 8
   enhancements, 7
   features, 2
   tools, 10
   Visual Studio debugger, 7
   wizards, 10

Visual Studio Analyzer, 10
Visual Studio debugger, 7, 20
   Continue feature, 21
   Edit feature, 21

W

Web Browser control, 459
   adding, 461
   creating, 463
   implementing, 465
   implementing HTML views, 469
   properties, methods, events, 460
windowless controls, 335. *See also* ActiveX controls
windows, 6
   adding child windows to rebars, 96
   child window titles, 145
   splitter windows, 151, 152
   suppressing child window creation, 145
Windows common controls, 220
   creating, 222
   MFC classes, 220
   processing notification messages, 225
   setting attributes, 224
WinInet classes, 470
   connecting to Internet, 470
   writing FTP applications, 477
   writing Gopher applications, 479
   writing HTTP applications, 474
WinSock API, 483
   MFC support, 485
WinSock classes, 480
   MFC support, 485
   sockets, 480
   TCP/IP, 482
   WinSock API, 483
WizardBar, invoking Dialog Editor, 9
wizards, enhancements, 10
Workspace window, 6
writing
   FTP applications, 477
   Gopher applications, 479
   HTTP applications, 474

Microsoft MSDN Training
The **Complete** Training Solution for Developers

Print Edition: Study at your own pace.

The Microsoft Mastering Series books allow you to get up to speed on new technology whenever and wherever you need it. These books provide in-depth, hands-on training in an affordable package. They are designed for the "code warriors" who enjoy digesting lots of code or are looking for a solution to a specific problem.

▶ More information: http://msdn.microsoft.com/training/options/book.asp or http://mspress.microsoft.com

MSDN Training Online: Get in-depth coverage of the latest technology now.

Mastering Series web-based courses are offered by training centers around the world. They allow you to combine the best of self-study with the advantages of classroom training — without the hassles of travel or being away from work.

▶ More information: http://msdn.microsoft.com/training/options/web.asp

Classroom Training: Learn from experienced developers and trainers.

Instructor-led training classes are the premium way to get training. You learn in hands-on labs with detailed guidance from veteran developers, at thousands of Microsoft Certified Technical Education Centers around the world. The combination of in-depth training and experienced trainers gives you the clearest possible picture of how to use new technology in the real world.

▶ More information: http://msdn.microsoft.com/training

What's right for you?

If you need help sifting through the many training opportunities available for developers, the professionals at any Microsoft Certified Technical Education Center can recommend the most appropriate training program, tailored specifically for you and your needs! They'll help you decide which critical products and technologies are most important to you. And they will assist you in determining what training formats best suit your preferred learning style and resources. To find the Microsoft CTEC near you, visit the Microsoft Find Training web page at:

http://www.microsoft.com/isapi/referral/product_select.asp?train=84

msdn training

Make the *Career You Deserve* with Microsoft Training Programs

Why get trained?

As a trained IT professional, you can:
- Take advantage of extensive opportunities in a growing industry
- Stay on top of changes in the industry
- Polish old technical skills and acquire new ones

As an IT manager, hiring trained IT professionals provides you with:
- Greater assurance of a job well done
- Improved service, increased productivity and greater technical self-sufficiency
- More satisfied employees and clients

What's right for you?

The professionals at any Microsoft Certified Technical Education Center can recommend the most appropriate training program, tailored specifically for you and your needs! They'll help you decide which critical products and technologies are most important to you. And they will assist you in determining what training formats best suit your preferred learning style and resources.

How do you get the best training?

With instructor-led, online, and self-paced training and instruction available at locations throughout the world and on the Web, you are sure to find what you need among our industry-renowned comprehensive solutions to give you the right method of training to produce the best results. And a combination of training formats sometimes called hybrid training may be more effective than a single methodology.

Where do you get the best training?

Choose from Microsoft Certified Technical Education Centers, Microsoft Authorized Academic Training Program institutions, Microsoft Press, and, Microsoft Seminar Online to get the job done right.

Microsoft Authorized Academic Training Program (AATP) helps full-time and part-time students in participating high schools, colleges and universities prepare for jobs that demand proficiency with Microsoft products and technologies.

For more information, go to:
http://www.microsoft.com/astp/

Microsoft Certified Technical Education Centers (Microsoft CTECs) are full-service training organizations that can deliver system support and developer instruction in a variety of flexible formats.

For more information, go to:
http://www.microsoft.com/train_cert/

Microsoft Seminar Online delivers a virtual seminar experience right to your desktop, anytime, day or night.

For more information, go to:
http://www.microsoft.com/seminar/

Microsoft Certified Professional Approved Study Guides (MCP Approved Study Guides), an excellent way to stay up to date on Microsoft products & technologies, are rigorously developed & reviewed to ensure adherence to certification objectives.

For more information, go to:
http://www.microsoft.com/train_cert/train/mcpasg.htm/

Microsoft Press delivers "anytime, anywhere learning" via a full line of Microsoft Official Curriculum (MOC) self-paced training kits enhanced with print & multimedia that prepare you for the MCP exams.

For more information, go to:
http://mspress.microsoft.com/

MICROSOFT LICENSE AGREEMENT
Book Companion CD

IMPORTANT—READ CAREFULLY: This Microsoft End-User License Agreement ("EULA") is a legal agreement between you (either an individual or an entity) and Microsoft Corporation for the Microsoft product identified above, which includes computer software and may include associated media, printed materials, and "online" or electronic documentation ("SOFTWARE PRODUCT"). Any component included within the SOFTWARE PRODUCT that is accompanied by a separate End-User License Agreement shall be governed by such agreement and not the terms set forth below. By installing, copying, or otherwise using the SOFTWARE PRODUCT, you agree to be bound by the terms of this EULA. If you do not agree to the terms of this EULA, you are not authorized to install, copy, or otherwise use the SOFTWARE PRODUCT; you may, however, return the SOFTWARE PRODUCT, along with all printed materials and other items that form a part of the Microsoft product that includes the SOFTWARE PRODUCT, to the place you obtained them for a full refund.

SOFTWARE PRODUCT LICENSE

The SOFTWARE PRODUCT is protected by United States copyright laws and international copyright treaties, as well as other intellectual property laws and treaties. The SOFTWARE PRODUCT is licensed, not sold.

1. **GRANT OF LICENSE.** This EULA grants you the following rights:
    a. **Software Product.** You may install and use one copy of the SOFTWARE PRODUCT on a single computer. The primary user of the computer on which the SOFTWARE PRODUCT is installed may make a second copy for his or her exclusive use on a portable computer.
    b. **Storage/Network Use.** You may also store or install a copy of the SOFTWARE PRODUCT on a storage device, such as a network server, used only to install or run the SOFTWARE PRODUCT on your other computers over an internal network; however, you must acquire and dedicate a license for each separate computer on which the SOFTWARE PRODUCT is installed or run from the storage device. A license for the SOFTWARE PRODUCT may not be shared or used concurrently on different computers.
    c. **License Pak.** If you have acquired this EULA in a Microsoft License Pak, you may make the number of additional copies of the computer software portion of the SOFTWARE PRODUCT authorized on the printed copy of this EULA, and you may use each copy in the manner specified above. You are also entitled to make a corresponding number of secondary copies for portable computer use as specified above.
    d. **Sample Code.** Solely with respect to portions, if any, of the SOFTWARE PRODUCT that are identified within the SOFTWARE PRODUCT as sample code (the "SAMPLE CODE"):
        i. **Use and Modification.** Microsoft grants you the right to use and modify the source code version of the SAMPLE CODE, *provided* you comply with subsection (d)(iii) below. You may not distribute the SAMPLE CODE, or any modified version of the SAMPLE CODE, in source code form.
        ii. **Redistributable Files.** Provided you comply with subsection (d)(iii) below, Microsoft grants you a nonexclusive, royalty-free right to reproduce and distribute the object code version of the SAMPLE CODE and of any modified SAMPLE CODE, other than SAMPLE CODE, or any modified version thereof, designated as not redistributable in the Readme file that forms a part of the SOFTWARE PRODUCT (the "Non-Redistributable Sample Code"). All SAMPLE CODE other than the Non-Redistributable Sample Code is collectively referred to as the "REDISTRIBUTABLES."
        iii. **Redistribution Requirements.** If you redistribute the REDISTRIBUTABLES, you agree to: (i) distribute the REDISTRIBUTABLES in object code form only in conjunction with and as a part of your software application product; (ii) not use Microsoft's name, logo, or trademarks to market your software application product; (iii) include a valid copyright notice on your software application product; (iv) indemnify, hold harmless, and defend Microsoft from and against any claims or lawsuits, including attorney's fees, that arise or result from the use or distribution of your software application product; and (v) not permit further distribution of the REDISTRIBUTABLES by your end user. Contact Microsoft for the applicable royalties due and other licensing terms for all other uses and/or distribution of the REDISTRIBUTABLES.

2. **DESCRIPTION OF OTHER RIGHTS AND LIMITATIONS.**
    - **Limitations on Reverse Engineering, Decompilation, and Disassembly.** You may not reverse engineer, decompile, or disassemble the SOFTWARE PRODUCT, except and only to the extent that such activity is expressly permitted by applicable law notwithstanding this limitation.
    - **Separation of Components.** The SOFTWARE PRODUCT is licensed as a single product. Its component parts may not be separated for use on more than one computer.
    - **Rental.** You may not rent, lease, or lend the SOFTWARE PRODUCT.
    - **Support Services.** Microsoft may, but is not obligated to, provide you with support services related to the SOFTWARE PRODUCT ("Support Services"). Use of Support Services is governed by the Microsoft policies and programs described in the

user manual, in "online" documentation, and/or in other Microsoft-provided materials. Any supplemental software code provided to you as part of the Support Services shall be considered part of the SOFTWARE PRODUCT and subject to the terms and conditions of this EULA. With respect to technical information you provide to Microsoft as part of the Support Services, Microsoft may use such information for its business purposes, including for product support and development. Microsoft will not utilize such technical information in a form that personally identifies you.

- **Software Transfer.** You may permanently transfer all of your rights under this EULA, provided you retain no copies, you transfer all of the SOFTWARE PRODUCT (including all component parts, the media and printed materials, any upgrades, this EULA, and, if applicable, the Certificate of Authenticity), **and** the recipient agrees to the terms of this EULA.
- **Termination.** Without prejudice to any other rights, Microsoft may terminate this EULA if you fail to comply with the terms and conditions of this EULA. In such event, you must destroy all copies of the SOFTWARE PRODUCT and all of its component parts.

3. **COPYRIGHT.** All title and copyrights in and to the SOFTWARE PRODUCT (including but not limited to any images, photographs, animations, video, audio, music, text, SAMPLE CODE, REDISTRIBUTABLES, and "applets" incorporated into the SOFTWARE PRODUCT) and any copies of the SOFTWARE PRODUCT are owned by Microsoft or its suppliers. The SOFTWARE PRODUCT is protected by copyright laws and international treaty provisions. Therefore, you must treat the SOFTWARE PRODUCT like any other copyrighted material **except** that you may install the SOFTWARE PRODUCT on a single computer provided you keep the original solely for backup or archival purposes. You may not copy the printed materials accompanying the SOFTWARE PRODUCT.

4. **U.S. GOVERNMENT RESTRICTED RIGHTS.** The SOFTWARE PRODUCT and documentation are provided with RESTRICTED RIGHTS. Use, duplication, or disclosure by the Government is subject to restrictions as set forth in subparagraph (c)(1)(ii) of the Rights in Technical Data and Computer Software clause at DFARS 252.227-7013 or subparagraphs (c)(1) and (2) of the Commercial Computer Software—Restricted Rights at 48 CFR 52.227-19, as applicable. Manufacturer is Microsoft Corporation/One Microsoft Way/Redmond, WA 98052-6399.

5. **EXPORT RESTRICTIONS.** You agree that you will not export or re-export the SOFTWARE PRODUCT, any part thereof, or any process or service that is the direct product of the SOFTWARE PRODUCT (the foregoing collectively referred to as the "Restricted Components"), to any country, person, entity, or end user subject to U.S. export restrictions. You specifically agree not to export or re-export any of the Restricted Components (i) to any country to which the U.S. has embargoed or restricted the export of goods or services, which currently include, but are not necessarily limited to, Cuba, Iran, Iraq, Libya, North Korea, Sudan, and Syria, or to any national of any such country, wherever located, who intends to transmit or transport the Restricted Components back to such country; (ii) to any end user who you know or have reason to know will utilize the Restricted Components in the design, development, or production of nuclear, chemical, or biological weapons; or (iii) to any end user who has been prohibited from participating in U.S. export transactions by any federal agency of the U.S. government. You warrant and represent that neither the BXA nor any other U.S. federal agency has suspended, revoked, or denied your export privileges.

DISCLAIMER OF WARRANTY

NO WARRANTIES OR CONDITIONS. MICROSOFT EXPRESSLY DISCLAIMS ANY WARRANTY OR CONDITION FOR THE SOFTWARE PRODUCT. THE SOFTWARE PRODUCT AND ANY RELATED DOCUMENTATION ARE PROVIDED "AS IS" WITHOUT WARRANTY OR CONDITION OF ANY KIND, EITHER EXPRESS OR IMPLIED, INCLUDING, WITHOUT LIMITATION, THE IMPLIED WARRANTIES OF MERCHANTABILITY, FITNESS FOR A PARTICULAR PURPOSE, OR NONINFRINGEMENT. THE ENTIRE RISK ARISING OUT OF USE OR PERFORMANCE OF THE SOFTWARE PRODUCT REMAINS WITH YOU.

LIMITATION OF LIABILITY. TO THE MAXIMUM EXTENT PERMITTED BY APPLICABLE LAW, IN NO EVENT SHALL MICROSOFT OR ITS SUPPLIERS BE LIABLE FOR ANY SPECIAL, INCIDENTAL, INDIRECT, OR CONSEQUENTIAL DAMAGES WHATSOEVER (INCLUDING, WITHOUT LIMITATION, DAMAGES FOR LOSS OF BUSINESS PROFITS, BUSINESS INTERRUPTION, LOSS OF BUSINESS INFORMATION, OR ANY OTHER PECUNIARY LOSS) ARISING OUT OF THE USE OF OR INABILITY TO USE THE SOFTWARE PRODUCT OR THE PROVISION OF OR FAILURE TO PROVIDE SUPPORT SERVICES, EVEN IF MICROSOFT HAS BEEN ADVISED OF THE POSSIBILITY OF SUCH DAMAGES. IN ANY CASE, MICROSOFT'S ENTIRE LIABILITY UNDER ANY PROVISION OF THIS EULA SHALL BE LIMITED TO THE GREATER OF THE AMOUNT ACTUALLY PAID BY YOU FOR THE SOFTWARE PRODUCT OR US$5.00; PROVIDED, HOWEVER, IF YOU HAVE ENTERED INTO A MICROSOFT SUPPORT SERVICES AGREEMENT, MICROSOFT'S ENTIRE LIABILITY REGARDING SUPPORT SERVICES SHALL BE GOVERNED BY THE TERMS OF THAT AGREEMENT. BECAUSE SOME STATES AND JURISDICTIONS DO NOT ALLOW THE EXCLUSION OR LIMITATION OF LIABILITY, THE ABOVE LIMITATION MAY NOT APPLY TO YOU.

MISCELLANEOUS

This EULA is governed by the laws of the State of Washington USA, except and only to the extent that applicable law mandates governing law of a different jurisdiction.

Should you have any questions concerning this EULA, or if you desire to contact Microsoft for any reason, please contact the Microsoft subsidiary serving your country, or write: Microsoft Sales Information Center/One Microsoft Way/Redmond, WA 98052-6399.

Register Today!

Return this
Microsoft® Mastering: MFC Development Using Microsoft Visual C++® 6.0
registration card today to receive advance notice about the latest developer training titles and courseware!

For information about products and training from MSDN Training, visit our Web site at
http://msdn.microsoft.com/training

msdn training

OWNER REGISTRATION CARD   0-7356-0925-X

Microsoft® Mastering: MFC Development Using Microsoft Visual C++® 6.0

_____   _____   _____
FIRST NAME   MIDDLE INITIAL   LAST NAME

_____   _____
INSTITUTION OR COMPANY NAME   TITLE

_____   _____
MAILING ADDRESS   SUITE/APARTMENT/MAILSTOP #

_____
ADDRESS LINE 2

_____   _____   _____
CITY   STATE/PROVINCE   ZIP/POSTAL CODE
                                             (   )
_____   _____
E-MAIL ADDRESS (INTERNET STANDARD, E.G. JOHNSMITH@BUSINESS.COM)   (AREA CODE) PHONE NUMBER

U.S. and Canada addresses only. Fill in information above and mail postage-free.
Please mail only the bottom half of this page.

For information about Microsoft Press® products, visit our Web site at
mspress.microsoft.com

BUSINESS REPLY MAIL
FIRST-CLASS MAIL   PERMIT NO. 108   REDMOND WA

POSTAGE WILL BE PAID BY ADDRESSEE

NO POSTAGE
NECESSARY
IF MAILED
IN THE
UNITED STATES

MICROSOFT PRESS
PO BOX 97017
REDMOND, WA 98073-9830